D0217127

# These Are Your Children fourth edition

# These Are Your Children

fourth edition

## Gladys Gardner Jenkins
University of Iowa

## Helen S. Shacter
Consulting Clinical Psychologist

Scott, Foresman and Company  Glenview, Illinois

Dallas, Tex.    Oakland, N. J.    Palo Alto, Cal.    Tucker, Ga.    Brighton, England

## ACKNOWLEDGMENTS

Sources of illustrations are listed below except for charts and diagrams used in the Reference Manual, which are accompanied by footnotes.
COVER—"Rocking Horse #2" by Henry Moore; courtesy of the artist.

Page 1—"The Family" group in granite by Vigeland, in the Vigeland Sculpture Park, Oslo, Norway; courtesy of the Vigeland Museet. 5 (top)—Courtesy of the Minnesota Historical Society; (bottom)—Rondall Partridge. 8 (top left)—Bonnie Freer—Rapho Guillumette; (top right)—Inger McCabe—Rapho Guillumette; (bottom)—Enrico Natalie—Rapho Guillumette. 9 (top)—Inger McCabe—Rapho Guillumette; (bottom)—Arthur Tress—Photo Researchers. 12—Paolo Koch—Rapho Guillumette. 15—Raimondo Borea—Photo Researchers. 18 and 19—Scott Foresman Staff. 21—Eric Futran. 26—"Infant" by Vigeland; photograph by David Finn. 36 (top)—Courtesy of Landrum B. Shettles; (center left, bottom)—Courtesy of the Carnegie Institution of Washington; (right)—Arnold Ryan Chalfaut. 37—Tom Eagland. 39 (top left, top right, center left, center right)—Courtesy of the Carnegie Institution of Washington; (bottom)—Eve Arnold—Magnum. 43—Ken Heyman. 46 (top)—Dorothea Mooshake—Photo Researchers; (bottom)—Ed Lettau—Photo Researchers. 47 (top)—Ken Heyman; (bottom)—Bill Strode—Black Star. 53—Brian D. Palormo. 55—Jan Saudek; photograph courtesy of the Permanent Collection of Photography, Exchange National Bank of Chicago. 63—Scott Foresman Staff. 65—Erika—Peter Arnold. 66—Paul Sequira. 67—Gerry Cranham—Rapho Guillumette. 69—Erika—Peter Arnold. 71—Fred Lyon—Rapho Guillumette. 73—Ken Heyman. 75, 77—Erika—Peter Arnold. 90—Robert De Gast—Rapho Guillumette. 91, 94—Ken Heyman. 97—Alice Kandell—Rapho Guillumette. 98—Hanna Schreiber—Rapho Guillumette. 100—Ken Heyman. 101—David B. Barr—Black Star. 103—Courtesy of Children's Television Workshop. 105—Hella Hammid—Rapho Guillumette. 114—"Child Playing" 1942 by Giacomo Manzu; courtesy of Galerie Welz, Salzburg. 120—Lynn McLaren—Rapho Guillumette. 124 (top)—Lucia Woods—Photo Researchers; (bottom)—Scott Foresman Staff. 125 (top)—Alice Kandell—Rapho Guillumette; (bottom)—Scott Foresman Staff. 127—Arnold Zann. 139—Jean Claude LeJeune—Black Star. 140—Linda Schwartz. 141—Chester Higgins, Jr.—Rapho Guillumette. 143—Lucia Woods—Photo Researchers. 144—Garvino Peterson—Photo Researchers. 146—Ken Heyman. 154—Bonnie Freer—Rapho Guillumette. 156 (top)—Allen Swerdlowe; (bottom)—Raimondo Borea—Photo Researchers. 157 (top)—Gerald Holly—Black Star; (bottom)—Allen Swerdlowe. 159, 166—Inger McCabe—Rapho Guillumette. 167, 169—Brian D. Palormo. 171—Ken Heyman. 173—George W. Gardner—Photo Researchers. 180—Trina Lipton—Photo Researchers. 181—Wm. Franklin McMahon. 183—Inger McCabe—Rapho Guillumette. 184—Chester Higgins, Jr.—Rapho Guillumette. 192—Paul Sequira. 194 (top)—Chester Higgins Jr.—Rapho Guillumette; (bottom)—David Krasnor—Photo Researchers. 195 (top)—Peter Miller—Rapho Guillumette; (bottom)—Wm. Franklin McMahon. 197—Stephen Shames—Black Star. 204—"Bust of a Girl at a Window," 1943 by Giacomo Manzu; courtesy of Galerie Welz, Salzburg. 211—George Gardner. 213—Nacio Jan Brown—Black Star. 214—Bonnie Freer—Photo Researchers. 217—Nacio Jan Brown—Black Star. 222—Ivan Massar—Black Star. 227—Eric Futran. 228—Nacio Jan Brown—Black Star. 232—Eric Futran. 243—John Veltri—Rapho Guillumette. 245—Allan Price—Rapho Guillumette. 246—Michael Abramson—Black Star. 248—Bob Smith—Rapho Guillumette. 249—Scott Foresman Staff. 256—"Competition Entry for the Sibelius Monument," 1960 by Harry Kivijarvi; photograph, by courtesy of the artist. 265—Paul Sequira. 266—Wm. Franklin McMahon. 270-271 (top left, top right, bottom left, bottom center)—Linda Schwartz; (bottom right)—Eric Futran. 278—Inger McCabe—Rapho Guillumette. 280—Hella Hammid—Rapho Guillumette. 281—Ken Heyman. 284—Hella Hammid—Rapho Guillumette. 286, 288—Paolo Koch—Rapho Guillumette. 296 and 297—Scott Foresman Staff.

Library of Congress Catalog Card Number: 74-83835
ISBN: 0-673-07931-7

# preface

The material of THESE ARE YOUR CHILDREN is a practical body of information based on both clinical evidence and scientifically controlled research findings in child development and child experiences. The presentation is systematic; the content is based on scientific study; the tone is warmly human. This book presents an account of how children develop through sequences and patterns of growth and how they react to their total environment—personal, physical, and social.

The approach of this book distinguishes and describes four basic aspects of child growth: physical, mental, emotional, and social. The complete developmental picture is traced through the successive stages of life, from conception to birth, during early childhood years, through the preschool and school years, then into preadolescence and adolescence. The interdependence and interaction of all four aspects of growth are stressed; this concept is basic to comprehension of the total personality of the child.

The text is divided into five main parts, followed by a reference manual which provides aids for studying children. A carefully compiled bibliography documents the text and furnishes suggestions for supplementary reading and study.

Part One introduces the basic principles of sequential growth and gives emphasis to the individuality of all areas of development. Heredity as an influence on development is considered, and the important impact of family and community patterns are examined. There is stress on the need to consider a child's cultural environment when trying to understand difficulties and problems of childhood.

Parts Two through Four trace the several stages of growth from prebirth forward. In these successive chapters, three through fifteen, characteristic reactions are described as they develop at different ages, and are seen as factors in adjustment to family members, to children and adults outside the home, to the community, and to the special circumstances of a child's life. The continuity of growth is stressed, as is its uneven progress—sometimes rapid, sometimes slow, sometimes with plateaus. Stages of growth are not set apart in definite periods, but succeed one another almost imperceptibly. Attention is directed to the fact that the several aspects of growth—physical, mental, emotional, and social—seldom keep step with one another. The impact of this phenomenon on the adjustment of children and on the expectations of the adults in their lives is likely to be disconcerting and distressing when it is unrecognized or disregarded.

Part Five considers cooperation between home, school, and community and examines a number of problem areas in child adjustment: poor socialization, rejection of authority, emotional disturbances, physical and mental handicaps, hyperactivity, among others. They are discussed in relation to many of the difficulties in the growing up process.

Complementing and illustrating the text is a series of studies of individual children. These are briefs of actual cases treated by one of the authors; the children were seen in clinics, in schools, and in private practice. In the accounts, various alterations were carefully made so that no identities are revealed. Nevertheless, the essential situations and the parent-child and teacher-child interactions described are of real individuals.

The studies are varied, some of rather unusual circumstances and others of readily recognizable situations. Some show how important needs of children may be unwittingly overlooked by adults, resulting in confused and unhappy youngsters. Others involve conditions or handicaps which may retard a child's development until they are recognized, and special aids and procedures are introduced. In these presentations are practical implications toward wise guidance of children, noting desirable adult attitudes both within the home and at school.

A Reference Manual follows the main body of the text of THESE ARE YOUR CHILDREN. It is completely revised and provides significant concepts which are currently held in the field of child development. The manual has five sections:

> The "Individual Study Guide" gathers facts essential to conduct a psychological study of a child. Pertinent areas of growth, development, and experiences are organized to provide the specialist with as complete a background picture as possible, leading to an understanding of the disturbing elements of a problem situation. The Guide is not designed for the students' and teachers' use since special training and experience are required to conduct a psychological investigation. However, it helps students and teachers to be aware of what can be involved in the development of problems and when professional help should be sought.
>
> The "Guide for Parent-Teacher Conferences" suggests a method for conducting a conference to enable both parties to learn more about a child than each individually might recognize, and to plan jointly both for immediate and for future progress of the child.
>
> A section on "Theories of Development" presents concise statements of four influential positions in child development: Erikson's eight stages of psychosocial development; Havighurst's developmental tasks; Piaget's stages of intellectual development; and Kohlberg's levels of moral development.
>
> "Charting Development" provides selected charts, graphs, tables, and other material illustrative of developmental and reaction patterns

*in various circumstances at various periods of child growth.*

*Last, "Summaries of Normal Development" provide an overview of children's growth, outlining general patterns of development from infancy through adolescence and noting the special needs of each developmental period.*

There are significant characteristics and reactions common to each stage of growth before and shortly after birth, during the earliest years, the middle years, and the preadolescent and adolescent years—so in a sense all children are alike. But infinite variations are found in the degree to which these characteristics and reactions are manifested, so realistically *all children are different. All need understanding as individuals.* At home and at school, within the family, in the classroom and out at play, children go through varied experiences. How they surmount problems and difficulties and what they enjoy in activities and interests depend to a large extent on the interpersonal climate in which they live and grow. For that climate to be salutary and conducive to the kind of life their parents and teachers would wish for them, understanding is required.

There has been much thoughtful concern about the children and young people of our time. Troublesome questions continually arise as to how some of the puzzling aspects of their ways came to be, and how the more worrisome ways might have been forestalled. That all children may achieve total well-being, with a feeling of security, a satisfying sense of achievement, and self-assurance is an ambitious hope. Reaching in this direction is this fourth edition of THESE ARE YOUR CHILDREN.

# contents

# These Are Your Children fourth edition

part 1

# ALL OUR CHILDREN

These are our children. These are the boys and girls who are growing up at home, in the classroom, and in the community. These are the youngsters who we hope—through the guidance of all of us working together—will become healthy, useful, and happy adults, for their own sakes and for the sake of the world of tomorrow.

We are coming more and more to realize, as our knowledge of children increases, how great must be our individual concern with the development and guidance of all our children. Encouraging as progress over the years has been, a large number of children still grow up in homes that cannot, or do not, give them proper physical care, love, and attention, or they attend schools that neglect their physical and emotional needs and fail to stimulate their mental development. We have a responsibility to help all children develop to their fullest—those who are slow learners as well as those who are capable students, the disadvantaged as well as the privileged, the neglected as well as the cared for. They cannot do this without the help of adults who will work together to provide an environment which is suitable for the continuing development of each child.

This is particularly true today when guiding a child is complicated by continuing social and scientific change. It is no longer possible for parents to bring up

1

their children on their own, as may have been possible in the past. The impact and pressures of contemporary society are so strong that it is increasingly necessary for parents, teachers, and the other adults in the community to carry a joint responsibility for the welfare of all the children. The first and major responsibility for child care remains with the parents, but they must have the continuing support of the school and the community.

While the children who are described in this book may not represent backgrounds, experiences, or cultural and ethnic patterns of the children in all the communities in our country, the principles of understanding and the processes of growth that are presented apply to all boys and girls, whatever kind of community they may live in and whatever type of racial or cultural background they may have.

# chapter 1

# Children in a Developing World

The heritage of the children of our country is that of the whole world, for there are few parts of the world left unrepresented in some neighborhood or school of our country. Many of the boys and girls in our schools come from minority groups that have contributed richly to our culture, as the customs and traditions of their backgrounds have become part of the distinctive culture of our country. Yet many people think of these boys and girls, and even speak of them, as black children, or as Indian, Japanese, Mexican or Filipino, or with the name of whatever country their ancestors came from, and mentally set them apart as if they were different from one another and the majority of children in our country. These are our children too, children of our nation.

In spite of such obvious physical differences as color of skin, texture of hair, shape of eye, or size of body, the similarities among children are more basic than the differences. All have the same fundamental needs, motivations, and drives, although no two children have them in the same proportion or express them in exactly the same way. All children need an environment that helps them grow physically and mentally to their fullest potential; the security of being loved, cared for, and accepted by parents, friends, and the community in which they live; and opportunities to learn and to be rewarded by a sense of accomplishment. All children need these things and many more, but each child needs them in different, constantly changing degrees.

Of far more significance than the differences of racial background are those differences of community, culture, opportunity, and experience which shape a child's reactions, determine in large part patterns of behavior, and foster the development of unique traits and characteristics. Many children of all racial backgrounds still grow up in deprived communities in which few of the essentials for healthy development exist. Children in city slums or in poverty-stricken areas of a community where there is no work for their parents, have a very different environment from children in the suburbs.

A child in a slum area may, of necessity, have developed different values than a child in whose home the necessities of life and protection have

3

been taken for granted. The child who must fight for a place on the street, who has little certainty of shelter or food and little or no privacy, lives in the immediate present, demanding immediate gratification. There is little incentive to look ahead and plan for improbable satisfactions in the future.

There still are communities in which, although material needs are satisfied, new ideas are met with suspicion and adults cling to the past and try to ignore the changes of the present. Some parents simply have no interest in education for themselves or for their children. The child who grows up in a home where education is valued and learning is encouraged, where new ideas are met with eagerness and explored, has a start on the road to learning which has been denied to far too many of our children.

If we would understand the children we teach or the needs of children in the larger community of our country, we must be aware of the influences of the culture in which children grow up. We can never ignore the background of a child. If we would help a child grow and develop as fully as possible, we must begin where each child is.

PRESSURES OF CHANGE  The children of today are the same as the children of yesterday in the stages of development through which they will pass as they grow up, but their environment is increasingly complex. The patterns of the past continue to be disturbed, and new directions are not entirely clear. We cannot guide our children today toward a stable, comfortably predictable future for which we can help them prepare step by step. In the glimpses we have of what the future may be like, we do know that the children who are growing up today must be prepared to think clearly for themselves, evaluating new knowledge not only in science and technology but also in human relations.

The people of the world have an ever increasing need for understanding one another and for learning how to think together and work together for our common welfare. What affects children across the world affects our children and hampers or encourages their own best development. The boys or girls who grow up unable to appreciate and work with people whose appearance, language, or customs are different from their own will be severely handicapped in the world of tomorrow.

Our children must be helped to learn how to meet new problems and as-yet-unknown situations. They will need adaptability, stability within themselves, skills with which to open up and use new knowledge, ethical values to guide them, and the courage of the pioneer. If we as teachers and concerned adults are to be able to guide children in this direction, it is important for us to remain aware of new developments, opportunities, and possible strains and pressures which may affect the lives of the children in our care.

There has never been a time in which more attention has been paid to the welfare of children. We are aware of their *health needs* and are attempting to meet them through many services in school and clinic and through public health nursing. Physically our children are taller and heav-

4

ier on the average than they were in the past. As a group they mature physically at a slightly earlier age. Our infant mortality rate is showing a steady decline, although it still remains high in poverty areas. There is rapidly increasing knowledge of ways to prevent many of the potentially damaging childhood diseases. Physical handicaps are more widely recognized, and more care is given them. Mental handicaps have been taken out of the realm of superstition and disgrace and are under scientific study. More attention is being given to the emotionally disturbed child, to the mentally ill child, to the child with learning disabilities. An increasing number of physical and mental health services are available to help children as well as to help parents in better understanding their children's needs and problems. There has been real progress. Nevertheless, much still has to be done if these services are to reach all the children and parents who need them.

The *rights* of children are gaining legal recognition. Concern for children's rights should not be overlooked in regard to questions of custody—protecting them from being used by disagreeing parents. Children's rights are also being recognized in cases of child abuse—parents can no longer do as they will with their children. In many states children are entitled to the protection of a lawyer if they have committed a delinquent act which requires a court appearance. The rights of children, within our schools, to be free of harassment, harsh punishment, or the curtailment of basic liberties is being supported by law. These are important indications that children can no longer be considered possessions of their parents or subservient to adults. They have rights as individual persons which must be recognized and safeguarded by all those who have the responsibility for the care of children.

Although thousands of our children are not yet receiving an adequate or appropriate education, there is an awareness of the *educational needs* of many different kinds of youngsters and a movement in the direction of finding better ways to meet these needs. Much thought and experimentation are going into the effort to find more effective ways of teaching, new ways of grouping and of school organization, and new curriculum goals, so that the individual differences among children can be taken into account more fully during their school years.

There are, however, too many boys and girls who are defeated and discouraged by their school experiences. There are too many children who drop out in school and become seat-sitters as well as a large number who leave school as soon as legally possible. Some of these children can master the tasks which their schools set for them; some of them are bright, alert youngsters whose needs are not met in some of our classrooms. They, too, may turn away from school, reacting to feelings of boredom and the irrelevance of their studies to their lives.

The problems of vandalism, delinquency, drugs, and alcohol among restless junior and senior high school students cannot be ignored. These problems are found not only among disadvantaged youth but may involve boys and girls from all varieties of communities. This has become a national problem confronting all of us.

Many of our boys and girls are growing up prematurely through expe-

6

riences which they are not yet ready to fully understand or use wisely. Even comparatively young children of junior-high age are all too frequently caught up in the excitement of social and sexual stimulation and adult demands for material possessions.

EMPLOYMENT AND MOBILITY Toward the end of the school years, we find a reverse situation. Our older boys and girls are far too often pushed backwards toward dependency, as it becomes difficult for them to enter into an adult world which is not prepared to receive them with adequate jobs and participation as working citizens. Many young people are faced with no employment at a time when work habits should be established. After-school jobs and summer jobs are almost impossible to obtain in many communities.

*Problems of employment* are not only affecting older adolescents in their search for work, but many of their parents are also experiencing employment difficulties which affect the lives of children, creating tension and anxiety within families. It is becoming increasingly difficult for family businesses, such as the small shop or plant, to hold out in competition with large corporations. The number of workers needed on farms has diminished as intricate farm machinery continues to take over most farm tasks. Family farms, unable to compete with large corporation-owned farms and agribusiness, are rapidly disappearing. In addition, many job qualifications are changing as new technological methods are introduced, leaving jobless those whose skills are no longer required or whose skills have become obsolete. This is a growing problem for many families, particularly when parents are reaching an age when learning a new skill or moving into a new field of work is no longer easy. The rapid obsolescence of skills and changes in job patterns is also causing concern among adolescents, many of whom fear that they may be interested in or preparing for jobs that will no longer be in demand when they leave high school or college. The uncertainties of employment involve serious problems that must be faced now, among them the effect on the stability of a family.

*Mobility* is a part of the pattern of modern life. About 20 percent of our people move within a given year. Roots must be pulled up, friends and schools changed. No longer is this true only of the migrant worker or of the laborer who must go where there is work. Executives are transferred from one locality to another. Scientists and technicians are frequently sent to other plants. The personnel of government and the armed forces may travel, with their families, all over the earth.

Some children, in families that are secure within themselves, can gain an enrichment of experience through such moves. But for others, the constant mobility spells insecurity, loneliness, and a feeling of constant unrest and anxiety. The need to move may put an added strain on the family group at a time when the stability of the family unit, which is so essential for the children, is being threatened for other reasons. There are many boys and girls who have never experienced the stability that can come from growing up in a community where there is a feeling of belonging.

The family unit may take a variety of forms. Today many families are isolated from close contact with grandparents and relatives. Alternative patterns as single-parent units or communal arrangements are also becoming more visible variations.

9

Some have never had the opportunity to move through a well-planned educational program but have changed from school to school, sometimes several times a year. Many boys and girls do not know their relatives. They rarely feel the support that can come from close relationships with grandparents, aunts, uncles, and cousins. Family history is being lost. The family home rarely exists as a gathering place of the generations. The small family group is on its own. In time of crisis, its members often must turn to impersonal community agencies to secure advice and help.

THE FAMILY UNIT  Although the family of father, mother, and natural children is still the usual family relationship, the impact of the *increasing variety of family forms* cannot be overlooked. The term "family" may have to be extended to include parenting people who carry the responsibility for caring for children during their growing years with ties of affection. An increasing number of boys and girls are growing up in one-parent families due to divorce, the death of a parent, an unmarried parent, or a single adult who has adopted a child or children. Single parents are not always mothers; fathers are increasingly gaining custody of their children if they are considered to be the better parent. A growing number of children may be cared for by a group of parenting people, as communes of many varieties are increasing in number. This way of sharing responsibility for children will affect the life styles of these boys and girls as well as their parents.

Due to the growing awareness of the vital need to *curb the growth of population* in our country, the size of the family is changing. The two-child family is becoming the accepted family size. There is a growing tendency for those who want large families to adopt children so that there are an increasing number of families with both natural and adopted children. There also is a steady trend toward interracial adoptions so that children in a family may have different racial backgrounds.

Many children will experience the need to adapt to a new family unit as parents divorce, remarry, and sometimes divorce again. Not only do these children have to accommodate to new parent combinations but also to new relatives; a child might have not only four but six or eight grandparents. As family relationships must be realigned, problems of loyalties have to be confronted.

Family patterns are also undergoing change. A steadily increasing number of mothers of children under eighteen are working outside their homes. When both parents work, or when a single parent works, there necessarily are shifts and changes in the routines of the home and the care of the children. Many more children are likely to be on their own before and after school hours and during holiday periods. Infants and small children in increasing numbers will spend their early years in day-care centers. These centers will need to rethink the role which they must play as supporting agencies to the home, if children are not to experience neglect.

10     SEX-ROLE EXPECTATIONS  The concepts of the roles of men and

women are also changing rapidly. Role stereotypes are being challenged; although the biological role remains the same, the cultural expectations which surround those roles are being reconsidered. Questions are being raised about the patterns of behavior and the stereotyped interests which have been encouraged as appropriate for each sex. There is a growing realization that roles of men and women, other than the biological ones, can be interchanged. Men and women can aspire to the same goals if their interests and abilities lead them in the same directions.

Changing sex-role concepts will have a profound influence on what is taught in our schools to both boys and girls and on the vocational choices toward which they have been steered in the past. The relationships within the family group are also being modified, including the expectations of the roles of father and mother, husband and wife. These changes cannot help but influence the feelings which boys and girls will have about their own maleness or femaleness and the interrelationships which develop between them. It also will affect the guidance we give to our children regardless of their sex, the opportunities which we offer to them as persons rather than as boy or girl.

A CHALLENGE TO VALUES   In any period of change there is likely to be a confusion of ethical values. It is usually a time of questioning and of rejecting many previously accepted beliefs and standards. There is often a loosening of the moral code. Many grown-ups are no longer sure of their own beliefs. This adds to the confusion of boys and girls who must look toward their parents and other adults for guidance. It makes it more difficult for children to gradually learn the patterns of behavior and the ethical values which are essential in any society that is to survive.

Children today receive their impressions of the values of their society not only from parents, teachers, and other adults in their own immediate environment, but also from many sources far removed from the home. The mass media, which are so much a part of life today, touch the lives of even our very young children. They can extend the horizons and enrich the lives of boys and girls. But they also can, and often do, add to the confusion of youngsters as they bring an intensity of experience into the home. Our children are constantly exposed to false concepts of success created by a materialistic society; to undesirable behavior both on the part of other boys and girls and grown men and women; and often to experiences in human relationships that they are not yet ready to interpret or evaluate. Many of these unwholesome and false concepts are developed through the media before our boys and girls have been helped to develop a sound basis of ethical values which they can use as a base from which to judge what they see and hear.

Children are not small adults. They do not think, feel, or react as adults do. They do not have the knowledge, judgment, or background to choose experiences that will be beneficial to them and reject those that may be harmful. Therefore, we cannot judge or measure children by adult standards. They need adults who can thoughtfully lead the way through the confusion of our times. The first responsibility of those who sincerely want to help children grow up ready to take their part in this changing world is to try to understand the world of children: the general pattern according to which all children grow and, within this framework, the individual needs and characteristics of each particular child for whom they are responsible.

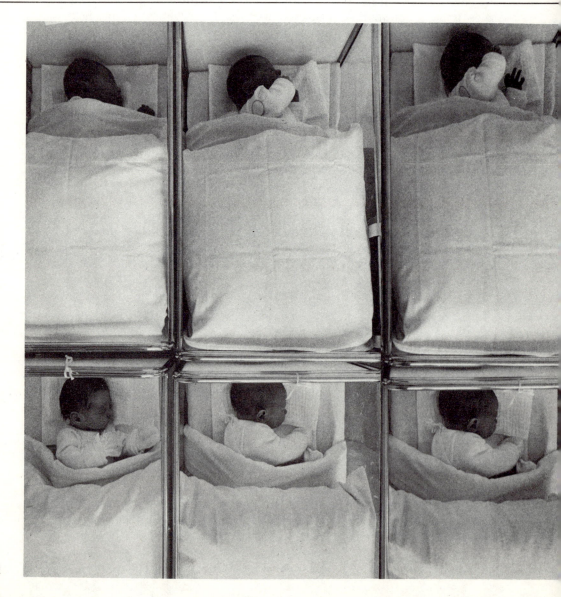

# chapter 2

# All Children Are Alike-and Different

BASIC INFLUENCES ON DEVELOPMENT—HEREDITY AND ENVIRONMENT  It is essential that we be aware of the differences among children that are due to their endowment, for these innate differences are the keystone on which a child's development will be built. Some children will always learn relatively slowly; others will learn rapidly and easily. Some will have an unusual capacity for understanding abstract concepts and working creatively with ideas; others may have the coordination to develop special physical skills.

Certain basic traits of temperament are apparent at birth. There are babies who are placid and others who are vigorous. Some are more sensitive to stimuli than others. Some have a quick reaction time while others respond more slowly. Some react to frustration with lusty crying and active body movements; others do not seem so readily disturbed. Even in the first days of life, there are babies who have more energy and drive than others.

But whereas heredity determines the potentiality that can be developed, the environment determines *how* or even *whether* that potential is developed. Even before birth the environment is an important factor. All children bring their own potentials into an environment that is uniquely their own—different even from the environment of brothers and sisters.

We are aware of the tragic results of brain injury at or after birth. Such injury can make it impossible for a potentially fine mind to realize its original possibilities. We know that a crippling illness or accident can limit the use of a body that could have developed normal coordination; deafness can silence a musician; blindness can prevent an artist from expressing on canvas his great innate ability.

In the same way, an unfortunate emotional environment can keep a child with normal potential from becoming a mature, emotionally healthy adult. The child who feels unloved and unwanted may grow into a discouraged, self-doubting individual or an aggressive bully. A child who has been dominated by an oversevere parent may be unable to make independent decisions. An impoverished educational background can impede the development of a scientific genius, or slow the mental development of a normal boy or girl.

The influence of heredity and that of environment on the development of a child's personality cannot be separated. They are closely in-

13

tertwined, one influencing the other. It is often difficult to decide whether a particular developing trait is due to initial endowment or to factors the child has experienced—or failed to experience. Mental retardation, for example, may result from limitations present in the original cells at conception, from malnutrition, particularly protein deficiency, from severe cultural deprivation, or from brain damage due to illness, accident, or biochemical deficiency. It is futile to argue whether heredity or environment, nature or nurture, has the greater significance for a child's development, because both affect the child's ability to grow into a mature adult.

Probably no one realizes all possible potentialities. At birth, the child possesses the capacity for far greater development than usually will be achieved. With understanding and help, even the mentally retarded, severely handicapped, or culturally deprived child can often develop far beyond the point that might otherwise have been reached.

Obviously, no matter what we do, we cannot change the heredity of a child. Our sphere of influence is necessarily limited to the environment. But this limitation encompasses a wide variety of overlapping factors, often broadly classified for the sake of convenience as the *physical, mental, emotional,* and *social* growth and development of children.

The development of a child is a complex and individual matter, and the factors that interact to help or hinder this development are infinitely varied. It is impossible to control them all, nor should we even try. Learning to cope with problems and disappointments is one of the important tasks of growing up, and the ways a person copes with problems are as much a part of personality as are unique abilities and interests. But we can—and must—try to protect children from situations that are completely beyond their ability to handle independently, such as the devastating effects of disease or malnutrition, lack of educational opportunities, or severe emotional setbacks.

AN OVERALL SEQUENCE OF GROWTH   It is difficult to help any child grow to full potential without understanding the overall sequence and pattern of growth characteristic of all children. *These Are Your Children* is concerned with this foundation of knowledge and understanding. But although we talk about stages of development, we need to remember that there is no sharp cutting-off point at which one stage ends and another begins: one stage passes naturally into another. At any point in development, a child still evidences some of the needs of a previous stage of growth, even while shooting forward in other aspects of development into a more advanced stage. The toddler occasionally behaves like an infant, though at times carrying out activities more typical of the runabout. The adolescent sometimes returns to the dependency of a grade-school youngster and at other times displays the responsible behavior of a young adult.

All normal children follow an essentially similar *sequence of growth,* yet because of great variations in endowment and experience, no two children, even in the same family, pass through this sequence in just the same

14

way. Some meet life eagerly, head on; others are more phlegmatic, less easily interested or excited. Some are easily guided; others are aggressively independent. Some have great vitality; others have less stamina. All these factors influence the point at which a child reaches any particular level in the sequence of growth.

Thus if we are to understand and help children as they grow, we must accept the fact that within a range termed "normal" some children will develop much more rapidly than the average, others much more slowly. In the total progress of growth, they all will reach normal adulthood. But in every group of children some may be as much as several years ahead of their age group physically, mentally, emotionally, or socially, while others may be as far behind. So when we talk about "the six-year-old" or "the eight-year-old," we are talking of averages—the stage of development *most* children reach around six or eight. Some children will reach "six-year-old-ness" at five or even four, others not until seven or eight or even later.

INDIVIDUAL RATES OF DEVELOPMENT   We must try to understand a child's *individual rate of development.* Is this child fast-maturing? If so, there may be a need for opportunities to go ahead of others in that age group. Is the child slow-maturing? Then caution must be exercised so that pressure of over stimulation are avoided. We are usually aware of the need to allow mentally retarded children to take things at a different pace from that of their age group; but we are not always so keenly aware of such special needs among children in the normal group who are maturing more slowly or rapidly than the average. If children are functioning well at their own level, their efforts should be accepted and respected.

Growth does not always go ahead smoothly. It is continuous, but not necessarily steady. Sometimes for weeks or even months the child's development seems to be at a standstill. At other times a youngster appears to slip backwards in behavior, seeming less independent today than last month. Sometimes, in both physical and psychological growth, these slower growth periods occur before a new spurt. There is slower physical growth, for instance, before the spurt preceding puberty.

Some children seem to grow at a relatively constant rate, so that at any given age they appear to achieve a level of development that is consistent for them physically, mentally, emotionally, and socially. For example, at the chronological age of twelve, these children display the physical, mental, emotional, and social characteristics more or less typical of a twelve-year-old. There are indications that such children may have less difficulty in growing up and adjusting. They also may show fewer behavior problems than do those children who grow at a more uneven rate.

OBSERVING ALL AREAS OF DEVELOPMENT We must take into account all areas of a child's development if we are to understand and meet the needs of each individual child. For instance, if a child has developed rapidly mentally but remained immature socially, it would be unfair to judge by the area in which there is advanced behavior and expect the child to live up to the same level in all other activities.

In order to evaluate a child's growth, we should avoid looking at the immediate present, comparing this week with last week or today with yesterday. We should *take the long view*—look back six months or one or two years and observe the growth that has taken place. The nine-year-old may baffle adults with poor language usage and untidy appearance, but know more about truthfulness and honesty than was evident at six or seven, be more cooperative in work and play, and be more self-reliant. How fast and how evenly a child develops is significant, but more important still is the fact that there is progress from one stage to the next without the youngster being blocked along the way.

Although a child's personal pattern of physical maturing seems largely predetermined, growth can be encouraged by an environment that provides ample physical and emotional care; it can also be hampered by sickness, malnutrition, and inadequate emotional relationships. A child will grow in some fashion whatever care is provided, but optimum growth possibilities cannot be fulfilled unless there is adequate care suited to individual needs.

PHYSICAL GROWTH Physical growth is easily observed. We can tell whether a child has gained weight by checking weight in proportion to body type and observing the nutritional state as shown by weight gains and skin and muscle tone. We can examine teeth, find out the stage of skeletal development, and test coordination. In these ways we know whether a youngster is unusually mature or immature physically—that is, how the child is growing in relation to the average at a particular age. Such knowledge can guide us in planning a program that will further develop

16

the strong points and correct the deficiencies in the child's physical growth. Physical examinations also can help determine whether a child can be expected to do schoolwork at the pace of the same age group. If there is a lag in physical development, a youngster may be unable to keep up with others in handwriting, for instance, which demands fine coordination of the muscles of the fingers. Or there may be an inability to climb and run as well as schoolmates or to handle tools as skillfully as they do.

All children need ample physical observation and care; fatigued, poorly nourished, or physically ill children cannot grow as fully as they might or accomplish the schoolwork that is expected of them. Knowledge of a child's level of physical development, good food, fresh air, protection from disease, correction of physical defects, plenty of exercise and outdoor play balanced by rest and relaxation—all these are essential for optimum growth, not only of a child's body but of the total personality.

MENTAL GROWTH  A child's mental growth and capacities can be observed through standardized psychological tests, carefully given and interpreted by a trained person. We know through such tests and through observation that all children of a given age have not reached the same point in mental growth. In any first-grade class, we may find children with mental ages ranging from four-years-old to, in exceptional cases, ten-years-old. Parents and teachers must recognize these wide differences in intelligence and in capacity for mental growth if they are to give all children the opportunity to grow and achieve.

It is important that the experiences offered to children fit their own maturity levels. Children cannot learn either reading or independence until they have reached the stage in their growth at which they are ready to learn these things. If too much is expected of them before they are ready, they will fail, and their failures may seriously discourage their future progress.

On the other hand, children's growth may be slowed if parents or teachers fail to recognize their readiness for the next step. If children are kept dependent when about to take some independent step, they may either rebel against restraints or yield to adult pressure and lose interest. The infant-child who reaches for a spoon is moving toward independence. If a parent refuses to give the spoon for fear the child will be messy, the child may later refuse to use it when the adult decides it is time to learn to use it. If a youngster is keen to take the next step in arithmetic but is held back until the slowest member of the class is ready, there may be a loss of interest or the child may just fool away the time in school.

EMOTIONAL GROWTH  Emotional growth is not easy to understand or even observe scientifically. Growth—or the apparent lack of growth—in this area may be misinterpreted or overlooked. The behavior of children reflects their emotional development. If children seem generally interested in life, reasonably happy and relaxed, free from undue strain and tension, and able to meet situations appropriate to their age, their emotional needs are probably being cared for adequately.

Children are alike—and different. Physical, mental, social, and emotional growth proceeds at an individual rate for each child. Children are constantly growing, developing, maturing, but not always at a constant rate. As youngsters change, needs and behavior patterns change, too. Home, school, and community must respond with understanding guidance to these varying patterns.

All children have certain basic emotional needs that must be met if they are to be emotionally stable. Children need the security of knowing that they are loved, that they belong and are wanted. They also need the self-confidence that comes from being able to meet situations adequately. Successes must at least balance failures as they try to cope with the normal problems and frustrations of growing up.

If needs are met, children are able to develop through the stages of childhood into adequately mature adults. If one or more of these needs is consistently overlooked, emotional growth may be retarded, and they may have real difficulty in achieving emotional maturity. A baby who does not feel the security of being loved may refuse food and show serious malnutrition, even though there is excellent physical care available in the home. Or an older child, anxious because of a new baby in the family, may return to outgrown baby ways. The schoolchild who cannot read is often one who is discouraged because of feeling unloved and unwanted at home. The bully is often the rejected or unsuccessful child who has been made to feel that as a failure, nobody cares.

A knowledge of the stages through which we can expect children to pass will help us recognize behavior that indicates some problem in a child's emotional growth. A three-year-old may wake frequently from sleep—this is normal for three-year-olds. But if this waking continues over a period of time and is often accompanied by nightmares, we should begin to look for the cause or causes of tensions and anxiety. Perhaps too much is being expected of the child, resulting in anxiety. Similarly, if the adolescent moodily shuts others out or temporarily slumps in schoolwork, it may be just a part of growing up. But if there develops a *pattern* of withdrawing from friends and family or of neglecting studies, we should look for the causes. Behavior in excess of the normal reaction is the child's way of showing that for some reason growth is being blocked or hampered.

Many environmental factors influence emotional growth. For this reason, if growth is to progress as well as possible, adults close to a child should be sensitive to behavior that suggests that the child's needs are not being adequately met. When a child is tense, anxious, unhappy, and out of harmony with parents or surroundings, growth cannot proceed as well as if the child were reasonably happy, secure, and self-confident. For example, a child experiencing too much competition with older brothers or sisters and discouragement from constant comparisons may simply stop trying to compete, or may feel unloved in comparison to a brother or sister.

The self-images which children develop are built through the attitudes expressed toward them by those with whom they are most intimately connected—family, relatives, playmates, neighbors, and teachers. Children see themselves as they think others see them. Those who work with children are increasingly aware of the significance of children's concepts of themselves as they affect behavior, motivation, and ability to live up to individual potentials.

Children's opinions of themselves largely determine their attitudes toward the growing demands that are put upon them. If they are self-con-

20

fident, they will have the initiative to move ahead, to explore the environment, to try new things, to meet and attempt to solve problems. But if children doubt themselves, if they already have met too much discouragement, too many defeats, too much adverse criticism, they may become so insecure that they will be afraid to meet the demands of growing up.

Even well-meaning parents or teachers sometimes damage a child's self-confidence through excessive criticism for mistakes and failures, without giving balancing praise for successes and assurance that the child is liked in spite of mistakes that have been made.

SOCIAL GROWTH Social growth closely parallels emotional growth, for it involves children's feelings and relationships with people among whom they are growing up. No child lives in a vacuum. All children must learn to get along with others, to accept growing responsibilities, and to live and work with other people at the same time that they keep their own identities as individuals.

Children vary in the ease with which they develop socially. These variations, in part, reflect differences in personality: some children are more outgoing than others. There are differences in environment: some children have had warmer family relationships and greater opportunities for satisfying contacts with other people. There are differences in ability and in training: some children have skills in games and sports that make other children enjoy their company; others are shy or less skilled and find it difficult to make friends with other children.

Any assessment of social growth is relative, because it may change according to the situation in which a child happens to be. A child may be comfortable and happy at home, but unhappy and uncomfortable at school with a particular teacher. Sometimes a child does not fit in with the group of youngsters on the block, and may feel temporarily left out and inadequate; yet the same child might get along well with other children who have the same interests and abilities.

Group acceptance is seldom a safe criterion of social adjustment. It is essential to know more about a child and the total situation before judgments are attempted. If a child's growing social development is healthy, there will be an ability to relate to some other people, whether to a large group or a small one is not so significant as the capacity to relate to family members and to some other children.

No child can develop normally as an isolate. All children need contact with and acceptance by other people. Children develop socially as they play and work cooperatively with others and assume increasing responsibility for their share of a group enterprise as well as for their own personal activities. The child who is a loner is a child who may need special help. But the label of social immaturity is one that must be used with the greatest care.

There are tests to assess social adjustment and to give insight into a child's feelings about other people. But such tests are not infallible. They can give some indication of a child's possible problems or anxieties in relationships with others, but the results are not an accurate indication of a child's social adjustment.

## BEHAVIOR IN THE NORMAL AND ACCEPTABLE RANGE

Unfortunately, much of the behavior typical of normal children is exasperating to adults who do not understand the stages of development through which children normally pass (and sometimes even to adults who *do* understand). Recognizing that some disruptive behavior is necessary to children's growth doesn't necessarily make the behavior less irritating, but it does enable adults to cope with it more calmly and intelligently.

The active, fifteen-month-old baby who touches, feels, and mouths everything within reach is exploring an unfamiliar world and not just being a nuisance and "getting into everything." The restless six-year-old who is boisterous and who finds it difficult to sit still may annoy adults, but is perhaps simply responding to a tremendous drive toward activity. The child who is passing through the growth spurt at the beginning of adolescence may be awkward and trip or drop things, not because of carelessness but because the body is growing unevenly.

Often the child who is labeled naughty or badly behaved is a child who is misunderstood by adults. They may be pushing too hard and expecting too much, or they may know too little about children to realize that this is a normal reaction of many children in similar circumstances— that the child is not deliberately naughty but is trying to assert individual feelings as a person. If we can learn what may legitimately be expected of our children we will save ourselves and them unnecessary heartache and bewilderment. We will not make the mistake of regarding as wrong or abnormal the behavior that is perfectly normal for the child's age and development.

But even though we know what behavior is normal for the child, we cannot assume that all *normal* behavior will be *acceptable* behavior. Adults cannot assume a "do-nothing" attitude. They must curb, guide, and help children grow toward behavior that is acceptable as well as normal. For example, the noisy activity of a healthy group of children may be encouraged on the playground, but not in the classroom where it would be disturbing to others.

APPROACHES TO UNDERSTANDING  Numerous research centers throughout the country contribute to our growing knowledge of children—their needs and development. Most of the studies are of two types: *cross-sectional* and *longitudinal.* Cross-sectional studies compare and study large groups of children and isolate those characteristics that almost always seem to appear at certain age levels. Longitudinal studies follow individual children over a period of years, so that their patterns of growth can be observed and charted. Both types of studies have made valuable contributions to our knowledge.

Another approach to understanding children's behavior is from reports of psychiatrists, clinical psychologists, and social workers. Although the methods of these three professional groups are not identical, they all emphasize the understanding of each child as a *unique individual* with personal needs, a personal growth pattern, and personal problems. (This is in contrast to the normative approach of longitudinal and cross-sectional studies which reports on the "average" child.) These professional people are interested in the general pattern of child development not only theoretically but also because they are often confronted with practical problems that need a solution. Through clinical experience and research, they have found that they must have all available information about a child's heredity, potential endowment, and environmental influences. What happened as the child grew up that either resulted in healthy development or warped the child's personality and prevented the growth of existing potentialities? Largely through the influence of these clinicians and their awareness of the effect of the child's total endowment and environment on adjustment, our emphasis today is on *the whole child*—on individual problems and needs.

Clinical specialists have supplied valuable information concerning children's feelings about their relationships with parents, brothers and sisters, teachers, and children of their own age—and also about the effect of the child's self-concept on the development of personality. Their interviews, in which children are helped to talk about feelings, memories, and reactions to the experiences of life, have been useful in understanding basic needs and the way that tensions and anxieties can block or distort growth. Material gathered in this way is more subjective and less easily measured than that which has come from research studies, but it is of great importance in appreciating our children's points of view and reactions. It also adds to our understanding of normal and abnormal emotional growth patterns.

We need both types of understanding—one to give us the general pattern of development and the individual variations that are normal within the pattern, and the other to give us insight into the child's emotional life and its interplay with the growth process.

FOCUS ON THE INDIVIDUAL Children are alike—and different. Alert teachers and parents will always keep the individual child foremost in their minds, seeing the child against the background of the overall developmental picture. If growth seems to differ greatly from the expected pattern of a specific age group, it is wise to look for a reason. We need to be aware that some problems arise from a particular phase of development or a temporary environmental situation, but that others have a serious emotional basis. Children with the first type of problem often can be helped within an understanding home or school, but more seriously troubled children may need the more specialized help of community or state agencies or of a private psychologist or psychiatrist.

Children are constantly growing, developing, maturing. As they change from year to year, their needs and behavior patterns change, too. In growing up, youngsters need the understanding guidance of both parents and teachers, together with the kind of environment in home, school, and community that makes the most healthful total growth possible.

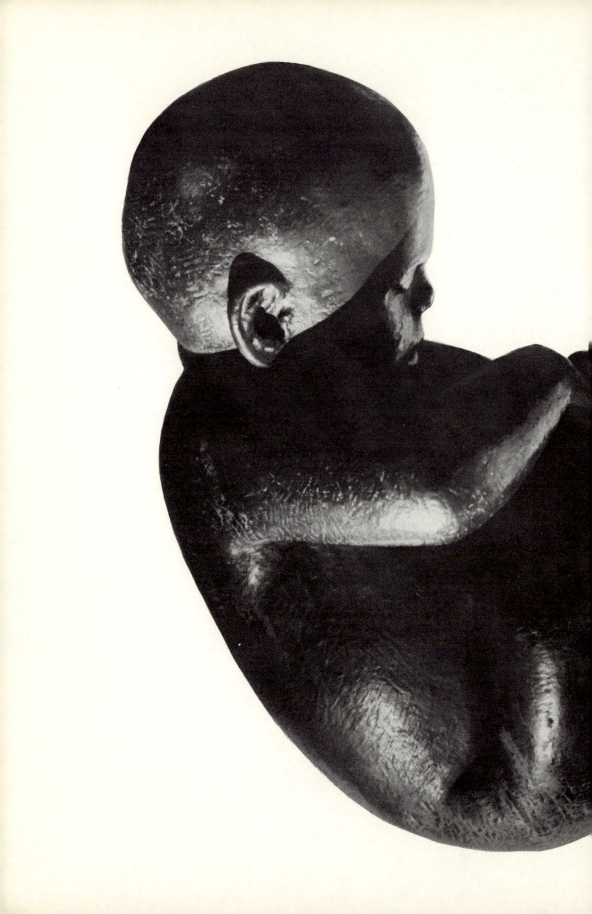

part 2

# EARLY CHILDHOOD YEARS

The birthright of all our children is to become fully the unique person each one was meant to be. From conception every child has been a separate and distinct entity, in spite of the close prenatal connection with the mother. After birth this separation will widen as each child takes new growth steps toward independence, though there will long continue to be the need for both physical and emotional dependence upon responsible parenting people.

After birth, infant-children pass through another period of rapid and spectacular growth. This will be marked by the continuing development of the physical structure and the increasing effectiveness of the functioning of the body. They will move out of the misty, undifferentiated consciousness of the newborn into a world of color and movement. Gradually they will be able to explore their nearby world by touching, tasting, hearing, smelling, and seeing. The use of all their senses is the forerunner of the later development of the simple concepts that will make it possible for the child to begin to think and reason. Gradually there will come a differentiation of self from nonself and the capacity to relate to other human beings.

Infancy also is the period when each child begins to experience the first pressures of the cultural patterns which will have a profound influence on both growth and learning. By the end of the

27

first and during the second year of life each child must begin to learn that there are limits and sometimes various and contradictory expectations of what is acceptable behavior. Part of growing up will be learning to find ways to cope with the myriad demands made by the process called socialization.

As babies develop during the first two years, they will walk upright and begin to use language, enabling them to grow in independence and to participate with increasing adequacy in a world of people. The dividing line between infant and toddler is a shadowy one. Once a little child has crossed it, parents may suddenly realize that their little one is no longer a baby. Certainly being able to walk is part of being a toddler, but also it is a time when there are growing signs of less dependency. It is a transition, often a short one, between being a baby and becoming a runabout child. Language is being understood and words are spoken. Actions are beginning to have direction. Toddlers show many signs of knowing what they want, and make attempts to gain it. They are no longer babies nor quite young children, but they are clearly on the way.

The first two years of a child's life seem amazing because of the constant change and development, but the years from about two to five are equally amazing because of the growth in knowledge, independence, and the ability to cope with new situations. It is a period when growing children are beginning to form basic attitudes about themselves, the people around them, and the world in which they live. The attitudes they develop about themselves and other people will color their behavior not only during these three years but later on as well.

Because of their physical activity, which is so characteristic, we often call these the runabout years. Runabout children are gradually moving away from the self-centeredness of the baby, although they still see things in terms of themselves and have difficulty in realizing that other people have different points of view. They are beginning to learn to share and to understand that other people's personal and property rights must be considered—that they must sometimes give up their own way to fit into a pattern more comfortable for everyone. This is the beginning of complicated learning that will continue throughout life.

During early childhood, children also must master concepts of the world about them. What are stars and flowers? Where does water come from? What is hot and cold? There are hosts of ideas we take for granted that children must question and understand before they enter school. The beginnings of the concepts of time—today, yesterday, tomorrow, weeks, months, and years—are developing. Children must begin learning numbers and letters as symbols. They must learn to understand what is big, what is little, and what is real rather than make-believe.

In their social growth, they have to learn what it means to be a boy or girl, a man or woman, how to play with other children, and how to cope with problems when grown-ups are not around. They must learn to listen and not always interrupt, to wait for attention, and to ask instead of snatching. They need to learn, too, a few manners that make getting along with other people easier. They have to develop concepts of relationships.

28

What sort of relationships exist between fathers and mothers and children, neighbors, teachers, doctors and nurses, mailcarriers, and other community helpers? Often they act out these relationships in their imaginative play. They must master the ability to live in a family and share mother and father with other children and adults. Later they need to learn to share their teachers and their friends with other children.

Probably more learning takes place during these years of early childhood than in any other period of a child's life. This is not the formal learning that we associate with the school years, but rather the accumulation through experience of a child's first knowledge of the world. This is a time of absorbed watching, questioning, and exploring. Young children are alive with curiosity. *How, why, what, where* are constantly in their vocabularies. Yet they still live in a magical world—anything seems possible. Through their gradually increasing knowledge and experience they will move closer to the world of reality, becoming better able to distinguish that which is fantasy and imagination from that which is real.

There is no time in life when the world is as fresh and wonderful as it is to children during these runabout years. They are fortunate if they grow up among adults who treasure for them this period of childhood and provide for them the opportunities to explore their world widely and safely—adults who give them time to grow without pushing them ahead into experiences that they are not yet ready to assimilate.

This is indeed important. The ability to learn, to modify behavior through experience, is innate within every child, but barring severe handicaps, how much learning will take place during these early years and in the years ahead will be determined largely by the amount of appropriate stimulation which is received, and the opportunities and encouragement which are provided by the child's environment. This does not mean that environment alone will produce effective learning. The biological maturation of the nervous and muscular systems, the readiness of the organism to achieve certain forms of learning must also be taken into account. No amount of teaching will make it possible for a newborn baby to learn to distinguish its mother as a special person, a three-month-old to sit up or walk, or a toddler to reason abstractly. Children must pass through many phases of maturation before there will be a readiness to use words, or the ability to bring ideas together in order to be able to cope with problems.

The ability of a child to think, to bring ideas together in some form and carry them out in action is known as cognitive development. It involves perceiving, storing impressions in memory and being able to retrieve them, bringing impressions together into ideas or concepts, and seeing relationships and generalizing from them. It involves the ability to bring ideas together into some kind of logical formation which can lead to the adjustment to new experiences and to the solving of problems. It requires the ability to relate what happens in the present to past experiences, and later to be able to project into the future and to deal with abstract concepts. The use of language and of symbols is required to make it possible to deal with knowledge beyond actual experience. The path from the early thought processes in the nine-month-old baby to those of an in-

29

telligent adult is complicated. There are many theories as to how all this occurs, but there is agreement that cognitive development helps make us distinctly human beings.

It is thought that these years of early childhood, from the first barely sustained attention of the newborn to the accumulation of the many functioning concepts of the five-year-old who is off to kindergarten, are the most significant years in the cognitive process. During these early childhood years, the foundation for later and more intricate cognitive development is laid. A child who is deprived of the necessary learning experiences during these years may remain lagging behind in these areas throughout life.

# chapter 3

# The Very Beginning

THE BEGINNING OF LIFE   The main concern of those who work with children is with the growing and developing child after birth. Indeed, many people are accustomed to speaking as if life begins when a baby is born. Actually the process which results in the individual life of every child begins at conception with the uniting of the sperm of the father and the ovum of the mother. These two minute cells contain all the potentials of a new person. As soon as they unite, the miracle of growth begins. During the following nine months development will progress steadily, in just as vital a fashion as development after birth. What happens to the growing organism within the uterus is highly significant in its effect on normal growth and development after birth. We cannot ignore this period of intrauterine growth if we are to understand fully the continuity of development that begins nine months before a child is born.

Each child's potential characteristics are determined at the time of conception. Within the nucleus of each sperm and ovum are microscopic rods called chromosomes. These rods include tightly coiled spiral molecules of DNA (deoxyribonucleic acid) made up of ladderlike chains of atoms. DNA in the chromosomes is the material basis of heredity. The actual carriers of heredity, or genes, are areas within the spiral molecules of DNA. These genes determine the characteristics that will be passed on to the child from parents and from other ancestors through the parents. There are specific genes for such inherited characteristics as color of eyes, texture and color of hair, pigmentation of skin, length of fingers, shape of nose and ears, height, and body build. Complex factors such as the potentials of intelligence and temperament in such areas as activity, introversion or extroversion, and emotional responsiveness seem to be influenced by the genes. There also is some indication that artistic, musical, and mathematical potentiality may be transmitted by genes. The baby's sex is determined by a special Y chromosome from the father. No method has yet been found to effectively control the determination of sex, although there are indications that it may be possible in the future.

The genes control the way in which the body grows and the development of particular body functions. This amazing process is carried out by "directions" which are given to the cells through a coding in the chemical structure of DNA. The discovery of DNA and its influence on the development of life and the control of growth has brought a new understanding of the functioning of the chromosomes. It has opened up new fields of exploration which, in the years ahead, will provide much more accurate knowledge of the passing on and selection of inherited characteristics and the whole process of life itself. It may be necessary to modify many of our present concepts of hereditary factors in the light of new findings.

Each parent has twenty-three pairs of chromosomes, but only one of each pair is included in any given sperm or ovum. Each man may have over eight million combinations of chromosomes in his sperm cells, and there are just as many different possibilities for a given ovum. Since pure chance seems to determine which member of each pair winds up in a single sperm or ovum, the heredity of each child (except identical twins) will be different. This is the reason why children in the same family can be so different from one another, although they also may have some characteristics in common. They have the same parents but they have not received the same chromosomes or chromosomal patterns and, therefore, do not have entirely similar genes. Identical (or monozygotic) twins have identical chromosomes, because only they develop from the same fertilized ovum.

The selection of the particular genes takes place when one sperm out of the many available thousands reaches, by chance, the mature ovum that is ready for fertilization. At birth within every girl baby's two ovaries, there are about one-quarter of a million immature egg cells; of these about 400 will mature during the reproductive cycle. Once a month, midway between the menstrual periods, an egg becomes mature and leaves the ovary. This is called ovulation. The egg, or ovum, makes its way slowly through the fallopian tube toward the uterus, or womb. Usually only one egg is discharged each month, but occasionally two or more become mature. If two should be fertilized, fraternal (or dizygotic) twins are born. In rare instances, women have given birth to as many as seven babies. Although one egg is usually released, thousands of sperm from among the millions stored within a man's testicles may be discharged at any one time.

Both the mature ovum and sperm have short lives. Conception can take place only within about two days after ovulation, and it is a fresh and vital sperm that is most likely to fertilize the ovum. This means that a child can be conceived during approximately the fertile two-day period in any month.

ORDERLY GROWTH, SUITABLE ENVIRONMENT  Following conception, growth follows an amazingly orderly course as the fertilized egg cell develops to form a body pattern which will be ready for birth as an infant in about 265 days. There is a special timetable for the development of each part of the growing body. If development does not occur in its normal sequence at the appropriate time, the result will be seen at birth in defects such as a harelip, cleft palate, defective heart, or deformed limbs.

32

During these 265 days, called the prenatal period, the developing baby is known by several names. In the *germinal period,* which is the first two weeks of development, the developing cells are called a *zygote;* during the next six weeks, the *embryonic period,* an *embryo;* from eight weeks until birth, the *fetal period,* a *fetus;* at birth and for two weeks afterwards, a *neonate.*

Nature has provided not only a plan for growth but also a suitable environment for growth. Within the uterus, the developing baby is suspended in a membrane sac and immersed in amniotic fluid within the sac. The thickened, soft, spongy walls of the uterus provide further cushioning, while the mother's wide, supporting pelvic bones serve as a shield.

Although before birth the developing fetus is completely dependent on the mother for survival, there is no direct connection between the blood stream of the mother and that of the fetus. The connection, or exchange, is through the placenta. This is a spongy, complex tissue which develops after conception. It is composed of a mass of blood vessels and connecting tissues which are attached to the wall of the uterus. It is connected with the fetus by the umbilical cord, which is attached to the abdomen at the point that becomes the navel. Blood vessels of the fetus run through the cord into the placenta. The circulation exchange is through the membrane of the placenta, one side of which is bathed with maternal blood. This membrane permits oxygen and necessary nutriments from the mother's blood to reach the circulatory system of the fetus. It also enables carbon dioxide and other wastes from the fetal circulation to pass into the maternal blood stream.

There is no direct connection between the nervous system of the mother and that of the fetus. The old superstition that a mother's thoughts can harm or mark her child is untrue. What she sees, hears, thinks, or reads cannot directly influence her child before birth. The fetus does respond, however, to vibrations from the outside world and sometimes appears to be more active if exposed to loud noises. Increased fetal activity may also be evidenced when the mother is tense, excited, or excessively fatigued. For example, there is some evidence that adrenalin, which is released into the mother's system when she is under extreme tension, may pass through the placenta into the circulatory system of the fetus resulting in increased fetal activity.

INTERRUPTIONS IN ORDERLY GROWTH  In spite of nature's protective mechanisms, the fetus is not invulnerable. Even before birth the environment can interfere with the optimum development of capacities, even with the ability to be born alive.

We do not know all the factors that may interrupt the sequence of normal growth, but we do know that there are specific environmental factors which, if they occur at a certain stage of development, may damage a particular organ as it develops. For instance, the otherwise benign infection of German measles, if contracted by the mother during the first three months of pregnancy, can have serious effects on the baby's eyes,

33

ears, or heart, or even result in mental deficiency. Other virus and bacterial infections and toxemia during pregnancy also may affect the development of the embryo and fetus. The spirochetes of syphilis can be passed on from the mother to the fetus causing either a miscarriage or a congenital infection which results in a baby born with syphilis. If the mother is treated for syphilis early in pregnancy, preferably before the eighteenth week, the baby may escape the syphilitic infection.

Both the embryo and the fetus are more sensitive than the mother to large doses of X-ray or atomic radiation. Such doses can produce defects, particularly in the nervous system. The widely publicized effects of the drug thalidomide on prenatal development adds to the evidence of the vulnerability of the embryo during these early weeks. Many of the babies whose mothers had taken the drug early in pregnancy were born with an absent or defective limb. As a result, the possible effects of other drugs are being carefully studied. Doctors are warning mothers-to-be that other drugs may be harmful to the embryo and that all drugs should be avoided during pregnancy unless they are taken on the advice of a physician.

There is growing evidence that the mother's nutrition may affect the growth of the fetus, particularly if there is a deficiency in protein, in vitamins, especially vitamin B, and in minerals. Babies born in a poverty-stricken environment frequently are smaller in all dimensions than those born in a more favorable environment. Inadequate maternal diet also appears to be related to stillbirths, some congenital defects, and some types of retarded development. A spontaneous abortion or a miscarriage may occur if the damage to the embryo or the fetus from the mother's malnutrition is great.

The Surgeon General's report on "Smoking and Health" indicates that women who smoke during pregnancy tend to have smaller babies and a significantly greater number of premature deliveries than nonsmokers of a comparable social group. Whether the mother's smoking is permanently detrimental to the child's development is not known; however, size at birth and premature delivery do have permanent effects upon the development of some children.

A growing awareness of and alertness to environmental and congenital factors that can harm fetal development should eventually reduce the number of children born with handicaps. Research in this field is progressing rapidly. It is already possible to detect some defects or problems in the development of the fetus before birth. One of the major breakthroughs has been the ability to detect the extra chromosome which results in mental retardation from Down's syndrome, frequently called mongolism.

It is also possible to avert the consequences of the Rh factor, which occurs if the blood type of the mother is Rh negative and that of the father Rh positive. This is a serious condition which develops in some pregnancies, beginning with a second child because of incompatibility between the blood of the mother and that of the fetus. This condition can lead to miscarriage, stillbirth, early infant death, or brain damage if the infant does survive. Damage can be prevented if the blood types of the par-

34

ents are checked before or early in pregnancy. If the incompatibility develops, a blood transfusion replacing all of the baby's blood can be given to the fetus before delivery, usually about the seventh month. Progress is also being made in the inoculation of the mother following the first pregnancy. This holds promise at preventing the development of the incompatibility.

PRENATAL DEVELOPMENT  Even before the mother is aware that conception has taken place, the growth of the new individual is proceeding at a remarkable rate. During the weeks that pass before the first evidence of pregnancy (usually the cessation of menstruation), development has already progressed from the first to the second stage of the prenatal period—from a zygote, smaller than the dot over this *i*, to an embryo ten thousand times larger, complete with rudimentary eyes, ears, mouth, and brain, simple kidneys, a liver, a digestive tract, a blood stream, and a tubelike heart that begins to beat on about the twenty-fifth day. All this in a body about one quarter inch long.

At the end of the first two months, when the embryo becomes a fetus, the body structure begins to be recognizable. The ears and eyes have begun to grow. The teeth are forming. The blood is circulating and the heart is beating, though it cannot be heard yet. By the end of two and a half months, the fetus has a head, nose, mouth, fingers, and toes. The other organs have started to develop and bones are beginning to harden into the skeleton that will later enable a baby to stand up and walk. The growing organization of the nervous and muscular systems is apparent to the mother a few weeks later, when she begins to feel movement inside her. At first, activity is in the muscles of the head, arms, body, and legs. A little later the eyes and hands also move; some fetuses even suck their thumbs.

In three and a half months the gums are developed, and there are signs of the coming teeth. Fingernails and toenails are forming. The heartbeat can be heard at about the sixteenth to the eighteenth week, and at this time the mother begins to feel more activity and more strength in the fetal movements.

The last three months of the prenatal period are marked by steady growth and a continuing refinement of structure and function. The seven-month-old fetus has a good chance of surviving if born prematurely. However, the premature baby may be very small in size, frequently weighing only two or three pounds, for the development of fat takes place in the last months of pregnancy. The low birth weight and incomplete development of the premature may result in permanent handicaps affecting future physical and neurological development.

During the last two months growth is rapid; length increases from fourteen to about twenty-one inches, and weight increases to about seven pounds at birth. At birth the newborn is often wrinkled and red, sometimes the head is temporarily misshapen due to pressure during the birth process. In fact, parents may feel some shock and concern over the appearance of their newborn child if they have been anticipating a smooth, pink-skinned, chubby baby.

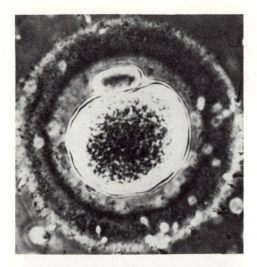

At conception (upper left), sperm attempt to penetrate the egg. Fertilization is completed in about thirty-five hours, when a sperm reaches the nucleus of the ovum. In the third week (middle left), the two lobes of the brain and the developing spinal cord and vertebrae can be distinguished. At forty days (lower left), many of the internal organs have developed in rudimentary form. The root-covered capsule shown here in cross-section houses the embryo during the first and second months; the roots provide nourishment as well as anchorage to the uterus. At approximately two months (lower right), the physical structure of the baby will be essentially complete. When the fetus is ready for birth (opposite page), contractions of the uterus gradually push the child through the birth canal. As shown, fathers may be present at the birth of their babies as well as offer supportive help during labor.

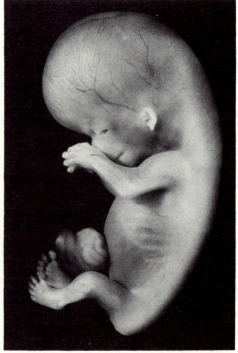

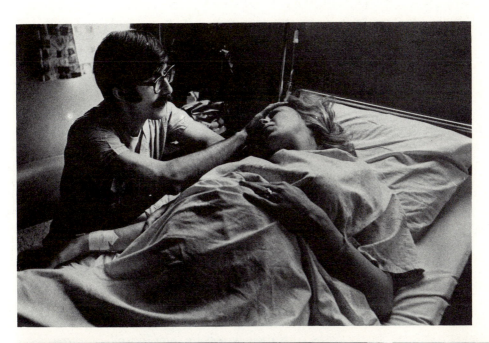

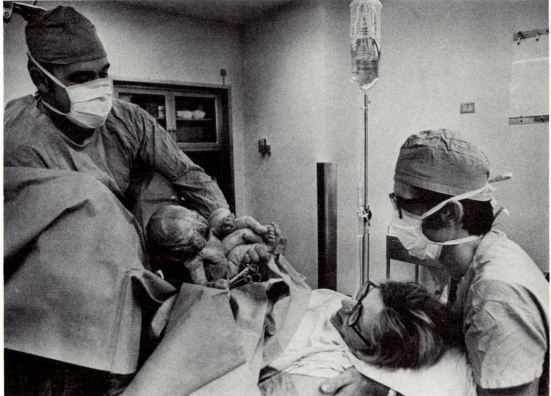

THE BIRTH PROCESS When the fetus is ready for birth, the mother experiences contractions of the uterus, which are called labor pains. Through the pressure of these contractions, which begin gradually and increase in intensity and frequency, the membranes that have supported and protected the fetus are broken. The amniotic fluid leaves the mother's body at some time during this process. The baby (or the neonate as it technically should be called for the next two weeks) is gradually pushed by the contractions through the birth canal, which is enlarged at this time by its special capacity to stretch.

The birth process may be relatively easy or difficult, depending on the size and structure of mother and child, the elasticity of the mother's muscles, the physical condition of the mother, and the position of the child. The mental attitude of the mother may also influence the birth. Tension caused by fear and anxiety at the time of the birth may make the birth process longer and more difficult. Studies also have shown that a mother prepared through special exercises and an understanding of the birth process usually will have an easier time during the birth than a mother whose muscles have not undergone preparation and whose lack of understanding of the normal stages of the birth process causes her to approach the delivery of her child with fear. Such preparation for childbirth may be given through a prenatal course recommended by an obstetrician, or one offered by a hospital in the months before delivery. Fathers are encouraged to attend such classes with their wives. In some hospitals, fathers now may be present at the birth of their babies, and are encouraged to give supportive help to their wives during the period of labor. Consequently, there is increasing recognition of the importance of prenatal care to prepare the mother for the birth process and also to prevent those complications of pregnancy that are likely to harm mother or child.

The period of birth usually varies from twelve to twenty-five hours for the first baby. With some babies, however, the process is much more rapid than this, and with others it is considerably slower. The duration of labor typically is shorter for subsequent babies than for the first one.

ENTERING A NEW WORLD The baby's environment changes dramatically at birth. In the uterus the temperature was stable; the baby was cushioned and protected; the mother supplied all of the needs for survival. But at birth this close connection with the mother is abruptly broken; the baby must breathe air for survival, and this adaptation must be made quickly. Babies normally cry as they enter the world. This cry is an important signal that the lungs have inflated and begun to function. With the start of breathing, the valves of the heart alter the circulatory pattern and the blood flows to the lungs instead of the placenta.

The placenta, which is no longer needed, is expelled following the delivery of the baby. It is then called the afterbirth. The umbilical cord, which is still attached to the baby, is tied and cut off. This is done without pain to the child, since the cord contains no nerves. Now the baby must take food, digest it, and excrete wastes. Responses to changes in body temper-

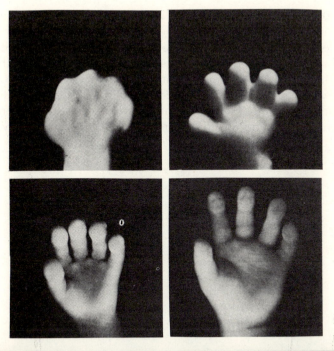

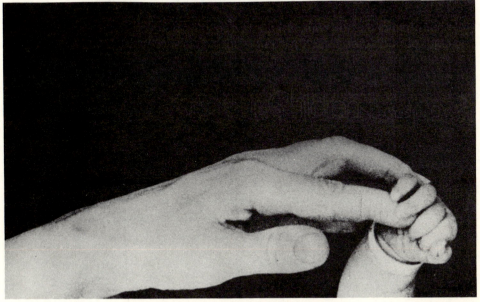

ature also are necessary as are reactions to an environment which is no longer quiet and protected but contains many varieties of stimuli. From the moment a child is born, adaptation is essential to survival. This need for adaptation is present throughout life; indeed, without it life would cease. It is this necessity and capacity to adapt that has enabled human beings to conquer the environment and to meet life's problems.

We do not know much about the effect birth has on the child. Most babies come through in fine condition, but a few suffer brain damage in the process; such birth injury is one cause of cerebral palsy. Studies indicate that children whose birth was difficult are more likely than other children to develop symptoms that may include poor coordination, undue restlessness, hyperactivity, and distractibility—possibly as a result of slight, often undetected injuries to the brain. But birth is a normal process for which the mother's body can be well prepared, and, ordinarily, delivery will take place without damage to the newborn child.

# chapter 4

# The Infant-Child

PHYSICAL DEVELOPMENT AT BIRTH  Many people think of a newborn baby as a complete miniature person equipped with small replicas of adult organs, ready to function immediately and efficiently, as though all that takes place in the years ahead will be growth in size. This is not quite so. Although all the organs are present and ready to function at birth, the heart, lungs, and digestive tract must undergo further development before they will function maturely. The bones of the baby are softer than those of adults, and their proportions and shapes are different. Nerve and muscle structures are still incomplete. Although the brain of the newborn baby has a structure similar to the brain of the adult, many nerve tracts have not yet acquired their outer sheaths. The process of myelination, or the gradual acquiring of the sheaths, is essential for the development of the motor skills which are the basis of the beginnings of intelligence in an infant-child. Myelination usually has taken place by about the fourth month. The four pieces of bone that make up the skull have not grown together yet, so there is a soft spot on the top of the baby's head known as the *fontanel*. This will close sometime between nine months and two years. The tooth buds are present, but there are no teeth except in rare instances.

Girl babies are further advanced physiologically than boys. Because of this advancement, their teeth usually appear earlier, their body organs mature earlier, and X-ray studies show that their bone development usually is ahead of that of boys. Infant girls have proportionately more fat than boys, but infant boys have a greater proportion of muscle tissue than girls and are usually heavier and longer at birth than girls.

At birth, a baby is able to suck. When a nipple is placed in the newborn's mouth, sucking movements result, weak at first but becoming increasingly vigorous. If the region about the mouth of a baby is touched there is movement toward the direction of the stimulus. This is known as the *rooting reflex* which serves to guide the baby's mouth toward the nipple. A newborn, when held close to the mother or any other person's body, will usually begin to root and try to suck, abilities which are necessary for survival.

If a newborn is startled by a loud noise or a sudden loss of support, particularly of the head, the arms spontaneously fly out and then return

41

toward the chest in a clutching fashion as if there were an attempt to regain support or hold on to something. This is called the *Moro reflex;* it disappears about the third month. A newborn's grasp on a finger is also surprisingly strong. For a few weeks after birth many babies can support their weight for two minutes or longer by such grasping. These two reflexes are probably survival mechanisms from a long ago, primitive past when an infant had to be able to cling to the mother in order to survive.

The newborn's senses function at birth or shortly thereafter, but vary in activity. New babies hear well. They are easily startled by a sudden or loud noise, and seem to respond more intensely to a high pitch rather than a low one. They can be soothed by a gentle voice, but cannot understand words nor even connect the voice with a person. Although we do not know what a newborn baby actually perceives, we do know that soon after birth a baby's eyes are able to follow a slowly moving light, and that the pupils dilate in darkness and constrict in light. There is growing evidence that a baby may see more than had been supposed. Some interesting experiments on the observation of eye-movements in the newborn and young infants suggest that the baby reacts differently to white or black or patterned stimuli. For instance, the eyes of the babies studied seemed to scan the edges of a black triangle on a white surface—the contrast seemed to hold their attention.

The sense of touch is evident at birth. Body contact with the mothering person seems soothing to the baby. A sense of pain also is evident soon after birth, but seems to vary in different infants. Although a sense of taste does not seem present at birth, within two weeks some observers have found that a baby will grimace at a taste of citric acid and make sucking responses to sugar. Although the sense of smell does not seem strong, a baby will turn the head away from a strong, unpleasant odor such as ammonia.

Soon after birth newborns can flex and extend their limbs, kick their legs and wave their arms, but these movements are random, unorganized. The baby can neither control nor direct them until further development occurs.

Most of the time the new baby sleeps; many may even have difficulty staying awake long enough to nurse. Even at birth, however, differences are evident. Some babies are easily startled and wake easily, others are rarely disturbed. These differences may affect the interaction between parents and child in the months ahead. Some parents may find it difficult to live with a restless child who wakes easily and disturbs their own activities and sleep.

ADJUSTMENT TO THE ENVIRONMENT  Newborn babies relate to their environment in the outer world through their sensory experiences. They cannot think, they can only feel and respond with involuntary, reflex actions. They respond to discomfort by crying when they are hungry, wet, cold, or uncomfortable. If the cry is answered and the baby is made more comfortable, tension is released and a feeling of comfort is restored. If the cry is unanswered, the discomfort persists and tension mounts within the baby resulting in prolonged and sometimes intense crying. This is a baby's first means of communication, a spontaneous cry of distress. The studies of the late Dr. Aldrich at the Mayo Clinic on the crying of the newborn were among the first to help us understand the automatic nature of the infant's cry and the response when the cry is answered. Contrary to popular belief, such attention will not spoil the baby who is not yet capable of voluntarily planning to cry in order to attract attention.

A desirable environment for both physical and emotional growth is one in which the baby is not only cared for physically, but also feels the warmth of human contact from a mothering person who not only answers the baby's cries, but also soothes, comforts, cuddles, and talks to the baby. Even when given adequate physical care, a baby left lying in a crib without human response is deprived of the mental stimulation and emotional warmth which are essential for normal development.

Usually it is the mother who provides the first warm relationship with the baby, although it may be some other nurturing person. Newborn babies do not recognize their mothers as persons, for they begin life in a world in which one thing is not clearly differentiated from another, but they do respond to gentleness or roughness of touch, the way they are held or moved, and the ease or difficulties of nursing. Studies have shown that if a mother is tense, overanxious, or abrupt when she handles the baby, the infant may respond with greater restlessness and crying. A mother communicates with the baby through body contact. If she can learn to be relaxed and at ease when she handles the baby, the infant usually responds positively, seeming more content, relaxed, and comfortable.

43

NURSING THE BABY During this first month babies begin to explore the world with their mouths, one of the most sensitive sensory areas. Nursing brings comfort and contentment and is one of the ways through which closeness to the mother is continued. Later, babies will not only use their mouths in rooting for the nipple and receiving food but also will mouth toys, fingers, or whatever is within reach. This is one of the ways in which exploration of the world through the senses begins.

If first experiences with nursing are difficult or frustrating, babies may respond with restless crying and may experience greater difficulty in developing feelings of trust and security. Some babies do not learn to suck easily and must be helped with the sucking process; others may develop colic, which makes them uncomfortable and, as a result, irritable. These conditions can be so disturbing to both baby and mother that sometimes tension develops, making it more difficult for the mother to give the gentle, relaxed comfort and care a baby needs. This potential problem needs to be recognized, since the mother may need help in adjusting to a child who has feeding difficulties at the very beginning of life, if she is not to feel mounting irritation and frustration over the extra time, comfort, and care such a baby needs.

Whether or not bottle-fed babies receive sufficient gratification of their emotional needs has been a matter of considerable discussion. Equally competent pediatricians differ in their opinions on the subject. A baby seems to gain physically just as well when fed by bottle as by breast. Some feel that breast feeding has a psychological advantage—that it brings about a closeness between mother and child that is valuable for the baby's emotional development and the development of maternal feelings toward the child. This would seem to be true only if the mother wishes to nurse the baby: If a mother breast feeds without really wanting to, the feeling of harmony between mother and child, one of the most important benefits of nursing, is lost. A mother who bottle feeds can establish much the same closeness and warmth by holding the baby when giving the bottle, or holding and cuddling the baby at other times.

SELF-DEMAND FEEDING Because there are individual differences in food needs which are apparent even at this early age, it is wise to adjust the schedule to meet these individual needs. Instead of feeding the baby at certain prescribed hours, which was the recommended practice for many years, the baby's feeding schedule usually can be adjusted to hunger needs. Such a plan is called *self-demand feeding*. It is known that some babies are hungry in two hours, some in three hours, and others in four hours. Self-demand feeding recognizes these differences, so a baby is fed according to a personal pattern. However, if a mother should be overly anxious or unable to differentiate between hunger cries and cries that may signal other needs, or if she is so tense about her baby that she offers the breast or bottle at every cry, it might be better for the relationship between mother and child if the baby were on a more definite schedule. Most babies soon find their own schedule and within a month or six weeks settle down to fairly regular feedings.

Studies made of babies on self-demand schedules seem to show that, on the whole, they are contented and responsive babies who cry less than many babies fed on a more rigid schedule. Self-demand babies also regulate the amount of food they need; consequently, the mother does not have to feel that she must force a certain amount of breast milk or formula upon the child, regardless of whether or not hunger seems to have been satisfied.

GROWING AWARENESS AND RESPONSIVENESS During the second month babies become increasingly alert. Their muscles are stronger. They begin to kick and exercise more than they did when they were newborn. They fuss more if they are restrained. They are not as compliant when being dressed or changed. Arms, legs, and fingers are less curled up than at birth. The head still looks too big for the body and is still wobbly when unsupported, but two-month-old babies usually are able to lift their chins and during this month also will be able to lift their chests. They take more milk or formula at a feeding, and may even sleep through the night without waking from hunger.

Many babies have already found their thumbs and suck them contentedly. Often a crying spell stops as a thumb is slipped into the mouth. Again there seem to be individual differences in the amount of sucking babies need; some babies suck their thumbs constantly, others rarely. The amount of a baby's sucking may be determined in part by the length of time spent at the breast or bottle; there is some indication that slow-nursing babies do not suck their thumbs as much as fast nursers. Thumb-sucking may also serve as a release for some inner tension or need for comfort, or it may merely provide a pleasurable sensation to the child's sensitive lip and mouth areas. We do not know just why many babies seek the comfort of a thumb; such sucking is considered harmless, and usually it decreases gradually as the child becomes interested in other things. Parents' efforts do not seem to affect the amount of sucking that is done.

Sometime during the second month, the baby gives the first real smile of response. This always delights parents, even though the smile is not really a recognition of them as individuals. At first babies smile at anyone who pays attention to them; it has even been reported that some babies will smile at a full-face mask that moves in front of them. Again there are individual differences, for some babies are much more responsive and smile more readily than others.

The infant's smile is not only delightful but important, for it is one of the first real responses to someone else. But even though the baby's perceptive powers are increasing, there is not enough experience or memory to separate people or objects from one another with any real meaning. That will come later.

During the second three months it is exciting to watch how babies grow. They are awake much more of the time and seem to enjoy being near people. They respond to mother, father, and other children in the

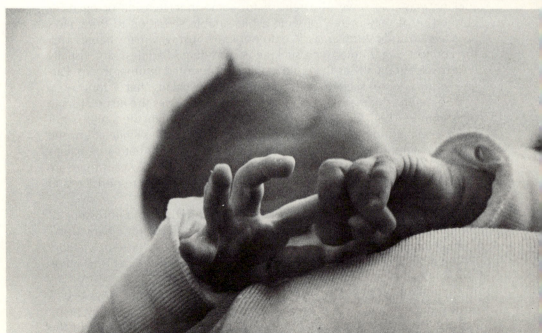

The infant's growing awareness and responsiveness is exciting to watch. Adjustment to the environment expands as parents and infant-child interact with each other. Physical care as well as mental stimulation and emotional warmth are essential elements in this interaction.

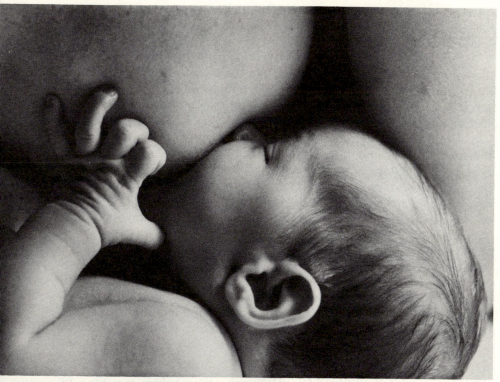

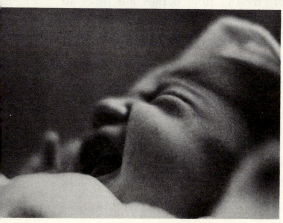

47

family, and will often smile and respond to strangers. There now are babbles and coos and smiles and even the beginning of laughter. It is possible to carry on "conversations." This is another step in communication (the cry was the first). Babbling is important for later language development, for this is the beginning of the mastery of sounds that will later be used in forming words.

Some babies from the very beginning are more responsive than others. Their responsiveness gives pleasure to those who care for them which in turn calls out their responsiveness toward the baby. Unresponsive babies frequently get less stimulation from others than they need—they are more often left alone in their cribs for much of the time. Such early difference in babies can color the beginning of their relationships with others which is so essential for their emotional growth.

It is during the second three months that babies begin to relate to the mothering person in a special way. Often the persons who care for them the most intimately can soothe and quiet them when other people are unsuccessful, or the baby turns toward the mother or mothering person with special smiles or holds out arms to be held. There are indications that babies thrive best when there is one central mothering person to whom they form an attachment by the middle of this first year. This attachment provides the feelings of security and trust which make it possible for the baby to grow into warm relationships with other people all through life.

This does not mean that other mothering people, including fathers, may not be an important additional help in providing a warm and loving atmosphere in which babies may learn to relate to others. It is possible, in fact, that the important need is for warm, personalized care and that such care could result in a feeling of security and trust without a central mothering person. So far, the evidence would seem to indicate that both are needed. Studies do show that babies who must be placed in institutions in which they are cared for by many different individuals who have no ongoing personal attachment to them, do not thrive as well as babies who have more personal mothering care.

IMPROVED COORDINATION By the time babies are three to four months old, the nerve cells of the brain are more efficiently related to the different muscle groups, so that some voluntary actions begin to be possible. This improvement in coordination follows a downward sequence, starting with the head, then the upper body, and ending with the legs. Babies are able to turn their heads and reach out to obtain something long before they can walk.

Now at the sight of the breast or the bottle, a baby's mouth may be opened in readiness. By this time babies are beginning to take a greater variety of soft foods, for the neuromuscular development of the tongue and throat now makes possible the swallowing of foods other than liquids. However, if new foods are offered too soon, the baby may not be able to handle them and will push them out with lips or tongue.

Eyes are beginning to focus better. The cross-eyed look so disturbing to many parents of newborns is less frequent. Most babies still sleep much of the time, usually falling asleep as soon as they have been fed. Crying is still the means of communicating a need, and it is wise to answer it and supply the attention, comfort, or change of position that seems to be needed. Babies are now able to change their own positions in a limited way. They can wriggle and twist around and possibly even roll over. They can hold their heads more steadily and look around a bit when they are laid on the stomach. The muscles of arms, legs, and trunk are larger and stronger. The whole body is more active, with many random movements of arms and legs. Occasionally a three-month-old baby will catch hold of a toe or a swinging toy, but he cannot yet plan to do so. Movements are still automatic rather than voluntary. The mind cannot yet guide the body.

If needs are being satisfied, babies now cry less for immediate attention and often will lie happily looking at their hands and feet or watching the sunlight and shadows in motion on the ceiling or the movement of the branches of trees. They may watch a mobile with fascination or reach for the toys on a cradle-gym. Around the fourth month as coordination improves, babies begin to really play with their fingers and toes; they may be able to grasp a rattle or clasp their hands around the bottle. Arms and legs are straightening out to some extent and body proportions are better. The top-heavy look is disappearing.

Four-month-old babies are not content just to lie on their backs when they are awake, but try to turn over, and sometimes they may succeed. By the fifth month they will be able to turn over with ease. It is a big step toward independence when babies learn to change their own position. By this time babies also enjoy being held in a sitting position for a short time. When supported on the lap or against a shoulder, they can hold the head erect and fairly steady and enjoy watching what is going on.

By five months babies laugh aloud and respond gaily when played with. They enjoy being in a padded playpen or on a blanket on the floor. They are beginning to reach for toys and often succeed in grasping and holding them; they may even try to wriggle toward them. If propped up they will sit like a frog with the head pushed out. Some babies cut their first tooth during this month. Most babies begin teething, and some are irritable because their gums are sore, although the extent of such irritability varies greatly with individual babies. It is during this month that babies begin to chew on anything they can put into their mouths. They also may drool, because they cannot manage an increasing amount of saliva.

SIX MONTHS—A MIDPOINT   Six months is a real midpoint in the development of the first year. From here on, babies rapidly leave behind the helplessness of their first months and grow toward greater independence of action. They may try to sit alone; when they succeed, they will be able to see the world from a completely new position whenever they wish to do so. They take increasing delight in watching activities around them. Now they can enjoy the playpen for a longer period and usually can sit for a short time in a high chair or in a small, low chair. Their neuromuscular

49

development has reached the point where most of them can not only hold things but also have fun banging them on the ground and on the chair, or shaking them and dropping them. They often may seem absorbed for a minute or two as they look at something. Many babies are beginning to take sizable steps forward in amusing themselves. Most of them get up on all fours and rock back and forth as if they were all ready to be off and creeping. Occasionally a baby does begin to creep at this age.

Six-month-old babies know their mother well and sometimes cry if she goes out of the room. They notice the difference between familiar people and strangers. At this age babies may experience a period of shyness, showing fear or crying when a stranger approaches, or perhaps turn away and bury their heads in their mother's neck. Some observers place this period of shyness at five or six months, others at as late as eight months. But sometime during the middle part of this first year, most babies will "freeze" and then burst out crying at the sight of a stranger, perhaps even at the sight of their mother in sunglasses that make her less recognizable. During this period of being shy, babies should not be forced to go to strangers but rather should be allowed the security of nearness to their mother or those whom they know well. If they must be left with someone else, it should be someone who has spent at least a little time with them and so is not totally strange.

At six months babies enjoy going out and look with interest at people and dogs and cars or whatever catches their attention, although their interest spans remain short. They soon tire and often drop off to sleep.

By this time babies are able to take food off a spoon with their tongues and lips instead of having it put into their mouths. In fact, they often open their mouths and reach eagerly toward a spoon. They also are beginning to show food likes and dislikes, turning the head away or fussing if there is an attempt to make them eat when they do not want to. During this month babies are likely to cut two lower front teeth, the lower central incisors, indicating that they are moving out of the sucking stage into the biting stage.

ON THE MOVE   At about seven months the baby's back has become flat and strong, and the back and abdominal muscles are much better developed. It will soon be possible to sit up without help. Many seven-month-old babies are starting to get around more, and even try to crawl.

There are many different ways of crawling. Sometimes babies begin by just rocking back and forth on their knees before they find that they can move. Some babies hitch themselves along on the floor, some roll over and over, others arch along on their backs. Some go backward at first instead of forward. But whatever means they use, seven-month-olds usually are eager to try to get around. Many babies of this age also try to stand by grasping the edge of their playpens and attempting to pull themselves up from a kneeling or sitting position. Some seven-month-olds are successful, and very occasionally a child this age will even start to walk.

Seven-month-olds want to touch and handle and taste everything

50

within their reach. They put toys in their mouths, feel them, bang them on the floor, or on the tray of the high chair. This is just the beginning of an interest in touching, feeling, and mouthing everything within reach, an important stage in learning.

While the seven-month-old still picks things up with the whole hand and holds them tightly in the fist, the eight- to ten-month-old baby will become able to bring the thumb and the index finger together to pick up a small object. At this stage, the person who is caring for the baby must be careful to see that there are no buttons, pins, or other small objects within reach, because whatever can be picked up will probably be put into the mouth. Now babies can help feed themselves by taking up small pieces of food from the tray. The index finger is used to point and poke. From now on the infant will use fingers and hands more and more skillfully, manipulating everything eagerly, using both hands to reach, hold, and bang, and using fingers to pick up or explore available objects.

During the eighth and ninth months, growth begins to slow down. The baby's movements are no longer random. More and more time is spent practicing sitting, creeping, pulling oneself up, and getting ready to walk. Babies at this age are very active; they can creep rapidly, and get into all sorts of mischief if not watched carefully. Scoldings are useless, for babies are not able to understand what they may or may not do. Less sleep is needed, and one nap a day often is enough. The child's appearance changes greatly in these two months. There is more hair, and the face is beginning to lose its baby expression and take on the more individual characteristics of later childhood.

PROGRESS TOWARD CHILDHOOD  Babies at ten months seem more like children than they did at eight months. They can sit up alone whenever they want. They can usually stand with support, but should not be urged to do so until they show that they are ready and want to stand. They may be able to pull themselves up to a standing position, but they have difficulty getting down again. Sometimes they stand holding on to a chair or to the edge of the playpen and cry for someone to come and put them down; if no one does, they just topple over. A few babies begin to walk at ten months, although most are not ready for this development until some months later.

Ten-month-old babies show progress in still another way. They start to notice the different tones of voices and to know when there is approval or disapproval of what they have done. They begin to respond to "No, no" and may even pull back their hands and look at the person who is taking care of them if they are reaching for something they are learning is forbidden. This is the time to begin teaching some of the simple things babies must gradually learn, if they are to be able to live in harmony with other people. But even though they may seem to understand at the moment, they cannot be expected to remember very well from one time to the next. They cannot take responsibility for their actions. The "no" will have to be patiently repeated in each situation.

At ten months babies will respond and stop what they are doing if they are scolded and punished, but harsh tones frighten them and may develop anxiety and tension. Such teaching through fear, though sometimes effective, can block rather than encourage learning. The change from the permissiveness shown toward a younger baby must come gradually, or infant-children may become overly disturbed by the "dos" and the "don'ts" which seem to color life as they get a bit older. At this age babies are easily distracted, and their attention generally can be turned quite easily from something forbidden to something that they are allowed to have or do. This is a better way of teaching.

GRADUAL WEANING By ten months most babies are able to bite and chew well enough to eat solid food and can drink milk from a cup instead of a bottle, so that the gradual weaning process, which was probably started earlier, can soon be completed. Babies who were nursed have usually been weaned from the breast before this time—usually to a bottle—sometimes to a cup. Some babies, however, still want a bottle, especially at bedtime, well on into the next year. There is no "right time" to completely do away with the bottle, and, in most instances, a child should not be forced to give it up until there is emotional readiness. Most ten-month-old babies have reached this point, but many normal children still cling to the bedtime bottle at seventeen or eighteen months, seeming to need the comfort and security that it implies.

Weaning is one of the major adjustments babies must make. It not only involves a change in the way they get their food and the kind of food they will be offered, but it also makes a change in their relationships with their mothers. Younger babies associated eating with emotional satisfaction and closeness to their mothers. Later, when they are physically able to sit up in a chair and receive food entirely from a cup and spoon, with perhaps a bottle of milk at bedtime, the physical closeness to their mothers that they experienced as they nursed or took their bottles in her arms, and the comfort they derived from this closeness, are taken away from them.

If this step away from physical closeness is taken too suddenly or too soon, the baby may be greatly disturbed. This is why it is wise to take weaning slowly and in many steps. Even with the preparation that most babies receive today—being offered food by spoon as early as four or six weeks, and later being given occasional sips of juice and milk from a cup—doing away entirely with the breast or the bottle often is disturbing. A baby's emotional readiness for the final weaning needs to be taken into account. Some babies seem to need both the sucking and body closeness longer than others; some push the bottle or breast aside, preferring to drink from a cup, even before the mother is ready to complete weaning; some go through a period of clinging closely to the mother and not letting her out of their sight. Extra holding and cuddling at times other than meals may help the child's emotional adjustment. If babies are shown affection in other areas and at other times, weaning may be distressing but not unduly disturbing. It is the overall relationship with the mother or mothering

52

person which is the most important factor in emotional growth, not the effect of one experience, even if that experience may be distressing.

Babies may now reach for a spoon and try to feed themselves. If they are given a spoon they can grasp, they may be able to get some spoonsful into their mouths, doing a messy job but one that often delights and absorbs them. They also will try to eat with their fingers. This attempt to feed themselves, although perhaps not very satisfactory in the eyes of adults, is another important step toward independence. It is always a little sad if an adult is so concerned with cleanliness that the spoon is taken from the baby so a quicker and neater job can be done.

As with all growth steps, independence in eating comes gradually. Little children cannot always be expected to feed themselves just because they have shown an interest in trying and have had some success. They should be allowed to feed themselves as long as they are eager to do so; when interest lags, the parenting person should take over. Insistence on continuing first efforts will often discourage children and make it harder for them to try later.

NEW PLEASURES AND ACCOMPLISHMENTS Ten- or eleven-month-old babies usually respond to people whom they know, but sometimes they are hesitant about strangers, although not quite as shy as they were a few months ago. They are very responsive to their mother and want

53

to be near her. They often hold out their arms to be picked up. They like to sit on someone's lap, to romp and be played with. They enjoy watching other children. Toys may be thrown over the edge of the crib, high chair, or playpen with gleeful laughter. They also may throw things in anger. If allowed to explore the kitchen floor, they head for the cabinets and take out all the pots and pans. Now that they can use their hands more skillfully, they especially enjoy putting things into a container and taking them out again over and over—a spoon into a cup, clothespin into a box. They frequently amuse themselves happily while a parent goes about working, as long as they can watch or can see other children when outdoors in the playpen or yard. Cats, dogs, and birds fascinate them; they watch them with interest and try to reach and play with them. Passing cars and people also hold their attention. However, they will no longer stay contentedly in the playpen for long periods. They need to explore and can safely be allowed considerable leeway if they have a play space in which dangerous objects are out of reach.

They enjoy playing games and will display their abilities on request. This is the time to teach pat-a-cake and peekaboo. They love rhymes when they are chanted or sung and often enjoy listening to music. They are imitative and will repeat sounds like "da-da." Perhaps they may begin to wave "bye-bye." The child who is deprived of this kind of play may not develop as rapidly as might otherwise be possible. Care, of course, must be taken not to overstimulate or tire the child. Neither should responses be demanded of an unwilling baby.

A child's early accomplishments will depend partly on adult encouragement and partly on the maturity of growth. It is particularly important for adults to be constantly aware of the great variation between children in timing and achievement that may be expected even in this first year. There is a wide range of the normal, particularly in walking and in language development. Some children walk as early as ten months; others, equally intelligent, walk as late as sixteen or seventeen months. Some children begin to say words before they are a year old, while others use no words until they are eighteen months or older.

## THE FIRST YEAR—LAYING EMOTIONAL FOUNDATIONS

During these first twelve months babies have grown more rapidly than they will at any other time in their lives, excluding their prenatal development. Usually they have tripled their birth weight, and their length has increased by one third. They have developed from helpless, newborn infants, completely dependent upon others for care, even for a change of position, to infant-children who are able to move around, explore their environment, and assert themselves within that environment.

Year-old children express their wants through their actions. They show their anger when they are frustrated, or their pleasure when they are happy. They respond to other people and usually like to be with them, although they may continue to have moments of shyness or fear if they are approached too quickly or noisily. Each child has a definite and recogniz-

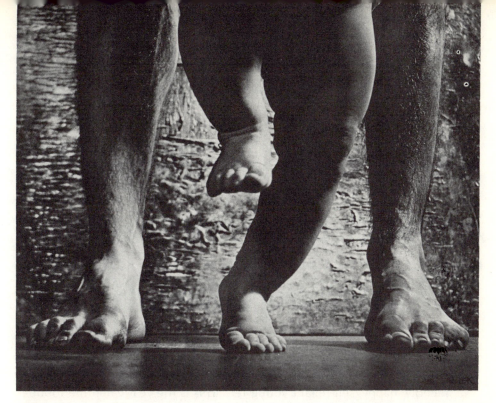

able personality. They are able to begin to learn through their interaction with their environment and with those around them who are caring for them. There is an emerging awareness of self as distinct from others.

The first year has been, to some extent, the "receiving" year in which the baby has been almost totally dependent upon others for survival. Yet even in this year parents and child have interacted and have influenced one another. The child has not received passively but has had to cooperate in order to receive. Milk had been offered, and the baby had to suck to take it. This is the beginning of cooperation. During this first year the parents and their baby have been learning to get to know one another, they have been learning to work together to establish a relationship in which they can cooperate with growth. During the time that the parents have been learning about their baby, the baby has been learning about them.

Parents and babies do indeed influence one another. Babies have very different temperaments which are evident even in the first two months of their lives. Studies have shown that some babies are cuddlers, others are noncuddlers who do not mold their bodies as readily into the arms or against the body of a mothering person. It is easier for parents to relate warmly to a baby who snuggles close to them rather than to one who stiffens up and seems to reject body contact. In the same way some babies smile more easily and frequently than others. Smiling babies call out smiling responses in those about them. Most babies are rhythmical in their biological functions so that the parents can arrange their own lives around the fairly predictable needs of the baby for food, sleep, and elimination. But there are babies who are not rhythmical—they are erratic sleepers, they want to be fed at irregular hours, their bowel movements are unpredictable. It is much more difficult to fit the routine needs of such babies into the needs of the rest of the family. A difficult baby is not necessarily the result of poor or inadequate parenting. The interaction of the personalities

55

of parent and child can be very real from an early age and in some cases disturbing to both parent and child. The cues of some babies as to their needs are often more difficult to understand and interpret than those of others. However, if parents try to learn to understand the kind of baby they have and try to meet the individual needs of their baby within the pattern of the emerging personality, the relationship can become a mutually satisfying one.

During this first year babies have not only been passing through a period of rapid and spectacular physical growth and development, but also have been experiencing those feelings which will lay the foundation for their ability to learn to trust and feel secure with other people. A child who is neglected or denied the warm, affectionate care which is needed for emotional growth during these early months of life may not be able to relate easily to other people later in life. Those parents who have been able to give to their baby the kind of affection, attention, and stimulation which all babies require, will have made a good start in building a warm and harmonious relationship. These babies who have been helped to develop a feeling of trust in their parents are likely to become capable, friendly, happy, self-reliant youngsters. This is the year when the foundations for learning to love and be loved are first laid.

By the end of the first year the once almost helpless baby has come a long way. Parents will need to realize increasingly that they no longer have a tiny infant, willing to play safely in the crib, high chair, or playpen, but a young explorer who needs scope and equipment for expanding activities.


## Study of a child

*EVERY BABY IS UNIQUE*
*Individuality Needs Recognition*

Today, the concept of individual differences is an accepted fact: We know that no two children are ever entirely alike. Their differences may encompass all areas of growth and development. Physical appearance and body build, mental alertness and potential, emotional qualities and responses, social attitudes and reactions—in the combination of characteristics each child is unique. As a total personality there is no duplicate. Frequently, however, parents forget this in caring for their children. As a result, they are likely to be concerned when ways followed easily and satisfyingly with one youngster do not seem to work well with another.

When their second baby girl arrived, the Aldens were delighted. They had enjoyed their first little girl, now a healthy, good-natured, alert three-year-old. They expected that Deborah would be just as responsive to their love and care.

"And everything will be so much easier with this one," Mrs. Alden said confidently to her husband. "When I think how awkward and jittery I used to be with Ellen, it almost makes me laugh. I won't have to worry about things now. I'll know just what to expect and what to do."

The father's memories of the first months of Ellen's babyhood were somewhat vague. But he knew that she had been a good baby who seldom cried and who seemed to be very willing to do whatever was expected of her. He supposed that her mother's care of Ellen had a great deal to do with this, and complacently agreed that all would go smoothly with the new baby. Three years ago business had kept him away from home so often that he had not had much part in caring for Ellen. He now anticipated less traveling and was glad that his work would keep him away less often. He wanted to watch Debbie grow, spend time with her as she progressed from babyhood, and have a share in meeting her needs. He expected no difficulty.

The first surprise came when Deborah was only a few weeks old. Coming home one evening in an especially jovial mood, Mr. Alden opened the door somewhat noisily, whistling at the terrier pup who eagerly came to greet him. There were several reactions—the dog barked with delight, the baby cried, and his wife protested in an annoyed tone of voice.

"You woke the baby! And I've had such a time getting her to sleep! Couldn't you be more quiet?"

"You don't mean a little whistling and a bark woke her up! Why, Ellen slept through records playing and the telephone ringing and even a couple of tables of bridge. The baby was probably just waiting to say 'Hello' to her daddy," he added, striving for a light tone as he noted his wife's displeasure.

"I had just managed to get her to sleep," her mother said wearily. "She's so restless and cries more in one day than Ellen ever did in a week at her age. She's awake when I expect her to sleep, and when she finally does drop off, the least little thing wakes her up again. She never seems to sleep very long at a time."

As the days went by, the parents were increasingly aware of differences between Ellen and the new baby. Ellen had been a placid infant who drifted off to sleep between feedings. Debbie was restless and easily startled; she often awoke crying. Ellen had generally accepted her bottle and emptied it in the expected time. But, evidently quite content with her schedule, she had rarely shown any impatience to be fed. Debbie, on the other hand, usually cried demandingly and lustily long before her bottle was given to her. Then after emptying it thirstily, she showed none of the satisfied readiness for a nap that had been customary with Ellen. Instead, she puckered her face, mouthed her lips and tongue, and, with clenched fists waving, often cried until her mother felt exhausted listening and wondering what she should do. More and more Debbie sucked her thumb as solace before she finally fell asleep. Thumb-sucking had very rarely been Ellen's way of going to sleep.

When cereal had first been offered to Ellen, she had tasted it tenta-

57

tively, but had not objected to it. Just as with her bottle, she took what was given to her. Not so Deborah. She spit out her first cereal, turning her head and crying when her mother attempted to give her more. A number of days passed before she would accept the new taste and texture.

But although Debbie proved difficult to manage in many situations, in other ways she pleased her parents greatly. She reached for and held a rattle, she turned over, and she held her head erect at a considerably earlier age than had Ellen. A bigger, stronger infant, she reacted quickly and was alert to many stimuli to which Ellen had given little attention. Her behavior with people also was not what her sister's had been. Ellen had smiled happily and calmly at every face she saw and had often cried when left alone again. Debbie reserved her smiles for her parents and gave an amusing impression of aloofness as she stared gravely at an unfamiliar adult. She made no protest, either, when she was alone again, but she was more restless and kicked more vigorously after the visitor had gone.

Interested as they were in all such reactions, her parents' primary concern was with Debbie's restlessness and her sleeping and eating behavior. Her mother particularly was upset that she no longer knew "just what to do." Indeed, she was finding that she no longer even knew what to expect.

A long discussion with the pediatrician brought some new insights. Mrs. Alden had less contact with the doctor than when Ellen was an infant because, with her experience, she felt sure she knew how to handle a baby.

"Maybe I'm imagining things, but I'm worried," she told the doctor, after recounting some of the episodes that had been bothering her.

"I don't think it's imagination," said Dr. Thomas. "Your two babies are two individuals. You've been setting up standards for one on the basis of your experience with the other. And obviously the two are very different. Think of Debbie as herself, not in terms of her sister. Don't try to compare them, because no two babies are really alike. And as they grow older, the differences will still be there, often more so.

"It seems to me, first of all, that the baby should have a larger feeding each time. I know Ellen was satisfied with what you gave her and the baby has been getting just as much and has, as a matter of fact, been gaining weight. But she is Debbie, not Ellen. The way she acts shows that she wants more to eat. Certainly she wants to suck more! Let's try increasing the formula as a first measure. That thumb-sucking you're worried about will possibly be less in evidence—may even disappear—when she gets more sucking activity. Thumb-sucking in a baby can mean a need for more nourishment or a need for more sucking or a need for more loving and comforting.

"All behavior has a reason. A certain amount of crying is to be expected from every baby. But when one cries as much as yours has been doing, it's a pretty sure sign that something should be changed—perhaps the baby's schedule as well as the amount of her feedings. Remember we talked some time ago about not being too rigid in planning a day's schedule? Let *her* tell you when she's hungry. It sounds as if she uses a lot of

58

energy trying to tell you when she wants to be fed. Then when she finally gets her bottle, she's not only upset at having had to wait—and probably also at feeling neglected—but she's tired out with all the crying she's done. And to make matters worse, she's still hungry when the milk is all gone."

"It would be easy enough to give her larger feedings," said Mrs. Alden. "But if I don't schedule my day, I'll never get everything done. Ellen never had any difficulty getting used to a schedule. I can see the sense of giving one child more milk than another has needed. But if I give the baby more, then she won't need it when it's *time* for it."

"The time for it," said Dr. Thomas, "is when she tells you by crying and by being restless. She'll get very upset if you make her wait too long. All babies need the same general care and attention, but every child has individual rhythms, which parents have to watch for and respect if they want to have a satisfied baby as well as a healthy one.

"Of course it's hard to say positively, but I would guess that your schedule and Ellen's own feeding rhythm were about the same, whereas Deborah's seems to require shorter periods between feedings. Then, too, Ellen appears to have a different temperament as well as different body needs. She can be satisfied more easily, isn't upset as quickly, and, in general, accepts circumstances more placidly.

"Really, there are a great many differences between your two children. This baby is developing muscular control earlier than your first child did. And she probably doesn't require as much sleep. She reacts more positively to stimuli, too. And it seems she's showing signs of differences in social behavior.

"Don't try to make her fit Ellen's pattern; she's a different person, an individual, and parents really must learn to accept individuality, unless they want to worry needlessly—and unless they want to risk making their children less relaxed and happy than they'd like to have them. Babies whose own rhythms happen to match pretty closely the schedules set for their care, follow regular schedules easily. But others won't let routines be imposed on them without some noisy protesting. That's hard on their parents, but it's hard on them, too."

Mrs. Alden was skeptical. "I know there's been a great deal said about former ways not always being good for children—like keeping rigidly to routines, and expecting all children of the same age to do the same things in the same way. But why can't I learn about one baby from having taken care of another?"

"It isn't comparing one baby with another that tells us how they grow and develop or tells us the best ways to handle them," the doctor responded. "It's work with hundreds and hundreds of babies that counts. Studying a large number of children over a long period of time tells us, in general, what to expect and what not to expect. It corrects some things we've taken for granted; it suggests better ways to help children grow and develop. But with all our knowledge, we always need to adjust considerably in planning for a particular baby, to meet particular needs. I'm not suggesting that you feed Debbie every time she cries, but that you adjust your schedule to her rather than try to force her to adjust to an arbitrary schedule.

"Different methods are advocated from time to time. If we didn't learn new ways and better ways, we'd keep repeating many mistakes," the doctor continued. "Each baby is likely to respond in an individual fashion to whatever care is given. One gets along well because of the procedures followed, but another gets along well in spite of what's done. And some others won't get on satisfactorily at all unless the approach is varied to meet their special needs.

"There is one thing you can bank on with all babies—they need to feel secure, important to their parents, and sure of their love. That need is the same for all, for both Ellen and Debbie. Make sure Debbie feels that you love her very much. Let her always have the comfortable assurance of being loved. Later, when you must criticize and sometimes even punish her for unacceptable behavior, let her still sense that you love and accept her, although you can't accept her behavior.

"All normal children within any age range show many similarities. But no two in a group are entirely alike. Every procedure suggested for caring for children will have to be changed here and there, perhaps even entirely discarded to fit the individual needs of a child. New ways in child care will be advocated as we gain new information from research about child development and adaptation. But there's no substitute for the emotional security which must be given a child to feel the assurance, the sense of belonging, the contentment necessary for healthful growth. And such feelings come from the feeling tone between parents and children.

"When your baby cries because she is frustrated by her schedule, that frustrates you, too, and destroys the pleasantness of the feeling tone. Making the schedule fit the baby rather than forcing the baby to meet the schedule is important. And, as a matter of fact, it will help both of you. You'll feel easier, so you'll find Debbie easier to handle."

Mrs. Alden smiled as Dr. Thomas stopped. "It's a lot easier to cuddle and love a baby when you aren't worn out and worried by her crying and restlessness. Yes, I think I see now what's been happening. Debbie's constant crying has made us impatient with her, and I suppose she senses it. But we love her just as much as we do Ellen. It is something of a circle, isn't it? But I think I see a possible way out now, thanks to our discussion."

# chapter 5

# The Toddler

PART BABY, PART CHILD   There is no exact day or month when an infant-child becomes a toddler. Some children get up on their feet before their first birthday, others not until they have reached seventeen or eighteen months. The toddler age usually begins somewhere between a year and eighteen months and ends between two and two-and-a-half years. It is an in-between stage. Toddlers have neither attained the maturity or the growing self-sufficiency of the runabout. They are still part baby although already part child.

During the toddler period, children learn not only how to walk upright but also how to talk. Both are of the utmost importance, for they enable them to participate adequately and independently in the activities they will encounter as they grow up. The child who cannot walk and the child who cannot hear and so imitate the sounds of speech are both severely handicapped and must have skillful assistance if they are to survive in a world of mobility and speech.

This also is the period when children first feel the pressures of the cultural patterns they will be expected to follow. Most parents in most cultures seem to accept the necessity and advisability of protecting, loving, and caring for a baby. However, they differ over the age at which constant and immediate responsiveness to the baby's demands for attention should be gradually modified toward guidance in the kind of behavior that will be expected as the child grows up. Although many parents begin gentle teaching toward the end of the first year, in our culture this process of socialization usually starts during the toddler period. During the second year, children are asked to give up doing some of the things they want to do and to begin learning to conform to some of their parents' expectations. They must learn that there are things they may not touch, taste, hold, or take apart; that there are places they may not go; that there are actions, such as learning to use the toilet, they will be expected to perform; and that there are kinds of behavior that will be unacceptable to other children or adults. The almost complete permissiveness of the first year must give way very gradually to the necessity of teaching children what they may or may not do. But these limitations on freedom should be balanced, whenever possible, by allowing little children to do things their own way.

The willingness of toddlers to cooperate and give up their own pleasurable and impulsive feelings depends upon a happy, loving relationship with parents and others who take care of them. Battles, scoldings, and slappings, far from making toddlers learn acceptable behavior, make them more difficult to teach and may retard their growth toward independence by making them insecure and anxious. Part baby and part child, toddlers will gradually begin to learn what grown-ups want to teach them if those who take care of them will love them, have fun with them, patiently teach them as they seem ready to learn, and encourage independent behavior without forcing them out of their baby ways too rapidly.

GUIDANCE TO MEET GROWING AUTONOMY The way guidance is begun and the way it is enforced during the toddler years will have an important influence on youngsters' social development in the months and years ahead. If those who teach these little children are overly severe or if their expectations are beyond the level at which toddlers can achieve, tension, negativism, rebelliousness, timidity, or fear of people may develop. If this happens, the desire to learn and to cooperate may be damaged or destroyed. Toddlers who are continually scolded and restrained hold back instead of reaching out for new experiences. Growing up may become too difficult, and babylike patterns may persist.

This does not mean that toddlers should never be frustrated or denied what they may want, for encountering limits and consequent frustration, and learning how to cope with them, are an unavoidable part of growing up. It does mean that frustration and denial should be kept at a minimum and balanced by the pleasure of achievement during this second year of life. All children have to give up doing some things their way in order to learn how to cooperate with and respect the rights of other people. Such lessons are hard for toddlers, since they are not capable of understanding why things should be done in a certain way. Often they are bewildered or unwilling to give up their own way and will hit out against adults who frustrate them. Biting, kicking, breath-holding, or head-banging are ways of showing resentment at this age. As one mother described it, "She expresses anger by banging her head right on the floor. Sometimes when she gets mad, she just slaps me right on the face." Another mother described her angry toddler as throwing a block across the floor and banging a peg in obvious anger. Displaying anger is a young child's natural response to frustration. If it becomes a continuous response, however, it is a signal to parents or to others who are caring for the child that they are expecting too much too soon or are trying to teach too much at once. It is easy to make the mistake of trying to teach toddlers too many things at the same time, overburdening them with learning before they are able to assimilate all that the adults about them feel they should both know and remember. Perhaps other cultures are wiser than ours in this respect.

At the same time that toddlers are beginning to feel the pressures of adult demands, they also are beginning to be aware of their own autonomy. To some extent, they can reject or accept demands. Toddlers can run the other way when they are called; they can refuse to go to the toilet at the proper time or place; they can push food aside or throw a dish on the floor; they can say "no" quite emphatically; they can, by the end of the toddler year, drag a chair over to a shelf and climb up to get what they want.

In short, toddlers begin to assert themselves and to resist attempts to distract them—attempts that were often successful a few months ago. Many parents consider this second year of life the most difficult in their relationships with their children. It is during this year that disharmony and a battle of wills often begin between parents and their children. Sometimes parents begin to lose confidence and wonder whether they know how to bring up their children. Their self-doubt may result in increased anxiety and tension which is readily sensed by a child. This may result in problem situations, a cycle of interaction between parent and child that can slow up and interfere with a child's emotional growth.

During the child's first year, the parents usually controlled the situation. The baby could be placed in a safe spot in a crib, high chair, or play-pen. A crying baby could be picked up, and with a little ingenuity, attention usually could be diverted and crying stopped. The baby could not get around alone, so a parent could meet the baby's needs with a feeling of comparative success. But during this second year, toddlers notice and want to touch, taste, and feel the many appealing objects everywhere about them. This is an essential part of learning. At the same time they are too young to take responsibility or to be held responsible for what they do. They may have seemed to have learned not to touch the hot water faucet or the burner on the stove, and to stop at the curb, but toddlers are not able to really understand and remember what they may or may not do. Some adult must still take full responsibility for their safety, while patiently

63

continuing to teach the desired behavior as each situation arises. This can be frustrating for both adults and children. Adults so often feel that having repeated themselves so many times, surely their children will remember.

APPROACHES TO "DISCIPLINE" The toddler who does not understand why a pleasurable activity is forbidden may become angry and throw a temper tantrum. By eighteen months, or thereabouts, youngsters also may have temper tantrums if they are unable to make some object do what they want it to do. They may kick the box or the doll or the truck that they cannot manipulate and may throw themselves on the floor kicking and screaming. Although disturbing to adults, temper tantrums might be called a normal means of expression for most toddlers. After about two-and-a-half, most children usually will be able to express themselves and handle themselves in better ways, and tantrums should occur less frequently. During the toddler months it is best, when possible, to ignore the temper tantrum while it is occurring, or if that is not possible to remove the child to a quiet place where feelings can be worked out without too much disturbance to others. Shaking, scolding, spanking the child during a tantrum only intensifies the child's upset feelings. It is important, however, not to reinforce the use of temper tantrums, even at this early age, by giving in to the child or giving that which was wanted and denied. A temper tantrum is a form of aggressive behavior. If aggressive responses are rewarded, the child gradually learns that this is a successful kind of action and aggressive responses will become a usual part of the child's behavior.

Because toddlers sometimes do prove difficult to manage, many adults feel that the time has come to use "discipline" meaning "punishment." But toddlers are not ready for punishment; it bewilders them. They are not old enough to understand cause and effect, which is necessary if punishment is to be used as a remembered deterrent for future actions. Although even a little child can be taught to some extent by fear, the anxiety and distrust developed by the seeming hostility of the punisher when such forms of teaching are employed is often destructive.

These are the months when it is best, if possible, to teach with a light touch. Toddlers respond to humor, to fun and games better than to commands or to direct interference with their activities. Reasoning is not very effective at this age, although a simple statement such as "You cannot bite Betty, it hurts her" coupled with removing the child from the situation for a few minutes can be the beginning of gradually helping a child to the realization that actions do have consequences for other people. This will be an important first step in developing moral values. If toddlers refuse to do something necessary or seem tired or cross and cannot be distracted, it is usually best to go ahead with what must be done as quickly and gently as possible, without scolding or argument.

Although at times a direct "No" or "Don't touch" must be used, toddlers respond best to the positive approach: "You may have this" rather than "You can't have that." There is no reason why learning should not be a happy experience. To hop like a bunny to the bathroom is fun—and

64

hands are then washed with gaiety rather than tears. A tired child comes in from play much more readily with a ride on the shoulders than being dragged by the hand. By using a light touch in teaching little children what they are expected to do, those who take care of them are making it easier for them to learn, and more pleasant for them to respond. In this way learning is being reinforced and is more likely to become a permanent part of children's behavior.

ACTIVITY—THE KEYNOTE  Activity is the keynote of the toddler period. Now that youngsters are able to get around by themselves, they are off in every direction, as any parent who has tried to watch and keep up with an eighteen-month-old child well knows. Attention span is usually short. Toddlers go from one experience to another and usually are easily distracted by new sights or sounds, although at times a particularly fascinating activity, such as exploring a hole with a finger or looking at colorful pictures is completely absorbing. They are learning to throw, and they toss things indiscriminately—a ball, a beanbag, a spoon, or a dish. They do not throw a ball as older children do but use the whole body, letting the ball go in any direction whatsoever and usually laughing with glee as they toss it. Though they cannot throw with any sense of direction, they enjoy playing throwing games.

This has been called the "dart-and-dash-and-fling" age. These children seem to be in constant motion, for they rarely stay still when they are awake. They like to open drawers and pull all the contents out onto the floor. They overturn wastebaskets and rummage through them. They try to climb the stairs. By the end of this year, they clamber onto tables and chairs. At first if they succeed in getting up on a couch or bed, they are apt to roll off or come down again headfirst. Soon, however, they learn to turn around and slide off backwards. It is necessary to be constantly watchful,

65

even when as many dangers as possible have been moved out of the way. At this age children show no discretion in where they go or what they do.

Toddlers are full of curiosity. They still learn by touching, feeling, and mouthing everything within their reach; but now that they are on their feet, they can explore their world more fully. They no longer enjoy the playpen but prefer to range through the house or yard. Knowing how much freedom to allow these young explorers and when to curb them for their own safety and for the sake of the rest of the family is a real puzzle to parents.

A NEW LOOK—AND DEXTERITY  Along with growing independence, toddlers are losing their baby appearance. Hair has become much thicker and features are taking on their own individuality. One can begin to see what they will look like as they grow older. The face is taking form and the jaw is shaping for the teeth. By the last part of the second year, most toddlers will have a complete set of deciduous, or baby, teeth. Bones are increasing in size and number and calcification is taking place. There will be a growth of about four inches in height during this year.

At first toddlers walk with their feet wide apart, their stomach sticking out, sometimes with their arms held up for balance. They cannot run or turn corners, and often stumble and fall. But by the end of the toddler year, they have a much more grown-up walk. They are steady on their feet and have learned to walk backward, to run, and even to turn corners without falling down.

As youngsters near two, they also begin to show much better coordination in using their fingers. They usually are able to put the big pegs into a peg board, and a little later can slip a ring over them. They place one block on top of another and often manage a tower of five or six blocks. They can turn the pages of a book, if it is made of heavy material, and they like to look at pictures and feel and pat them. But toddlers do not use their small finger muscles nearly as often or as well as their large muscles. Some of their greatest fun lies in pulling, pushing, lifting, and dragging things

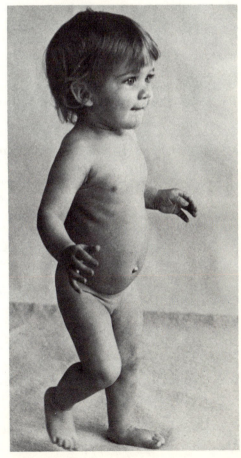

around. They enjoy sand and water, and delight in dumping and pouring them. For the most part attention span remains short, although sometimes there may be a surprising temporary absorption in what is being done.

Music often calls out an alert response in toddlers—they may even try to dance to a marked rhythm that appeals to them. They often try to turn the radio or television on for themselves. They like to have someone sing to them and play rhythmic games. Although peekaboo and pat-a-cake still are fun, they revel in the more boisterous play of being picked up and carried over a shoulder or of rolling on the floor and roughhousing. They laugh uproariously and have such great fun that their excitement sometimes gets out of hand. Adults should take care not to overstimulate them, especially before meals and at bedtime.

TIME—THE HERE AND NOW   One source of frustration that toddlers constantly experience is the difference between their concept of time and that of adults. During this period, children live in the "here and now." They have no conception of past or future time, and no capacity to wait for something they want *now*. They do not understand about waiting and will be quite disturbed if it is necessary. If a parent says "outdoors," the toddler may head for the door. Further, toddlers do not understand the pressures time imposes. If they are engrossed in what they are doing, the fact that shopping must be done means nothing. Here may begin another cycle of battles between parents and their children. Parents move quickly—time is of the essence to them. Toddlers move slowly, absorbed in the moment—perhaps trying to put the lace through the hole in a shoe, perhaps looking at something in the crack in the sidewalk. The parent wants the youngster to ride in the stroller, but the toddler wants to explore, by climbing up every step or picking up little objects from the sidewalk. This puts a strain on the patience of the parent.

When possible, it is best to cooperate with the child's exploring. When that is impossible, diversion may work, since attention usually can be drawn toward some other equally fascinating object. When parents' schedules necessitate moving the child along faster and diversion no longer works, picking a toddler up from behind seems more effective than a head-on approach. If the interruption is too abrupt, however, the child often responds by screaming and kicking a direct protest. The toddler has little capacity for self-control.

Wise parents recognize and make allowances for this difference between an adult sense of time and that of a child. They also recognize the importance of the attempts to "do it myself," even though the little one may be slow and inept; these attempts are necessary for the growth of independence.

INDEPENDENCE—IN SPURTS   Sometimes children of this age show great interest in trying to do things for themselves; at other times they want help. It is not wise to *insist* on self-help. If youngsters are encouraged and praised for what they do, they will try of their own accord to

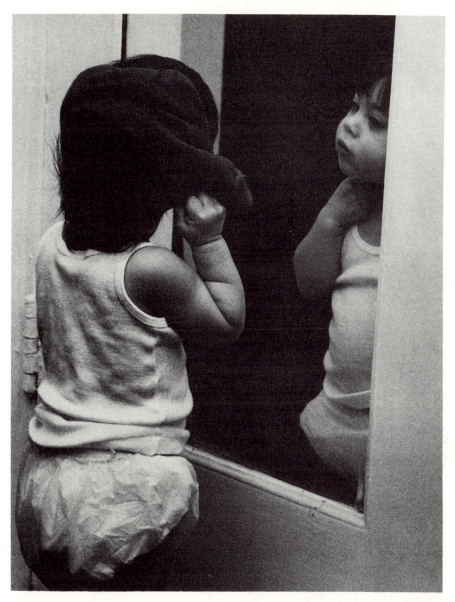

become increasingly independent as they grow more capable of using their fingers and hands.

Most toddlers try to undress themselves and have some success in getting off their shoes and socks, and perhaps their shirts and pants. Dresses and overalls present greater difficulties, and slipover sweaters and most snowsuits are almost impossible to manage. Some toddlers can put on their shirts; they may even manage to put on a sock after a fashion, but the heel is likely to be on top. If they struggle into their pants or pajamas, both legs are often in the same opening. But they are trying and should be allowed and encouraged to do so whenever possible, even though their efforts are not a complete success by adult standards.

69

Toddlers make a mess when they try to feed themselves, for their eye-and-finger coordination is imperfect. Often there is more food in hair and on the floor than in their mouths. By the time they are between two and two-and-a-half, however, they may have learned to manage spoons and cups more efficiently.

EATING PATTERNS—AND PROBLEMS   Feeding problems often develop during this period. The first year babies triple their birth weight; the second, they gain only three to five pounds. Obviously they neither need nor want the quantities of food in proportion to their size that they did as babies. This drop in appetite often worries many parents who begin trying to make their children eat more than they want, with the result that they rebel and a problem is created. For instance, a parent who still insists on a quart of milk a day for a child leaves little appetite for solid foods which also are a necessary part of an adequate diet.

Toddlers accept and enjoy a much wider variety of foods and can eat many of the simpler foods from the adults' table. But they also are showing preferences; by two they express their likes and dislikes and push their plates away if they contain something they do not want to eat. Most toddlers do not seem to relish foods mixed together, as in creamed or casserole dishes. They are conservative and want to see the meat, potatoes, and vegetables as separate items on a plate, and enjoy finger foods which they can pick up. Frequently they finish one food before they start the next.

Children of this age often go on food jags that are disturbing to their parents. They refuse certain foods and want large quantities of others. Parents who have been taught to believe in the clean plate—the eat-everything theory—sometimes find a feeding problem developing when they make an issue of the child's eating everything. Toddlers do not understand parents' concern, but they do sense the resulting anxiety. Often they refuse to eat and begin to associate unpleasant feelings with mealtime. Offering foods that the child enjoys eating within a reasonably balanced diet is emotionally healthier than battling with the child whose understanding necessarily is limited. The most important thing during this period is the child's attitude toward eating.

NAPS AND BEDTIMES   Toddlers still need a great deal of rest. Most of them take a nap right after their midday meal and sleep around the clock at night. If a child will not take a nap without a struggle, bedtime might be earlier. Such a child should have a quiet period in the afternoon, playing with toys on the bed or listening to records, or just resting. A toddler who does not take some time out in the middle of the day usually is fussy by suppertime.

Bedtime, too, may begin to present difficulties, for children may not go to bed as readily as they did a few months earlier. If they have taken a long afternoon nap, they may not be ready to sleep again until eight or nine o'clock. If they are put back to bed too soon, they may be restless and demanding. Parents often find it necessary to change their schedules to better accommodate the child's changing needs. The toddler usually wants bedtime to follow a certain routine, and even then makes demands for drinks of water or trips to the toilet. Often they are attached to a particular toy or blanket and will not go to bed without it.

FEARS OF THE WORLD AROUND Because toddlers are aware of the world around them before they are quite able to understand it, they seem to develop many fears. Noises frighten them: They may cry or cling at the sound of a loud siren or at the sudden whir of the vacuum cleaner. Wind, heavy rain, thunder, fire engines, or even the flushing of a toilet may be frightening to them. Sometimes they seem afraid at bedtime and cling to their parents who try to leave them; or they may wake up as if they had been dreaming, and still be afraid even after mother or father has come.

They may begin to be afraid of the dark and insist that the door be left open with a light in the hall at bedtime. Large, unfamiliar objects may make a toddler run to the security of adult arms. They have no conception of size, and sometimes will refuse to get into the bathtub for fear they may slip down the drain. Nor do they like things to be changed. They may resist going to bed if their crib has been moved or if they are in a new room or a new house.

Children should not be laughed at or scolded for these fears. When they are afraid, they need the reassurance and comfort of being near someone they trust. As they are soothed it is wiser to explain, or better still, show what made the noise or what was frightening. When they understand more clearly, some of their fears will disappear. But nearness to their parents does much more to quiet and relax toddlers than explanations. They are still very dependent on parents for feelings of well-being and security.

Toddlers sometimes evidence another kind of apprehensiveness—a timidity, anxiousness, and general fearfulness. This type of fear is not likely to be cured by explanations or reasons. Usually it suggests that parents may be putting too many demands on youngsters, expecting too many achievements for the level of development or too much self-control. They may not know what can reasonably be expected of toddlers. They may be using too many "dos" and "donts" or expecting that because their child now understands what they say, there should be the ability to conform to their demands and invariably remember their admonitions from one time to the next.

Sometimes apprehensiveness appears when toilet training is begun too soon or with too much emphasis. And sometimes it results from parents who give the impression that they find their child a nuisance who is not really wanted. Or again, they may not realize that cuddling and other clear evidences of affection are important if a child is to be secure, happy, and responsive.

Demands made of toddlers are multiplying so that sometimes these little ones are unsure of what they should do. Their uneasiness is increased if they have been unsuccessful in meeting their parents' expectations, with the result that scoldings and signs of disapproval also have increased. Little children are often worried and anxious for fear that if they fail to please their parents, their parents will no longer love them and may leave them. This fear is sometimes behind the two-year-old's restlessness at bedtime, particularly if there has been scolding or punishment during the day. Toddlers may try to climb out of bed or call out to reassure themselves that their parents are still there—that they have not gone away.

TOILET TRAINING  Toilet training is one of the major demands put upon the toddler to conform to the ways of our culture. In other cultures, this particular type of conformity is not given the importance it is accorded in most of the United States. Sometimes adults, in their desire to make the young child conform, forget that two considerations must be

taken into account if toilet training is to be successful. First, the child must be ready for training. Not only must there be understanding of what is expected, but there also must be muscular coordination necessary to control the bowel and bladder muscles and to release them voluntarily at a given time and place. Second, successful training depends on the child's willingness and interest in cooperating. Until a toddler seems physically and emotionally ready to cooperate, toilet training should not be begun.

Training used to be started early in the first year, but today training is usually not begun until the middle of the second year, and it is some time during the third year or occasionally even later that training is completed. This shift in the cultural pattern has occurred as a result of our recent understanding that the child is not ready for training before this second year. Success in toilet training usually depends on the child's relationship with those who are trying to train him and on their ability to accept accidents casually, to express encouragement, and to praise success. Tense, anxious parents who communicate to their child their tension over toilet training can begin a cycle of difficulties in guiding the child in other areas. Rebellion or anxiety over too severely enforced toilet training may cause a child to be defiant or overanxious in any situation where an adult makes demands. Consequently, the relationship which toddlers have developed with their parents is important at this time. If it is harmonious and happy, youngsters, once ready physically, usually can learn to use the toilet without too much effort. But if tension already exists between parents and child, or if anxiety, severity, or overinsistence characterize training, the process may be very upsetting to the child.

73

BOWEL TRAINING BEFORE BLADDER TRAINING  Toddlers usually are ready to start bowel training a good many months before they can be expected to control their urination, because the stool, when it is ready to leave the body, causes a more definite pressure and generally comes at regular times. Many toddlers have only an occasional bowel movement in their diapers after eighteen months, though it may be several months longer before they can tell when they need to go to the toilet or go alone. Bowel training may not proceed smoothly, however, and there may be relapses, just as in other forms of learning. It is much more difficult to train a child who has irregular bowel movements. This is not the fault of the child but is part of the youngster's individual makeup.

Learning to keep dry is much more difficult. Urination does not always occur regularly and is easily affected by the quantity of liquid drunk, by temperature, by excitement, by an approaching illness, or by the size of the bladder. At some time during the second year, children become interested in the puddles they make and will point at them or get a cloth and busily try to mop them up. This is an important step in their awareness of urinary functioning—even though it may irritate those who feel that the child should have told them ahead of time instead of waiting until the puddle had been made.

Children differ greatly in their responses to toilet training. Some tiny children seldom have accidents; others continue to soak many diapers a day. Parents need to notice at what intervals the child usually urinates and then place the child on the toilet near those times. This is apt to be about a two-hour interval, although the time varies with different children and even with an individual child from day to day. Toilet training may be achieved quickly, or it may be a very slow process. Toddlers should never be forced, scolded, or punished for lack of success. If they do not seem to get the idea, it is better to wait and try again a little later. Many parents find the last part of the second year best for starting toilet training.

By two-and-a-half years accidents are usually becoming less frequent. Many children can tell by this time when they want to go to the toilet or may even go of their own accord. They should not be expected to keep dry at night until after they have learned to stay dry during the day, and occasional accidents, both night and day, must be expected throughout the preschool years. If a child who has been rather consistently dry begins to have lapses over any considerable period, however, it is well to look for the reason behind the need to return to baby ways.


LANGUAGE DEVELOPMENT  During the toddler year, the baby's babbling sounds start to form into words. These little ones are not only learning to master their bodies through walking, climbing, pushing, pulling, and using their hands, they also are learning to form words and to use these words for objects they want or see.

It is interesting to notice that both these efforts—walking and talking—require tremendous energy and concentration, for studies show that many children do not acquire these skills simultaneously. The child who talks early and well often walks at a later date, whereas the child who is an active, early walker often is slower in learning to talk. Children vary as to which they learn first. Some children walk first and talk very little; others talk first and then walk. It appears that youngsters need to expend their energy in one direction or the other, but that typically they cannot master both feats at once.

Language skill, like other accomplishments, is an individual matter, and wide variations are to be expected among normal children. Some eighteen-month-old youngsters can say as few as four words, others ten or eleven; some have been reported as using "too many words to count." Some normal two-year-olds use only six words; others over two hundred fifty.

But real speech begins only when the child has meaningful associations for the words used. One mother did not feel that her toddler was talking until he held up his duck and said, "Uck." The repetition of words as sounds is a step toward the mastery of language. A little child may say "ma'ma" long before making the sound in response to seeing her or wanting her. Many children make chains of sound in rhythmic patterns when they are tiny, as if they are copying the rhythm of the speech they hear.

The words children use are determined by the culture in which they grow up. All babies, wherever they are born, seem to make the same basic speech sounds. But the sounds the children will continue to use as words or will combine to form words will be those they hear in their environment. For example, a child of American parents brought up in a Japanese family will speak Japanese if that is the language consistently heard.

Many toddlers experience considerable frustration during their second year as they try to make themselves understood through words. Many children who are trying to express themselves verbally with indifferent success may work themselves into tantrums because they are not understood.

Many factors enter into language development. Some children seem to have their wants met so thoroughly that they apparently feel no need to use words at an early age. Some, growing up in highly verbal families, talk more readily than most children. Others, growing up in families that speak rapidly or indistinctly, or in families that pay little attention to the child, may be slow in speaking.

Parents can help their children master language by speaking clearly and simply. Either baby talk or speech that is too involved may impede the child's learning to talk. Parents also can help by chanting rhymes and reading simple stories aloud and by naming objects as they give them to the toddler, though they should never force a child to say the word for what is wanted.

The devotion of toddlers to those who care for them is important in helping them develop motivation for speech learning. Clinically, we see children blocked in language growth because of tensions that exist between them and their parents. Parental acceptance and encouragement of the baby's babbling and cooing is an important step in the child's speech development. Support is even more vital when the child is trying to form sounds into words.

REACHING TOWARD SOCIAL RELATIONSHIPS  Toddlers are still infant-children in some ways. They still need a baby's care, but they also need encouragement and opportunities that are within their capacity for success. One of the steps toward growing up that toddlers hesitatingly try to take is reaching out toward other children. They do not know how to play with them, but they are beginning to like to be near them when they play. By the age of two, most youngsters enjoy *parallel play* with another child—the two sitting contentedly side by side in the sandbox, each one doing what he or she likes. They enjoy each other's companionship even though they don't actually play together. But though the two children like being together, they will still snatch one another's toys whenever they have a chance.

Social relationships of toddlers are awkward, and they cannot safely be left alone with others their own age, for youngsters of this age may push, hit, hurt one another, or even bite. The toddler can rarely share or take turns. This is the period of "mine," with everything still related to the self. The child clutches a teddy bear or toy tightly if someone else wants it. They have not yet reached the age when they can understand that there will still be something for them if they let go of what they have or share it with another. Occasionally, they may make a gesture away from themselves—reaching out toward another child by offering a toy or a cookie to bite. But often they quickly snatch back the toy if the other child takes it, or cry if the other child eats the cookie. Toddlers still need to have a substitute placed in their hands if they are to relinquish what they hold.

During this year, toddlers seem to feel safe only when they are close to their mother or some other accepted adult. Around eighteen months and again at the end of the year, they go through a period of accentuated clinging. At two this is particularly noticeable, perhaps because they seem so much more grown-up that their parents expect greater independence of them. But far from showing more independence, they cling and often cry when the person with whom they feel secure leaves.

There are an increasing number of children who, because their mothers work outside the home, must be in a day-care center or in the

care of some other parenting person during the day. Studies show that if those who care for toddlers are warm, encouraging, happy people who can give the individual care needed, the experience need not be upsetting to the child. However, the parents will need to remember that the toddler's attachment to them, particularly to the mother, will still be very strong. They must be ready and able to receive their child back into the home at the end of the day with warm affection. Some toddlers may seem demanding and clinging on their return home. This can be annoying to tired parents, but it is a normal expression of a need to feel close to them again. It is wise to plan the evening schedule so that there is time allowed for them to be available to meet the needs of their child.

The fact that toddlers still have a special attachment to their mothers does not mean that fathers are not important parenting people too. An increasing number of studies are showing the significance of the father-child relationship in the development of children. Fathers can be warm and nurturant, able to meet the needs of their little children. Children need to learn to love someone other than their mothers, to feel close to them if they are to be able to gradually grow in independence from their mothers. It is important for fathers to feed, play with, put to bed, and cuddle their children, so that their toddlers learn to love and trust them as well as their mothers. The toddler also can enjoy brothers and sisters, grandparents, and other familiar people. Through these relationships longer times away from mother are tolerated and feeling safe with other people grows. The development of this feeling of trust in others is one of the most important things learned this second year.


## Living with a child

### THE IMPACT OF HABITS
*Feelings and Actions Interact*

Early childhood experiences which seem to have been long since forgotten are not infrequently the source of troublesome and uncertain feelings and actions of both young people and adults. Parenting individuals at home, in day-care centers, in schools, and on playgrounds need to be alert to the long-lasting impact of habits learned in the early years, and particularly of attitudes that develop in connection with the habits. Both habits and attitudes may arise in the development of daily functions important for good physical health, for example, eating, elimination, and sleeping routines. They may stem from adult management which is not always consistent. Adults in charge of little ones are sometimes warm and accepting, sometimes critical, or impatient, or overly protective. The mood and behavior of a parent or parent substitute influences and modifies the reactions of children even in their infancy.

A patient, affectionate adult usually is rewarded with a responsive, smiling, serene baby. A tense, impatient parenting person will generally find the baby restless, whining, unresponsive. Both physical health and growth and emotional health and development are affected. The early years require wise handling on the part of adults. Training infant and toddler in acceptable ways needs patient understanding.

For many parents, perhaps one of the most troublesome aspects of early childhood is training in habits of elimination. Current opinion deplores too early or too insistent an approach in helping a child learn bladder and bowel control. Yet even while accepting this opinion, few parents know exactly what is meant by "too early," and not many are likely to feel that their methods are "too insistent." Very often a young parent of a first baby has only the vaguest idea of how to go about the whole procedure and what to expect of the child.

Ronny's parents had been looking forward to the time when he could get about by himself, say at least a few words, eat without being spoon fed, and keep dry. He had finally fulfilled their anticipations in all but the last, and they were commenting ruefully about it one morning.

"He's always so wet when he wakes up!" said his mother. "His diaper and his sleepers and even the sheets are just soaked. And during the day he has so many accidents. He doesn't seem to get the idea of what the bathroom is for, even when I get him there in time. Little Mary Elroy, down the block, is almost always dry," she continued, "and her mother says that she never has a bowel movement except on the toilet. Ronny almost never does. Do you suppose there's something wrong with him?" She was genuinely concerned, so much so that she passed on some of her feeling to her husband.

"Mary's younger, too," he responded. "But you've talked to the doctor, and he didn't think it serious."

"Yes, I've asked him about it, and he said to stop worrying. He said there's not a thing wrong with Ronny—that most girls learn to stay dry several months before most boys do and that what may be right for Mary isn't necessarily right for Ronny. But I'm not convinced."

And she was not. She was quite sure that Ronny was not responding adequately to her training efforts, and she found this frustrating. Now that Ronny was two, she felt he should be able to keep dry.

As a matter of fact, some two-year-olds have been toilet trained. But while the young child needs fewer and finally no diapers, the early learning may have been accompanied by such stern and insistent adult procedures and attitudes that the child acquires emotionally unhealthy feelings.

Without realizing it, Ronny's mother had surrounded the task of toilet training with an aura of unpleasantness. It had become her custom to place Ronny on the toilet seat firmly and none too gently, saying, "Get through quickly now, Ronny. No fooling around." And some minutes later she was likely to add that he was delaying her work. "Hurry, Ronny! I've a lot to do."

Ronny probably did not entirely understand his mother's words, but

79

no doubt he understood her attitude: "This is certainly a nuisance, a bother, this business of a bowel movement." When he had no success in following her admonition, she would take him off the toilet seat with a little shake, and sometimes even a slap emphasized her displeasure. Often, only a short time later, his mother had to change his soiled diaper. Was this perhaps Ronny's unconscious way of retaliating?

One morning Ronny was successful, much more quickly than ever before. His mother was not in the bathroom when he finished, and he managed to slide down from the seat. He leaned over the bowl and examined with interest this product of his which his mother seemed so concerned about. After a moment, he reached in and was smearing the lid when his mother appeared. She pulled him away, exclaimed crossly, and with a look of disgust scrubbed his hands thoroughly. Throughout this process she kept up a running comment about how naughty he was, how much work he made for her, how slow he was in learning to behave. Her voice was sharp and impatient.

Ronny was frightened and cried, confused by his mother's reaction to what had happened. He had accomplished what she had always urged him to do, and now he was being punished for it. Not long after that episode, there was another problem: Ronny became constipated. Was it perhaps his unconscious fear of further punishment that made Ronny retain his stool? That is not inconceivable.

His mother might have managed more wisely if she had been less tense and felt less inadequate about the toilet-training procedure. She might well have said a word in praise of Ronny's success, then cleaned him and the toilet lid with the firm but not cross comment that "You don't play with a BM. You just flush the toilet." Later, play with plasticine or finger paints or sand and water would have provided satisfaction for Ronny's desire to squeeze and smear a soft substance.

Bladder training, after a time, was proceeding fairly successfully, and Ronny had become quite dependable. "Wear big boy pants," he said proudly to his father, and was pleased with his father's praise.

One afternoon Mrs. Hyde was expecting a few friends. Ronny had been freshened up, so his mother was annoyed at seeing a large wet spot on his clean pants.

"Oh, Ronny, not again!" she protested. "It hasn't been ten minutes since you were in the bathroom! You're a naughty, naughty boy!" In her exasperation at just then seeing the first guests coming up the steps, she slapped the child. He burst into tears, and she was chagrined to have her friends find her red and cross and the baby wet and sobbing. "It was an accident," soothed one of the guests, herself the mother of three. "Don't punish him." But Mrs. Hyde could not believe that such a lapse was really an accident. Surely it was carelessness or deliberate naughtiness. Ronny could certainly have kept dry if he had really tried.

She was expecting too much of Ronny. Had she stopped to think she might have realized that he would sense her nervousness and tension preparing for infrequent guests—and that he would be excited by the morn-

80

ing's activities. She would have been wise to have put rubber pants on him as a precaution that particular afternoon, even though training pants had definitely been in order for some days.

Normally the bladder grows to sufficient size during the first two years of life, so that voiding approximately half a dozen times daily becomes routine. But this will vary under excitement or stress, when irregular and more frequent urination is very likely to occur. Indeed, such a reaction may be experienced at any age, throughout life.

There is really no *right* time for a child to learn to control elimination. This varies with individual children. Some develop earlier than do others the voluntary control of the muscles involved in urination and defecation, and the essential coordination of the nerves and muscles governing these functions. Children who walk and talk early are likely to indicate their elimination needs at an earlier age, too. A tense, restless child generally achieves the dry habit later than does a calm, placid one.

Even the most conscientious training will be ineffective until the child is physically and psychologically ready for it. And since it is the child who must learn to control eliminative processes, it is futile and unwise to expect this before the necessary level of development has been reached. Infinite patience is generally necessary.

"A child must have control of the sphincter muscles at the outlet of the bladder and of the rectum," the doctor had said, "before he is ready to respond to any training to keep clean and dry. Be patient until then, and until Ronny can verbalize well enough to tell you in his own way when he needs to go to the toilet. For quite a while any success in training him will be *your* success in judging just when to take him to the bathroom and in keeping calm and matter-of-fact about the whole process."

Casual, easygoing parents often have much less trouble with toilet training their children than do tense, determined, worried ones. Mrs. Hyde's approach was not only making her unhappy but was threatening Ronny's development. He was becoming uncertain of what was expected of him and of parental approval.

Parents' reactions during toilet training also influence other attitudes in their children. In our society, there is all too often a feeling of shame or of disgust connected with the excretory functioning of the body. Inevitably the child acquires such feelings if the parents make it evident that that is the way they feel. Facial expression and tone of voice will convey meaning even more exaggerated than words. Yet the functioning of the organs of elimination is necessary for the child's good health and is a normal bodily activity. It is neither a dirty, nor a nasty, nor a shameful activity. Nor is the product of the body, which is excreted because it is not needed, dirty or nasty or shameful.

A very real complication often arises from the fact that the organs of elimination are located adjacent to the sexual organs. The feeling that the child learns to associate with the former may become associated with the latter, bringing still another difficulty from faulty attitudes toward excre-

81

tory functioning. Sexual functioning, too, may be drawn into the feeling of shame or disgust, of dirtiness or nastiness. Even in adolescent and adult years, these feelings of early childhood may persist. Later sexual maladjustment may result when early training to be "clean" has incorporated a kind of "training" wholly unplanned and unrecognized by the adult caring for the child.

The concern of the Hydes about their child could have been lessened if they had known more about how toddlers grow and develop, and what they could wisely anticipate and expect. They failed to realize that parental patience—in terms of recognizing individual readiness for new learning—is reflected in the child, and that the interpersonal relationship of parent and child influences not only the immediate present but future activity and attitudes as well.

Ronny Hyde was doing all right for Ronny Hyde. How the child on the next block reacted was inconsequential. Children need to be allowed to follow their own timing in mastering various aspects of bodily control, whether moving their bowels or learning to skip, whether building a tower or learning to control urination. Children are anxious to learn new skills, and take pride in achievement. Like their elders, they learn better with encouragement than with pressure or impatience with failure. They will be quicker to take responsibility for conforming to social ways if they are made to feel that adults know they want to do the right thing, and that before long they will learn to do so.


## Caring for a child

### A HOME AWAY FROM HOME
### Care for Children of Working Mothers

Currently, more and more women are working outside their homes. Whether they are employed full- or part-time, there is a growing need for facilities to care for their young children. Runabouts and toddlers and even younger infant-children must be provided for, and often for the entire day. Parents must leave their children early enough to get to work on time, and generally cannot call for them until somewhat past work hours.

The Jordan's baby was eighteen months old when they felt they could no longer manage without two regular paychecks. Mrs. Jordan had been working part-time for awhile, and her mother had taken care of the infant. They now persuaded the grandmother to come for the whole day. However, the latter soon found that an entire day was too taxing for her. Billy had learned to walk, and was an active, curious, demanding little boy.

"I have to be after him all the time," worried the elderly lady. "I'm afraid he'll hurt himself, or break something. He's after everything around, and he just won't listen when I say 'don't touch' or 'no, no.' Sometimes he won't eat more than a bite of his lunch, and sometimes he just throws it

82

on the floor without even a taste. It makes such a mess! And I can't always get him to take his nap, and then he's so crabby. It's just too much for me," she said helplessly. "If he'd just sit still sometimes and be good!"

But of course healthy little children rarely sit still. They are investigative, and they turn from one thing to another, often with disconcerting rapidity. "Being good" needs understanding interpretation.

Disappointed as they were at the grandmother's decision, the Jordans nevertheless realized that there was a vast difference in caring for an infant who sleeps much of the day and gets a bottle at intervals, and a toddler who is strong and determined and fast-moving. A neighbor suggested that her twelve-year-old daughter could baby-sit when she came home from school in the afternoon, relieving the grandmother. But a brief trial of this arrangement proved it a poor expedient.

Not infrequently when she reached home, Mrs. Jordan would hear through the door Billy's screams and Mary's scolding voice. Later she would find the child cross, whining a great deal, hitting out at his mother or father when they prevented him from reaching for something breakable or scolded him for throwing something on the floor. They were often at odds with each other as to how to manage their child, and their frustration and irritability were reflected in the child's responses to them.

From the social worker at the clinic where Billy was taken for routine immunizations, his mother learned of a day-care center where they might find help. When told of it by his wife, Mr. Jordan wavered between feelings of relief that she could continue to help out with the living expenses, and skepticism that the plan was feasible for them.

"He's pretty little to be off by himself. He'll be scared. And anyway it'll probably cost more than we can manage."

But they agreed that they should look into it. A Saturday appointment was arranged with the director of the center, and both parents went to talk with her. It did seem a possible solution, and Mrs. Jordan was pleased. But her husband was not wholly convinced.

"What'll it cost?" he asked Mrs. Wilson, the director, and stated bluntly that they needed almost their entire joint earnings for rent and food and carfare to get to work.

"There is a sliding scale," he was told. "I know it's not easy to get along, but our families pay according to their ability to pay. You'll talk that over with our social worker. The family income and the size of the family are always considered in the fees set. We seldom have to turn anyone away who needs us. We have an arrangement so that we can call on financial help when it is really needed.

"But tell me more about your little boy. How old is he?"

"He's real little, not two even. I—we wondered if he was *too* little. He's just a baby, you know, and might be scared. I mean, without somebody he's used to, and away from home, and with lots of children around." Mrs. Jordan was both eager and concerned.

"Until a child is three or more," said Mrs. Wilson, "he's really not ready for us here. But," she added quickly as she noted their disappointed

83

glances toward each other, "we have home-care arrangements for younger ones. Just six or seven children in a home, with a woman who knows how to manage little children so they're happy and comfortable and can learn new things."

Mrs. Wilson explained about their home-care centers: a number of homes, each chosen carefully after registration by the state had been obtained. Each had to be kept clean, and be big enough for the children to have room to play both indoors and outside.

"And we feel it's very important to have just the right kind of women to take over the children's care. We try to be sure they are kind and patient with little children, and want to help them grow and learn in ways that are healthful.

"Every day the children have a hot lunch sent over from our kitchen here, where we have a dietician. That way we're sure each child has the proper nourishment. After lunch there's a short time to play, and then they take naps. Each child has a cot and a blanket. Of course, a very little one would have a crib."

Mrs. Wilson went on to tell the Jordans about some of the things the children do during the day, and told them, too, about the brief training course each home-head must complete before she is finally accepted.

"We give them information which we think is important for them to know so that the children who come to them have the best possible supervision and care. It's not only details about health and safety we talk about. They learn about the songs and rhymes and games little girls and boys enjoy, and how to teach them.

"Each home is supplied with materials to make simple things; picture books, coloring materials, and toys are all provided, too. So you see each home center has all the equipment that the children need. And each woman in charge, with an assistant, has all the information we can give to help make each day a good experience for every child."

The Jordans would have registered Billy immediately if that had been possible, but some preliminaries had to be considered first. There was the interview with the social worker, a health history to be recorded, and a conveniently located home center with room for another child to be contacted. When all arrangements were completed, including a meeting between Mrs. Jordan and the head of the Blake home center, Billy and his mother went for his first morning away. His mother had managed a half day off from her job to stay with Billy while he had a chance to get his first taste of the home center. The youngest of the little group, at first he was content to sit on his mother's lap and just look around. After a bit, a brightly colored train off to one side attracted his attention, and he squirmed down to the floor to get it. Soon he was rolling it back and forth, at intervals looking up at his mother.

Mrs. Blake had been watching from across the room, and now came over. With a word or two and a pat on his head as she passed Billy, she went on to talk with his mother.

"He's my youngest," she said with a smile. "He's made a good start.

84

You'll be surprised how many new things he'll learn in a little while."

"He's still so young," his mother responded. "We thought he was too little to learn much."

"Well, for one thing, from what you've told me," answered the home-head, matter-of-factly, "he's learned to slap when he isn't pleased, and he's learned that he can take anything he sees that attracts him. He can learn other ways. He can learn what things he may pick up and feel and examine and what things are not for him to touch."

"My mother says he just won't listen when he's told not to touch something," ventured Mrs. Jordan.

"We grown-ups probably say 'no' so often it loses its effect," was the reply. "Sometimes it's better to just offer something else to take his attention away from what's breakable. And sometimes if we pick up the vase or ornament or whatever and hold it while the child strokes it or pokes at it or presses it, his curiosity is satisfied without damaging a valued object. And a little child will generally turn cheerfully to something else, particularly if we substitute something attractive to children.

"That's one of the things we're told in the lectures we hear before we can have children at home with us," Mrs. Blake explained. "And then we try to tell our parents here, in turn, some of the ways to make taking care of little children easier at home. And this helps not only the parents; it helps the children.

"We mustn't always step in, though," she continued. "We must give children a chance to learn by doing things for themselves. When we're in a hurry and get impatient because a child seems very slow and awkward—zipping up a jacket, for instance, or maybe drying his hands—and do such things for the child, a chance to learn is being missed. All children need practice to improve their muscular control. Then they won't be so slow or seem so awkward. And they develop a feeling of independence and self-confidence if they're given a chance to learn and to succeed. You see, we don't have to hurry here. We don't have to get to work; we're already at work. So we can let them take their time, and we help them only when it's necessary.

"Don't worry. Billy will get along fine, I'm sure. Now, since he's been used to having you go off each day, pretty soon you might go over and say good-by, and tell him you'll be back later to take him home. I don't think there'll be any difficulty. Look, he's found some blocks he's banging together now."

His mother followed her usual procedure when she had left her own home for work and he had stayed with his grandmother. Billy watched her cross the room and go down the hall, looked toward Mrs. Blake uncertainly, one block held up in his hand. She took up two other blocks and said with a smile, "See, I can do that, too!" and brought them sharply together. Billy chuckled. "And I can make a tower," she went on, placing one block on top of the other, then placing a third. "Can you do that, Billy?" Billy promptly imitated her, and laughed aloud when another block was added and all fell. He started to rebuild, engrossed.

The days went by with few difficulties, Billy falling into the routines of

85

the home center easily. His naps were longer than those of the other children, but his crib in a separate room made that small difference simple to handle. He needed more help at lunch, but, that, too, was easily managed. Skeptical as his father had been at first, he was greatly pleased at the small evidences of progress Billy showed, and also greatly interested in the procedures followed at the home center. He spent more time with his son before he put him to bed at night, and many mornings he dressed and fed the child before going off to work. The parents often spoke wonderingly and rather laughingly of what they called Billy's "schooling." And in many ways, it *was* learning, in the best sense of the word, education gained from experience.

Billy was learning from contacts with other children and with adults other than his family. Ways of doing ordinary everyday things which had been done in a hit or miss fashion were now done more effectively. He learned some things were permissible and others not, that sometimes he could not do as he wanted at the moment, but had to wait a bit. And there was a smile or word of praise for something done better than previously, for attempts at a new endeavor, for correctly following a simple direction.

At regular intervals there were meetings at the home center to which all parents were asked to come, and it was always stressed that if only one parent could attend on a given evening, at the next meeting the other parent, hopefully would have a turn. Fathers came with increasing frequency, and more and more often would join the discussion, offer a helpful suggestion from their own parent-child experiences, and would pick up their children after work for an opportunity for time together.

Often adults assume a child understands simple concepts readily used by adults, and become impatient when mistakes are made. When the meaning of up and down, soft and hard, dark and bright, few and many, for example, is demonstrated and learned through group play, with rhymes, with active movements, with music for rhythms, learning is fun and the words and numbers gain meaning. Eye-hand coordination develops and improves when, for instance, there is play with differently shaped blocks which fit into openings or recesses of the same shapes. Color differentiation and naming also are part of everyday experiences when children use crayons or finger paints or work with colored construction paper.

These activities are examples of what many people consider "just playing" or "keeping the kids out of mischief." In truth, they are a significant beginning to learning. Such awareness makes learning to read a more meaningful process, a more enjoyable task, and is important preparation for later school studies when preschool years are long past.

Not all day-care and home-care centers are organized the same way, of course. Not all have similar facilities. Local conditions and individual circumstances determine the way each functions. Some are partially funded by the government. Some are connected with the public school system, this relationship existing chiefly in large cities and often on a research basis. The aim is to go beyond the usual public school function of providing education for children: It attempts to bring the parents into the situation directly, having them spend time observing schoolroom procedures, bringing wise methods of child management to their attention, and also suggesting ways of using some of the school's procedures at home. Other centers for early childhood care are church sponsored, and still others are connected with philanthropic social agencies. And in many instances, they are the outgrowth of neighborhood interest and the determination of parent groups to bring into families' lives some of the advantages not offered in their particular area.

Both public and private facilities have the same aim: to make it feasible for women with children, who need to or wish to work outside their homes, to do so with the assurance that their young children are safe and well provided for. But it is not only the parents who are aided. The children can benefit greatly. These are the days when learning and habits and attitudes which persist for long years ahead are developing. Home-care centers can play an important role in such development.

# chapter 6

# The Runabout Years

PHYSICAL GROWTH  During the runabout years, physical growth continues at a moderately rapid rate. The appearance of the children continues to change from the soft roundness of the baby to the beginning of the long-leggedness of the school-age child. The permanent body build of each child is becoming increasingly evident. The head and the upper part of the body have now assumed their adult proportions, so the child no longer looks top-heavy. Legs and arms are rapidly lengthening out. Bone growth is proceeding, and cartilage will be almost completely replaced by bone by the end of this period. Girls are ahead of boys in their skeletal development, but usually they are a little lighter and shorter than boys. Height and weight show a gradual steady increase. By the end of the fourth year boys are about forty-three to forty-four inches in height and weigh around forty-three pounds. Girls usually reach about one half of their adult height by the time they are two, boys by the time they are two-and-a-half. By the age of three all the early teeth will usually have developed. The heart rate, respiration, and blood pressure are more stable, so that children are able to play for longer periods without growing fatigued. The weight of the muscle tissue is increasing, particularly in the large muscles. Boys continue to have more muscle tissue, girls more fatty tissue. The nerve fibers of the brain are nearly mature by the end of this period, and the brain will have reached around 90 percent of its adult weight.

These are the most important years for laying the foundation for physical and mental growth. How well children fulfill these normal growth patterns will depend not only upon maturation but also upon the kind of diet and physical care they receive. Protein is needed for building new cells upon which normal growth depends. Carbohydrates, minerals, and vitamins also are necessary for healthy growth. Children whose diets are deficient in any of these elements may lack energy and be apathetic in their responses. Such children lack the vitality and alertness of the normal, healthy, runabout child. A lack of knowledge of diet, which may result in overfeeding at this age, may lead to obesity which in turn can keep a child from running and playing in a normal fashion. Overweight during these years can be the beginning of a serious and handicapping problem, both physically and socially as the child is growing up.

"I'LL DO IT MYSELF . . ." Not only are runabout children showing physical changes between the years of two-and-a-half and four going-on-five, but other developmental changes are evident. Although a two-and-a-half-year-old has lost a baby straddle and walks and looks like a child, there still is a bit of the baby left. They still like to be cuddled and to be close to their parents, and their parents still enjoy picking them up and cuddling them. But now these youngsters are learning to assert themselves. They sometimes insist that things be done their way. They may refuse to come when they are called. They indicate their new feelings of self with a frequent "No!" or "Do it myself!" Such independence may be disturbing to some parents who respond with scoldings or punishment. This is not deliberate disobedience; the two-and-a-half-year-old does not understand what obedience and disobedience mean. Rather, it is a step toward growth in independence. Many children of this age resent interference with their physical activities or their absorption in something which interests them. If they are frustrated they may still bite or kick or hit or throw themselves on the floor in a temper tantrum. At times these youngsters may have a quick change of mind, for they have discovered that there are choices to be made. They may push away their soup and demand cereal, or take out blue socks and then insist on red ones. If parents give in to all the constantly shifting demands, there will be constant turmoil, and reinforcement for the little ones' demanding ways. It is best to present children of this age with few choices and to keep routines as simple and clear as possible. Statements made with an air of casual expectancy work best: "It's time for lunch now," or "I'll help you put away your toys." Two-and-a-half-year-olds will not always conform, to be sure, because they are developing minds of their own, but reasoning or arguing with them usually makes them more confused and unable to decide just what they do want to do. When possible, these little ones should be allowed to do things their way. Parents should not be severe or rigid with these youngsters. Teaching with a light touch holds for the two-and-a-half-year-old just as it will throughout childhood.

90

THREE AND FOUR   By the time they are about three, children usually go through a period in which they are less negative and much easier to take care of. They even seem to want to do things the right way and often ask, "Is this the way?" They understand words so well that they can be given simple reasons and explanations. They are less resentful of interference and can be more easily interested in a new activity. They may still be upset when things fail to go their way, but temper tantrums are less frequent. Instead of hitting out when they are angry, they may begin to call names or say, "I don't like you!"

By the time they are four, runabouts have lost that last bit of baby softness and roundness. They are a great deal larger, sturdier, and more

self-reliant. They are well aware of themselves as persons and respond best when they are treated as individuals. At four, children often are not nearly so pleasant to live with as they were at three. They are going through a noisier, stormier, more active year. Frequently, they are "out-of-bounds" in their behavior. Many family problems begin at this point. Four-year-olds seem so grown-up that parents are apt to expect too much of them and be less patient with them. They may try to clamp down on their noisiness, manners, language, and personal care. Life often becomes filled with "dos" and "donts," with children's resultant aggressiveness often turned toward their parents. Children become difficult to teach. They call names and say: "I hate you!" "You're a mean mommy!" "I'll get you!"

Some four-year-olds are sufficiently adventurous to run away from home. Usually this is not deliberate naughtiness or disobedience but simply a desire to see something going on a few blocks away, or boredom with what is happening in the yard.

The four-year-old's boundaries need to be widened a bit. Their own yards are no longer enough to hold their interests. They may need freedom to visit a nearby friend. They are beginning to understand about crossing streets carefully and can often be trusted to cross a quiet street to play at a friend's house. Many four-year-olds enjoy and develop well in a preschool experience. Parents need to meet the four-year-old's growing independence rather than create problems by continuing to treat them as though they were babies.

VIGOROUS OUTDOOR PLAY The runabout years are years of bodily activity and vigorous outdoor play. Youngsters of this age would like to live outdoors, and they become restless and even irritable if they must stay indoors for too long a time. During this period children make great physical progress. The coordination of their large muscles improves strikingly, and they need ample opportunity to use and develop them. Although physical skills will depend upon maturation, after that time skills largely depend upon the opportunity for practice. A child who has no opportunity to run and climb may lag behind other youngsters who have the opportunity and encouragement for such experiences. The child who lacks the opportunity to use physical skills may not develop as much vitality and physical strength as other children of similar age. Such a child also may become handicapped in relationships with other boys and girls, for the physical skills of normal play which open the world of childhood relationships may be lacking. This can seriously retard social development.

All runabout youngsters like boxes and barrels to clamber over, ladders or jungle gyms to climb, and slides to scoot down. The littlest ones enjoy climbing up the ladder to the slide almost as much as coming down, while four-year-olds may experiment coming down headfirst or backwards or even try climbing up the slide. Three-year-olds usually discover the trapeze, and by the time they are four many youngsters can hang by their feet and do stunts. Swings often are used during these years; even two-and-a-half-year-olds begin to learn how to pump, and four-year-olds go "high in the sky." Although some youngsters have a good deal of difficulty when they first try to ride a tricycle, they soon find it a favorite and use it constantly. They would even bring it into the house, if their parents would permit it. Until they are about four, children enjoy sand and water play. When it is available, they spend a great deal of time dumping and hauling and pouring sand. But many four-year-olds have outgrown the sandpile; they want to rush about in more active, noisy play. Runabout children like to use their bodies in rhythmic games. Even the two-and-a-half-year-old can run and jump and walk on tiptoe, gallop like a pony, or clap hands to rhythms.

During these years the child's small muscles are not as well coordinated as his larger ones. Eye-hand coordination is imperfect, and it is a strain for the child to perform small tasks requiring close concentration. Two-and-a-half-year-olds may be able to thread large beads, and three-year-olds to enjoy a small pegboard; four-year-olds often like cutting and using sewing cards with large holes. For the most part, however, the use of the large muscles should be encouraged rather than putting too much emphasis on the use of the smaller ones.

GETTING ALONG WITH OTHERS  It is important for the runabout child to learn how to play with and enjoy other children. Studies show that those children, who, beyond the third year, are deprived of such experiences, who are kept too close to parents or some other care-taking adult, may be slowed up in their normal social development. Such children may find it difficult to relate to other boys and girls when school days begin. During these years, they may continue to need the security of a nearby adult when they are playing with other boys and girls, but they are gaining the ability to cope with one another in most situations. The runabout years are the special years for learning how to get along with other children.

Two-and-a-half-year-olds, on the edge between toddlers and runabout children, usually have not learned how to play well with other children. They like to be with others as long as there is a parenting person to whom they can run for security if another child upsets them. They still have to learn how to share and take turns, to ask for what they want instead of using the more direct tactics of toddler days. They may want to show a toy to another child, perhaps even have a fleeting idea of sharing it, but they will still clutch it and hold on if the other child tries to take it. These children are experimenting with friendship, but are not yet ready to manage many situations in which there might be conflicts. They may get into difficulties, or withdraw from other children, if there is no adult nearby to help solve the problem. How the problem is solved, even in these young years, will begin to set a pattern for later relationships. If an aggressive attack on another child is rewarded by success in getting what was wanted, aggression may become a useful tool in learning how to cope with similar situations. An adult who stands by during an aggressive attack reinforces the child's learning that aggression gets you what you want.

93

Helping children see how their actions affect others, helping them find a way to work out the problem, even at this age, are more constructive ways of helping little children learn how to get along with one another. It is at this age that patterns of coping begin to be established.

By the time the runabout is three, *cooperative play* is usually beginning. Several children may play house or bus together. Even three-year-olds, however, have no real understanding of cooperation. Whenever their interest changes, they go their way and do what they want regardless of the wishes of the others. But they are beginning to understand about sharing and taking turns. They may be seen waiting for their turn at the swing or drinking fountain.

They are learning to ask for what they want instead of just taking it. It still is hard for them really to be generous or to give up something they want, but they may offer a playmate something other than the toy they are using, "Here, you take this." Although they still need an adult in the background to help them learn how to play with other children, how to share and take turns, they are better able to take care of some of their quarrels and disputes themselves.

The three-year-old sometimes selects a special friend and plays happily with this youngster, ignoring other children or even pushing them away. The special friendship may not be of long duration—it may be Mary today and Timmie tomorrow. It makes no difference to three-year-olds whether their friend is a girl or a boy. They enjoy children of both sexes equally, and both boys and girls play the same games.

By the time they are four, youngsters usually want to dash out of the house the first thing in the morning. Their friends are now becoming more interesting to them than adults, and they have special friends with whom they like to play. Although they play with either boys or girls, their best friend is apt to be of the same sex, perhaps because they have learned to enjoy the same activities. Four-year-olds enjoy each other. They boast and brag, make noise, talk at great length, and are full of wonderful plans.

At the same time there is a lot of name-calling and quarreling, sometimes with words and sometimes with hitting and fighting. They often say, "Go away, I don't want to play with you!" or "You can't play here!" Sometimes they run to their parents with bitter complaints. They tattle a great deal, partly for reassurance that they are right about something. It is a form of checking up on what they are learning about right and wrong. On the other hand, they do not need nearly as much adult supervision, nor do they run to their mother quite as readily as they used to do when things go wrong.

94

SEX TYPING   During the runabout years some girls are already showing increased interest in dolls, whereas boys turn more frequently to cars, blocks, and trucks. In part this is due to the long-established cultural patterns which make it seem undesirable for boys to play with dolls and girls with trucks. Parents and other adults may curb the cross-sex activities of even these little children. Toys are provided which are felt to be sex-appropriate. Particularly with boys, play is checked which seems to be more suitable for girls. Many a little boy has had a doll taken away from him and has been told, "Boys don't play with dolls." In part, sex-typing play also may occur because these are the years when girls are expected to identify with their mothers, and boys to identify with and copy their fathers. It is difficult, however, to separate the two as the sex roles of parents are, in many aspects, based on cultural expectations. In most cases, the roles of mother and father have been defined by custom, but, for many parents, these roles are changing. As an increasing number of mothers go out to work and their lives begin to resemble those of the father, patterns of sex-role expectations and identification for children also may become less rigid. If left to their own desires little children are known to choose their toys and games with little consciousness of their sex role.

THE NEED FOR ADEQUATE REST   Although runabout children, as their activity increases, are apt to resist having to stop their play for a nap, they still need a midday rest. It is not wise or possible to insist on sleep, but children can learn to have a quiet playtime, preferably on their beds after lunch. Records, stories, coloring books, puzzles, and peg toys are all useful in keeping children quiet while they rest. Some parents find that a special box or shelf of toys for resting time is helpful. If the adult rests, too, so that the pattern of the house is one of quietness and relaxation, the child is more likely to rest willingly. The neighborhood parents can help one another by agreeing to keep their children at home for a time after lunch each day.

Bedtime is an individual matter, depending on the child and the situation, but most runabouts will be ready for bed between seven and eight o'clock and will sleep around the clock. Two-and-a-half- and three-year-old youngsters will want a bedtime ritual, but four-year-olds are usually a bit more flexible and often go to bed quite willingly, even though things are not done in just the same way each night. They still want a playtime with their mother or father, but are able to accept any one of a variety of activities. It may be riding in the car, making puzzles, building with blocks, playing a simple game, or listening to a story or a record. It is the closeness to their parents that counts, rather than the activity itself.

It is not unusual for three-year-olds to get up and wander about the house, or want to get into their parents' bed, or just lie in their beds and talk to themselves in the middle of the night. By four, children are apt to be less restless at night. If four-year-olds do wake, it is usually because they have had a bad dream or are disturbed about something. They now need only a small amount of help in going to the toilet at night; they may even be able to go alone. They also usually amuse themselves when they wake up in the morning instead of calling for someone to come.

LEARNING THROUGH PLAY  During the runabout years play is a form of learning. As far as possible within the limits of safety, common sense, and the rights of others, play should be spontaneous. Children should be allowed plenty of time to play what they want to play. Telling them how and what to play tends to destroy initiative and imagination, reducing the value of play as a learning situation. Children learn best when they are doing things they like to do and feel a need to do, rather than things that are forced upon them. This does not preclude providing stimulating situations and materials which a child can use in play.

During these years, children need a variety of creative mediums—paints, crayons, large pencils, finger paints, clay, records, rhythm instruments, costumes, wood, a hammer, and nails. Using these things should be fun. At this age completion of a project is not as important as the satisfaction of creativity. Completion of a task will come later. Children's ability to begin creative play spontaneously is often killed by well-meaning adults who make them self-conscious or who impose their own adult standards of neatness, accuracy, and completion. This is a period of experimentation, not of finished or perfect results. It is fascinating to watch the two-and-a-half-year-old absorbed in drawing or painting on large sheets of paper with big lines and splashes of color, smearing finger paints with bold strokes and sweeps, or energetically kneading, rolling, and pounding clay. By three, the youngster may be able to draw a recognizable man or house or to make a crude object out of clay. Four-year-olds often chatter as they work, describing what they are doing, admiring their work, and expecting others to admire it.

Blocks are fun, too. At first the youngster builds simple towers or houses, later towns or a farm or a zoo, depending upon the experiences they have had. Many creatively combine blocks with other toys such as dolls, farm animals, cars, trucks, or airplanes. Older runabouts also enjoy simple singing games and using rhythm instruments. Dramatic play is an important part of helping runabout children relate to their world. During these years they take the roles of those about them, trying them out—mother, father, even baby, mailman and grocer, bus driver and doctor—their roles are endless as they play out the life around them. Many a parent has seen themselves as their child sees them if they listen to their youngster playing house. By the time they are four they are inventing wonderful and exciting games of cowboy or spaceman, doctor or an imaginary character from TV. These games may even carry over from day to day. Older children often assign roles to one another—"You be the doctor, I'll be the nurse, you be the sick one" or "I'll be the cowboy, you be the bad man!" Leadership is developing. An especially creative child may emerge as the planner of games. Sometimes there is a struggle as to who will be the bad man—who, the cowboy.

Another important element which comes out of play is the release

96

which it offers to little children for their feelings as they try to adjust to the demands of the world in which they must live. We sometimes forget that it is not easy for a child to become socialized, to give up his free and comfortable ways of doing things, and to conform instead to such requirements as going to the bathroom, eating certain foods in certain ways, and sharing parents and toys. Children need opportunities to release their feelings, to feel free to do what they want, to follow their desires and interests.

They can find this in their play. They often use active, creative play to express their real feelings, even their anger. This gives release and helps them cope with their world. Although some adults look upon play as a waste of time, play is essential to the all-round growth of children. Indeed, when more formal learning becomes desirable, children master their lessons better when there is a relaxed atmosphere and early lesssons are taught, when possible, through play.

PRESCHOOL  An increasing number of runabout children will spend much of each day in a day-care center or a preschool. The preschool is a children's world rather than an adult one. In it, children can find learning materials that individual parents may be unable to provide. They have an opportunity to learn to give and take and to interact happily in a group of other youngsters their own age. In the story period or at "telling time," children learn to listen to what someone else is saying. At juice and nap time and in taking turns, they learn cooperation and consideration for others.

A desirable preschool provides new opportunities for growth by setting the stage for constructive play. The equipment, the toys, the opportunities to use clay and finger paints freely and to pound nails and build with the large nursery-school blocks, and—most important—the opportunity to share these experiences with others add to the value of play as youngsters learn to express themselves and to try out their newly developing abilities.

97

Many of these activities can be carried out at home, too, and should be encouraged, but parents rarely have the time to permit children the same degree of freedom to explore and to try out many ways of expressing themselves that the preschool teacher can provide.

The preschool teacher ideally maintains a healthy balance between free play and the kind of activities that offer children an opportunity to explore their world more fully, through developing an interest in nature, in simple scientific experiments, in beginning experiences with form and number, and in the symbols that will soon take shape as words. Although runabout children usually are not yet ready for formal lessons in reading or numbers, they are being helped to build basic understandings that will prepare them for their later school experiences.

A few children are ready for preschool when they are two-and-a-half; most are not ready until three. Not all children need preschool, for some have neighborhood groups that satisfactorily provide freedom to play under the wise guidance a child needs. But when children are ready and able to enjoy other children, preschool may be a rich experience for them, providing a stimulating environment in which to grow and learn. The best preschools are flexible and friendly. The teachers keep in close touch with the parents and work together with them in understanding and meeting the needs of the runabout child. Preschools also bridge the gap between home and school, so that there is no sudden break when the child first leaves the family circle. Parents often come to school with their child until the runabout is at ease in the new surroundings, and in many preschools parents are participants in the daily program.

The day-care center differs from the preschool in that most of the children remain there for the greater part of the day. As the center will be a home for little children during most of their waking hours, it should be chosen with the greatest of care. It should be a homelike place with enough warm and nurturing staff to give personalized care to each little child. This means that there should be a ratio of at least one adult to every four children under two years of age, one adult to every six two-year-olds, and one adult to every eight three- to five-year-olds. An adequate day-care center not only will provide for the physical care and safety of the children, but also will have the equipment and program of a good preschool. Attention will be given to the socialization of the youngsters and to the stimulation of their developing mental capacities. There should be close involvement between the parents and the staff of the center so that the needs of the individual child can be better understood and met. The day-care center also can be helpful in parent education for those parents who need some help in understanding their little children.

Day-care centers are increasing in number to meet the needs of the many little children whose parents both work outside the home. Unfortunately many of the centers are not providing the best care for children. There is no evidence that quality day care is harmful to children, but inadequate day care may be as limiting to development as an inadequate or disadvantaged home. The awareness of both local communities and the federal government that day care is becoming a necessity for many parents who must work is a hopeful indication that more attention will be given to developing standards for day-care centers and helping train those who will staff them.

Preschool or day-care experiences can be of special benefit to those children who have physical or mental handicaps, such as those who are blind, deaf, mentally retarded, or physically crippled. For these children, specially planned programs can provide an opportunity for play with other boys and girls. This cannot always be arranged at home, yet it is of as much importance for the social development of handicapped children as for other youngsters. When possible, these youngsters benefit from contact with normal children. Some preschools plan for and are willing to admit a limited number of handicapped children. For those whose handicaps are more severe, special centers are beginning to be developed. These may be sponsored by parent groups or community funds, and, in an increasing number of cases, by local or county school systems.

For the disadvantaged child whose own home cannot provide the stimulation and opportunities for the creative play and learning of the more advantaged home, the preschool, or more often the day-care center, may provide many of the needed experiences. Children growing up in these early years in an environment which is lacking in the necessary stimulation for mental growth start with a severe handicap, and unless help is provided such children may never come close to fulfilling their full potential. A good program during these early childhood years can begin to provide this help.

Although they are ready to step beyond their home into the world of playmates and even preschool, runabouts still remain deeply attached to their parents. They are the ones they turn to spontaneously for comfort and care. A child needs the active interest and affection of both parents for best development.

Children are confronted with the task of learning how to share their mothers and fathers with other people during the runabout period. They must permit the triangle of mother, father, and child to expand and include, first, brothers and sisters and members of the family group, then the various adults in their environment. They must feel secure enough with their parents to be able to reach out toward other people and be willing to include them. This is not easy at all for a child to do.

Children learn to love through their closeness to their parents; they feel possessive about them. One of the greatest tasks for runabout children is to develop an increasing ability to share their parents with their brothers and sisters. They need, for instance, to be helped to realize that their parents will continue to care for them even though a new baby comes, and that they have sufficient love to go around. Sibling rivalry is never completely overcome, and much of the quarreling and tensions that begin during these preschool years are due to this basic and fundamental rivalry of children for the love of their parents. If parents understand this, they will feel less guilt and sense of failure as their children quarrel. They then will be free to meet rivalry situations more constructively.

BECOMING MORE INDEPENDENT Runabout children like to try to do things for themselves. Even two-and-a-half-year-olds may try to wash themselves when they are in the tub or struggle to put on their socks or pull their shirts over their heads. By the time they are four, children are fairly efficient at dressing and undressing themselves; sometimes they take over and "surprise" their parents by appearing in their room fully dressed. True, shoelaces will be untied, and clothes or hair may not always be neat, but on the whole they do a good job.

During these years children also are learning to feed themselves more skillfully. At two-and-a-half they may still need some help with their meals, but by the time they are four they are usually capable of eating most food without help. Their table manners are far from perfect, of course, but parents or adults who are working with children need to retain a light touch in teaching conduct at the table, since an overemphasis on table manners or eating correctly can make a child dislike mealtimes. It is better to let them eat in their own way, still using their fingers if they want to. Children are highly imitative, and if they see good manners at the table, they will gradually try to copy them. When they behave particularly well at the table or say "Please" or "Thank you" or "Excuse me," a word of praise will help them feel proud that they have done something admirable, and they will try it again one day.

Runabout children also like to "help." Even the two-and-a-half-year-old may try to set the table or help dust or make a bed, while the four-year-old can empty wastebaskets or dry the silverware or serve the juice in preschool. But a child at this age cannot take responsibility for doing "chores" or even for completing those that have been started. But though interest may fade quickly, the desire to help is real and can be encouraged. Even if they do put the forks on the table upside down or run away after they have emptied just one wastebasket, they try to help again if they are rewarded with a "Thank you for helping me" or "That was a big help!"

Adults need to be careful not to judge a child's early attempts to be helpful by adult standards. Demands that a job be finished or done just right may destroy a child's desire to help—a desire that is not easily re-created. It is wisest to let children do what they will to help, then run off, and help again some other time.

101

Although they are steadily becoming more independent, sometimes runabout children will want mother, father, or teacher to take over or to give them considerable help in doing things they are able to do for themselves. This is especially true when they are tired, out of sorts, emotionally upset, or ill. Understanding adults will give help when it is wanted or needed, but will praise and encourage self-help when it occurs. Too much insistence on complete self-help discourages the runabout child just as it does the toddler.

## LANGUAGE DEVELOPMENT AND COMMUNICATION

Language develops rapidly during the runabout years. Most children add from five to six hundred words a year to their vocabularies between the ages of two and five, and they probably understand a great many more. The grammatical structure and the dialect will be that of their parents and the cultural group in which they are growing up. Occasionally, children may begin to stutter because they have much to say and cannot find the right words or get them out quickly enough. Usually, this stuttering will disappear if those who listen to the child do not comment about it, ask for repetition of words, or ask the child to speak more slowly. This type of stuttering is not so serious as another kind that also may appear during the preschool years—stuttering caused by adults putting too much pressure on the child.

It is often difficult to understand the speech of two-and-a-half-year-olds, but by the time youngsters are four they usually talk clearly enough to be understood. Some normal youngsters use poor speech even into their school years. These children may need help in overcoming their speech difficulties or incorrect speech habits; such help should be given by a trained person. Frequently, schools will have speech therapists available.

Four-year-olds not only use language well but seem to be fascinated by words. A group of four-year-olds can often be heard using all sorts of silly words and sounds and then bursting into gales of laughter. Many children of this age begin to acquire words parents do not like. They may discuss their toilet functions openly and chant toilet words. Usually it is best to ignore what children are saying and turn their attention to some other activity that will interest them. This phase, though distressing, generally does not last long. If a child has picked up words that are really disturbing, it sometimes helps to explain their meaning and matter-of-factly discourage their use. But if too much is made of a youngster's interest and play with "bad" words, they are likely to discover that these words upset their parents and so use them when they want to make them angry.

By the time children are four, they are learning to use words to express ideas and feelings. This is an important step in socialization. Sometimes they can settle disputes by words rather than by the more primitive methods of hitting and snatching that they used when they were younger. They also find words useful in helping control their impulses. Since they now can verbalize their feelings and their needs, temper tantrums when they are angry or frustrated are less frequent.

Clear and simple speech on the part of parents remains essential for the child's language development, and stories—both read and told—assume increasing importance. Most runabout youngsters listen eagerly to stories and enjoy books filled with pictures. They should be given time to turn the pages slowly, not be hurried from one page to another. Children who do not have books to look at and are not read to during these years often have more difficulty in learning to read when school days begin.

Fantasy and fairy tales, except of a simple variety, do not belong in the library of most runabout children. The children are learning to know the real world about them. They have not mastered it and are not ready to cope with stories of the supernatural, the fairy world, or the world of magic. That will come somewhat later. Runabouts do, however, enjoy make-believe stories of animals who talk and play like children. They never weary of being told tales about themselves or their playmates. They listen attentively to the running story their parents can make up of what they did. They like stories about other children with whom they can identify, who are doing things they can understand. Some nonsense rhymes and jingles, as well as simple poems and songs, appeal to them.

Some imaginative four-year-olds will begin telling stories of their own and will want to share them with their parents or other children. Sometimes, too, their imaginations run away with them, and they add all kinds

103

of imaginative details to actual happenings. In this case, some adults feel that a child is not telling the truth and should be reprimanded. It is easy to forget that the line between reality and fantasy is not definite yet. Instead of scolding and destroying imagination, which is a valuable asset all through life, it is usually best to say, "That is a good story you told me—what really happened?" In this way a child is helped to gradually learn the difference between fantasy and reality.

Language development is not only learning to speak and use words in an understandable fashion but is also a basic part of the developing mental abilities of children. Until a child can use language and think in the symbols of language, there can be little progress in problem solving, thinking, and reasoning.

Although there are other ways of communication, language is the one most frequently used. But communication involves not only the ability to use words, but also the capacity to listen to the other person in order to be able to respond. Little children need to learn to listen if they are to interpret what they hear. This is the beginning of understanding of both written and verbal communication which will become such a necessary part of their lives. Adults also need to learn to listen to children in order to be able to understand their needs, their feelings, and the concepts which they are beginning to form. Such listening takes practice on the part of the child and patience upon the part of adults, but it is important in establishing genuine communication between parents, and others who care for young children, and the child. Dr. Wendell Johnson, one of the most famous speech therapists of this century, said it this way:

> "Listen to the child well, to what he is saying, and almost saying, and not saying at all. He has something he wants to tell you, something that has meaning for him, that is important to him. . . . Respect him as a speaker. Listen to him enough to hear him out. It is wonderful for him as a growing person to feel that he is being heard, that others care about what he is saying. Assume he is doing the best he can and that it is more important for him to want to talk to you than to sound correct."*

## MAKING THE MOST OF CURIOSITY

Curiosity is an outstanding trait of runabouts, and one of the most interesting sides of their personalities. They want to know about everything. As toddlers, children tasted, felt, touched everything within their reach. Now they want to *find out* about the things they touch and about the things they see and hear as well. As they grow up, they may not continue putting unfamiliar objects into their mouths, but they will want to touch and examine them and will ask questions many times over. They need time to look at whatever interests them, whether it be in pictures or in reality. Because they need time to absorb what they see and hear, adults should avoid rushing them along. It is often distracting to children to have someone continually point things out to them. They want to see for themselves and ask their own questions.

*Johnson, Wendell, Brown, Spencer, Edney, Clarence W., and Keaster, Jacqueline. *Speech of Handicapped Children* (3rd ed.). New York: Harper & Row, 1967.

Before children can develop concepts or ideas, they must have had many opportunities to get to know the things around them by actual touching, seeing, hearing. They learn first through their senses. Gradually, through their widening experiences, they learn how to bring together their impressions of things seen and heard and touched to begin forming ideas or concepts. These become the tools with which they will think and enlarge their knowledge. But children cannot learn how to use the symbols that are words until they have had some experience with the objects those words represent. The word b-a-l-l can mean nothing to children, for example, until they have felt and touched and used a ball. If adults are willing to answer questions and provide them with opportunities to find out about things themselves, they will be amazed at how much runabout children are able to learn. From the time youngsters arrive at this "What-is-it?" and "How-does-it-work?" stage, adults will be kept busy answering their questions. They should encourage this wonderful and useful curiosity. The questioning mind may be a nuisance at the moment, but it is a valuable asset later on.

When adults answer children's questions, they should answer them simply, clearly, and without elaboration. They should not try to explain too much. If children want more information, they will ask. Sometimes youngsters ask questions to reassure themselves that they are right: "That's a big building, isn't it?" Sometimes youngsters repeat a question over and over, making it a part of themselves, or they may come back to the same question many times. If those with the child cannot answer a question, they should say, "Let's find out." This is a useful approach to develop, in anticipation of the many times in the child's life when there will be a need to find out. If the question is one that can be answered by seeing or doing, this is the best way to explain, since children learn from simple, concrete experiences. Climbing into a small boat, going to a farm to see the cows being milked, taking a trip to the airport, visiting the place where father or mother works, watching a steam shovel at work—all these are rich experiences through which children can find out about their world.

If adults are to help children make the most of their curiosity, they first must help them cultivate the attitude of wanting to know. This attitude is of great importance in the preschool years. If children find that it is all right to explore, that their questions will be answered, they develop an inquisitive, adventurous approach to life that will be invaluable to them. It is important to let children try things out for themselves as much as possible. "Can you do it yourself?" is a good key to follow. Let them try to ride the tricycle before showing them how to do it. Let them experiment with taking appropriate things apart. Don't help them unless they ask for help or show that they are getting too frustrated.

Young children are capable of absorbing much more information than most adults realize, if the information is given to them in terms they can understand and at a time when their own interest is awakened and they are ready and eager for it. Many adults do not take children's interests and questions as seriously as they should. They are apt to push the eager question aside or answer it carelessly, even incorrectly. But it is important that questions be answered as accurately as possible within the limits of the child's understanding. The concepts that are built should be correct from the very beginning. Whenever possible even little children should be helped to see the reason behind things; this is the start of an understanding of cause and effect, an important part of growing knowledge.

This is particularly true when the questions asked may involve the development of attitudes which may remain with the child over the years. Some of the questions which three- and four-year-olds ask are difficult for parents and others who are responsible for runabout children to answer as the answers involve not only facts but personal feelings. It is difficult to explain death to a little child when a pet dies, a dead bird or animal is discovered, or even more so if a relative or someone whom the child knows has died. Three-year-olds have little understanding of death; they may realize that the bird "is all gone," just as a doll or toy might be broken. Four-year-olds have a limited concept of death. There may be games of "bang bang—you're dead" as they copy what they see on television. There may be some temporary grief at the loss of a pet, but they do not understand the irreversibility of death. If a near relative or a friend dies, they will miss them, but may still talk of their coming back. Religious concepts of God and heaven are not clearly understood. Sometimes a child may be angry because the loved person has gone away. Some children of this age are quite matter of fact; if the relationship is not so close that the child feels the hurt of separation, the death may be ignored. This may be hard on parents who look upon death with a much greater depth of feeling. Although little children should not be overburdened with sorrow, the normal grief and sadness should not be kept from them. The simple explanation "We feel sad because we will miss Grandfather" is a healthy feeling for children to begin to understand.

Questions about the beginning of life also are difficult for many parents to answer, for their own attitudes toward birth and reproduction are involved with feelings that have grown from their own childhood experiences and attitudes which have been learned and held for many years. Such feelings often are reinforced by the cultural patterns within the community. Some parents can talk openly and comfortably about these things, others find themselves embarrassed and ill at ease.

Children normally ask many questions about reproduction—not only about where babies come from but why their mothers are different from their fathers, why girls can have babies and boys cannot. These questions vary with the age of the child. They will ask the same questions many times over as they grow and feel the need for more information. At whatever age they ask them, parents should answer the questions simply, honestly, and—if at all possible—at the time they are asked, remembering that a child often learns more from the way something is said than from the actual words. A good general rule is to answer only the specific question a child asks. When they want more information, they will ask for more—if they feel that their parents are willing to answer their questions. Too often in our eagerness to teach the child, we give far more information than is sought or can be absorbed. Too much information given too soon only bewilders and confuses. During the runabout years, providing simple information in answer to the questions is usually the wisest course to follow.

These are the years also when little children are beginning to identify their own sex. This is important for their future sexual adjustment. Although the cultural sex role may be changed, the biological sex role remains the same. It is important that little children do not feel confused as to whether they are a boy or a girl. They also need to begin to understand that they will become men or women. By the time school days begin little girls should have learned to identify physically with their mothers, with other girls, and other women. Boys should have a physical masculine identification with their fathers, other boys, and other men. They should know that there are bodily differences between men and women, that women can carry babies within them and men cannot.

A PATTERN TO FOLLOW   Runabout children have much to learn, and often they have to learn in an adult world under adult pressures. It is no wonder that many problems begin during these years. Children must have guidance. They must learn what is acceptable behavior and what is not. They need patterns to follow. But patterns should be presented gently, consistently, without undue pressure to conform to adult ways, and with an understanding of the child's ability to learn. As little children respond to the steady guidance of warm and loving parents and other adults to whom they are attached, they begin to develop the conscience that will guide them as they must make choices of what is right or wrong in the years ahead when parental people are no longer always at hand. Runabout children do not know what is considered acceptable or unac-

107

ceptable behavior; they learn this gradually as they model after and identify with those whom they love, and as they receive approval and encouragement for the kind of behavior that those who care for them are trying to teach.

If parents are stern and too demanding during these early years, children may become too concerned about their behavior and may be over-inhibited when they grow up. Such children will be unable to meet life with the initiative required to master skills and to meet new situations without undue strain and without ultimate rebellion or timidity.

If, because they are too busy or unwilling to be bothered, parents are inconsistent in their guidance—strict today and permissive tomorrow—children cannot know what is expected of them. They will be likely to learn to test the limits imposed on them to see what they can get away with: Is mother going to be strict today; does father mean what he says, or is he just threatening again? This is a poor and confusing beginning for any child. There is no consistent model to follow.

If parents are aware of the growing independence of their runabout children, and gradually help their youngsters take some responsibility for their actions through kindly, affectionate, and consistent guidance, children will be able to develop enough self-confidence to feel that it is safe to grow up. These children also will have the initiative to begin to go ahead on their own. When these early years are over, children who have learned to trust those who guide them will be ready to leave the security and shelter of the family and those they have known well, and be eager and ready to become a part of the larger and less familiar kindergarten group.


## Living with a child

### PRESCHOOL EXPERIENCES FURTHER DEVELOPMENT
*Group Participation Benefits Runabouts*

Most children go to school by the time they are six, but many go to kindergarten when they are five. Increasing numbers of communities are providing the advantages of prekindergarten experience. Where such provision does not exist, church groups, philanthropic organizations, and groups of interested parents often establish centers for runabout children. Thus more and more four- and three-year-old youngsters are spending part of their time away from home. The give and take of companionship in active child play furthers social and emotional development as well as physical development. Many three-year-olds respond positively to group play, and most four-year-olds are happy participants.

Susan O'Neil was just four. She lived in a city apartment with her parents and had always seemed a cooperative child. She usually played by herself, enjoying her toys and books, and readily accepted the daily routines at home. But her mother was noting changes. Susan's play seemed noisier, often boisterous, and vigorous objections were voiced when she was asked to be quiet. Then there were intervals when she just sat passively, looking at nothing, lost in daydreams. Sometimes she appeared to carry on a dual conversation with herself.

Now and then there was a playmate for a short time. A friend of her mother's might drop in with her preschool-age child, or Susan might go with her mother to the home of a family friend. But when she was with other children there usually was turmoil. She would demand whatever toy the other child played with, and of course there was resultant squabbling. She wanted to choose what they would play, and her ideas were not always accepted. Not infrequently angry shouting or crying punctuated the visit, and neither mother looked forward to repeating it.

One evening Mrs. O'Neil told her husband of a brief call she had made that afternoon with Susan. "We stopped at the Dales' for not more than fifteen minutes. That was long enough for Susie to knock over Freddy's fort, and there was a fight when he objected to her appropriating his new ball. I'm sure they were glad to see us go!"

Shortly afterward Mr. O'Neil came home and found Susan busily engaged in drawing on a large sheet of paper. He studied her efforts a moment, then said with interest, "Look, Susie, this should be this way. And you made his legs too long; I'll fix them for you. And whoever saw a blue dog!" With a few strokes he transformed the dog to his liking, filling it in with brown crayon. "There you are! Here's your dog," and he held out the picture. But Susan struck at it. It was no longer *her* dog. "I don't like it," she protested, and ran out of the room crying.

One day following an invitation to a birthday party Susan and her mother arrived at Mary's house, and Susan looked with interest at the wrappings and toys strewn about. Mary was opening her gifts promptly, with more curiosity than care. Susan held on to her box.

"Give Mary her present," coached her mother, "and say 'Happy Birthday.' "

Susan obediently repeated the phrase, but held on to the box, still interested in the presents which stood among the papers and ribbons. Mary, growing impatient, took hold of her birthday gift. Susan immediately wrapped both arms around it. A momentary wordless struggle ended with a hard push by Susan and a wail from Mary. Mary's mother picked her up, while Mrs. O'Neil tried to make Susan understand that it was Mary's box, Mary's birthday gift. "Don't you remember," she coaxed, "you thought Mary would like it." It was relinquished with reluctance, Mary's tears stopped, and the arrival of another child and another gift was welcome.

Shortly, a film cartoon was shown, and all the children settled down on the floor to watch. Around Susan there arose a succession of small disturbances.

"Get outa my way," Michael complained as Susan, ignoring him, moved over for an unobstructed view.

"Mommy, she poked me!" whined Jane, when Susan shifted to a more

109

comfortable and advantageous position.

But such problems were forgotten when the lights were on again and the children were called to the table. For most of them, that was the party. Whatever manners they had learned were forgotten as ice cream in animal shapes was placed before them. Again Susan was a storm center.

"I want the elephant," she announced, and tried to change her chocolate bear for Teddy's strawberry elephant. Teddy promptly objected.

And as Susan's hand reached out, "Here, you give me that!" yelled Charles, grabbing his cookie out of her reach.

"That's mine! You snapped yours!" Kathy protested when Susan tried to pull another snapper after demolishing her own.

It could hardly be called a peaceful party, at least around Susan.

A little while later a father arrived for his daughter. Noisy youngsters engaged in an energetic game blocked the doorway. Susan happened to be the nearest child, and he appealed to her.

"Do you know where Lisa is?" he asked hopefully.

Susan recognized the name. "I'll get her for you," she offered. She went to the room where she had seen Lisa playing, and, casually pushing another child out of her path, pulled Lisa up forcibly. "Your Daddy's here. Come on!" But "You let me alone!" shrieked Lisa, while the boy Susan had pushed hit her. Susan hit back, and a lamp went over. "I was just bringing her to her Daddy," Susan sobbed, upset at the accident, as her mother and Mary's mother converged on the scene.

Describing the party to her husband that night, Mrs. O'Neil said, "We must do something. When Susan's with other children her behavior is so different than when she's at home. It worries me. I wonder if preschool wouldn't be a good idea. I think she needs to be with other children more. She just doesn't know how to get along with them."

After further discussion, he agreed that they should investigate possible preschools and an appointment was arranged with the head of one not too far away. Mrs. O'Neil indicated her worry about Susan. Determined to tell all her concern, she added, "Sometimes she sits and gazes into space and talks to herself as if she's two children. And she makes up such exaggerated stories!"

Miss Adams was reassuring. "Susan sounds like a great many children who are with grown-ups most of the time. They get along well when most of their wants are met without argument. They seem to be conforming to the household routines, but actually the household is conforming to them. Then when not everyone acts the same way, they are upset. Susan needs to learn that she has to give in sometimes. She hasn't had to at home, I expect.

"She should be learning to do more for herself, too. She is well able, I'm sure, to dress herself, yet you tell me only that she is 'good' when you dress her. And she needs to learn certain things her home can't teach her. Playing with children, learning group social skills, takes practice in a child's own age group. That can't be provided by a child's parents, interested though they may be.

110

"I think you're right. Susan not only seems ready for preschool, I believe it would be very helpful for her to have the kinds of experience it offers."

Upon returning home, Susan's parents discussed reactions to the preschool.

"You should have seen the way the children took off their own wraps and hung them up, and put them back on again later when they all went out to the playground. And they practically managed without help in the bathroom, and when they had milk or orange juice. They chose what they wanted to play, and shifted to something else when they felt like it. And when a teacher brought a few of them together and read them a story and showed them the pictures in a book, they were so interested. They were having such a good time—and it all seemed so good for them."

Susan was more curious than hesitant about starting to school. And the family was both relieved and surprised that the new situation offered no problem about leaving home each morning. The noisy and boisterous Susan was really no different from the other children in the group. At four—a time of loud, strenuous activity—children welcome periods of vigorous group play, a wholesome release of energy. This helps them at other times to listen to stories or to music, or to participate in quiet table play with crayons, clay, or scissors.

It was not in being boisterous that Susan was unlike other four-year-olds, but rather in being overly dependent—in allowing herself to be dressed, washed, and sometimes even fed. Very soon after entering the preschool, as she saw how much more self-sufficient the other children were, she began showing not only a desire to help herself but an eagerness to do things well. There were some things which gave her trouble—fastening the top coat button, managing boots that just wouldn't go on—but when she accepted help it was to learn how to manipulate difficult tasks.

Progress was soon apparent, also, in her relations with other children. During her first days at the preschool Susan pushed and shoved to lead a line or to get to the table first for milk. She seemed surprised that a teacher discouraged this: "We take turns. We'll all have a chance." And she was disconcerted when one of the children stared at her disapprovingly, or when another, just as eager to be first, shoved her even harder.

One day Susan impatiently pushed away a child who came to join her in clay modeling. She wanted all the clay for herself. But she soon found that she had more than enough, and that there would be more "cakes" for her "bakery" if Lucy shared the activity. Later she beamed with pleasure at the smiles she received when she pulled her clay apart and gave some to two other children. There were fewer quarrels about possessions and less snatching and clutching.

At first, when she came home from school Susan replied only briefly to her parents' questions. But she soon had a great deal to tell about. "Guess what! We made a garden!" "You know where we went? To the zoo!" The exaggerated tales of earlier months were no longer heard. Real playmates and real experiences had greater appeal. She had little time or

111

need for daydreaming.

Some activities generally frowned on at home were readily allowed at school. She could march and stamp her feet; there were no downstairs neighbors to be disturbed. She could bang at the workbench with real tools. When a sound appealed to her, there were others to join in chanting repetition. "Woozy doozy!" she sang out one morning, and Amy laughingly replied, "Woozy snoozy!" More and more rhyming syllables were added by other children, and no one said to stop being silly. The rhythmic pattern amused them for a little while, then was forgotten as they shared another interest, climbing on the jungle gym.

If the children were in a group with a teacher and one of them wandered off, Susan learned not to shout accusingly, "Katie's gone away!" Time after time the teacher either called the wanderer back quietly or left the child alone. Learning from her teacher's ways, Susan soon discovered that behavior other than aggressiveness could be effective in persuading others.

When a child misbehaved, Susan would say, "He's a bad boy," or, "She's naughty, isn't she?" But the teacher would calmly remark, "Tommy hasn't learned how to do that yet," or "I'm sure Cora will try not to do that again." Gradually Susan's condemning, critical comments stopped.

Most children profit greatly from the experiences provided by group participation. Their interests expand as they encounter new ideas and learn new skills, social skills among them. Group contacts provide opportunities to learn to work and play with other children while adults guide and help and encourage.

Susan, especially, needed such experiences, and through them she learned to meet many kinds of situations. She recognized group standards, and, accepting them, she learned to adapt. She showed increasingly good nature as well as skill in working out disagreements and disappointments. In short, she acquired appropriate four-year-old maturity.

Habits and attitudes as well as facts and skills are important acquisitions for young children. They profit from activities within their own age group, particularly through experiences which differ from those within the home. This furthers maturation and enhances growth in self-confidence.

part 3

# MIDDLE CHILDHOOD YEARS

There is no sharp dividing line between the years of early childhood and the beginning of the so-called school days. Often children already have had Head-Start or other preschool experiences. School is not a new experience to many of them but, in most cases, a transfer from one kind of school to another. The new school experience is usually in a bigger building. They now will be in contact with children who are considerably older than themselves. They must get used to the noisy and sometimes rough life of the playground, and the need for some rules in the school building. Classes will be larger and often less personal. They must learn to cope with many situations without the close support of an adult.

There will be other changes as well. They will gradually become part of a special world which few adults can ever really enter. During the school day, these growing children will usually do those things that adults expect them to do—but in their private lives, and among their friends, they will begin to stay apart from the adult world. They will be fascinated by it and try to understand it; they may even be eager to enter it someday. But their own feelings, the understandings they have with their friends, the games they play, and the secret words they share are those passed on from child to child and shared with only the most perceptive adults. Young children run home eagerly to tell all about

115

preschool or even kindergarten, but by the time they are six or seven they seldom share their world in all its vivid living with an adult.

Although five- and six-year-olds usually are in the elementary-school building, their needs are different from those of the older boys and girls. They need flexible schedules with many opportunities to move around and to learn from active experiences. The curriculum must be such as to encourage those who are ready to begin to master the symbols of words and numbers, without discouraging those who are not yet ready. The thought processes of most six-year-olds seem more nearly like those of the five-year-old than of the seven-year-old. This should be recognized and taken into account in planning the curriculum. For this reason, in some countries seven is the year chosen for the beginning of formal education. Five- and six-year-olds are getting ready for this next step.

Between seven and twelve, there is a tremendous growth in the ability of children to begin to use logical thought in the solving of problems. They are becoming increasingly able to understand cause and effect. They still need many opportunities for concrete experiences, to continue to touch, examine, and observe, but they are mastering the use of symbols to represent words and numbers, and to use them in thinking and reasoning.

They are now able to pay more sustained attention to similarities and dissimilarities of objects, and to generalize and organize their concepts into categories based on these similarities and differences. They are learning rules and relationships and continuing to learn concepts of right and wrong. At first moral behavior is rigid and cannot be changed, but by the end of these years these youngsters will have become more flexible as an understanding of the relativity of situations develops.

Throughout these years, they are absorbing and accumulating facts and are becoming able to put these facts together to form ideas and to raise logical questions about that which they observe or are taught. They are able to learn through the vicarious experiences brought to them through books and mass media and to transfer these representations to the world of reality. The capacity to store facts and impressions in memory and to call upon them as needed is rapidly increasing. They will be able to understand the principles of weight and size and that these do not change even though the form may change. They can come to understand that many processes, such as addition and subtraction, can be reversed.

The capacity to understand and use these processes was not present in the early years of childhood. These abilities are part of the developmental growth of children. Certain forms of learning cannot take place until children are developmentally ready to comprehend and use them. The effectiveness of the learning of the elementary-school years is dependent in part upon this readiness which occurs, to some degree, in all children of normal intelligence.

School years have their ups and downs. For some children they are almost entirely satisfying and rewarding, and for some they are generally disappointing and discouraging. For the great majority of children, however, there are both good times and bad. Most children start school eagerly. They want to learn. They want to read. They want to enjoy school. Yet

116

somewhere along the way we lose too many of these eager youngsters, so that there are those who no longer learn willingly—they have lost their curiosity and come "like snails unwillingly to school." It is our task as parents and teachers to reduce this number of unwilling or discouraged learners as much as we possibly can, so that all our children can take advantage of the years of education that are offered to them.

It is often right at the beginning that we allow youngsters to falter, when they are just starting to master the tools they will need for further learning—basic skills in reading, writing, spelling, and arithmetic. We give lip service to individual differences in children's ability to master schoolwork, but this is of little value unless we apply what we know about each child to the work that we expect will be accomplished. It is essential, if we are to educate all our children, that our expectations for them fit their abilities, so that each one may be encouraged to go on learning—so that none becomes discouraged by an inability to meet unrealistic goals.

It is also the adults' task to help each child develop responsible attitudes, not by scolding because there is seeming irresponsibility, but by giving opportunities to act in a responsible manner and by encouraging and recognizing responsible behavior. It is during the elementary-school years that children either learn the meaning of responsibility or develop the attitude of "getting by." Sometimes we limit our concept of responsibility to the carrying out of certain specific tasks at home or at school. We forget that responsibility also means getting up and going to school, accomplishing assignments, going home after school, acting fairly with other people. These kinds of behavior need recognition, too. Children learn to be responsible when responsibility has meaning for them.

During the years from six to twelve many parents overload their children with activities that involve additional responsibilities—for getting to lessons, for practicing, for accomplishing. It is no wonder that sometimes a child of this age cries out, "You never let me do what I want!" or, "I never have time for myself!" Between school and homework and extracurricular activities and organized club groups, many children literally have no time for themselves. Perhaps we have overdone the emphasis on opportunities and achievement to the detriment of individuality, creativity, imagination, initiative, and even the ability to entertain oneself. This question requires serious thought on the part of parents and teachers. How much assigned responsibility can children carry during these important years without having to sacrifice something else important to their best development—some freedom to follow their own interests, some time to do what they want?

Differences in background must also be taken into account in planning for children during these years. Some children come from homes in which there are books, encyclopedias, and other resource materials; library cards are well used and parents are available to help and encourage. Other children lack such resources; they also may lack a good place to study and do their homework because of crowded living conditions that make any quiet or private time impossible. There may be no nearby library available, and the one that is available may have poor resource material. Not all parents are helpful, and some do not have the background to be helpful

117

where school subjects are concerned. Some children are made to feel uncomfortable about the clothes they wear or the race to which they belong, others may seem different in other ways from the majority of children in their classroom. Some children are rejected by others, even by some of the teachers. All of these conditions must be recognized and taken seriously indeed by those who hope to help children learn during these years. Children do not come to school from a vacuum—they bring with them what happened at home that morning, what has happened in the past, what they expect may happen in the future. All of these experiences will determine, in part, the enthusiasm which children have for learning and their immediate abilities, not their capacities, to learn.

Our problem as adults is to recognize how much learning of different kinds we can expect of children. We must help each child find a place in the schoolroom and attain maximum growth without experiencing strain, tension, or humiliation. We must provide schools which encourage curiosity, making the acquiring of knowledge an exciting and desirable activity. If children have a feeling of accomplishment and acceptance during their elementary-school years, they are more likely to continue being eager to learn and willing to put out the effort that will be required to continue their schooling instead of becoming truants and dropouts even by the fourth grade.

# chapter 7

# Starting Kindergarten

HOW DIFFERENT THE FIVE-YEAR-OLD   Probably during no period of life do children accomplish as much as in the runabout years. The distance they travel in growth and development, in learning and absorbing, readily becomes apparent when we look back over the years from two to five. At two, little children were barely beginning to talk; they uttered words, but rarely a sentence. They could walk, but still fell down if they ran or turned quickly. They needed their parents or some other adult to take almost complete responsibility for their physical care. Their concepts of right and wrong did not exist yet. They lived in the immediate present, relating themselves to neither past nor future. They had not learned how to play with other children and could not really cooperate or even share. They knew nothing about the world outside their immediate environment; without their parents or some other responsible person, they would have been utterly lost.

How different are five-year-olds when they start off for kindergarten. In three years they have developed a definite personality. The person they will be is beginning to show, not only in their appearance but in their way of meeting situations and in their approach to life. Their speed of learning, their potentialities of intelligence, some of their special skills and talents are noticeable. Some of those individual characteristics that make each child different from everyone else are already evident.

Children usually go to kindergarten eagerly, looking forward to the new experience. They may hold a parent's hand tightly as they approach the building the first day, but rarely do they try to turn back. Not only do they want to know what kindergarten is like, but they enjoy other children and want to be with them. They are relating what they see to their past experience and are anticipating the future. The five-year-old is no longer a baby but a child who is ready for new and wider experiences.

A PERIOD OF SLOW GROWTH   The five-year-old has entered a period of slower physical growth, very different from the rapid growth of the first eighteen months. The five-year-old may be expected to grow two or three inches during the year and to gain from three to six pounds, although children vary in the amount they gain, depending partly on their total body size. Although boys are often slightly taller and heavier than girls, at this age girls are usually about a year ahead of boys in their physiological development. The skeletal development of a five-year-old girl approximates that of a six-year-old boy.

The physical growth of five-year-olds is uneven. Their legs are lengthening more rapidly than other parts of the body. Their lungs are still relatively small, and the heart is growing rapidly. Their large muscles are still much further developed than the small muscles controlling the use of the fingers, so that kindergarten children should be encouraged in activities which use the large muscles of arms, legs, and trunk. Many children are not ready for such activities as writing. They may enjoy painting with a large brush on a large surface, but holding and manipulating a pencil and trying to make small letters sometimes will cause undesirable strain and prove frustrating for some children.

A child's handedness usually is determined by five and should not be changed. Ninety percent of youngsters are right-handed. Left-handed children need special help in learning to write. They will need to be shown how to hold a pencil and the angle at which to place the paper.

The five-year-old's hand and eye are not yet completely coordinated. Kindergarten children may have difficulty when they try to reach for things beyond arm's length and may sometimes spill or knock them over. They normally are far-sighted and should not be expected to spend much time looking closely at small things.

ACTIVITY WITH A PURPOSE Five-year-olds are active children, but less restless than when they were four. Though noisy and vigorous their activity usually has a definite direction. They are better able to use and control their bodies purposefully and often skillfully. Individual differences may be marked, however, and becoming increasingly obvious, for some children will always have better coordination than others. Five-year-olds can run, skip and dance, climb, and enjoy games in which there is plenty of movement. They need equipment that gives them an opportunity for purposeful, planned activity—a tricycle or small two-wheel bicycle that they can handle, a wagon to pull or push or to use in hauling their playmates around, plenty of large planks and boxes to build bridges, boats for sailing, or just something from which to jump. They need ladders or a jungle gym to climb, unless they live near a tree of just the right height with large spreading branches.

The five-year-old is learning to throw and catch a ball and may greatly enjoy trying to toss it through a low basketball hoop. The more adventurous five-year-olds experiment with roller skates and ice skates and enjoy trying to jump rope, though their efforts are often less than successful. By recognizing this developmental need for activity and cooperating with it, both parents and teachers can encourage activities that will strengthen the large muscles and develop body control as well as give the children constructive channels for expression.

QUIET ACTIVITY Periods of strenuous activity need to be balanced by periods of quiet activity including periods of rest. Five-year-olds get tired easily in spite of their vigor and their eagerness to use their bodies—or perhaps because of it. Some five-year-olds will withdraw from play of their own accord and either just watch or seek a quieter activity; occasionally they will even lie down. Others show fatigue by being cross or irritable.

Most five-year-olds sleep about eleven hours at night. Few children at this age take regular afternoon naps, but many of them will take a nap one or two days a week, as weariness seems to accumulate. In a kindergarten program one or more rest periods are advisable, depending on the length of the kindergarten day. If children attend morning kindergarten and are at home during the afternoon, they should have a "quiet-play" rest time even if they are unable to sleep. If they attend afternoon kindergarten, usually it is wise to bring them in from play at about eleven in the morning for a quiet period or a rest before lunch and school.

During these periods of quiet activity, children need to feel free to move from one activity to another. They cannot be expected to sit still for a long time, although their attention span is increasing rapidly, so that they may remain interested and absorbed in the same project for twenty minutes or even longer. Five-year-olds find blocks, paints, clay, "work-with" tools, and puzzles all satisfying to their growing interests. They may work for a period of time at the easel or settle down at the puzzle table; they may make a clay bowl or spend time with blocks, working out a plan they have in mind. Many of them no longer run from one activity to another,

121

experimenting with this and that. They know more fully what they want to do today and will even carry over a project until tomorrow.

Five-year-olds usually have an idea of what they want to do before they go to work. In painting they may begin by announcing what they are going to paint. Often they will be very critical of their own work, expressing dissatisfaction with it or asking for directions. An increase in perceptual acuity shows in their drawings and paintings. Details such as windows, flowers, and a door into a house, eyes, hair, and fingers, or people with contrasting size, indicate the growing ability to observe details. Many five-year-olds have passed the stage of just smearing and dabbing paint; they want to create something and have a definite feeling of accomplishment when the picture is finished. They enjoy showing the product to their teachers for their praise and taking it home for their parents to admire. It is best not to ask a child "What is it?" for it may be disappointing to the youngsters who feel you should be able to see what the picture is about. It is better to say "Tell me about your picture."

LISTENING AND LEARNING  Whether at home or at school five-year-olds will respond eagerly to "Let's have a story." They enjoy stories that answer their questions about things they see around them—steam shovels and cars, airplanes and boats. They also like stories about the activities of children and about family life. But stories about families should include many kinds of families, not just the family of mother, father, and children, for many children today are living in one-parent families and other kinds of family situations. The traditional family story can make many children feel left out. Stories about children might also include some situations in which children have problems to work out, such as how to play together without getting angry or excluding another child. Five-year-olds are learning how to control their own impulses and how to get along together. Attitudes are forming toward the acceptance of other children who may be different from themselves. Their ideas about how to be friendly children are forming. Well-chosen stories can lead into simple discussions about relationships and are enjoyed by the children.

Five-year-olds are ready to begin to broaden their horizons beyond their own families, blocks, and neighborhoods with tales about other lands and other parts of their own country. City children can learn about country children, and country children are interested in what city children do. Stories about children in other countries which stress the similarities between children everywhere as well as the differences are a valuable beginning in helping children learn to understand many kinds of people. In addition, television continues to open up the world to young children. By five many children have moved from one place to another; some have even traveled and can share their experiences, from camping out to flying to another country. Such experiences can supplement stories.

There is a continuing delight in imaginative stories, especially those about animals, but five-year-olds usually are not old enough to enjoy the more fantastic or involved fairy tales. They listen to poems with pleasure, the rhythm adding to their joy in listening. Humor and repetition in both stories and poems are also fun. These youngsters typically become quite absorbed in a poem or story and resent interruptions—they may "shush" a restless or talkative child. They also resent changes in a favorite story or poem. They expect pictures in a book and are disappointed if there are none.

Many five-year-olds are ready for simple, basic principles of science and mathematics. Their interest can be stimulated through hearing stories in these areas, but they also will need opportunities to follow an aroused interest through watching and taking part in simple experiments. They love nature stories, particularly if these, too, are supplemented by such activities as watching and caring for animals, plants, fish, and, when possible, insects, taking nature walks, and collecting natural objects. Stories can arouse curiosity; if this is encouraged the children will ask many questions of "how" and "why" and will be eager to take part in discovering the answers.

Stories which are a valuable part of the five-year-olds' year help children learn the pleasure of books, awaken and stimulate their imaginations, and also lead them into the world of books as a source of knowledge. This is important for all young children, but especially for those who may not have had an opportunity to listen to stories and learn about books at home.

Some children in this age group are able to take part in activities that will lead to reading during this year. In vocabulary alone, the child of today who has watched television is usually about a year ahead of kindergarten children of pretelevision days. A small number of five-year-olds are ready to read, and some do read; others pretend that they can do so by telling a story as they turn the pages of a picture book. If the desire to read comes from the child, the opportunity to learn should not be denied. However, many kindergarten children will not be ready and may become overanxious if they are pushed before they are physically and psychologically ready to master the complex use of symbols.

A good kindergarten program will always try to meet the needs of the individual child. It will avoid a formal program that pressures children to learn to read during the kindergarten year and thus discourages the many who are not yet ready for reading. Much valuable learning can be accomplished without the use of the printed word. Informal reading may be a valuable addition to the kindergarten for a few children, but it is not necessary for the development of a vital program for all children.

Physical development as well as mental ability must be taken into account before a formal reading program is started. This may be particularly true for boys, many of whom have trouble learning to read in the elementary school. In general, boys are more active than girls and have a harder time sitting still and listening and applying themselves to formal schoolwork. They seem to learn better in an active program in which they can learn by doing. Because boys often are as much as a year behind girls in their physical development, many may not be ready for reading as soon.

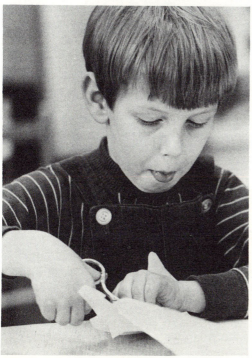

Kindergarten is a new experience most children eagerly anticipate. Growth in independence and experiences in shared activities increase during this year. Though vigorous in their activities, five-year-olds are less restless, and activity usually has a definite direction. They are better able to use and control their bodies skillfully. Though kindergarten children cannot be expected to sit still for a long time, although attention span is increasing rapidly, they may become absorbed in a project that satisfies their growing interests.

Physical development also must be considered in using workbooks in the kindergarten. Some children may be ready for the experience, but others may become so discouraged that their future confidence in themselves as learners is impaired.

MUSIC, DRAMATIC PLAY, AND SOCIABILITY Five-year-olds enjoy rhythms and songs. They like to make up dances to music and enter enthusiastically into singing and rhythmic games. They also enjoy taking part in a rhythm band. Many of the children are beginning to follow a tune and will even correct a child who does not know it. Often a five-year-old chants a short original rhythmic song.

Five-year-olds love dramatic play. They are ready to act out a story they have heard—very simply and with plenty of action and spontaneity. Their love of dramatic play is the keynote to many of their activities. They act out their interests in their homes and the places they go by playing house, being mother or father, playing doctor, or playing store. Both boys and girls enter into this home-centered dramatic play. They also show their interest in the exciting world in which they live by playing various roles as astronaut and jet pilot.

Kindergarten children are greatly interested in group activities and group play. They like to play with other children, but they are not very good about really cooperating with others. They stay in the group as long as they enjoy it, but their interests are self-centered. If they tire of group activities, they become restless or seek something else that pleases them more, even if it means leaving the group without a father in the home or a delivery truck for the supermarket.

The kindergarten child is capable of taking part in large-group activities if they are well supervised, but they get along better in small groups of five or six children, or with just one other child. At this age, three is often a crowd; a child can adjust to one playmate or the other but often not to both. Thus on a rainy day it is wise to invite one other child over rather than two.

Five-year-olds are improving in taking turns, in respecting other peoples' belongings, and in asking to use things rather than snatching or hitting. Their sense of property is developing. They will quarrel and fight, but they are learning better ways of getting along and are increasing in their ability to handle situations themselves. Usually adults can remain in the background while children of this age work through their own problems as they play together. Interference is needed if one child is being discriminated against, or if there is danger of physical hurt.

PUTTING NEEDS INTO WORDS Five-year-olds are beginning to use language fluently and correctly. They usually pronounce words clearly and are easily understood. They talk freely, carrying on conversations and expressing ideas. They love to tell stories, and they will recount to their teachers incidents that happened at home or will tell their parents about the happenings of the day at school. They have learned to put their needs into words. Parents and teachers can help by listening to youngsters when they try to tell about incidents or personalities or objects, by encouraging conversation in the family, and by avoiding overemphasis on correct speech. That will come later and largely from example. Speech at five should be spontaneous.

Five-year-olds are becoming able to put their fears and their anxieties into words. They sometimes will spontaneously tell what is bothering them; or a parent or teacher, seeing or sensing that the child is disturbed, may be able to help the youngster talk about the things that are of concern.

Adult assistance in understanding and interpreting what children see and hear is particularly important to the child today, when the whole world is brought into the living room through TV. Kindergarten children, with their growing awareness of reality, may be confused by the behavior of adults they see on the television screen. At an age when their conscience is developing, when they are trying to learn to control their own impulses and to behave as their parents have taught them, they see grown-ups on TV fighting with and screaming at each other and generally behaving in ways that they have been told are unacceptable. Studies show that children may copy the actions of those they see on television, modeling many of their aggressive actions. Documentaries and news reports of current events also often bewilder small children, and sometimes this information provides real cause for concern and anxiety.

127

Parents in the past were able to protect their children from the impact of anxiety-producing reality while they were very young, but today's children must meet life head on and need the support of adults as interpreters and protectors; they must be sure that someone will take care of them. Most children can absorb most of their concern over bewildering or distressing events if they receive adequate answers to their questions, so that what they see and hear is not distorted. But a child who already is disturbed or insecure will need special help and understanding. The questions of the observing child today may have much more serious import and need more thoughtful answers than those of most children who grew up before television became a household fixture. The choice of which programs these young children watch is indeed important, and deserves more adult thought than is usually given to it.

By the time they are five, children who are tense, overanxious, excessively rebellious, or unusually withdrawn can be identified. The problems of such children should be taken seriously, not pushed aside with the vague hope that they will outgrow them. These children should receive thoughtful attention and, if it appears necessary, special outside help.

ENJOYING INDEPENDENCE Children of kindergarten age are quite independent and enjoy doing things for themselves—if they previously have not been pushed too hard or had too many discouraging demands made on them. They usually can wash themselves, although their mothers or fathers will have to help in neglected or hard-to-reach spots. They are able to take care of their own toilet needs, although sometimes they will need a reminder, for they find it hard to leave their play. They feed themselves easily and with a minimum of mess. They still like to eat many things with their fingers, but they are becoming increasingly skillful with fork and spoon and may use a knife. They have definite likes and dislikes in food.

Youngsters of this age can dress themselves, although they get things twisted sometimes. They cannot always tie their shoelaces or manage tight buttons or small fastenings. They may need help getting into difficult winter clothing, especially when they are tired or out of sorts. Parents can help by trying to provide clothing with self-help features—ample armholes, large buttons or snaps in places the child can reach, boots that are loose enough to put on easily, and cardigans rather than pullover sweaters. If these provisions are made, dressing can be a source of fun and pride to a child.

When one takes care of a child from babyhood, it is hard to keep pace with such growing ability. Many a parent does not even know, until a visit to kindergarten, that a youngster can put on coat and boots. Parents need to refrain from quickly doing something for a child their kindergartener can accomplish—even though slowly and ineptly. Yet such help robs their child of satisfaction in successful accomplishment, satisfaction all children need for building self-reliance and the courage to meet difficult situations. Five-year-olds want to test and rely on their own powers, and they should be encouraged, though never pressured, to do so.

Five-year-olds also show their independence by liking to be trusted with errands or by performing simple tasks at home and in kindergarten. They will go proudly to a nearby store and bring home a loaf of bread, change and all. They usually will carry out directions faithfully and be elated by their success.

This is the age, also when children are beginning to be able to take some responsibility for their own actions. Many of them have learned to cross a street safely on their way to school. They are beginning to know the difference between right and wrong as their consciences continue to develop. Until now they had been dependent on their parents or some other adult to tell them what is acceptable behavior; now they are beginning to understand for themselves, although often they will turn to an adult for guidance and reassurance. Five-year-olds still think of "good" and "bad" in terms of specific situations—it was "bad" to do this or "good" to do that. They need frequent reinforcement from the approval of grownups.

Because five-year-olds still want to please those they love, they can be taught how to adjust to the needs of the group and to respect reasonable authority. Most five-year-olds want to do what is expected, particularly in kindergarten. They often ask whether they are doing something the right way, or they may turn to parents or teacher with "Can I go; can I do this; is this the right way?" Most five-year-olds like to fit into their environment and infrequently rebel against it, unless there have been too many demands and frustrating experiences, so that the child already is rebellious and beginning to have hostile feelings toward others, especially grownups. Since five-year-olds want to please others, care needs to be taken lest they become too conforming and lose their spontaneity and initiative. An overdeveloped conscience can become a handicap. If approval is given for conforming to the needs of the group, it also should be given to initiative and creative behavior. If limits must be set and learned there should be ample opportunity for freedom of choice and activity within those limits. This is a year in which there is some danger of overstressing conformity to the detriment of future creative learning.

Five is a good year to enter kindergarten. Five-year-olds are better able to settle into the necessary routines of the larger group than they were at four. Five seems to be almost a resting point between the out-of-boundness of many four-year-olds and the confusion of some six-year-olds as they are confronted with the many new experiences of moving into the larger world of first grade. The child who goes to kindergarten during this year of equilibrium has a better chance of learning to adjust to the schoolroom situation with a minimum of strain than does the six-year-old who goes to school for the first time without a kindergarten experience.

Frequently questions are raised as to whether children who have been to preschool can profit from the kindergarten year or whether it will be repetitious. It is true that those children who have been to preschool already have had the experience of being with other youngsters in a group situation. Hopefully, they will have learned how to share and take turns, to

129

listen to others and enter cooperatively into some planned activities. However, most five-year-olds, even if they have been to preschool, can benefit from the kindergarten experience as a prelude to the more organized expectations of most first-grade programs. The preschool usually has appropriately offered a much more flexible program of activities. Most preschools also provide a lower ratio of children to adults than is possible in kindergartens. Parenting people always have been nearby when coping became difficult, or when comfort was needed. In the larger school situation, even in the kindergarten, children must learn how to cope with many situations without the ever-ready help of the preschool personnel. This step toward increasing ability to cope is a bridge between the free activities of the preschool and the beginning of the formal learning situations of the school years. An effective kindergarten will provide both experiences.

The varied experiences of the kindergarten are of particular value as changes in the patterns of cognitive development begin. The younger child could only absorb and focus on that which was an immediate experience. Five-year-olds are beginning to combine that which they know, that which they experience in the immediate present, with that which has gone before. They are starting to look ahead to tomorrow. They are able to begin to combine ideas and concepts and use them to cope with new situations or to solve simple problems. They are beginning to understand, within simple situations, the meaning of cause and effect. Memory is increasing. These are steps toward the ultimate ability to bring together ideas in logical thought. Children still need many opportunities for the use of all the senses in manipulating, experimenting, discovering through concrete experiences. They are not yet capable of understanding abstract ideas. Kindergarten can provide the materials and the guidance toward those experiences which are not always available to the child at home.

The majority of children do go to kindergarten. For many children this will be their introduction to the school years ahead. The kindergarten experience may determine the feelings which the children will have about school. If the kindergarten provides a happy learning experience, children will look forward to first grade, but if they have been unhappy and the experience has been unrewarding they may be fearful about the next step in school.

## Study of a child

### MILD BRAIN DYSFUNCTION
*Even Slight Damage May Affect and Retard Development*

When children do not respond and react as most youngsters of their age, the reason is not always readily established. If they appear normal mentally and strong and healthy physically, with no serious sensory defect or crippling condition, parents are not likely to consider that the cause of

130

the puzzling behavior may be slight organic impairment, with resultant brain dysfunction.

Often it is not until kindergarten age that behavior deviations become apparent and really disturbing. The school is likely to notice them first; parents generally become aware of them only when the school helps focus their attention on the child's total growth and reaction pattern. Earlier, parents are likely to feel the child is restless and overactive, shows little aptitude for games usually mastered easily by children of similar age, and flits quickly from one activity to another, showing poor concentration and little persistence. These responses are wearing for the parents, but they seldom attach any special significance to the behavior.

It was not until Danny Ward was five and in kindergarten that doubts arose about his development. Miss Rosen, his teacher, at first thought of him as a friendly, pleasant, though exceedingly restless and fidgety little boy. She soon recognized that he was less skillful on playground apparatus and with block construction than most of the other children, and that he was less fluent in relating his experiences. But in the first few months of school she was not particularly concerned about Danny; she was aware that some youngsters need more time and practice in learning skills than do others.

As time went by, however, Miss Rosen came to realize that Danny's pleasant smile was vague, that his restlessness seemed uncontrollable, and that his motor and verbal skills did not improve despite her patient help and repeated demonstrations. Furthermore Danny's speech was hard to understand, and although she encouraged him to enunciate correctly, he was either incapable of reproducing sounds correctly or reverted to incorrect ones as soon as her careful coaching ended.

Now and then Danny attempted simple songs and rhymes which the other children had learned readily, but for the most part his attention was not held long enough to learn the melody or words. Even when he did have some small success, he sometimes forgot the song or verse the next time it was repeated.

Danny's play with clay and finger paints was very immature, but it was far more successful than his efforts to draw or color pictures. Long after other children's drawings were recognizable as trees, flowers, people, rabbits—whatever the subject—Danny's could not be identified. Generally Danny was willing to try to follow his teacher's directions, but his efforts brought him little or no success. This did not appear to bother him. He seemed unaware that he had copied a letter incorrectly or produced an unrecognizable picture. He would often ask Miss Rosen, "Shall I write my name now?" To her encouraging assent, he would make an unintelligible mark on his paper and hand it to her with a satisfied smile. He seemed to want to please his teacher, to do as she directed.

Danny knew the meanings of many words, but his concepts were often faulty or bizarre, resulting in vague or far-fetched responses. He could see, but he saw inaccurately—shapes and letters appeared incomplete or distorted. Matching pictures apparently was an impossible task for him.

131

In the most ordinary daily activities, Danny had trouble getting along. He was inept and untidy at lunch, while the other kindergarteners were capable and reasonably neat. He needed a great deal of help with his coat and his boots, though most of the other children managed theirs alone. When his parents or teacher encouraged him to try again, he frequently yawned as he answered, "I'm too tired." If then they did not help, he was likely to lose his temper, and angrily run away.

He was seldom actually relaxed, even during story time. Picture books did not interest him for long. During games he often wandered from the group. Many times during every school day he distracted other children from group activities by his constant squirming, his incessant getting up and down, his monotonous repetition of a phrase or a question, or by poking or pushing a child near him.

After several months of consistent, patient effort to help the boy, Miss Rosen felt that everything she had done was fruitless. Speaking to Dr. Carol Gray, the school psychologist, she wondered if Danny were not a candidate for a class for retarded children.

"How could he possibly go to first grade?" she asked, both discouraged and concerned. "Should he stay with me another year? And if he did, would it do any good, do you think? He certainly hasn't made much progress this year, not at all like most of the class."

"Suppose we see how he does on some tests," Dr. Gray suggested. "From your description, giving him a psychological examination won't be easy, but the results could help us in planning for him."

Somewhat to his teacher's surprise, Danny's test results were not those of a mentally subnormal child. "Still," said Dr. Gray, "I certainly agree that Danny could never get along in first grade next term. He has definite limitations, and he is a difficult youngster to handle in a group. I'd like very much to talk with his parents. I'd like to know how he is at home and how his parents think of him. And I'd like to know something about him as an infant and as a very small child, before he came to kindergarten. He may just be extremely slow in developing. And there may be unwise management at home without the family realizing it. I'd like to know his pediatrician's opinion and whether he's had an eye examination and a hearing test, although I didn't note any obvious physical problem that might be contributing to the situation. An electroencephalogram might possibly further our understanding of the boy and help us plan wisely. Any serious neurological disorder would be indicated by the brain waves, but I suspect he has only a very slight impairment. Call the Wards, Miss Rosen, and set up an appointment on one of my days here next week."

Mrs. Ward arrived at the designated time for a conference. She was cheerful and interested, with no sign that she expected any difficulty about Danny's going into first grade in the fall term. She was puzzled and alarmed when Dr. Gray suggested a second year in kindergarten.

"But he'll be six even before this term is over," she protested. "Don't children start first grade at six? His brother wasn't six until November of the year he started school."

"I see Robert is in fourth grade now," Dr. Gray observed, looking at the record she had at hand. "How would you compare the two children when you think of their baby years, Mrs. Ward? For example, did they walk and talk at about the same age?"

"Danny was twenty months before he walked," Mrs. Ward replied. "But really, that doesn't have any bearing on going into first grade, does it? And I thought we weren't supposed to compare children," she added defensively, ignoring the comparison that she herself had already voiced.

"How about talking?" continued Dr. Gray, for the moment overlooking both question and comment. "When did Danny start to talk?"

Mrs. Ward thought for a moment. "Well," she said slowly, "there were a few words at—oh, about the time he started to walk, I think. But—well—I guess he was past three when he really began to talk. I know that even now he doesn't always express himself clearly. He's always in such a hurry to tell something or ask for something. You know how children are." She smiled a little uncertainly.

"And your older boy?" Dr. Gray asked. "When did Robert walk and talk?"

"Earlier. Earlier for both," Mrs. Ward said frankly. "We always thought he was exceptionally bright, so it didn't worry us when Danny seemed different. We just let him go ahead at his own rate."

"But can you recall whether Robert was at all like Danny in other ways—playing with blocks, looking at books, drawing pictures? Did he listen to stories? Recite Mother Goose songs and rhymes? Could he count and name colors? Did he undress and dress himself?

"Because here in kindergarten," Dr. Gray added gently, "Danny has not been doing what the other children do, or what Robert did when he first came here, according to his record. We don't compare one child with another child and look for each to develop at the same rate and in exactly the same way. But we do consider as evidence of normal development what thousands of children of the same age are like and can do. And we are concerned when there are marked differences in a particular child. We want to help Danny. I've already used some tests with him, and they show he does not lack intelligence. But he isn't able to do what is expected of children who will be ready for first grade in the fall. It would be much better for him to wait before going into the regular grades. That would give him a chance to learn some things he hasn't mastered yet. And with your permission, I'd very much like to talk with the pediatrician who has seen Danny these past years."

"Are you suggesting," Mrs. Ward asked hesitantly, "that you think Danny is—backward? Is there anything really wrong?" She and Dr. Gray talked for some time and considered a detailed history of Danny's growth. Mrs. Ward acknowledged that Robert's growth had been vastly different. Although Dr. Gray was sure that the results of the psychological tests indicated that Danny was not retarded mentally, she felt certain special training was necessary if he were to progress and learn as other children do in school.

"Right now he's not responding like a child who is almost six," Dr.

133

Gray emphasized. "He is learning very slowly, and he needs a great deal of individual attention. There are things you can do for him at home which I believe will help considerably. We'll talk over those steps and work with you all we can."

Understandably, Mrs. Ward was greatly distressed. She grasped eagerly at the suggestion that she and her husband discuss the situation in detail with their pediatrician, and have an oculist experienced in examining young children check Danny's vision. After a difficult examination period, the oculist stated that he had found no problem with Danny's eyes.

When the Wards consulted Dr. Donnelly, the pediatrician, he agreed that Danny and his brother had shown different developmental pictures. He reported that no endocrine deficiency was involved in Danny's case and that, as far as he could determine with the restless and uncooperative Danny, there was no hearing loss.

"He's always been a hyperactive child," said Dr. Donnelly. "He can't help the extreme restlessness that his teacher noticed; his nervous system is geared that way. I'd say that the cause is probably some relatively slight brain injury that occurred either before he was born or during birth. It's very difficult to tell exactly. You haven't mentioned before some of the things we've been discussing. Suppose we schedule an examination to check for any possible neurological problem; that will give a more exact picture than any description of his behavior."

Because they understood only vaguely the suspected basis for Danny's behavior, the Wards listened intently as the physician explained some of the known facts about the brain and its functioning. Unfortunate as Danny's condition was, they were encouraged to hear that improvement generally occurred when there was only slight malfunction.

"You see," said Dr. Donnelly, "the effects of slight damage to the brain are not necessarily apparent in the early months of a child's life. Even when a toddler shows certain behavior reactions, we keep looking for change, hoping he'll outgrow them. When a youngster is strong and well we're optimistic. And Danny has been healthy right from the beginning. Sometimes brain damage results from disease—meningitis, for example; sometimes from a serious accident, with a severe concussion or skull fracture. We know neither of these possibilities was true with Danny. That's why I say injury may have occurred either before or during birth.

"It's the kind of condition that may be present in so mild a form or to so slight a degree that in many ways the child seems entirely normal. Yet in other respects his behavior may be puzzling and actually evidence abnormal development. Fortunately, though, damaging results may often be overcome, not be permanent disabilities.

"Brain dysfunction shows up in various ways. Sometimes the child may be unable to learn. Or he may be very distractible, or irritable, or disinterested in his surroundings, almost withdrawn. It's impossible to say what behavior will appear. Often there's faulty perception. He may not see a diamond as a diamond, for example. He may not visualize the corners at all. Or a printed letter may look very different to such a child than it does to other children. So he'll have trouble learning to read and to write, to recognize numbers, and so on.

"Conceptual disorders are common among brain-injured children. For instance, when brain tissue has been damaged, a child does not seem able to group or classify objects logically. Given a number of familiar objects, such a child might say that of three things, a gong and a ball and a bell, the ball and bell went together because 'in the bell there's a little ball,' meaning the tip of the clapper. This is a far-fetched relationship. Most normal children would give the more logical grouping of gong and bell, because each makes a sound or gives a signal.

"Motor behavior is generally clumsy and awkward in these children. They have difficulty in making precise movements with both large and small muscles. And they can't coordinate their eyes and their hands. For example, when they're asked to make a mark on a certain part of a picture, the mark is likely to be off to one side, or above or below—not because they don't understand the instruction, but because the necessary messages to and from the brain aren't transmitted normally.

"The condition is very puzzling, you see, because it exists in varying degrees and in varying ways. Speaking generally, we know that brain injury shows itself in motor impairment or in impaired mental or emotional processes—sometimes in more ways than one. It's not surprising that a mild condition of this kind frequently goes unnoticed, and a child is often punished for not paying attention, for being restless, for talking incessantly, or for not learning normally, when actually it can't be helped.

"But fortunately Danny can be helped. And the earlier the condition is recognized, the more effective the steps taken to help. Your school psychologist seems to be on the right track. Seeing your boy over a period of several months has given the school a chance to observe how he acts, how he learns, how he is impeded in learning. Try Dr. Gray's suggestions. But be patient. Danny can make progress, I'm pretty sure, but remember it will probably be slow progress."

The school's counsel and the physician's concurring opinion were not easy for the Wards to accept, but they could not deny the facts as Dr. Gray presented them, and they recognized in Dr. Donnelly's explanation of brain dysfunction some of the difficulties that they now saw were true of Danny. Although they had been aware of the wide difference between their two boys, their acceptance of one being very bright and the other less capable had made them less observant of Danny than they might have been.

The Wards now accepted Danny's need for consistent, patient help in acquiring, at least to some extent, the skills he had not yet mastered. They were determined to do everything possible to remedy and improve Danny's ways. His teacher and the school psychologist helped them outline a definite plan to provide the kind of help the boy needed. For many months, Danny and his mother worked together several times each day to help Danny help himself. At first, he was rarely interested for longer than

135

ten or twelve minutes, but gradually he was able to concentrate for somewhat longer periods.

Before long Danny had learned to put on his sweater and jacket, to undress with just a little help, and to participate increasingly in the dressing process. He was also successful in other efforts: He learned the names of many objects he had scarcely noticed before, he described pictures briefly, he recited a few rhymes. His building with blocks improved so that he delighted in making towers "so high." Six-year-old Danny was beginning to master the many little accomplishments most children acquire at three and four. Perceptual problems were more difficult to improve, but the parents continued hopeful and encouraging and patient.

When the Wards reproached themselves for having neglected their son for so long, they were relieved to hear Dr. Gray say that it was questionable if many of his recent achievements could have been learned much earlier.

"Some, yes," she said. "But a child must be ready to learn before he can be taught. See what he can do now, compared with just a few months ago. His second year in kindergarten will without question be more profitable for him than his first, and more rewarding for his teacher and for you, too. Let's look forward to the following year, when there is every hope that Danny will be ready to start first grade and make progress there, perhaps with some special help continuing. You must recognize that his difficulties will not end quickly. It will take time and effort for real improvement in some areas. In the meantime, keep on working with him—ten, fifteen minutes at a time. He tires quickly, and he is very distractible. But whenever he makes a step forward, show him how pleased you are. Praise and encouragement help everyone."

When there is reason for concern in children's responses and reactions, establishing the basis for their behavior is of primary importance. Only with an accurate diagnosis, an understanding of a child's potential, and a realistic acceptance of limitations, can wise programs be initiated to help overcome difficulties. Remedial measures used in such programs may be medical, psychological, or educational—a combination of them is the usual picture. Unwitting neglect of any aspect of help is as much to be avoided as are unreasonable expectations; working toward goals beyond possible achievement can result only in disappointment, distress, and continuing difficulties. The rewards of the patient aid given both at school and at home will be better work habits, better work results, and the inner satisfaction that comes with sensed achievement. These children should be encouraged to aspire to goals that they have a chance of accomplishing successfully. Their self-confidence will be furthered, and they will be encouraged to make continued efforts.

136

# chapter 8

# A Period of Transition

BEING SIX   Being six years old has a special significance for almost all children. They have looked forward eagerly to the time when they could proudly say, "Now I am six, and I go to school."

Six is one of the turning points in the lives of children because here they step beyond the family circle into the larger world of the school and the community. Until now their relationships usually have been limited to their families, the few children on the block, and perhaps playmates in preschool or kindergarten. In each of these situations their parents have been closely involved. But now that they are six, children must find their own places and make their own friends under new conditions. At home children are loved and accepted because they are members of the family group; but when they start first grade and are away from home much of the day, they learn—as they began to learn in kindergarten and even earlier—that among their peers they must *earn* acceptance. Just being Billy Smith is not enough; acceptance comes because of the way you treat other people and because of a contribution made to the group.

The kindergarten year was one of transition between the home and the school, between the life of a child protected by the home and that of a first-grader encountering the often rigorous demands and competition of school life. Many factors combine to determine the child's adjustment to this new environment, but probably the two most important are *the pattern of individual growth* and *the background of home and neighborhood experiences.*

PATTERN OF INDIVIDUAL GROWTH   Progress in physical development varies among different children, but by six children have lost most of their baby contours. Although their growth at this age is less rapid than during earlier periods, their legs are continuing to lengthen and they are gaining in both height and weight. The child's body type is evident at six; the broad, solidly built boy or girl can be expected to weigh more in proportion to height than the slim, rangy youngster, and yet neither is underweight or overweight. While the child's body is gradually changing shape, so, too, is the face. The jaw is lengthening as permanent teeth replace baby teeth and as new molars come in.

The six-year-old's internal organs and framework also are growing and changing, even though this development is not easily observed. The heart is still in a period of rapid growth, but the brain has almost achieved its full weight. During this year, the child's eyes still are not mature in either size or shape, and their relatively shallow depth probably accounts for a continuing tendency toward far-sightedness. This defect usually is corrected naturally between the ages of eight and ten, when the child's eyes attain adult size and shape. Although eye and hand preferences are well established, a six-year-old still has difficulty in coordinating eye and hand movements. Muscular development also is uneven, the large muscles being more advanced in general than the small ones. Precise movements continue to involve a considerable effort and strain for the child.

Patterns of physical, mental, emotional, and social growth have many variations, fast and slow, steady and irregular. For example, a child of above-average mentality whose overall development is slow may be mentally ready for school at six, but emotionally and socially more like a four-year-old, as yet unprepared for the responsibilities of school. Similarly, a big, robust child may be far ahead of classmates physically, but socially and mentally immature. Too often we judge such a child by size alone and pigeonholing results.

Variations in growth patterns make it necessary to know not only what children of a certain age are like in general, but what each child is like in particular. Behavior problems at home and at school often develop because the adult in control, either parent or teacher, does not recognize a child's level of maturity. Many youngsters are regarded as incapable of adapting to first grade or as "difficult" children when, in reality, they are frustrated because they haven't reached the level of maturity attained by the majority of the class, or are bored because they have long since passed it. In a class for six-year-olds some children are still babyish, immature emotionally, and unable to adjust socially, whereas others are secure, self-reliant, and able to hold their own in their group.

HOME AND NEIGHBORHOOD EXPERIENCES   The home experiences of first-graders is the second crucial factor in their school adjustment. If their parents have shown them affection and acceptance so that they come to new experiences with the security of their home to help them, then they usually will be able to cope with school. If, on the other hand, they have been under strain during their early years—if their families have moved often and have failed to give compensating love and security, if they have had to live in cramped and inadequate quarters with money worries taking precedence over the child's need for attention and affection, if their parents have been overdemanding, or if they have serious marital problems—the child is likely to come to school tense and fearful. The boy or girl who has been too rigidly trained or made to feel unwanted will find it hard to adjust to the classroom, as will those children who have been overprotected and babied by their parents.

The experiences which children have had in their neighborhoods is also an influence in their adjustment to school. Some children have had unhappy experiences with other boys and girls with whom they have felt unable to cope. Such children come to school fearful of what other children may do to them on the way to school or on the playground. Some first-graders have had experiences of being rejected by their peers or by adults in their community because of racial, religious, or social differences between them. There are children who become bewildered in school and begin to feel inferior because their teachers, or other children, are critical of their language or behavior. Yet these were part of the neighborhood patterns they had known.

Obviously, then, all six-year-olds cannot be treated alike. *Each child is different, bringing to school a special native endowment, a special rate and pattern of development, and a special home and neighborhood background.*

AN AGE OF ACTIVITY    Although there is no typical six-year-old, certain characteristics seem to be predominant in this age group. One of these is the need for physical activity. At this age children rush about in their play, jump up from the table at mealtimes, and wriggle in their seats at school. Their whole bodies seem to be involved in everything they do. When they read, they move their lips, shuffle their feet, and twist their fingers in their hair. When they write, they screw up their faces, bite their lips, and pull themselves back and forth in their chairs. They may try hard to sit still, but they are unable to do so for long, because they have trouble controlling their movements voluntarily. Clearly, it is unwise to put a strain on these youngsters by expecting them to sit still for more than a short time. Unusual restlessness at home and at school often is a sign that the child has too little opportunity for physical activity.

Teachers and parents are not always sufficiently aware of the relationship between growth needs and behavior difficulties when they reprimand restless children or expect them to stay too long in their seats in the classroom. The inability of many six-year-olds to sit still for more than a short time is a by-product of the rapid growth of their large muscles, their high energy drive, the fatigue that follows the too concentrated use of the small muscles, sometimes the strain of using the eyes before they are fully ready for close work, and the difficulty of controlling and inhibiting movement. Differing energy drives among children make conforming to classroom demands more difficult for some children than others. A child who has a placid temperament or a low energy drive, or one who is well coordinated may have fewer problems in school than a child with high activity needs.

Six-year-olds carry over this pattern of activity even in their thinking. They learn better by participating actively than by sitting and listening. They count more easily if they have objects to move. They absorb ideas better when discussions and explanations are accompanied by, and grow out of, chances to handle all sorts of materials, to experiment with tools and art equipment, to look after details of housekeeping, and to care for a pet or a garden.

Six-year-olds enjoy using their hands. Although they like to try to make things, they usually are clumsy and cannot be expected to produce perfect results. Since the small muscles of the arms and hands are not completely developed, it is hard for many children to write or to do handwork that involves much skill or control. Even apart from their lack of skill, they usually cannot maintain their interest long enough to carry an activity through to a conclusion judged completely satisfactory by adult standards. Most children of six can, however, enjoy pasting and cutting; using paint, crayon, and clay; and handling simple tools which they now can use with

140

a fair degree of skill. Their work will be crude, but their creative efforts should not be discouraged by placing too much emphasis on perfection.

Children vary considerably in physical maturity, and standards should not be so high that those developing slowly are discouraged or pushed to the point of tension. We cannot force muscular development and coordination; we can only cooperate with the degree of maturity found at any level.

## PLAYGROUNDS—TRAINING SCHOOLS OF CHILDHOOD

Activities that require use of the large muscles should continually be stressed throughout this year. Six-year-olds should have plenty of opportunity for climbing and hauling, for running and jumping, and for free, active play. They like to use wagons and to build with large blocks and boxes and boards. They still are not well coordinated in their physical skills. They are learning to bat a ball or to jump rope, but they have far to go before they master these skills. Yet even if their movements are rough and jerky, six-year-olds enjoy learning new skills. Adults should encourage and provide opportunities for this learning but should not try to push children toward accomplishments beyond their abilities. A well-developed child may perform easily on the trapeze, but other children, not ready for such stunts, can only stand and watch with interest. Someday they, too, will try.

The playground has been called the training school of childhood. It shows not only the kind of activity children of six need and enjoy, but also the behavior patterns they are developing. They climb, jump, and run; they also shout and fight for their rights. They appear to have forgotten how to take turns, a social technique they had apparently mastered in preschool or kindergarten. Now each child wants to be first and will push, fight, and quarrel for the apparatus. Each wants to be the leader; each wants to win and finds it hard to lose. Children of this age need to be taught again how to take turns and how to get along together. Some of their rough-and-tumble play is necessary, however, for it is part of learning to hold one's own and of experimenting with independence. Competition often is keen, and many children boast and compare possessions, heights, and even families in trying to assert themselves and achieve status in the group.

Six-year-olds need adult supervision, though with a minimum of interference, to show them they don't have to be rough and rude in asserting themselves to meet the challenges offered by their playmates. Shy or slowly developing children, who might be overwhelmed by the usual playground activities, may need special help for a year or two until they are able to participate fully in an active group.

## INCREASING INDEPENDENCE AND IMAGINATION

Children of six are trying to free themselves of the behavior of little children. They do not want to be treated as they were during their preschool years. We would be concerned if this growth drive did not appear—children must drop baby ways and exchange their dependence on their parents and other adults for the increasing independence and vigor of childhood.

Group activities gain popularity in the first grade, although few children evidence group loyalty or responsibility. At six children often enter a game enthusiastically only to leave if they do not get the parts they want, or if they lose, or if something else attracts their attention. Such typical behavior shows that this still is a transition period between the individualistic play of the preschool child and the team play of the middle-grade boy or girl. Some immature children will remain at the level of individualistic play throughout the year, and for them group participation will be hard. These children should be encouraged to take part in group activities, but not compelled to do so.

In spontaneous play, girls and boys usually show different interests probably due to the cultural expectations learned in their earlier years—although some may be due to modeling after and identifying with their parent of the same sex. Occasionally girls join the boys in chasing and fighting games, and sometimes boys mix with girls in playing house or store, taking the parts of storekeeper, father, or delivery man. Best friends, however, are almost always of the same sex, and play in small groups is preferred. Although friendships are still shifting, they tend to last longer among the more mature children.

Dramatics have a prominent part in the spontaneous play of six-year-

142

olds, as in that of five-year-olds. This delight in simple, informal acting develops out of the interest or activity of the moment. Dramatic play is a source of learning as well as pleasure and therefore can be a valuable classroom tool. Dramatic play situations should be kept simple, however, since rehearsed or elaborately planned affairs are apt to destroy this rich, creative means of teaching and learning. A child of six quickly becomes self-conscious in a directed situation.

Love of dramatization carries over from play to conversation. Six-year-olds tell a story with gestures, often moving their whole bodies expressively as they talk. They like to add their own touches, and it is a mistake to scold them for telling something that is not completely true. Actually they are expressing their imaginations as they weave their stories. Children only gradually begin to realize the difference between reality and fancy. An adult can help them differentiate between the two by asking understandingly, "Was it really that way, Jimmy?"

Six-year-olds love to laugh and enjoy a joke. Affection, warmth, friendliness, and a sense of humor all help adults live happily with children who are six.

LEARNING AND LIMITATIONS Eagerness to learn is one of the most endearing traits of six-year-olds. Theirs is the age of *why*, and of trying to find clues and answers to their own questions. In this way children orient themselves to a world much bigger than the family or the block. They need to have adults encourage and respond to their efforts to express

143

themselves. How their efforts are acknowledged, their questions answered, and their curiosity stimulated will determine their subsequent attitudes toward learning.

Children at this age learn through concrete situations and direct participation. Their own environment challenges them first; they ask questions and seek answers to what they have seen and heard. This may include much that they have been exposed to through television and books concerning other lands and perhaps scientific activities such as space travel. To most six-year-olds, the distant past, even if vividly presented by television, still remains vague and only slightly understood. Time, like distance, is not a clear concept for them; they are interested in the present, in what is happening *now*. Six-year-olds cannot plan much for the future, nor should they be expected to accept responsibilities that involve perception of time. "We will do this after recess" is more meaningful to a roomful of first-graders than "in half an hour." Perhaps because time has so little meaning, many first-graders are likely to dawdle, and, if made to hurry, become irritated or upset.

Six-year-olds are showing an increasing interest in both birth and death. They are asking more questions than they did at four and five and will frequently persist if the answers which are given do not satisfy them. They ask questions about where babies come from, how they are made, and how they are born. The coming of a new baby in their own families or in the families of relatives or neighbors can be used as a rich source of experience in helping children understand the process of birth. Pets at home or in the classroom also can provide a valuable and wholesome learning experience, especially if baby animals are born. Six-year-olds will ask questions about the differences between the sexes; this often needs clarifying all through the early primary grades.

The six-year-old is beginning to realize that death is an ending. They know now that death is a fact, that old people, and pets, die and will not come back. Some six-year-olds worry for fear their mothers or fathers will die and leave them, particularly if there has been a death of someone they have known. Following an experience with death, some six-year-olds may become preoccupied with graves and funerals—they may even bring them into their play. They ask questions when they pass cemeteries. They now are able to relate death and killing. They do not yet realize that they will die someday. The questions they ask are difficult to answer in a way that little children, and six-year-olds still are little children, can really understand. The attitudes of the adults around them will determine to a large extent the feeling tone which six-year-olds relate to death.

Answers which are simple and honest are the most helpful. At the same time, the adult should try to be sensitive to the question as to whether it is one of curiosity or whether there is worry and concern related to it. The child needs reassurance that mother and father do not expect to die, as well as reassurance that there are others who love him and would take care of him if they did. It is important to emphasize to six-year-olds that they will be loved and taken care of whatever happens—for this is one of their concerns. If death should occur to a parent or one who is loved,

six-year-olds sometimes look upon it as desertion. Some children may grow angry at this seeming rejection by one whom they trusted, others may feel guilty and wonder if they caused the loved person to die. Adults need to be prepared for these reactions when their own grief may be foremost in their minds.

Stories about family relationships, new babies, and typical family experiences are helpful to children who are learning to establish their own relationships. Because many children today are growing up in homes that do not follow a traditional family pattern, care must be taken to reassure these youngsters by talking about the many different kinds of homes in which children grow up. There are homes in which there is only one parent or in which grandparents or other relatives are taking the place of father and mother. There are children who have been adopted, and others who are living with foster parents. There are many children from homes in which both parents are working. All these youngsters may be growing up in homes in which they receive loving care, and they should not be made to feel left out or different because their family is not like the typical family of mother, father, and children that is pictured in almost all readers and stories for young children. They should be helped to recognize that it is the love within the family group and the responsible care the adults give the children that makes a family and a home.

Teachers also need to be sensitive to the fact that some of the children may be experiencing unhappy home situations. Perhaps, they do not have loving parents; some children may be disturbed because their parents are involved in divorce; some may have parents who are unkind or even brutal. Discussion about families needs to be planned with all the children in mind. It is important to avoid stereotyped answers or setting up standards for family living which are impossible of achievement in many of the homes from which the children come. It is also important to avoid concepts of "What is a good father?" or "What is a good mother?" as these may make these young children question whether their own parents measure up or not. There are many "good" parents in homes which might not fit all the criteria presented in stories as "good" homes.

RESPONSIBILITY AND ROUTINE Six-year-olds like responsibility. Because they want to identify with adults and do what they think is grown up, they imitate the mannerisms and actions of their mother, father, or a teacher. They like to help set the table, wash the dishes, or make a simple dessert. At school they want to feed the goldfish, erase the board, and pass the papers. Even cleaning up is a coveted task if a word of praise makes the workers feel they have accomplished something.

Although the behavior of these children at home may disturb parents, they may appear quite grown up when they are out. This ability deserves praise but should not be taken to mean that they can act that way all the time if they want to. The effort of being grown-up all the time is too much for active, restless six-year-olds and should not be expected.

Six-year-olds have a hard time making decisions, and they should not be expected to make too many. Routines eliminate the need for some choices and give six-year-olds a feeling of security. Children of this age are reassured to know that meals come at certain times and that one activity follows another in regular order in the schoolroom. But this does not mean that programs for first grade should be rigid. On the contrary, freedom and adaptability within the program are needed, even while broad limits and sequences are clearly marked.

A TURNING POINT Primarily, six is an age of transition. These children are not more integrated, better-adjusted five-year-olds. They are different children, actually less stable, less decisive, and often less cooperative. They are being faced with many new experiences with which they must learn to cope. They are changing physically, mentally, emotionally, and socially. They are trying to identify with older children and even with adults. They want to be grown up, but at the same time they are small and dependent on the affection of the adults about them. Rigid discipline or a home or school atmosphere that is lacking in affection holds them back. They wilt under criticism and disapproval and become discouraged easily. Later they will be able to take criticism in stride, but now they need encouragement, praise, and understanding. Their explosiveness and violent changeability are normal and must be expected. Because their coordination is not perfected, six-year-olds still need help—help that may seem out of proportion to their size. Parents, for instance, should be on hand at dressing time or when a new toy won't work, and teachers may need to help when coat sleeves and boots or rubbers are hard to get on.

Emphasis on academic achievement can destroy a first-grader's confidence. Grades or marks should not be mentioned, but children should be helped to read and write and do numbers when they are ready—and not all first-graders will be ready at the same time. Any effort to force children to learn or to show independence before they are ready only defeats itself, rendering learning more difficult than it should be. On the other hand, if children who are ready to progress are not permitted or encouraged to do the work they are capable of doing because other children are not ready, they become bored and restless and find school lacking in challenge. Such children may turn to their own thoughts, interests, and home activities for stimulation and show little interest in what they are asked to do at school, or they may sit back and develop the habit of not living up to their potentials. If adults can catch the point of readiness, the child will pass more smoothly and efficiently from early childhood into a more complex and demanding period.

A flexible program to meet the needs of all the children in the first grade cannot be overemphasized. This is a time for learning, not for polished achievement. We adults often are impatient, expecting too much of six-year-olds. We should judge children's successes by their steady growth, by the progress they make over a period of months, rather than by a particular achievement at a particular time. If we expect more of six-year-olds than they are ready to give, we may set up tensions that will hinder their learning and affect their whole relationship to the school situation.

## Study of a child

### A CHILD CAN BE TOO "GOOD"
#### Compliance Can Conceal Confusion and Worry

Many adults consider a child's behavior undesirable and suggestive of poor adjustment only when it disturbs or annoys them or interferes with their own comfort. It is true that frequent disobedience or quarrelsomeness, temper outbursts or defiance may well evidence poor adjustment. Such reactions suggest a possible need for professional help, especially when the child's parents are at a loss to understand and correct them. But it is equally true, and not as often recognized, that a pattern of yielding, compliant behavior and submissiveness also may indicate poor adjustment and suggest the need for help. The quiet child may be quiet because of lack of self-assurance and deep-seated feelings of insecurity. A "good" boy or girl really may be too "good" and not a happy, relaxed child.

Johnny Gifford was six and had almost completed the first grade. He liked school and in the first months had not had any trouble with his schoolwork. But as the year wore on he gradually experienced increasing difficulty. He never seemed ready to begin when the other children were starting on a project. He was still assembling a well-sharpened pencil, a clean eraser, and fresh paper when they were well along with some task. And he seemed to make very slow progress once he did get started. Time and time again, dissatisfied with the results of his efforts he would erase the words and numbers he had written. Sometimes he would even recopy an entire page. The end of a period found him far from finished with work that most of the children had already completed.

Miss Eaton was a young teacher on her first assignment. She thought of Johnny chiefly as one among the thirty-five who never made her day difficult. She considered him "well behaved" and never worried about him. She was aware that lately Johnny's schoolwork had fallen below his earlier accomplishment, but it was acceptable. She had no doubt that he would be able to complete the grade requirements.

But when Johnny's report card indicated that he was slow and seldom finished his work, his mother was displeased. She appeared at the school the next morning and announced firmly to Miss Eaton, "He's never given any trouble before, and we're not going to have any now. I know he can learn as well as the others. If it's necessary, you can punish him to make him do better. Whatever he's doing wrong must be nipped quickly. He must get a better report next time."

Mrs. Gifford spoke quickly and decisively. Her chief reaction was indignation that her son was not bringing credit to his family. He had disturbed the routine of doing exactly as she expected, and she found this difficult to tolerate. She had always considered Johnny's docile obedience a reflection of the "good job" she was doing in bringing him up. Quiet, self-effacing Johnny had followed all the regulations imposed at home, and she was determined that he would meet her standards of schoolwork as well.

Miss Eaton felt challenged by Johnny's problem, partly because she thought she might have been somewhat at fault, partly because she sensed that the mother's attitude was somehow involved in the situation. She discussed the matter with the school principal, Mr. Jamison, and at his suggestion arranged an appointment for Mrs. Gifford to talk to them together. At about this time, however, Johnny developed a severe cold and stayed home during an entire week. Miss Eaton passed his house every day when she left school, and one day stopped in with some of his schoolbooks. Her report of the visit suggested a possible basis for Johnny's troubles and his tense, anxious manner.

"Johnny was lying on the living-room sofa," Miss Eaton related, "and his mother asked if I planned to stay for a little while. As I was there with him she would go out to do an errand. Her manner suggested it was almost as if he had caught cold to inconvenience her.

"When she had left, Johnny told me worriedly that because of his

149

cold he was making his mother do a great many extra things. It seems that usually he cares for his own room every morning. He makes the bed and dusts before he leaves for school. And he always sets the table and helps with the dishes. Another of his jobs is to keep the bookshelves in perfect order, dusting the books and ornaments and seeing that they are properly arranged. Every minute seems scheduled for him."

While Miss Eaton was chatting with Johnny, who had been delighted to see her, she picked up a book, glanced through it, and replaced it. A little later she noted a lovely pottery bird and admired the exquisite workmanship. Johnny became disturbed and restless, and blurted out unhappily, "The book should be on the next shelf, not where you put it. And the bird you were looking at—it should face the window, and you made it face the other way. My mother doesn't like it if things aren't right. She says there's a place for everything and everything should be in its place. She gets mad if I don't fix things right after I dust."

Johnny was apologetic for his implied criticism of Miss Eaton, but he apparently could not risk displeasing his mother. His teacher cheerfully arranged the articles as he directed, and Johnny relaxed. She asked him then if his father, too, was particular about everything, if he was strict. The reply was unexpected.

"Daddy tries hard," Johnny answered seriously. "But he's different. Mother says it's the way he was brought up. She says she's going to bring me up right. I heard her tell Daddy so one night," he added confidentially. "That was once when he wasn't being neat, and Mother told him I was just like him, and he was a bad example. But Daddy's nice. He's fun, and I love him."

Before Mrs. Gifford returned from her errands, Johnny's father came home. He entered cheerfully, tossing his coat on the end of the sofa, his newspaper sliding to the floor. "Hello, Johnny," he said, giving the boy a pat on the head. "Isn't it nice of your teacher to come to see you! Where's Mother?"

They chatted easily for a few moments and soon Johnny said, "Mother's taking a long time. I guess I'm making a lot of extra work for her." He looked anxiously at his father.

Mr. Gifford's expression became serious. "Have you been good?" he asked. More questions followed: Had Johnny taken his medicine? Had he eaten all his lunch? Had he been any trouble to his mother? "It's good that you have your schoolbooks now," he continued, with a faint smile for Miss Eaton, "so you can catch up with all the work you're missing. Mother's worried about that, you know. She wants you to be promoted."

Johnny sat up excitedly. "I have to be promoted!" he said shrilly. "I have to be! Mother said nobody in her family had ever *not* been promoted!"

Miss Eaton soothed him. "I'll help you, Johnny. You'll be back at school soon. And I'll leave these lessons for you to do while you're home."

When Mr. Gifford went to the door with her a few moments later, Miss Eaton told him about the earlier conversation. She was concerned that Johnny seemed to have a great many jobs.

150

"My wife's a wonderful woman," the boy's father said, a little uncomfortably. "I know she's set in her ways, but really, she means everything for the best. She feels our son should be taught early to do everything just right. She wants John to be different from his untidy father," he said with a self-conscious smile. "And she's right about his schoolwork, too. Of course he must learn to complete his assignments."

The principal felt that Miss Eaton's visit had been very enlightening. It suggested a home situation which was difficult for the boy and which perhaps was tied in with his school performance. After talking with Mrs. Gifford, he was sure his surmise was correct. He tried to explain to her how Johnny was caught between the opposing standards of his parents. Children want to please their parents; that is how they win the good will and approval so important to them. Thus when in the home there are two standards because the parents have opposing viewpoints, the child in the home becomes confused. In trying to please both parents, Johnny was having a hard time of it. Punishment was not the answer.

"Maybe you're right," said Mrs. Gifford finally, though grudgingly. "But Johnny will have to do as I say. I can't change at my age. I've learned to put up with his father's careless ways, but I won't have my child spoiled."

It was not easy to persuade her that her overexacting ways not only created too many demands on Johnny, but had confused him because of the friction they caused with her husband. She was urged to try to maintain a balance between her standards and her husband's. It was pointed out that at least outward accord between mother and father was essential to help establish a feeling of self-confidence and security in the child. Without these, his schoolwork was only one aspect of his life which might be affected. His adjustment was likely to suffer in other ways as well.

Parents are not always as rigidly demanding as Mrs. Gifford, yet their standards, whatever they may be, affect their children. In Johnny's case his mother was a stronger-willed, more dominating personality than his father. Johnny was zealous in meeting her demands and tried hard to live up to her expectations by being meticulously clean and orderly. Johnny's father was gentler and more affectionate. His ways were vastly different from his wife's. In seeking to meet his mother's requirements, Johnny often felt as if he were somehow criticizing his father. That made him feel guilty. Then when he occasionally left a toy on the floor or neglected to hang up his coat immediately on entering the house, he felt disloyal to his mother. That made him feel guilty, too. It was a problem he could neither understand nor resolve.

The dilemma worried the youngster considerably. And he did not leave the worry at home, where it originated. Often in school something would remind him of one or the other parent. He would begin to wonder a little anxiously whether he had done everything he was supposed to do before leaving the house that morning. And he would wonder about whether his father really was a bad example, as he heard his mother say so

151

many times. Then he would feel guilty to have had critical thoughts about his parents.

Johnny's docile behavior at home had been the outgrowth both of his guilt over his feelings and his fear of arousing his mother's anger. He had learned that if he did as he was told and said little, life moved more smoothly. But he could not control his feelings as he did his actions. Often he felt angry or rebellious even as he was carrying out instructions; frequently he disliked his mother intensely while he was doing exactly as she directed. He wondered about his father, who clearly did not live up to his mother's expectations. But he admired his father greatly and wished he could be like him.

It was a very disturbing state of affairs for Johnny. At school he had been obedient because he feared that his teacher as well as his mother would criticize him. His own demands on himself for perfect papers created a large part of his difficulty with classwork. And these demands reflected his mother's requirements, which seemed too much for the child and worried him constantly.

Johnny's outward docility was a symptom. It needed to be recognized and understood. The healthy, happy child is often casual and careless, but generally he is eager, responsive, and active. Tractable and submissive moments can be observed in all children, of course, but when there are no enterprising, alert, investigative moments—when the child never chafes or protests or murmurs—the situation is suspect. Handling the compliant child is easier than managing the rebellious one, at least for the time being. But the compliant child's very passivity, his yielding acceptance of the demands on him, are unhealthy. His withdrawn, meek, acquiescent behavior may cover angry and resentful thoughts, or puzzled and anxious ones.

A wholesome environment at home helps forestall such reactions. Expectations inappropriate to the child's level of development are unwise. Parental accord, at least in the presence of the child, is important. Naturally, differences of opinion occur and should be expressed frankly and talked through openly, but angry arguments and recriminations between parents confuse children and interfere with their healthy emotional growth. When a child is not merely well behaved but *too* well behaved— too submissive and compliant—there is trouble somewhere. The sooner the behavior can be understood and its cause corrected, the better the prospect for the child to reach inner contentment. This comes largely from the feeling of having both parents' approval and of being able to accept oneself.

152

chapter 9

# Slowly and Steadily Ahead

A NEW PHASE OF DEVELOPMENT  Seven-year-olds are much like six-year-olds in their physical growth, but in their feelings, in their attitudes, and in their capacities to begin thinking logically they have entered another phase of their development. Their experiences in the second grade are on a different level from that of the first grade. Teachers and parents should be aware of their new growth needs so they can anticipate and understand them.

Children's physical growth continues steadily and slowly; there is nothing spectacular about it. Their annual expected growth is two to three inches in height, three to six pounds in weight. Their legs continue to lengthen rapidly. Although their large muscles still are better developed than their small ones, children are gradually becoming more skillful in using their small muscles and in coordinating their hands with their eyes. Consequently, their writing is improving, although many still grasp a pencil tightly and show considerable tension when forming letters. Their eyes are not fully ready for close work, and they often may rub their eyes. This may indicate that the eyes are under some strain, and it certainly suggests the need for caution in emphasizing schoolwork that requires constant use of the eyes.

This is the period when children lose their baby teeth. They will have an increasing number of gaps as the months go by. Most children have already acquired their six-year-molars and are now getting their central incisors. Children usually do not experience great difficulty in cutting these teeth, although sore gums may cause an occasional child to be irritable.

The seven-year-old no longer takes an afternoon rest even on Saturday or Sunday, but they sleep approximately eleven hours at night, usually starting for bed between seven and eight o'clock. They tire easily and often show fatigue during the afternoon session of school; they should have a rest through a change of activity in the afternoon and should be encouraged to balance active play with quiet pastimes.

## PHYSICAL ACTIVITY AND LANGUAGE DEVELOPMENT
Healthy seven-year-olds are full of vitality and energy. Although they are not so continually active as six-year-olds and are more likely to balance

153

their activity with periods of relatively quiet play, they still like to do tricks—turning somersaults, hanging by the knees from a trapeze, or climbing to the top of a jungle gym, a tree, or a garage roof if one is available. They can ride bicycles and jump rope. On the whole, even though seven-year-olds attempt more kinds of activities, they are more cautious and less likely to take chances than when they were six.

Like six-year-olds, seven-year-olds often seem restless. They learn better if they are encouraged to be active while they learn. They still count more easily and effectively if they have objects to move. They understand better if they can work out ideas by developing and constructing projects. They want to use their hands to explore, to make things, and to learn. They enjoy painting, clay modeling, and carpentry and are learning to handle tools with increasing skill.

Language develops rapidly from six to seven. Seven-year-olds carry on vivid conversations. They like to talk although their conversations usually center around themselves and the things they have done or around their families and their possessions. They tend to dress up a story and usually tell it eagerly, often with accompanying gestures. They still enjoy dramatic play, both in school and in spontaneous play with other children.

Children now can use language effectively in expressing disapproval. Instead of fighting, seven-year-olds sometimes hurl words at their antagonists and walk off the scene. They express their feelings toward their parents and their requests in no uncertain terms if they think they are unfair or if they do not want to comply.

BOOKS, TELEVISION, AND MOVIES Seven-year-olds still enjoy songs, rhythms, and stories. They know the tunes of familiar songs and

154

comment if other children do not sing correctly. Their interests in stories have increased, as have their attention spans; they can listen or read for a longer period of time and can carry the thread of a story from day to day. Those who can read some books themselves may delight in reading alone, although seven-year-olds still enjoy hearing stories read by their teachers or their parents. They are well enough grounded in reality to enjoy fairy tales and myths and to recognize and accept the difference between an imaginary and a true story. Poems still are favorites, and the children will call for the ones they like; they may even know many by heart. Their interest in factual stories about real things is increasing; they want to know how machines operate, what electricity is, and all about rockets and space ships. Some of the children will bring to school a fund of knowledge they have obtained from watching television, from reading many of the fascinating but simple science books for children, or from talking with their parents or other adults. Many of the questions an alert seven-year-old asks require accurate, informative answers. Occasionally teachers will find seven-year-olds who know almost more than they do about a favorite interest.

Animal stories continue to be popular with seven-year-olds, but now they enjoy stories about real animals rather than fanciful, talking creatures. They like stories about other children, and some are beginning to be absorbed in the various series of books about boys and girls. This is the time to encourage going to the library and choosing the books they want.

Comics are a favorite of some of the children. While they may have enjoyed looking at comics for several years, they now can begin to read them, exchange them with their friends, and borrow them back again. Most children have a favorite or favorites, which may be read and reread.

Television is a major attraction. Many seven-year-olds come dashing in from play toward the end of the afternoon eager to hear the next installment of a favorite program, and some watch television three to four hours a day. Many children watch without being concerned by the violence or problems they see portrayed; others are upset and may even have nightmares following an overstimulating television program. And still others may internalize the aggressive behavior and imitate it at a later time. Sometimes it is necessary for parents, or for a teacher through discussion at school, to help choose the more desirable programs. Parents may find it necessary to limit choice by saying, "You may listen to any of these programs," instead of leaving the decision entirely up to the child. If television is used wisely and not allowed to interfere with outdoor play and other more creative activities, it can add an enriching dimension to a child's life.

Movies may begin to become part of the seven-year-old's life, but they are too stimulating for many youngsters of this age. If children attend movies, they should be carefully selected. Few movies are planned for children, and many introduce children to adult situations and experiences they are unable to understand. Both movies and many television programs can cause a confusion of standards as children try to gain increased understanding of grown-ups and their world.

155

Seven-year-olds are full of vitality and energy. A variety of activities are sought with other children, though active play is becoming better balanced with quiet pastimes. Spontaneous play with other children as well as more organized group games can aid the seven-year-old's exploring and learning.

STANDING UP FOR THEIR RIGHTS  Seven-year-olds are learning to stand up for their own rights on the playground and will sometimes stand up for the rights of another child, especially where property is concerned. Most seven-year-olds will fight for their rights if necessary, or else will walk off indignantly and refuse to play. A certain amount of aggressive behavior is necessary at this age, for the child must adjust to the rougher ways of the playground. In another year, gangs will be forming and the youngster, especially the boy, will find it even more necessary to hold his own with the crowd. The adult's problem is to help children stand up for their rights without becoming unkind, crude, or rough. This is not an easy task. Shy, withdrawn youngsters may need considerable help during this year and, in some instances, protection from situations that are still too difficult for them.

Children of this age like to be first. They like to win the race or have the biggest piece of cake or paint the best picture. They each want their turn and demand it if they don't get it.

DEPENDENCE AND INDEPENDENCE  Seven-year-olds are sensitive to what other children think about them and to whether or not they are liked. At the same time, they also are reaching for praise from adults and are becoming increasingly sensitive to their approval or disapproval. These two desires often conflict, because the patterns, values, and standards of the adults' group and those of the child's group frequently differ.

Because children are trying to imitate adult behavior and to relate to the adult world, it is more important than ever that their relationships with the adults about them be warm, friendly, and encouraging. Primary teachers have an especially important role to play in the development of children under their guidance, for the youngsters will seek a close relationship with them and will want to please them. If they are rigid or repressive, children will be less likely to develop into independent personalities and less able to think for themselves. Seven-year-olds often find it hard to take criticism from an adult, and sometimes cry or blame others. On the other hand, they accept leadership and friendly guidance. By encouraging and at the same time allowing some independence, teachers who are kind, understanding, and responsive will help children develop a great deal during this year.

It is important to recognize the seven-year-olds' drive toward independence—a drive often overlooked because of their outward dependence on their teachers and parents for directions and reassurance. Seven-year-olds want to grow up, to leave behind the manners and dress and behavior of little children, and to assume the standards of peers or of children a year or two older; yet they do not quite trust themselves and often seem anxious for fear they will do things incorrectly. If there is too much adult control, they will rebel against it, yet they continually turn to adults to make sure that they are right. If they are not reassured, they may temporarily give up trying until a little redirection or encouragement gets them started again. Teachers and parents need to be supportive in their attitudes and yet at the same time encourage independence and spontaneity.

A GOOD YEAR AT SCHOOL AND AT HOME  Seven is a good year for schoolwork because children are anxious to do well and to learn how things are done. It has been called "the eraser age" because many seven-year-olds erase as much as they write, trying constantly to make their work more nearly perfect.

Differences in ability to do schoolwork are becoming evident by this time. The children who are having difficulty will need support and encouragement if they are not to grow discouraged when they see others going ahead more rapidly. The attitude of both teacher and class toward the slow learner will be important. Seven-year-olds are not too young to learn to accept and respect differences in ability.

Seven-year-olds have learned to do many things for themselves—even though they often dawdle and dream while they are doing them. They still need a patient reminder that they will be late for school, or that dinner is almost ready and they should wash their hands. But they are beginning to see for themselves the need to wash their hands and even to help around the house. They like to have a job at home, just as they like to help at school. Again, they may not always carry out their tasks efficiently, but they are learning to do their share. They can take care of most of their physical needs. They can bathe and dress themselves, tie their shoelaces, and brush their teeth.

Although seven-year-olds are beginning to understand what time is and how to tell time, they still live primarily in the immediate present and cannot plan realistically for future goals. They may worry about being late for school, but they cannot take full responsibility for getting there on time. Occasionally, they move slowly as if time meant nothing, although sometimes they will hurry if they are told that they must leave for school—the dash into their clothes may be a sudden contrast to their dreamy slowness.

Seven-year-olds are ready for a small allowance. They understand what money is for, and that food and clothes and other things that they want must be paid for. They usually know the names of the more frequently used coins and their relationship to one another—that a nickel and five pennies are the same and that a dime is worth two nickels. When a weekly allowance is possible, seven-year-olds begin to learn about spending and saving.

REACHING OUT FOR NEW EXPERIENCES One of the most striking contrasts between six and seven is that whereas six-year-olds are content with whatever happens to be going on—being taken to the park or riding their bikes—seven-year-olds reach out for new experiences, trying to relate themselves to their enlarged world. They are often dreamy and absorbed, seeming to take things into themselves. They like other people and want to be with them; they are gradually becoming more sensitive in their feelings toward them and more aware of others' feelings.

An ethical sense is continuing to develop. They are able to take some responsibility for their own actions. They are concerned about right and wrong, often criticizing their playmates if they do things they do not think are right and perhaps tattling to their teachers or their parents. Sometimes tattling is an attempt to win adult approval, but frequently it is an outlet for children's anxiety and concern, an attempt to reassure themselves that whereas the other children are wrong, their own behavior is right. They also may ask, "Is it all right to do this? May we go there?" They are still seeking patterns of behavior and want to be sure that theirs are the right ones. They still do not completely understand truthfulness or honesty. They may pick up little things that they like—a pencil, a piece of chalk, an eraser—and slip them into their pockets. They are more truthful than they were at six, but they are still learning.

Seven is a responsive age, and it is easy to impose on the child's eagerness to please. Because they turn to adults for guidance, they can easily become too dependent on them, too inclined to give in to authority at the expense of their own feelings and drives. They are often overanxious for fear that they will not be able to achieve the standards set for them by their parents or teachers. Since they are becoming more critical of themselves and are sensitive to failure or being made fun of, this is no time for sarcasm, ridicule, or even too much teasing. It is up to adults to steer a middle course that gives seven-year-olds the support, encouragement, and guidance they need, while at the same time encouraging them to become independent and self-reliant.

160

## Study of a child

### WHEN A FAMILY CANNOT COPE
#### A Foster Home May Be Desirable

Certainly it is true that home usually is the best place for a child to grow up. Most parents love their children and want to provide adequately for their healthful development; few situations suggest taking a child away from the home. A youngster generally is better off living with at least one parent, if this is possible and if arrangements can be made for adequate care when the parent must be away or at work. But it is wise to consider every situation individually. Sometimes unusual circumstances make foster-home placement far more wholesome than a child's own home. Sometimes it is better for the child to leave the family, despite traditional counsel.

Russell Williams lived in an apartment in a pleasant neighborhood. There was a playground nearby, and a school was conveniently located. The family was able to provide more than the ordinary necessities. But by the time he was seven, Russell had a long history of troublesome behavior—a type of behavior more frequently found when a child lives under conditions of deprivation with little supervision, few comforts, and no recreational facilities. He was defiant and impudent at home and twice he had run away. He disobeyed constantly, told lies, appropriated whatever he fancied, and showed no remorse when scolded or punished. The family was understandably disturbed, but their disturbance showed in anger and harsh treatment rather than in an effort to understand the untenable situation.

His behavior was increasingly disturbing as time passed, and the child's aunt finally approached the school for help. She said that since he was three, there had been problems. He would throw his food on the floor, refusing to eat. Without apparent reason, he would throw things out of the window—fruit, the telephone pad, a number of towels. He was destructive with his toys, careless of his clothes, and adamant about refusing to accept any routine responsibility. He forgot errands and ignored meal hours.

The aunt considered that the climax of his misdemeanors was his taking a ten-dollar bill from her purse. He denied knowledge of the money until confronted with clear evidence that he had changed it for smaller bills and spent them for ice cream, cokes, and dime-store toys for the neighborhood youngsters. When it was useless to continue to deny having taken the money, the boy shrugged and refused to talk about it further.

All this was utterly baffling to Russell's family. It was only too apparent that their methods of constant scolding and frequent physical punishment, of depriving the child of an allowance and television, had been wholly ineffective. They were puzzled when the school said that the boy was not considered a problem—that his classwork was well done and that he had not been part of any disciplinary action. True, he often argued with

161

other children and was inclined to be noisy and talkative in class, but his behavior had not been very different from most boys his age. The school suggested that help should be sought rather than continue with a situation so disturbing to the family and so undesirable for the boy.

The pediatrician consulted by the family suggested seeing a specialist in children's adjustment problems, stressing that it was a problem of emotional rather than physical health. It is recognized that often a child who is considered "bad" in one situation will show acceptable behavior in another. This apparent paradox can be understood only when all the circumstances are known. It is necessary to study thoroughly both the child and all the conditions of the child's daily living—not only current conditions but those that have prevailed previously. It must be recognized that the behavior of a child at any time may be the result of what has occurred months or years before.

The medical report sent to the child psychologist showed that Russell's physical condition was excellent. His mental ability was found to be superior. But when his social relationships were considered, it was clear that his schoolmates disliked him and that he had no real friends. It became evident that Russell had taken the ten dollars to buy things for other children which would, in effect, buy their friendship. The psychologist sought to understand why such a step seemed necessary to the boy, why he had not been able to make friends without resorting to bribery. That brought into the picture the boy's family situation and the emotional interrelationships in the home.

The surface circumstances included a comfortable home and excellent medical care. But lacking was even one acceptant, understanding, sympathetic adult with whom the child might have had a close and warm relationship. Beneath the surface of his behavior were bitterness and resentment and unhappiness.

Russell's parents had been divorced after his mother deserted the family. The boy was then three years old. His father had never wanted a child and had always resented him as an added burden. When his wife chafed under the restrictions imposed by an infant, he was even more bitter. Yet when his wife left he saw no recourse but to make some plan to care for the child. He finally arranged to live with his mother, an aged and eccentric widow, and his older sister, also widowed, who worked in a library.

Undoubtedly, Russell was confused by the many changes that occurred during those days. When his mother had gone, a housekeeper had been found who would also care for the child. When the move was made to his grandmother's, he clung to the housekeeper, the most familiar and the most attentive of all the people around him. When she left—unable to get along with the demanding grandmother—he could not be consoled and cried for days.

Elderly Mrs. Williams had never been anything but coolly interested in her grandson. She had intensely disliked her daughter-in-law and had rarely seen her. She had agreed to share her home with her son only after considerable inner struggle, because, she said, she "knew her duty." Small wonder that the child feared his grandmother, who rarely smiled at him, and rarely expressed either affection or approval. Her "duty" did not include loving the boy. She was a rigid disciplinarian and was in complete charge. Russell's father was increasingly absent from home and, when there, never questioned the grandmother's demands or decisions. If she complained about the child, the child was spanked. When this had no effect, he was deprived of privileges or locked in his room.

Russell's aunt protested once or twice when she noted marks on the boy's body after his father had punished him. But she had little to do with the child and was often away weekends and evenings as well as during the day.

When she spoke to the psychologist, she mentioned that on several occasions after he had been punished, Russell had failed to come home until very late at night. "His father punished him severely," she said, "but it didn't do any good. The next day he came home even later!" It evidently never occurred to her that there was little at home to attract the boy.

When appointments were arranged with the psychologist, it was hard to convince Russell that he was there not to be punished but to be helped. His sullen manner changed slowly to responsive friendliness. He wanted to be liked. He spoke about wanting the children on the playground and down the block to be his friends, and he told how his grandmother had always interfered. She said he "showed his poor blood" by seeking the company of his schoolmates; she ignored his protests that errands and tasks always were required when he wanted to go out to play; and she never permitted him to bring a child to the house.

Russell had real need of other children, the need to be accepted by them. But they called him names when he did not join them at play, and he felt they did not like him. He was rejected at home, and to be rejected by the children, too, was more than he could bear. To treat them had seemed a way to entice them to be friendly. This was the background for his taking money from his aunt's purse.

It seemed impossible to convince the family that the child was not a confirmed delinquent, a thief, and a liar. They would not grant that the vastly different behavior he showed at school and at home involved them seriously. The grandmother refused to concede that she had played any part in the unhappy developments. The father admitted frankly that he stayed away from home so much because "The devil himself couldn't live peaceably with the old lady," and said that he did not entirely blame the boy for his misbehavior. Nevertheless, Mr. Williams was too involved in his own emotional problems to be really concerned about his son. The aunt bluntly summed up the situation: "I don't suppose we could expect Russell to grow up normally in our abnormal household."

Fortunately, it was possible to arrange for the boy to live in more favorable surroundings. A social agency was consulted and found an understanding family with two children of their own who were interested in car-

163

ing for another child. As is usual in such cases, the foster family would be paid for their part in supervising the boy and for providing him with room and board. In return they would be giving him a chance for more normal development. Mr. Williams also accepted the idea of continuing the boy's treatment to help him achieve an adequate adjustment.

For Russell, his own home clearly had not been best. One can only speculate about what might have been accomplished if the father had accepted his own need for psychiatric help, if the grandmother had been less rigid and resistant, or if the aunt had been warmer and more involved. Before reaching his eighth birthday, the boy had been antisocial, yet sought sociability. He had sensed rejection, and sought acceptance.

Because he was young, it was possible to help him, and after a period of time many of his scars healed. But for many months he needed professional help in learning to rechannel his emotional responses. He continued to do well in school, and he did better outside of school than he had ever done before. Because there was no longer any need to rebel against authority, he could accept deserved discipline and respect reasonable controls. He no longer felt the need to lie, nor did he appropriate what did not belong to him in order to buy friendship. He lived as an accepted member of a well-adjusted family. He felt loved and wanted. He had time to play and had friends who accepted him and liked him. Given an opportunity to develop in wholesome surroundings, away from his own family, all went well. The problem had been the home situation, not the child.

Unusual as Russell's circumstances may have been, less drastic conditions can lead to similar reactions. When a child feels unloved and unfairly treated, unhappiness and confusion often result in unacceptable behavior. The conditions of the home must be considered—and, if need be, corrected—if a child is to become a healthy individual.

# chapter 10

# An Eager Year

WANTING NEW EXPERIENCES Eight-year-olds are not little children nor are they yet quite so settled and responsible as they may be at nine. They resent being treated as small children and being talked down to by adults, but they still depend on praise and encouragement and need to be reminded of their responsibilities. Because they look so much more grown-up than they did at seven, adults often grow impatient when their actions are less mature than their appearance.

At home their manners may be lacking, but when they go out to dinner or to a party that they consider grown-up or exciting, they may surprise their parents with their courtesy and good behavior. They are not so dependent on their teachers for emotional support as they were at seven, but they often seem even more dependent on their parents. During this year, they make many demands on them. They continually want parents to play games, do things with them and for them, listen to their talk, and always be at hand when they want them. They are still family oriented. Perhaps this is part of being neither a little child nor quite ready to grow up. While they dislike being dominated or overdirected, eight-year-olds still need their parents' support and want to feel close to them.

Eight is an eager year. Children seem ready to tackle anything and often show more enthusiasm than wisdom in what they try. For this reason, they usually have more accidents than in other years. Eight-year-olds want new experiences; they want to try things out, to see how they work, to find out how they are made. Often they may attempt more than they can do, and so the results disappoint them or they are not able to complete their projects. But if this eagerness is wisely directed, it can be a profitable year in the child's development. Adult guidance that cooperates with the children's enthusiasm and channels their curiosity and vital interests can be invaluable to them. On the other hand, the adult who dominates, overdirects, and overcriticizes can cause tension and anxiety in children of this age. Parents and teachers who are working with eight-year-olds need to be aware of children's sensitivities; the children want to be guided and helped in achieving their goals, yet they are unable to accept much criticism. They cry easily if corrected too harshly.

PHYSICAL GROWTH AND PHYSICAL PROBLEMS Physically, eight-year-olds continue to develop steadily but slowly. Their arms are continuing to lengthen, and their hands are growing larger. Their eyes are beginning to accommodate more readily to both near and far distances, so that they are better able to handle reading and other schoolwork that requires close focusing of the eyes. Eye-hand coordination also is improved. Near-sightedness often develops during this year, however, and eyes should be checked regularly and glasses prescribed when necessary.

At eight the permanent teeth are continuing to appear, usually the incisors first and then the lower bicuspids. By this time the novelty of brushing teeth has worn off and many children grow careless. They need to be reminded to take proper care of their teeth and should be taken to the dentist for regular checkups.

Since the large muscles are still developing, children need continued opportunity for movement and active, outdoor play. They run, shout, climb, and punch one another. The small muscles are much better developed than they were at seven, and children are able to use them more effectively and with better coordination. They write much more evenly and can do craft work with tools that require some skill in manipulation.

During this year some children, particularly tall, thin youngsters, develop poor posture. This may be an indication of fatigue, of emotional tension, of poor nutrition, or not wanting to be taller than their peers. It is possible, however, to interest children in learning to sit and stand correctly—not by nagging and scolding but by building their interest in the development of their bodies and teaching them why good posture is desirable.

166

SOCIAL ACTIVITIES AND ORGANIZATION  Baseball, soccer, and other organized games delight both eight-year-old boys and girls. They try to learn the rules and may become quite bossy in insisting that they are followed. Sometimes a group will invent variations of the rules or make up new rules. On rainy days or in the evenings they are enthusiastic about table games, and construction toys are of interest. Model airplanes and cars are often desired—but are frequently disappointing because of the difficulty of putting them together. Many girls still play countless involved games with their dolls.

Eight-year-olds want best friends although they frequently will quarrel and argue. Children of this age usually can work out problems between themselves without regular adult interference. They are beginning to develop a sense of loyalty to each other. Many of their friendships will shift during the year, but some youngsters will remain best friends and carry their friendship over into another year. Difficulties in the ability to make friends are becoming more apparent. Some children have not learned the physical skills or the games which help open the world of childhood to them. Some are shy and find it hard to mix with other children; some have been made to feel unwanted, often because they cannot keep up with the other children. These children will need help during this year if they are to make friendly relationships with other children, and the other children may need encouragement to draw them into their games. Membership in a small adult-supervised group may be a first step for some of these left-out eight-year-olds.

Just as they want best friends, so children of this age also seem to enjoy having an enemy. Sometimes two children single out other children as enemies; sometimes a group of children singles out one child or another group. If hostile feelings get out of bounds, adult intervention and adroit redirection may be necessary, for children are learning consideration for one another. This is a good year for role playing or open-ended stories which help children develop an understanding of how others feel, and a responsibility for their actions toward them.

Until this year, boys and girls have played together some of the time, even though they usually have chosen their best friends from members of their own sex. Now we see a marked difference. Most boys and girls are pulling apart in their interests and their activities. Sometimes they even gang up against each other and call names or tease. They are entering the period when many of their interests will focus on friends of their own sex, the period of gangs and clubs. At this age the gang or club may not be well formed, and its purpose and membership may change frequently. But the children's desire to be a member of the gang is emerging and will grow more intense during the next few years. Boys and girls are beginning to want to be like their friends and to belong to a group. Parents and teachers sometimes find this stress on belonging difficult, for it becomes increasingly evident that these children may follow the pattern of their group rather than adult directions when the two do not coincide, particularly if they are unhappy in their relationships with adults.

There are, however, strengths to be gained from belonging to the group. Children need the security it gives, the opportunity to identify with others of their own age and sex, the opportunity to make and carry through plans and rules of their own. They learn the value of cooperation better in their own groups than in any other way. Eight-year-olds cannot take much criticism from adults, but they are capable of considerable self-evaluation at their own levels and are able to take and give criticism within their own groups. The wise parent or teacher will not try to hinder the establishment of gangs and clubs but will utilize their potentialities for helping children learn to relate to others and work cooperatively with them.

The adult-supervised group cannot take the place of the children's own group, but it can be of additional value during this year. Eight-year-olds respond positively to group activities of many kinds. Their teachers find them willing members of a classroom group and can plan and think more frequently in terms of the group as a whole than was possible in the first two years of primary school. Class projects, club activities after school, organized games, and recreational projects fit the children's needs and interests. They participate enthusiastically in some competitive games providing winning is not made so important that those who cannot do well are faced with humiliation. A well-planned program of both indoor and outdoor games provides not only fun but valuable learning for eight-year-olds. Through games they can enjoy wholesome competition and can begin to learn to be both a good winner and a good loser.

A program of after-school play activities is particularly valuable during this transition year, although eight-year-olds are not always mature enough to carry through these planned activities by themselves. They may start an organized game of baseball or soccer, but they get confused and usually end up in squabbles and disputes. They can work through some of their quarrels by themselves, but they usually are relieved if a friendly adult helps get them out of the muddle. When they are older, self-direction in such organized activities will be increasingly valuable to them.

Eight-year-olds resent being grouped with six- or even seven-year-olds—"those babies," as they call them—in school or recreational activities. Physically they may be nearly like the younger children, but their interests have moved far beyond the interests of most six- and seven-year-olds. Consequently, they often rebel against group activities in which they are asked to play with younger children.

DRAMATIC PLAY, MOVIES, AND TELEVISION Children's earlier interests in "acting" grow even stronger during this year, and their play frequently is dramatic. They may copy a favorite television program, or dress up, play house, or plan plays to put on for their families or friends. In addition to dramatization in their informal play, eight-year-olds also are ready to take part in simple dramatics in the classroom; they thoroughly enjoy putting on a play. These dramatizations should still be simple and within the abilities of the children, participation being more important than a finished performance.

169

Movies, comics, and television are a part of the eight-year-old's life. They like movies or television programs of Western and Indian pictures, stories of war, of space, and of adventure. But they do not want to be too scared and often close their eyes or cover their ears during a frightening scene. They also enjoy animal stories and some comedies.

Most youngsters of this age watch television in the late afternoon or early evening. They often rush home from school to see a favorite program and follow their favorite serials faithfully. Some spend as much time in front of the television as they do in school. This not only interferes with outdoor play but also encroaches upon the time available for reading books. For some children, television takes the place of books. Reading a book is a much slower experience and demands more imagination than television. Children who have trouble reading will probably prefer television to books, although this preference is by no means limited to slow readers.

READING INTERESTS AND PROBLEMS Some eight-year-olds read and reread comics, then exchange them with their friends and pore over the new crop. Children who have trouble reading will probably read more comics than books, but many eight-year-olds enjoy books as well if their interest and delight in them has been encouraged. Parents and teachers should be particularly aware of the attraction comics hold for children of this age and should help the children develop a wider interest in reading by introducing them to books full of adventure and humor. Fairy tales and stories about historical figures, animals, children, western adventure, and space travel appeal to eight-year-olds. Many children still enjoy reading aloud; others prefer reading to themselves.

This is the age when differences in reading ability begin to pose a real problem. The child who is having difficulty learning to read finds it continually more difficult to keep up with schoolwork and with the other children, because reading skill is now necessary for successful accomplishment in almost all areas of the curriculum. Such children often feel discouraged and defeated. They may develop a permanent dislike of school, even resulting in some cases in truancy. Their self-concepts and their progress may be so severely damaged that they develop permanent feelings of inferiority, unless parents and teachers are aware of their difficulties and help them overcome both the reading problem and the emotional problem connected with it. Merely holding a child back a grade will not meet the problem, nor will forcing or scolding, because various developmental and emotional factors usually are involved in a reading difficulty. A special reading or guidance teacher may be able to help identify these factors so that the children can deal with them and subsequently go on to improve their reading. Children who are having trouble reading need not only specialized attention in reading, but also a great deal of support from their parents and teachers. Certainly they need opportunities for success in other areas to keep them from feeling discouraged and ashamed of their failure in learning to read.

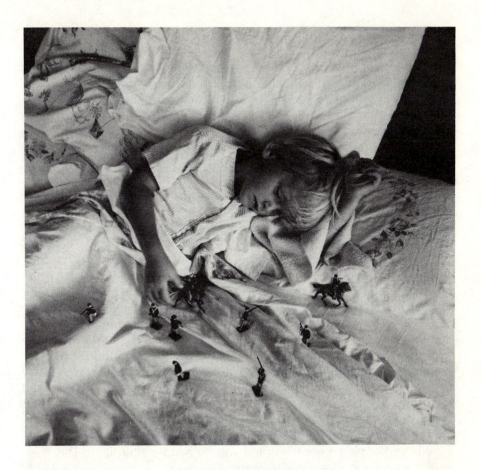

UNDERSTANDING NEW CONCEPTS Collections of all kinds intrigue eight-year-olds. Their pockets will be full of odds and ends, but their interests also are beginning to focus on more carefully planned collections. These may vary from bottle tops or playing cards to stones, bugs, or stamps. Their interests are not always prolonged, however, and their collections may change frequently. Parents can help by encouraging the collectors, by providing a place for them to keep their collections, and by not throwing away treasured objects because they seem useless by adult standards. Similarly, teachers can help by encouraging youngsters to bring their collections to school and tell the class about them. Children who are having difficulty in reading can often become excellent collectors and receive much-needed feelings of achievement as they share their collections with the class.

Money is beginning to play a part in the lives of eight-year-olds. They understand the purpose of money, and the simpler aspects of its use. They have some conception of saving for items that this week's allowance won't buy. If they do not receive allowances or if their allowances are not big enough for their needs, those with more initiative may seek opportunities to earn small sums of money. Eight-year-olds can plan ahead, counting the weeks it will take them to save enough to buy something they want very

171

much. Often they are unrealistic and start saving for unobtainable items. Often, too, they spend their money unwisely. But even if they make mistakes, they need the experience of having, when possible, a small amount of money of their own and spending it their own ways. Discussions at home and at school about how money can be used and saved will be interesting and helpful to them. The ideas presented in these discussions should be within the realm of reality for the eight-year-old—saving for a baseball bat is reasonable and comprehensible, whereas saving for a future education is beyond both their means and understanding.

Eight-year-olds are developing a better understanding about time. They can tell time and can relate it to the events of the day. They can wear a sturdy watch and be relied on to use it. They know at what time meals are served, when school begins, and when they must be in bed. Yet they are not always ready to take complete responsibility for going to bed, getting up, or arriving at school on time and must still be reminded by their parents if their routines are to function at all smoothly. They have the habit of putting things off. "In a minute" appears frequently in their vocabularies.

At eight, children also understand about days and months and years, and they are trying to relate themselves to a past and a future. They are showing an interest in things that happened "long ago," although they often are extremely confused about just when past events occurred. They may think that grandmother lived in the time of the Pilgrims, that she used a spinning wheel and was afraid of Indians. But at least they realize that there *was* a past in which people lived and did things. The world now extends beyond the present; they realize that people live and die, that there have been people before them and will be people after them. This is an adult concept and shows that they are growing up.

Eight-year-olds now realize that all live things die and are beginning to realize that they, too, will die someday. They are now aware that death is irreversible. Some children as they begin to absorb this realization dwell on death and dying. An insecure child, or one who has had a traumatic experience through the death of someone close to them, may develop a fear of death and will need help to overcome it. Others may talk freely about death and dying to one another, and may show great interest in the details of burial. The attitudes of adults about them and the religious interpretations given to children of this age may have a deep effect on a child's acceptance of death as a part of life, or intensify a fear. Questions should be answered simply and honestly. It is unwise to give to an eight-year-old ideas about death which the grown-up does not believe.

At eight children usually are showing an increasing interest in babies. They hover over them, delight in them, and often want to take care of them. They marvel over the tiny fingers and toes and are disturbed when the baby cries. A new baby in the family is no longer considered a rival, unless the eight-year-old is not sure of real acceptance at home. More often there is real interest and pride, a desire to show the new baby to friends, and pride in being asked to hold or look after the baby for a while.

Along with their interest in babies eight-year-olds are becoming increasingly curious about their origin and still are often confused about the birth process. Children who watch television, read papers and magazines, and listen to adult talk are often well aware that what they have been told as little children is not the whole story. They now not only ask questions about the differences between boys and girls and about where babies come from, but they will want to go into these things in greater detail. They may want to know the father's part and how the baby gets out of the mother's body. The questions they ask will need more complete answers than when they were younger. A helpful technique is to turn the question back to the child in a conversational way, asking, "What do you think about it?" In this way we are often able to go beyond the surface question and find out just how much the child really knows and whether confusing, inaccurate information has already been obtained. We then can correct mistaken notions and fill in the gaps in what the child already knows. There are books which are suitable to read and share with children which are helpful in answering their questions and developing healthy attitudes.

Even after children have been given factual answers, many times they still fail to understand fully and may return to get a clearer answer or more information as their concepts grow. If we keep the channels of talk open, so that children feel that it is all right to ask about these things, we will be able to meet their needs as they reach out again and again for more information. The attitude of acceptance, the comfortableness of the talk between grown-up and child in these matters will help to determine children's attitudes toward their own sexuality. If children do not receive correct explanations from the adults closest to them, they may gather sketchy or erroneous ideas from other children, for children do talk with one another about these things. Much of children's sex play and sex curiosity comes from lack of information, from unsatisfied but normal curiosity, or from wrong information and attitudes given to them by their playmates or from other sources such as television, advertising, and the many other ways in which sexual attitudes and practices are obvious in our culture. Because so much of this varied information is confusing to children we must be sensitive to what is underneath the questions they ask about both birth and death—there may be anxiety, guilt, or fear which we need to understand and try to alleviate.

AN EXPANDING ENVIRONMENT The thoughts of eight-year-olds are reaching beyond the immediate environment. Eight-year-olds are aware that children live in other parts of the country and of the world, some living much as they do but some differently, and they want to hear stories about them. They may pore over maps and pictures of other places. They notice racial, national, or regional differences among their own classmates. Sometimes, through the influence of the adults in their environments, they may have developed feelings and prejudices concerning these differences. Because they are noticing people, this is an excellent year to encourage a friendly interest in boys and girls of other countries, other races, and other backgrounds—recognizing the differences but stressing the many similarities.

Not only are eight-year-olds beginning to develop understanding, sympathy, and acceptance of other people and of their needs and rights, they also are beginning to understand themselves better. They see themselves in relation to other people. They realize now that some children do things better than they do, that others are not so capable, and that different people excel in different activities. They usually accept themselves and are not too concerned about their weak points unless the adults about them have put too much pressure on them, made too many unfavorable comparisons, or disturbed them with their concern over achievements or abilities. Eight-year-olds frequently show a capacity for self-evaluation and may even laugh at themselves. They often make excuses for themselves, but almost as often resolve to do better. They frequently set high standards for themselves and try to live up to them, as well as to the standards set by the adults around them. Some children develop considerable anxiety about their abilities to succeed in schoolwork or in games and sports. Some already are afraid they may not be liked by other children. This anxiety is apparent often among children who are successful as well as among those who are having some difficulty.

Eight-year-olds may not be as easy to guide as seven-year-olds. They may be more argumentative and have more spirit, but they also are alert to the world around them and interested in people. They may not practice their skills as carefully as they did at seven, but they are eager to find out about things and are stimulating companions. They may be careless about their clothes, be less willing to help at home, and be noisy and bossy; but they also are lovable and friendly. The third year in school can be a good one for parents, teachers, and children, for most eight-year-olds will respond well to sensitive, intelligent adult leadership and guidance.

## Study of a child

### THE SLOW-LEARNING CHILD
Appropriate Goals Depend on Potential

Not all children are bright children. Not all are even of average intelligence. But if the limitations of a child's intellectual endowment are recognized, a great deal can be done to help that child live as a social member of a group and experience the satisfactions important to every youngster. These satisfactions, which are basic needs, include successful achievement, approval by family and teachers, and acceptance by other children.

Edith was eight years old when her family moved. She had gone to school in a small town and now had to adjust to a large new school in a distant city. She knew none of the children, and she was understandably somewhat shy and hesitant. The school building was strange, the routines

175

were different, the whole situation was unfamiliar. But Mrs. Tyson, the third-grade teacher, hoped that as Edith became accustomed to things she would adjust to the new school and be able to meet the grade requirements. For Edith was friendly in a quiet way, seemed responsive to Mrs. Tyson's efforts, and was trying hard to do well.

The routine review at the opening of the school year was not too difficult for Edith, since Mrs. Tyson started almost from beginning fundamentals. The child was attentive and did her work systematically, and the results were passable. But as the difficulty of the assignments increased, her attention wandered frequently, and her obvious efforts to succeed in her schoolwork were no longer effective. Although her interest did not lag and she continued to be cooperative, the quality of her work fell.

Because no record had been sent from the school she had previously attended and because her mother had not noted that Edith had ever had any difficulty with schoolwork, Mrs. Tyson was uncertain whether the child simply felt strange and confused in a new environment, or whether she lacked the capacity to respond more adequately to the academic program. Over a period of time she observed Edith carefully, alert to the patterns of behavior that she was showing both in the classroom and on the playground. Gradually the teacher reached the opinion that a limited scholastic potential was at the root of Edith's problems. This conviction was soon substantiated by the results of psychological tests for both ability and achievement. These showed a mental age about two years below her chronological age and a level of achievement below her grade placement. According to the psychological diagnosis, Edith had "dull normal intelligence"; she was "a slow learner."

Outwardly, Edith was not different from the other children in her class. She was physically sturdy, and as tall as the average eight-year-old. Although she was more passive than most of the children, she was pleasant and friendly. But even though she was cooperative and worked industriously, she had little to show for her efforts. As the academic work in the class became more complex, she often failed to comprehend instructions. Like many slow learners, she tended to be satisfied with almost any result. Finishing a lesson always pleased her; whether she had completed it correctly or incorrectly did not seem as important to her as getting it done. She persisted with surprising determination although results were poor.

Edith's thought processes were slow, and her memory was uncertain. Even when she listened attentively, she needed repeated explanations to grasp a new concept and a great deal of practice to remember how to apply it. Her arithmetic papers always included many incorrect answers. Her spelling was better, but only passable. In reading, she sought help with new words, then often failed to recognize the same words when they appeared again in another context on another page.

Edith's muscular coordination also produced some difficulty. There was markedly poor development of the small muscles of her hands and fingers, making her awkward with pencil and crayon. When she wrote, she held her pencil in a tight, cramped position that resulted in crowded, uneven, sometimes barely legible writing. In rhythms she frequently was out of time with the music. She could not follow a rapid tempo or a change in the beat.

The same lack of muscular skill was apparent on the playground. Edith ran stiffly, and her reactions were slow. She did not throw a ball accurately, and when she tried to catch one, she often fumbled or dropped it. She was uncertain on playground apparatus and made mistakes when playing a game with specific rules.

Often Miss Tyson observed Edith on the edge of a group, watching the others. When she did play with other children, she was friendly but passive, never protesting the loss of a turn to a more aggressive child. With adults, Edith seemed a little shy and hesitant.

Edith's family was aware of her slowness and had been patient and understanding in the face of her limitations. Their continuing affection and attention had resulted in the positive attitudes the child exhibited. But now more than patience and understanding were needed. Special help in schoolwork was essential.

Recognizing that Edith had never acquired a really adequate foundation in reading and numbers, her teacher felt she needed a fresh start. In that way she could achieve a firmer mastery of the fundamentals and, at the same time, could experience encouraging success by working with material simpler than the regular class assignments. Because it was impossible for Mrs. Tyson to give Edith this necessary special help, a few periods each week were scheduled with a college student teacher aide who worked with Edith individually. An interview with the child's parents gave them specific suggestions for providing more help at home.

Going back to materials of second-grade difficulty, the teacher aide prepared a "book" with Edith which had story sequences, matching exercises, and vocabulary and classification sections interesting to an eight-year-old but simple enough for a child with very limited reading skill. Edith was encouraged to tell about some experience or incident, which they would then organize to put in the book. She looked through magazines for illustrations to cut out and paste on appropriate pages. Each story was utilized further as a basis for writing and spelling. This approach was also followed at home.

When writing was introduced, Edith was helped materially by the similarity of the symbols she found repeated in both her reading and her writing activities. She gained facility in recognizing words and phrases and in reproducing them. She learned to spell as she learned to read and write.

Edith was stimulated as she had never been before by the results of her efforts. She grew less dependent and learned to be more self-critical of her work. With the difficulty of her lessons scaled to her possible successful accomplishment, she was experiencing a totally new satisfaction. She could read, and read without help. She could write, and her writing could be read.

Simple concepts of primary science books were incorporated in Edith's work as time went on. And together she and her teacher arranged a number book, illustrating Edith's own experiences. She recognized that she was accomplishing something, that she was learning. Mrs. Tyson was generous in her praise of the little girl and gave her much encouragement when she produced increasingly better class exercises.

Edith also participated in regular classwork. She listened more carefully to discussions, understanding more than she had formerly. She even began to offer an occasional spontaneous comment. By the end of the school year Edith showed gains in more than academic skills and knowledge. She was becoming more self-reliant, more willing to stand up for her rights on the playground, and more aware of herself as a person in relationship to other persons. She continued to be friendly, but gained a quiet self-assertion.

Edith's parents realized that they could not expect her to learn as effectively as other children of her age or to participate in classroom activities on a par with them. But Edith was able to learn within the limits of her abilities and to participate in the class to the extent that she was capable.

Important in the total picture was the continued cheerful encouragement of her parents. Their praise for her efforts and their unmistakable pleasure in her progress was stimulating. Thus home and school complemented each other, with satisfying results.

# chapter 11

# In Between

GROWING INDIVIDUAL DIFFERENCES Nine for many children is a dividing line. The wide variations in development that will become increasingly noticeable at ten, eleven, and twelve may be beginning. In their interests most nine-year-olds are closer to ten- and eleven-year-olds than to seven- or eight-year-olds whom they think of and sometimes refer to as "those children."

Physically, most nine-year-olds are much the same as they were a year ago, but a little longer legged, better developed, and closer to physical maturity. During this year, girls who mature early may reach the growth plateau that precedes the pubertal growth spurt. Occasionally, a girl may even begin menstruation.

The whole body is continuing to grow steadily and is nearer its adult functioning. The lungs and the digestive and circulatory systems are still growing but are almost mature in function. The heart is not yet fully developed, and some children may strain it during this year if allowed to compete physically to any great extent with older children, or in organized competitive sports which overemphasize winning. The eyes are much better developed—although they usually will not reach adult size until ten, they are able to accommodate to close work with less strain. Children often get their first and second bicuspids at nine, and their teeth often need straightening. If this seems indicated, parents should consult a dentist promptly, since treatment is sometimes started during this year.

Nine-year-olds are becoming more skillful with their hands; their eye-hand coordination is greatly improved. Individual differences in coordination are increasingly apparent. Both boys and girls enjoy crafts and shop work, and some can carry out many kinds of careful, well-planned craft work. Others, however, still have trouble with handwork that requires any great degree of skill.

The nine-year-old's attention span has greatly increased. Even though these children are capable of sustained attention, adults should not plan activities of long duration for them, because interest and self-motivation are important determiners of attention span. Forced or required attention for too long a time is wearing to children and usually results in tension and restlessness.

Nine-year-olds have original ideas and interests and are capable of

179

carrying them out. They often make plans and go ahead without any adult direction or encouragement. They may carry on a project over quite a period of time, thinking through and planning each step with almost adult care. At the same time, as soon as a project ceases to interest them they may drop it without finishing it or giving it further thought.

Nine-year-olds still need and enjoy active, rough-and-tumble play. But sex differences are showing up increasingly. Both groups are talking more. They may rush onto the playground shouting but soon congregate in groups and begin to talk. Sometimes they just sit around talking at random; at other times they make plans or discuss the activities of their clubs or gangs. Their plans are often too elaborate to be carried out, but the talk is good and the youngsters enjoy it and grow with it.

INCREASING INTEREST IN SKILLS At nine children often are perfectionists. They are becoming critical of their own performances. They want to do things the right way and so may work hard to perfect a skill or to recopy, on their own, pieces of work that look messy to them. They are no longer satisfied just to paint a picture; they want to carry out an idea in what they paint. They often ask for help now and are interested in techniques and skills, not only in their schoolwork but also in their play. They want to be accomplished ball players, to pitch and catch like experts or at least like the older players they admire. Children need to develop skills that other children appreciate and admire, so this is a good year for parents to take time with both boys and girls, encouraging them and helping them to learn new skills.

Parents and teachers can overdo the teaching of techniques and skills at this age, however. For even though the children want to know how to do things, their abilities and capacities for sustained interest may not equal their initial enthusiasm. Adults must be aware of the children's present abilities and future capabilities in order to set standards and goals that will encourage them in their desires to learn. It is extremely important that any teaching of skills be done in a spirit of enjoyment. The adult who is over-

insistent, who drives too hard or demands a perfect performance, can destroy children's initial desires to acquire a skill and pleasure in using it, whether it be playing the piano or pitching a ball.

COMPETITIVE GAMES Nine-year-olds enjoy competitive games—team games and relay races, for example. But the competition easily gets out of bounds. Winning becomes very important to the children, and they can turn indignantly on the boy or girl who fails to make a point or "loses" for their side. Children who are skillful in games can take these jibes in stride, knowing they can do better next time and receive applause instead of blame. But a child who always misses or is clumsy can be deeply hurt. Such youngsters may pull away from the very physical activity that they need and become spectators rather than try to play. Nine-year-olds need help in learning sportsmanship. They should be encouraged to play their games for the fun of playing and to keep their competition within reasonable limits. Choosing up teams without occasional adult advice or supervision, for example, can result in excessive competitive pressures. Some children are seriously hurt by team captains who willingly choose only

181

children who play well and then grudgingly accept the others. It is no wonder that some children shrink at the embarrassment of always being the last chosen or the one left out.

READING INTERESTS AND ABILITIES Wide developmental variations in both reading interest and reading ability are clearly apparent by fourth grade. Many nine-year-olds are great readers, whereas others are hardly interested in books. A reading span of four to five years is not unusual in the fourth grade. Some children can read as well as adults; others are still at first- or second-grade levels. The choice of reading materials for children of this age must be wide indeed if some children are not to be bored and others discouraged by the level of reading to which they are held. The school or class library must contain books at various levels of reading difficulty and yet equal in their level of interest.

Nine-year-olds are beginning to put aside fairy tales and much of the fantasy and imaginative play of their earlier years. They are relating not only to their immediate environments but to their communities, their country, and even other countries. Their interests go beyond that of third-graders. Alert fourth-graders like to study maps and play travel games. They enjoy writing letters to children in other countries, either as a member of a group or as individuals. They may ask discerning questions about other peoples and about world conditions.

At nine, youngsters are beginning to be interested in their own country. They want to know about the different parts of their country and the different kinds of work that people do in it, though they are actually not so interested in the work as in the trappings: the cranes on a construction project, an astronaut's space suit. They enjoy trips to a dock, a factory, or a farm and ask innumerable and often surprisingly intelligent questions about the things they see. They are beginning to think and talk about what they may want to be and do some day. They are beginning to be interested in heroes and great people. They sometimes voluntarily choose biographies when they go to the library. Their interests in science are also increasing, and they often try experiments on their own or read widely among science books available at their vocabulary levels.

This can be a crucial year for some children. Those who have experienced difficulties in learning the basic skills during the primary years, particularly in learning to read, may find an increasing gap between themselves and other boys and girls of their age. Not only do many children become discouraged during this year, when reading assumes a major role in the successful mastery of so much of the curriculum, but their eagerness to try to learn may be destroyed and their self-confidence severely damaged. The concept of "I am a failure," "I am no good" may become deeply embedded in the minds of some of these children and may persist into the years ahead. It is unfortunate that too many youngsters reach the fourth grade without adequate help for their learning difficulties. Such help should have been begun in the first grade when there were noticeable indications that mastering academic skills might present special difficulties

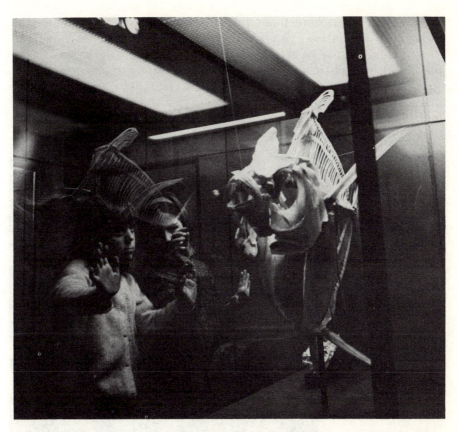

for these children. It is unfortunate, too, that difficulty in mastering academic skills is considered by many parents and teachers an indication that these youngsters are indeed failures. This is particularly unfortunate when it involves children from disadvantaged homes who have been handicapped from the beginning of their school years because of lack of those experiences which provide preparation for school learning, or those who have language or other cultural differences which set them apart from the more successful learners in the school situation. As a result it is often during this year, when self-awareness is more developed, that some children become rebellious and truant from school seeking to escape an environment which has not met their needs, while others withdraw into themselves and cease to try to learn.

THE LEFT-OUT CHILD Having friends and belonging to a group mean a great deal to nine-year-olds. Consequently, parents and teachers need to be particularly alert to notice and help the child who is being left out by classmates. Nine-year-olds generally are conformists. Often they leave out children who are in any way different from themselves, whether they are unusually bright or a bit slow, whether they speak with an accent or dress differently than they do, whether they have special talents or are handicapped in some way. In the earlier grades, children are not so keenly aware of differences as they are at nine. Nine-year-olds need help in learn-

183

ing to accept others. Sometimes they must be checked if they become too thoughtless and unkind.

The teacher may be able to help the left-out child win acceptance by placing such a child in a favorable position in relation to other classmates, so that they begin to like and appreciate the child they once rejected. She may, for example, seat the youngster next to a friendly child or skillfully initiate a group project in which the child can make a valuable contribution. Parents may help, too, by inviting other children to the home.

Both parents and teachers can help children accept those who are different from themselves by being aware of and consciously trying to avoid passing on their own biases or prejudices toward individual children or toward groups of people. If a teacher or parent rejects a child or a group of children, the other children can easily make such a child or children scapegoats for their own feelings, openly rejecting or tormenting them. Such behavior should not be tolerated for this continues to be an important period in a child's life for developing attitudes toward the rights and feelings of other people.

There are times, however, when it seems impossible to obtain acceptance for a certain child—sometimes even an especially attractive or talented one. Such a child will need special help, understanding, and support

184

in learning how to adjust to the group and to a difficult situation. Careful thought should be given not only to the problem of finding ways to compensate children who are on the fringe of the group but also to providing them with other outlets and successful experiences.

INFLUENCE OF THE GROUP    Clubs and gangs are stronger among nine-year-olds than they were among eight-year-olds. Although the membership and purpose are still of short duration and likely to change frequently, some firm and loyal friendships may develop during this year. The children are increasingly influenced by the group. They want to be like the others, to talk like them, to look like them.

Just as children copy each other in clothes and interests and mannerisms, so they may follow loyally the whole behavior pattern of their friends. Usually this pattern is not undesirable, but there is always a possibility that any group of children, primarily boys, may get into trouble or even minor vandalism, especially if they haven't enough opportunities for recreation after school. Parents and teachers should be alert to this possibility so that they can redirect the activities of youngsters who seem headed for trouble. Success in redirecting a trouble-prone youngster usually is possible only if an effort is made to redirect the entire group. Working with individual children or removing them from groups seldom brings satisfactory results, for the pull of the group is so strong that children who are forbidden to be with friends tend to feel defiant or rebellious and usually will find ways of rejoining them despite parental objections.

HALF MATURE AND HALF A CHILD    The fourth grade is an important year in children's development, for it marks their entrance into the upper years of elementary school. More will be expected of them in the way of being personally responsible both for their behavior and for their schoolwork.

Nine-year-olds are beginning to think for themselves, to develop their own ideas and points of view, to realize that sometimes there is more than one valid opinion and that perhaps their mothers, fathers, or even teachers do not have all the answers. They may be quite outspoken and critical of the adults they know, despite their fondness for them.

Nine-year-olds respond best to the adults who treat them as individuals and approach them in an adult way. They enter eagerly into making plans, whether for a project or party in the schoolroom or a trip with the family, and their ideas and suggestions are often worth considering. They are more cooperative and responsive when they are included in making the plans than when they are told "This is what we are going to do."

A child of nine also is willing and able to take some responsibility. They like to be trusted with handling the family baggage on a trip, going to a store, repairing something, getting the props together for a school play, or being responsible for a project. They often are shy when asked to take part in a play or program if parents or other adults are present, and they are apt to be embarrassed if they are praised in public. They do, however, like

185

recognition for what they have done and respond well to deserved praise. They also tend to be very fair and usually will refuse to accept credit for something they have not done. They will even give the credit publicly to a friend or to a person they feel deserves it.

Nine-year-olds will accept criticism or punishment if they think it is justified, but will be most indignant and outspoken if they feel that an adult or another child is being unfair. They frequently argue with other children over fairness in games, taking sides and upholding one faction or the other. This is a good sign, for it shows that they are really beginning to understand right and wrong and are trying to develop standards of acceptable behavior. They also are beginning to understand more about truth and honesty and about property rights and personal rights. They are increasingly developing sympathy for and loyalty to others.

Nine is a good year for helping youngsters develop standards for their behavior. This is best accomplished by using specific situations and experiences rather than by sermonizing. For example, if a child borrows something from a friend and then loses it, responsibility is learned by paying for it from an allowance or from money earned from doing jobs.

At nine, children more frequently are able to make up their minds and come to decisions than they were during the earlier years. They should be given as many opportunities as possible to exercise a measure of independence and make decisions for themselves. They will make mistakes, but they are ready to learn from occasional failures of judgment, as long as the learning takes place in situations where failure will not have too serious consequences. Fourth-graders are able to be on their own quite a bit. An overnight visit to a friend's house, the purchase of school supplies, or even a well-planned bus or plane trip is not beyond many nine-year-olds.

Nine-year-olds are not only responsible in many situations; they are also beginning to be reasonable. One can talk things over with them and present a point of view. They will listen to the reasons presented by an adult, but they also will want the courtesy of being allowed to present their own reasoning. If they are not too emotionally involved in a situation, they frequently are capable of modifying a plan or changing their minds if another course is suggested to them. They can accept the need to put something off, to reschedule the picnic for next week if the weather is poor today.

They also can understand a reasonable explanation in regard to the family budget. They may be disappointed that they cannot have new bikes now, but they can understand that the family cannot afford it. They are even able to see the necessity of contributing some of their birthday money toward the bike or of earning their share. They are best guided by a simple, clear-cut reason for a decision that must be made.

Because nine-year-olds seem mature and capable in many ways, adults sometimes overestimate their maturity and expect too much of them, becoming impatient when they seem childish in some of their reactions. They should remember that, despite their seeming maturity, they are still not far from being a young child. They may have a greater under-

186

standing of truthfulness, but under pressure may not remain truthful. They may be independent in many of their decisions, but turn to parents or teachers for help in some little thing adults feel the child should be able to handle. Because nine-year-olds are half mature and half children, it is best to let them lean in the direction of independence, to encourage them when they want to go ahead, but to willingly help them without ridiculing or criticizing them when they occasionally revert to more dependent, childish ways.

## Study of a child

*RUNNING AWAY—FROM WHAT?*
*Delinquency Threatens in the Absence of Emotional Security*

It is generally acknowledged that security is an important childhood need. But too often it is assumed that when a child's parents provide a home and clothes, and see to it that their child is well fed and reasonably clean, they have furnished that necessary security. Physical security, however, does not necessarily bring with it emotional security. And it is emotional security which children must have if they are to develop strong and healthy personalities.

Feelings of insecurity may influence a child's unacceptable behavior in ways not directly related to the child's basic problem. Sometimes social relationships are avoided because possible rejection is dreaded. Sometimes hours at school are dreamed away, and learning suffers. Quarrelsomeness, fighting, and insistence on stubborn behavior are other possible accompaniments of insecurity. Nightmares, digestive disturbances, extreme sensitiveness, puzzling fears—the patterns that may develop are almost infinite.

In the case of Mark, insecurity was symbolized by running away. He was a year behind in school, not because he was incapable of doing adequate schoolwork, but because he had been unable to withstand the impact of a home made stormy and puzzling by his parents' difficult relationship. He had become confused by the circumstances of his life and needed help before he could face his situation rather than flee from it. His parents, too, needed help, both for their own sakes and for the sake of their children. In order to insure a less disturbing situation for Mark—one that he could learn to handle—they needed help in working out their marital problems.

During his earliest years Mark had been pampered and indulged by his parents, and he had become accustomed to having things his own way. Discipline was rare and haphazard. His parents usually gave in to him if the boy nagged or pleaded. They seldom insisted on anything that he found distasteful. But the arrival of a baby sister when he was not quite six brought a number of changes. His mother was busier than he had ever remembered her being before, and his father seemed preoccupied. Both parents were less patient than they had been, and they were less apt to humor him. They also began to punish him and to criticize him more frequently than they had ever done before.

When Mark entered first grade, his parents said openly that they were glad he was old enough for school. "And you'd better behave there," they warned. Since he had not gone to kindergarten, this was the first time he had had to meet a situation without his mother. He did not like sitting quietly, taking his turn, or concentrating on what his teacher planned instead of doing something of his own choosing. School was an ordeal for him.

Mark's seeming inability to adjust to first grade led the school authorities, after a time, to advise keeping the boy home for another semester. They indicated to his parents that they favored delaying school entrance because Mark had not reached his sixth birthday and seemed to be very immature. His parents felt there was justification for the school's counsel and agreed to the postponement, although they were somewhat annoyed by it. So again Mark managed, in a sense, to get his own way. He stayed with his mother, and at the same time avoided a distasteful situation.

But staying with his mother was no longer the same for Mark. It was not only the new baby; it was a different feeling in the home. His parents were constantly arguing and exchanging recriminations; once or twice a quarrel more violent than most really frightened the boy. When one day his mother took the baby and left home, Mark was completely bewildered. A housekeeper stayed with him, but she did not like children particularly and was unreasonably demanding of Mark when his father was not at home. Mark could not understand why his mother was away for so long. His confusion was increased when one day the housekeeper failed to appear and his father brought another woman home to live with them.

A few weeks of unpleasant scenes followed: scolding, neglect, impatience, denial were daily worries for the child. He decided to find his mother and ran away. When the police brought him back, his father, really distressed and remorseful, was for a time gentle and more attentive. But Mark was unhappy and soon made another attempt to run away. This time when the police brought him home, his father whipped him and notified Mark's mother of what was happening, thinking she would send for the boy. Instead, she came home. The parents now decided that perhaps their marriage could be saved; and a reconciliation was effected.

About this time the new school term started, and again Mark was enrolled at school. His attendance was intermittent due to a succession of minor illnesses and also due to lax supervision on his mother's part. He had indifferent success with his lessons, and he was not promoted at the end of the term. So the following September Mark started first grade all over again. This time things were more peaceful at home, and he had learned to adapt somewhat better to being one of a group in the classroom. He mastered his lessons without special difficulty and at the end of the year was promoted to second grade.

But Mark's path still was not smooth. He was inclined to tease smaller children and to fight with boys his own size. He did not get along with his teacher, who criticized his work and frequently scolded him for fighting. One day, after the teacher had found fault with his reading, Mark failed to return for the afternoon session. Another time, when he had been reprimanded for being noisy and inattentive, he became sullen and did not come to school at all the following day. But although he had missed a number of days at school that year and had done only mediocre work, he was again promoted. School, however, became more and more distasteful.

At nine Mark started third grade. His absences increased, and he became adept at leading his mother to think he had been at school and his teacher to believe his parents had kept him at home. Actually he was wandering about. He was joining in the escapades of older boys and learning from them a vocabulary and attitudes and habits which were undesirable.

When the school's attendance department finally brought Mark's truancy to the attention of his parents, his father whipped him and told him to go to school. Mark did attend school the next day, but that night he did not come home until very late. His mother scolded him severely and Mark, seemingly contrite, promised to "be good."

But he had started a pattern which did not change for the better. He had often stayed away from school; now he often stayed away from home, too. His parents were angry and bitter at the sleepless nights spent and the time lost from work in looking for the boy. They saw no reason for Mark to behave as he did, and his father felt the only solution was to "try to beat it out of him." Mark felt increasingly unloved and unwanted. He liked home less and less.

By this time Mark, ignoring the school's repeated warnings, was absent from school more often than he was present, and he slept away from home as often as he slept in his own bed. His parents could not manage him. The attendance officer who had time and again picked Mark up was genuinely concerned about the youngster—so defiant, so glum and sullen in voice and manner, so insistent on staying away from both school and home. He referred the case to a social agency, and a case worker was assigned to investigate the situation.

For the first time since he had been a very small boy, Mark now felt that an adult was sincerely interested in him. He had many meetings with the social worker and, as his initial wariness gave way to friendliness, he responded well. He was gradually helped to verbalize his antagonism for his little sister, his resentment over his mother's having deserted him, his fear of his father's beatings, and his dislike for his teachers. The social worker helped him understand that there are some situations in life which cannot be changed, from which one cannot run away, and that one must learn to live with them. His sister was there to stay, *but his mother still loved him.* His parents were not always amicable, *but their quarreling between themselves did not mean that they were not interested in him.* His father had whipped him, *but he had been worried about him* and had not known how else to handle Mark's disobedience. His teacher was really interested in helping him learn, *and the criticism had been to correct him,* not to humiliate him, as he had felt.

The social worker spoke with Mark's parents and with his teacher, interpreting for them the boy's frustrations and insecurity and giving them suggestions for responding to him more wisely. He recognized that there was less open quarreling between Mark's parents, but because he sensed that their marital situation was still filled with hurt feelings and dissatisfaction, he strongly advised marital counseling. The parents were persuaded of the importance of spending more time with the boy, and of helping him feel an important member of the family group, so that Mark could sense his place in their affections and accept sharing them with his sister.

Change in Mark was slow but steady. Unacceptable behavior was less and less evident. Reassured, Mark no longer felt an urge to run away from his problems. Now he could go to school without resenting his little sister's staying home with his mother and without dreading that he would return to find his mother gone. He could come home after school feeling accepted by the family and no longer fearful of being beaten or criticized sarcastically. Once he felt secure in his parents' affection, he was able to accept the routines of school and home and to respond acceptably to the daily requirements of life.

There are times when every child experiences some degree of fearfulness and worry. Every child is likely to react to certain circumstances with resentment and jealousy. But in homes where a good parent-child relationship provides emotional security, the sense of being loved and wanted helps the child recover from the tensions that are inevitably aroused in the course of growing up. Without this bulwark, the child feels uncertain and unhappy. With it, delinquency is not likely to develop.

# chapter 12

# Rounding Out Childhood

LOOKING FORWARD TO GROWING UP   Ten-year-olds are rounding out their childhood years and are alert to what it means to grow up. They often seem to be looking forward curiously and eagerly to the years ahead. Most ten-year-olds are not yet caught up in the rapid physical, emotional, and social changes of puberty. They are usually only on the edge of being personally involved in them; they are not as preoccupied with themselves as they will be when they reach puberty. Consequently, they are detached enough to look at the adult world calmly, appraisingly, and often critically. They are not yet there, but they know that they will be someday soon.

Ten is a profitable year for teaching and learning. The children's interests in people, in their communities, and in world affairs are keener than most adults realize. Many ten-year-olds are interested in social problems in an elementary way and like to discuss them. They are becoming increasingly aware of differences among people, of social justice and injustice. They want to know why there are criminals and hungry people. Their ideas about democracy are forming. Their attitudes and prejudices are shaping up in wholesome or unwholesome ways. They are forming feelings about authority and cooperating with it. They are gaining concepts of law and order. Their ideas are broadening, and they are picking up a whole new fund of information from newspapers, magazines, and television. If adults will take their growing concerns and interests seriously and meet them at their level of thinking, youngsters can grow astonishingly in their social concepts. This is the year when social studies should probably become the core of the curriculum, for it is the year when the fresh awareness of these boys and girls can be channeled into a constructive approach to the meaning of real citizenship in our democracy.

During this year parents and teachers must try to help the children identify with the adult world in such a way that they are neither overinhibited by it nor resentful and rebellious toward it. Some children are too anxious to conform to the standards adults set; thus they tend to lose their spontaneity and bury their individuality. It is the adult's task to help youngsters develop responsible attitudes—not by scolding them when they are irresponsible, as they will be at times—but by giving them opportunities to act in a responsible manner and then encouraging and prais-

ing them for these actions. Ten-year-olds sometimes are so anxious to succeed and to receive adult approval that they may undertake more than they can manage.

RESPONSIBILITIES AND FRUSTRATIONS At ten children are a bit steadier, a bit more grown up than they were at nine. Their talents and skills are becoming more definite. By this time, we usually can spot the youngster with special abilities or outstanding interests. Such children will need encouragement and special opportunity to develop their talents if they are to fulfill their early promise. But *every* ten-year-old—whether outstanding, average, or slower than average—needs encouragement and opportunity to follow a special ability or interest. They like to do things well and want to learn new skills. Now they can look at their work more critically, without going to pieces if it doesn't come up to their standards. They can even say, "I guess I goofed." They are ready to plan their days and accept more responsibility for getting things done on time. They make good committee members and like to be given an opportunity to plan and carry through a project either with a group or on their own.

Despite a growing ability to take things in stride, some children are overly conscientious at ten and become worriers. They worry if they cannot get their homework done, or if they are not sure just what they should do. Because of some adults' emphasis on grades and academic success, fear of failure is becoming a real concern even to children who do well in school. If parents and teachers are aware of this fear of failure, they will try to be even more careful to assure each child enough successes to offset inevitable feelings of failure—and to see that these feelings of failure are occasional rather than constant. In this respect, it is important to set achievement goals in school realistically and on an individual basis. Continual failure in the classroom gives youngsters poor estimates of themselves which often discourage them or cause them to develop a rebellious "don't care" attitude toward those who put impossible demands on them.

Ten-year-olds are increasingly able to take care of themselves. They feel more secure in taking long trips away from home. They may go to the library and enjoy browsing on their own and even take responsibility for getting their books back on time or paying a small fine out of their own allowances. They can enjoy a museum on their own or go to a Saturday movie with friends. They want to go to the playground or park to play ball. They also enjoy camping, even if it means being away from home for a week or even longer.

Ten-year-olds are beginning to be able to take more responsibility for their pets, although they need still an occasional reminder. They are able to handle some household chores without too much fussing, although they do best when working along with an adult whom they like. They may want to be paid for some jobs now, because their wants are increasing and they like the feeling of earning their own money. This is a trait to be encouraged. There are many simple, extra jobs about the house or the neighbors' houses that a ten-year-old can do.

Pressures for achievement must be kept within realistic limits of what a child *can* achieve. Too often at this age, children begin to doubt themselves seriously and to develop inferiority feelings which may become permanent. Or their interests in learning may be discouraged by assignments too difficult or too easy for them, assignments that have been given to all children regardless of their abilities to complete. Many children, especially boys, begin to dislike school because they feel inadequate to accomplish the kinds of tasks the school requires. If sufficiently frustrated, they may play truant from school, take part in acts of vandalism, or establish predelinquent patterns of behavior. We don't yet have adequate information about the nonverbal boy, but we do know that many more boys than girls have difficulty mastering schoolwork as it is usually taught. There are, for example, four boys to every girl in remedial reading classes. This problem requires thoughtful consideration and continuing research if we want to avoid turning active, restless boys away from school toward more exciting activities.

193

Ten-year-olds, in rounding out their childhood years, find social activity a central concern. This is the club-joining age when loyalty to the group is maintained and responsibilities are shared. In addition to organized groups as in scouting, groups are still formed spontaneously and shift readily with changing interests. In spontaneous activities, boys tend to stay with boys and girls with girls. Boys tend to form more permanent groups than girls. Keeping up with activities and making a contribution to the gang are requirements for group membership for the ten-year-old boy.

Girls tend to be more selective than boys regarding group membership, and many girls gather in small groups of two or three. Being someone's best friend is an important experience for the ten-year-old.

FRIENDS AND FAMILY Healthy ten-year-olds are physically active. They like to rush around and be busy, so much so that they may easily overload themselves with activities. This is the club-joining age when both boys and girls enjoy the ritual and activities of their meetings. They become loyal members of their particular organization, willing to try to carry their share of responsibility and to keep promises made to the group, but they easily drift away if the program is not interesting.

The organized club does not take the place of the groups or clubs that children form spontaneously. These continue to hold appeal, although they tend to shift and change as interests change. Boys are likely to run together in a more permanent group or gang than girls and are less selective in their membership than girls. Boys usually will take in any one who can hold his own, make some kind of contribution, and keep up with their activities. Girls are more apt to gather in groups of two and three. Being someone's best friend is an important experience, although feelings are frequently hurt as best friends shift and change.

Ten-year-olds are growing in self-control. They may get angry and occasionally lose their tempers, but they do not flare up or cry as easily as they did when they were younger. Girls cry with frustration or hurt feelings more often than boys, who rarely give in to tears now unless they have been badly hurt or have had an overdose of frustration as in being pressured to succeed in competitive team sports. Ten-year-olds hurl words back and forth and call each other names. They frequently have their feelings hurt during such explosions, but they rarely harbor grudges and are usually quick to patch up their quarrels.

At home ten-year-olds still take part in family activities. Most of them want their parents to visit school and still talk things over with them. There is little indication of the rebellious need to break away and express their independence that may become apparent in a year or two. Youngsters still enjoy taking a special trip or doing other special activities with their parents.

At ten most youngsters are careless about taking care of themselves, their clothes, and their rooms. Their beds may look rumpled instead of neatly made. Many ten-year-olds drop their clothes on the floor, yet they may be very particular about what they wear.

HOBBIES AND INTERESTS This is still an age of collections. Ten-year-olds start many collections spontaneously and sometimes drop them just as quickly. The collecting of stamps, car and airplane models, rocks and crystals, or nature specimens may now shape into a permanent and valuable interest, even leading ultimately toward a career choice. Children should be encouraged in such hobbies and given adequate space and time to pursue them.

Most girls of this age are physically, mentally, and socially more mature than most boys. Although the two sexes mix in school activities and planned parties, in spontaneous activities boys stay with boys and girls with girls. Sometimes a boy and a girl of similar interests enjoy playing together when no other children are around, but in the company of others they often pretend they don't like each other. There is often considerable real and feigned antagonism between boy groups and girl groups. The girls may complain to grown-ups that the boys are interfering with their activities—a very real complaint at times.

Ten is the age, too, when hero worship flourishes. The early interest in biography has continued, but now these youngsters are personally identifying with these models—not only with persons in books, in movies, or on television, but also with living people whom they admire. They already are daydreaming about the great things they will do and about situations in which they and their hero or heroine are involved.

GROWTH IN ABSTRACT THINKING   Ten-year-olds are beginning to develop a capacity for abstract thinking. They are becoming increasingly concerned about what is wrong and what is right. They are sensitive to unfairness, cheating, and lying, and they turn on a friend or even an adult in righteous indignation if they detect or suspect this kind of behavior. They are beginning to ask searching questions and to be increasingly concerned about God and life and death. They ask many questions and want thoughtful answers—occasionally they reject an answer given by their mothers, fathers, or teachers. They are aware that people have many varying opinions, and that different adults, even among those they admire, have different standards of right and wrong.

At ten children often are bewildered by the many diverse standards they see being followed in the adult world. As they begin seriously to question and wonder about right and wrong, they need help and guidance, especially during this year when they still are strongly influenced by adults. Adults responsible for their guidance must let them know what their values are and why they believe in them, not through words alone but also through their behavior. This is a formative year. In the next few years children must struggle, as they grow up, to choose their own values and begin to live by them. They will be more likely to choose wisely if they have had sound guidance and a desirable pattern to follow during childhood.

A PLATEAU YEAR For most children, ten might be called a plateau year. It is a point of resting and of bringing together all that they have achieved and learned during the childhood years—of getting ready for changes that will soon take place as they enter puberty. But things will not go so smoothly for all ten-year-olds; some, particularly among the girls, will already be approaching the restlessness of preadolescence. Most ten-year-olds, however, are absorbed in their own affairs, and are vigorous in carrying them out. They seem to be coordinating and applying what they have learned during early childhood and, at the same time, to be reaching ahead toward their teen years and interests. Ten for most children seems a fairly steady, well-knit interim before the preadolescent and adolescent years begin.

Study of a child

POOR SOCIAL RELATIONSHIPS
An Unrecognized Organic Condition May Cause Puzzling Behavior

There is increasing acceptance of the concept that all behavior has some cause. But sometimes it is not understood—or at least not remembered—that no single cause can explain so complex a result as a child's behavior. Factors intermingle and their impact may be almost baffling when one tries to understand a child. When parents find themselves unable to understand and to cope with their child's problems, they are wise to seek the aid of experts. Both medical and psychological aid may be desirable, even essential, to correct an existing condition.

This was true in the case of Adele Moffat. Her parents were increasingly concerned that the child had no friends. To the suggestion that a birthday party be planned, Adele had said dejectedly, "Who would I ask?

198

Nobody'd come. Nobody likes me."

The Moffats realized abruptly that Adele had only occasionally been invited to a party or even to another child's house to play after school. They thought uncomfortably of the many mornings Adele had started for school alone, while other groups of youngsters went on their way, walking together. "I actually haven't thought much about it before," said her father, "but I wonder why she isn't getting along better with other children."

They had to acknowledge that their child often was a bit moody. Frequently she was inclined to go to her room rather than stay sociably with the rest of the family. Perhaps she should be coaxed to be with them more. They recalled how seldom Adele spoke during dinner. Usually Adele's brother, Richard, who was more than a year younger, monopolized the conversation. Even if Adele were asked a question directly, Richard would answer before she had a chance to reply. They wondered if Richard's talkativeness should be curbed a bit.

When guests came to the Moffat home, Adele rarely wanted to stay downstairs. Sometimes she would say she had homework to do, or just disappear without saying anything. Later her parents would find her alone in her room, reading and munching a candy bar. They had been accustomed to smile tolerantly. "We've just kept thinking she loved to read," said her mother. "She hasn't seemed much interested in anything else."

Discussing the situation, they decided perhaps she needed more stimulation and more attention. "Let's see if we can get her into some kind of activity outside of school," suggested her father. "Music, maybe? Or dancing?"

"Not dancing," was the decided reply. "I don't think that would do. She's not the dancing type. She's—well—sort of heavy for that. I'll see about music lessons."

Adele was not particularly interested, but made no objection to being enrolled in a beginner's class at a music school. The other children were about her age, and her parents hoped that she might become friendly with one or two of them. But, as the weeks passed, she made only slow progress with her music and none at all in making friends. Meanwhile, her schoolwork seemed to suffer, perhaps from lack of application—perhaps, her parents thought, from too heavy a schedule. She did seem tired often. After a particularly poor school report, the Moffats, wondering how matters might be improved, decided that the child's mother should make an appointment to talk to Adele's teacher.

Miss Tice, the third-grade teacher, was inclined to think the Moffats were asking too much of Adele. "She isn't as quick to grasp things as some of the children are," she noted. "She really requires more time for her schoolwork. Perhaps music lessons put her under considerable pressure. And you say she hasn't done very well with her music either. Does she enjoy it? Is she interested?"

Mrs. Moffat hesitated. "Sometimes I get discouraged," she said. "I think Adele does, too. She isn't especially interested in anything, though she does like to read—at least she has a book in her hands a good deal of the time, along with some popcorn or candy! She doesn't seem to have friends, either. How does she get along with the other girls in her class? Do they like her?" her mother seemed almost reluctant to ask.

The teacher was thoughtful for a moment. "I don't recall any special incidents with the other girls," she said slowly. "Adele is usually rather quiet. She doesn't volunteer much in class, but she seems to follow along with whatever we're doing. She never gives any trouble. On the playground," she continued, "I don't think she ever takes a very active part in games. She's more likely to be off by herself, watching, or maybe just standing at the door, waiting for the bell to ring to go back to the room. She's not very energetic, or very social. She seems to try in class; although as you know from her report, her work isn't very good. She hasn't been absent much. I suppose she's all right physically?"

Mrs. Moffat seemed a little startled at the question. "Why, I think so," she answered. "She seems all right. She certainly is big and husky. The only thing I can think of is that she's always so tired mornings when I call her. I know she gets to bed early enough. She's never been nearly as lively and active as her brother. We've often mentioned that. But we didn't think it was anything to be concerned about. After all, children aren't all alike. She's very like my husband's sister, as a matter of fact—big and slow and deliberate. But her aunt is always good-natured and easy-going and friendly; I'm sure there's nothing wrong with *her*. I just wish Adele were as cheerful."

"Well," said Miss Tice, "I'll see if I can manage to get her more interested in games at recess. Perhaps she needs more encouragement. I *have* noticed she's never picked first when the children are choosing sides. I think possibly it's just because she's heavy and doesn't run fast. She gets winded quickly. They do tease her a bit about that. I've heard them call her "Fatso" and "Jumbo" and names like that, but I don't think they mean to be unkind."

The Moffats discussed the meeting that evening. "Her weight might have something to do with her being slower than a child ought to be," said Mr. Moffat. "And if she's getting self-conscious about it and being teased at school, I suppose that makes things pretty unpleasant for her. Even so, I can't see any relationship between her weight and the sort of schoolwork she's doing, or not being popular or never being interested in doing anything. Well, I suppose it might be a good idea to see what Dr. Mann has to say about it."

The pediatrician had known Adele well when she was a small child, but since her general health had not presented any difficulty beyond an occasional cold, she had not seen her for a long time. She listened thoughtfully to Mrs. Moffat before seeing Adele.

"You're concerned about several things, aren't you?" she said. "Adele isn't doing very well in her lessons, or on the playground. She's inclined to be moody, she's not very social, and she has no friends. She seems to tire quickly and to be short of breath. And she's overweight. But you seem skeptical that Adele's weight has anything to do with your worries. Yet often we do find a connection between conditions that don't seem to have any bearing on each other. Suppose we look her over and see what a thorough physical check will tell us."

The Moffats' skepticism changed when, later, Dr. Mann discussed with them the findings of the examination and the laboratory tests. She had investigated in detail the total picture of Adele's body functioning and considered it in relation to the story her mother had told. Mrs. Moffat, impatient with herself for what she now realized was too casual an acceptance of her daughter's difficulties, was relieved that Dr. Mann's verdict was no more serious than it was. She was sure the problem could be solved once it was given proper attention. She urged that it not be ignored any longer, saying that both an inherited tendency and uncorrected habits contributed to Adele's excess weight.

"But the overweight is just one of the symptoms. That's primarily a matter of metabolism," she explained. "There are glands of internal secretion that regulate the body in many ways. When one such gland isn't functioning efficiently, it can both influence the functioning of another and directly affect the way the whole organism responds.

"The thyroid gland produces a substance called *thyroxin* which the body needs. When not enough thyroxin is manufactured, the individual shows it in several ways. These may hardly be noticeable when the lack of thyroxin is only slight, but they are very marked when there is a really serious deficiency of it. In mild cases the condition is not likely to be thought of as a factor interfering with health and happiness. But it *does* interfere—with work output, with the inclination to be social, with activity in many areas. It can be a very hampering condition. A mild hypothyroidism—that's what a mild underfunctioning of the thyroid gland is called—seems to be at least part of the cause of Adele's difficulties. There simply hasn't been enough thyroxin poured into her blood-stream to meet the ordinary demands of daily living. And so to you she has seemed tired, without the vigor and pep we expect in truly healthy children. In examining her, I noted that her skin was somewhat dry, and her hair, too. Not markedly so, but suggestive of something needing investigation. And all her movements, even her speech, are unusually slow, don't you think? She's not interested in active play and doesn't even have enough energy to be social.

"Of course, an overweight problem is not always a matter of underfunction of the thyroid, by any means. But it can be related. When persons are disinclined to be active, to move energetically, ordinarily they don't get enough exercise. That encourages a gain in weight. And when food intake is greater than the energy used, the pounds do mount up. This is especially true when there's an overindulgence in sweets. It's certainly been true with Adele. Fortunately, the lacking thyroxin can be easily cared for, and I'll give you a prescription. It's important to see that Adele takes the pills regularly."

"For how long?" inquired Mrs. Moffat, already relieved that there was something definite and simple that could be done to help Adele.

"Possibly always," was the answer. "We'll see. It's a simple enough way to supply what isn't being produced in as large an amount as the body

201

needs. I'll want to check her at regular intervals for a time, to be sure the dosage is correct for her. Sometimes we can decrease it after a while; sometimes we find more must be given. We'll repeat some of the laboratory tests now and then to be sure we're on the right track.

"And, of course, attention must be given to her diet, too. Not too many sweets. It's difficult to restrict a child entirely, but I'll give you a list of things to be avoided and a suggested diet. Encourage Adele to be more active, to participate more in outdoor sports. Don't hurry things too much, though. First let's give the medication a chance. When she's feeling less lackadaisical, she'll want to play more. I've seen a listless boy or girl surprise parents when active play became part of daily activities. Baseball and skating and bicycling and hiking—all the things that children usually love—will have much more appeal for Adele when she feels more normal." She paused for a moment.

"I think, though," she went on seriously, "that there's more than Adele's physical condition to be considered. You say she doesn't make friends, and her teacher told you that the other children tease her and leave her out of their games. I think you should give some attention to the emotional factors in this picture.

"Health isn't only physical fitness. Mental health is very important. Why don't you see if her school has a psychologist on its staff? Or consult one outside of school if you can. A child psychologist should be a great help here.

"Problems of this sort often seem to form a lengthy chain. The physical problem brings about a situation that affects emotional reactions and even intellectual functioning. We find social relationships tied in with it, too. Bring her in to see me again in three weeks, and, in the meantime, plan to look into the psychological aspects of Adele's problem."

The school psychologist had not known Adele previously. There had been no apparent reason at school to suggest the child's referral to her. Adele had handled her lessons fairly adequately, although when her record was checked carefully it was seen that she had a greater potential for achievement than her accomplishment suggested. Her overweight had always been thought a relatively minor problem. But the combined results of these elements had made for a situation that was on the way to becoming a serious one.

Adele was increasingly uncomfortable about her appearance, and the self-consciousness that resulted interfered with easy social relationships. Her apparent unfriendliness really was a defense; rather than be hurt by teasing or unkind remarks, she avoided other children. Her apparent slowness in understanding and responding to situations had little to do with innate capacity; it was actually a slow mustering of thoughts and responses. She had as much to say as her younger brother did, but before she could put her thoughts into words, he would have replied. Her hesitancy in expressing ideas was not because she lacked ideas; it was partly because her reactions were slowed by unrecognized physical handicaps, and partly because as a result she felt unable to compete with her brother and with other children. She was both chagrined and disheartened, especially when it seemed that her mother and father enjoyed Richard's companionship more than they did her's and when, alone in her room, she heard her brother laughing and talking with his friends. On the playground, too, she was slow-paced and sluggish, and her indifferent skill at games was emphasized by her shortness of breath after only slight exertion.

Adele was aware of her mediocre success academically and socially. She did not know why so often she was out of sorts and cross. She only knew she felt listless, uncertain of herself and unpopular—and that a chocolate bar or a handful of cookies helped her feel more comfortable.

After medical and psychological aid had been continued for some time, there were marked changes in the child. Her improved physical condition was reflected in increased participation on the playground. Her greater understanding of her feelings and behavior resulted in a more cheerful attitude and encouraged her to be a little more social. And, sensing a change in her parents' response to her, she felt a new contentment with herself and with her family.

The Moffats made a conscious effort to show the deep affection and love that they had for Adele. They drew her out gently and listened to her patiently, responsive to her need for their attention. They were careful not to continue giving disproportionate notice to the lively Richard. They no longer smiled tolerantly when Adele started to leave the room while they chatted sociably with visiting relatives and friends. Instead, they included her as much as possible in the conversation and felt when she did go to her room that she went because she was busy with something or it was time for bed. They knew now that formerly she had disappeared not because she really wanted to, but because she was so ill at ease.

Adele's weight loss was matched by the loss of discontent and uneasiness. As her appearance improved, she became more self-assured. Her interest in school grew, and her schoolwork gradually improved. She was no longer apathetic nor so frequently irritable. After a time, the changes in Adele were met with a change in the way other children reacted to her. When she was asked by two of her classmates if she would like to play with them on Saturday, all concerned counted it real progress.

No single factor should ever be considered the cause of poor adjustment. When a child's entire life situation is reviewed, many elements are disclosed as causative factors. Each element must be understood, and the interaction and interrelation of the various elements must be discerned. Only then can measures be planned to improve the total picture.

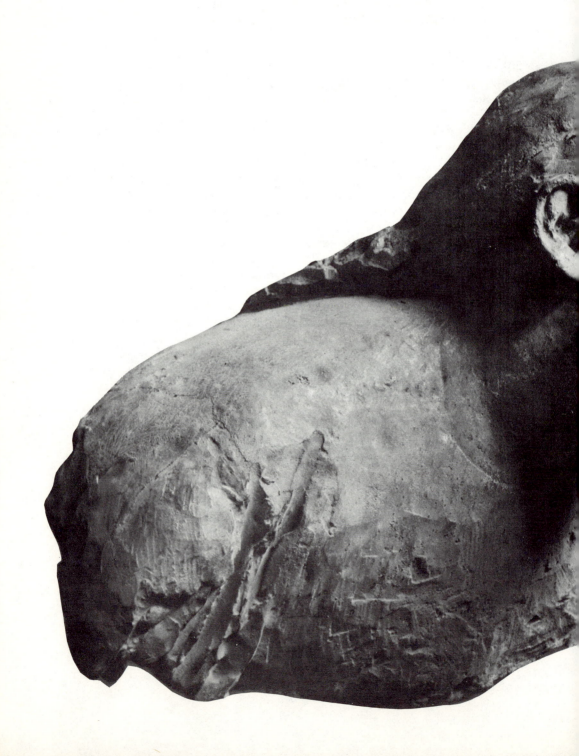

part 4

# ADOLESCENCE

Children in our Western culture are reaching puberty even earlier than previously reported. As a result the years between ten and twelve, which used to be considered years of childhood, have now become transition years between childhood and adolescence. By this time, many boys and girls have begun the cycle of puberty with its beginning of physiological and psychological changes. It is difficult to plan for them as children, but neither are they quite ready to leave childhood interests behind. We call them preadolescents to indicate that they are in between childhood and adolescence. This has been described as a period of disorganization as the patterns of childhood so often temporarily break down, and the hardly mature patterns of the adolescent have not yet been achieved. It is a period of getting ready for a new stage in their development.

When adolescence is attained, boys and girls must begin to reweave the patterns of their lives so that out of the disorganization of preadolescence may come the maturity they will need as adults. This change does not come about all at once. Adolescents must still go through a good many years during which they often will be immature and dependent. Yet parallel with this continuing immaturity will be evidence of increasing independence and often a surprising maturity of thought and judgment. During these years perhaps

205

more than at any other time, parents and teachers must try to keep a balance in meeting the adolescent's needs both to become more independent and, at the same time, to continue to turn, when necessary, to adults for guidance.

Because boys and girls mature at varying ages, we cannot say that adolescence begins or ends with any certain year. Some children mature rapidly and are ready for adulthood and its responsibilities when others of the same age still are immature, still working through the adjustments of adolescence. Youngsters differ, too, in the ease with which they make these adjustments. How they will adjust is determined by their attitudes, abilities, and personalities; and these factors, in turn, will have been affected by their past relationships and experiences. Many adolescents will have grown steadily toward emotional maturity; others will have had experiences that have delayed rather than furthered their development.

Our interest in the adolescent years and our recognition of the very real strains and adjustments involved have made us highlight this period, setting it apart from the rest of the growth process. As a result, the difficulties youth may have at this time often are so overdramatized and overemphasized that many parents and teachers and even some adolescents themselves almost have come to dread these transitional years. Yet they are valuable years, vital in the total developmental picture. Adolescence is indeed a period of heightened growth activity, but it must be regarded as part of the normal sequence of growth, continuous with what has gone before and with what will follow, not as an isolated headline. Rather than dreading these years, we should consider carefully the role that we, as adults, can play in guiding young people through the period of adolescence, so that they will be able to step with some confidence into their places in the adult world.

The current trend toward playing up and setting apart the adolescent years is unfortunate for another reason. It provides adolescents a cultural pattern—actually a blueprint for behavior—that is not always a desirable one. Through books, magazines, movies, television programs, the creation of a teen-age market, and even classroom discussions, we often push young people into thinking that it is natural for them to want to look alike, think alike, and be alike. We imply that they are expected to be rebellious and to break away from the influence of their parents and other adults, that the standards of their peers are more important to them than the standards of an adult world. But even though rebelliousness and the desire to conform are commonly observed conditions of adolescent development, they are not always as essential as the popular image of "normal" teen-age behavior would indicate. All adolescents do not feel the need to conform to their peers or to rebel to the same degree, and many of them find that the popular image makes it unnecessarily difficult for them to be themselves and to mature in their own ways.

Adolescents do, of course, face several major adjustments, and parents and teachers should be aware of these. The first, and perhaps the most basic, is the problem of finding a personally satisfying answer to the question, "Who am I?" In order to further the search for their own identities, it is necessary for adolescents to become less dependent on parents. In order to gradually identify with and assume a more adult role, they must be able to attain a certain degree of self-control and emotional maturity, to make decisions, to use good judgment, and to meet new situations without constantly turning to a teacher or parent or to peers for support and guidance.

Another adjustment adolescents must make is to the complicated physical, emotional, and social changes involved in recognizing and accepting their roles as men and women. Associated with this adjustment is the adolescent's desire to learn about members of the other sex and to establish comfortable relationships with them.

Young persons also must begin thinking about a vocational interest during their adolescent years, so that they can begin to plan toward establishing themselves as self-supporting, self-respecting adults. They must begin to find their strengths and weaknesses, their interests and aptitudes, as they come to the time when they must fit into a realistic situation, translating the daydreams of their childhood into actual possibilities for their adult life.

These are difficult, complicated adjustments. Young people need the wise support and understanding of their parents and their teachers as they try to work through the problems they must inevitably face at some time between the years of twelve and eighteen. Adolescence cannot be thought of as one period—but rather as two. The growing-up tasks of the young adolescent from twelve through fifteen (roughly our junior high school years) are different from those of the older adolescent who will receive adult status and citizenship at eighteen. Guidance which is helpful for the younger adolescent will differ from that which will be of value for the almost adult high-school student. It is unfortunate that the term adolescent masks the essential difference.

# chapter 13

# Growing Toward Adolescence

DIFFERENT DEVELOPMENTAL PATTERNS   Every fifth- and sixth-grade class will contain some children who are on the threshold of puberty and some who should be considered young adolescents. Youngsters who are still approaching puberty will remain much as they were in physical appearance and development. But those who are beginning the cycle of puberty will show changes in their growth patterns and often in their attitudes and behavior. Because of their different levels of physical maturity, children in these grades are difficult to plan for at home, in recreation groups, or in our usual school grouping. Parents, teachers, and community recreation leaders need considerable skill and understanding to plan programs that benefit and interest those who still are youngsters and those of the same age who have already begun to further mature physically and socially.

The age of maturation at puberty is built into the developmental pattern of each child. It is genetically determined and, except in rare cases requiring medical treatment, cannot be hastened or delayed. The hypothalamus in the brain triggers the increased production of the pituitary hormones and the increased release of the sex hormones which start the cycle of puberty. The first noticeable bodily changes usually occur between one-and-a-half and two years before the actual occurrence of puberty. Most girls reach this stage two years earlier than boys, although there is a wide difference in the age at which the cycle begins and the rapidity and closeness of the stages within the cycle. Some children will have reached physical maturity before others of the same age have even shown signs of beginning the cycle of puberty. Most girls begin this process around ten-and-a-half or eleven and menstruate between twelve-and-a-half and thirteen years. Most boys mature physically between fourteen and fifteen. The range is great, however; girls may menstruate between ten and sixteen and boys may mature between twelve and sixteen, with a few starting earlier and a few later. This variation among children points up one of the big problems of the preadolescent period. Even in the sixth grade, some girls will already be menstruating and others will be nearing their first menstrual period. It is much less usual for boys in the sixth grade to enter puberty, and comparatively rare for boys to be sexually mature by this time.

Both boys and girls go through a period of accelerated growth in height during the cycle of puberty. The growth of girls is usually more spectacular as it occurs before the menstrual period and slows down afterwards. Many girls in the sixth grade are experiencing the beginning of their rapid growth in height while most of the boys have not yet begun theirs. With boys, the growth spurt in height does not necessarily precede physical maturity; the peak may be reached later in their teen years. This may become a real problem for many sixth-grade girls who find themselves not only more physically mature than some of their classmates, but also taller and heavier than most of the boys in their classes.

There also is a tendency for most children to gain considerable weight during the prepubertal period. Naturally many children and their parents become alarmed for fear this increase in weight will be permanent. But if the child has not been overweight during the earlier years the excess weight usually will not be retained, unless the weight growth is complicated by emotional problems which lead to overeating, or if there is a lack of exercise.

At the same time that children are gaining in height and weight, their hearts are enlarging, and there is an increase in muscle weight. Since this occurs in girls before it occurs in most boys, there is a period of about two years in which girls may have more muscle weight and strength than boys. Boys move ahead of girls in muscle strength and weight after they have reached puberty. The head, hands, and feet increase in size and reach their adult proportions ahead of the other parts of the body. The girls' hips begin to broaden and their breasts begin to develop. The appearance of breast buds and the first signs of pubic hair are an indication in many girls that menstruation will begin in a year or two. The increase in size of the penis and testes and the first evidences of pubic hair are indications of the beginning of physical maturity in the boy. The relation of the timing of these growth patterns and physical maturity is less clear for boys than for girls. Since all the parts of the body do not develop at the same speed, the child may become self-conscious because of seemingly too large hips or hands or feet. Much awkwardness—the dropping and tripping over things—is due to this uneven physical growth.

EXPLAINING VARIATIONS IN MATURITY If parents and teachers are aware that pubertal changes may take place, particularly among girls, as early as the tenth or eleventh year, they can avoid many problems and better understand and help the early maturing youngsters. Early maturity must be recognized. A child who is beginning to experience the problems of early adolescence cannot be treated in the same way as others of the same age who are not yet adolescent.

Explaining the different times of maturing to children can spare them unnecessary bewilderment, fears, and feelings of inferiority at being different. Children should know what to anticipate in physical changes and in new emotional reactions and problems during the coming years. They especially need to realize that girls usually mature earlier and are, for a few years, often bigger and better developed physically than boys. Children need opportunities to talk through the problems and anxieties that may arise when they find themselves either far in advance of their friends or far behind them during these years of maturing. Group discussions in school or youth groups often can provide opportunities to talk about these problems, especially when the children who are physically more mature can be grouped together. Frequently this can be achieved by forming groups on the basis of common interests. The teachers' function within such groups should be to stimulate the discussion, listen to the children's reasons and opinions, provide needed information, and help them in their search for an understanding of themselves.

SEEKING NEW INFORMATION    The years from ten to twelve are probably the best time in which to make sure that children have the physiological information they will need to understand the coming changes in their bodies. This is also the best time to make sure that all boys and girls have the basic knowledge of how life begins. Youngsters should have this information by the end of the sixth grade. The information given to children of this age should be specific. They should understand the physiology and function of the reproductive organs of both sexes, menstruation, the birth process, and the sexual roles of male and female. It is preferable to give this information as part of a general course of study that deals with all parts of the human body, so that children will learn to think of their sexual organs as part of their bodies and not something on which to focus special attention.

Fifth- and sixth-grade children are building attitudes and values. They are trying to orient themselves to the world about them and to their places in it. With manifestations of sex everywhere about them, it would be unusual for children not to be curious about the beginnings of life and about the differences and relationships between the sexes. The ways in which we attempt, both in the schoolroom and the home, to fill youngsters' needs for certain kinds of experience at each level of development are important. We need to be aware of the normal curiosity which all children have about sex and of the questions and situations that are likely to arise in the normal process of their growing up. What counts is the way we answer their questions during each period of growth and the way we help them to understand themselves, to live successfully through each stage, and to progress normally into the next phase of development.

Understanding the child's present information and attitudes is of special importance during the preadolescent period when the mass media expose a child to confused concepts of the relationships between men and women and between teen-age boys and girls. On television and in movies materialistic values, amoral standards, and varieties of sexual practices are evident. Before boys and girls become adolescent they need help in sorting out ideas and information that will help them to build healthy sexual concepts as distinguished from those that will confuse them or foster unwholesome or oversophisticated desires and patterns of behavior.

Preadolescents are more likely to seek information from their friends than they are to ask direct questions of either their parents or their teachers. But adults should take the responsibility for presenting correct, factual material to preadolescents which will help them develop positive attitudes toward themselves as boys or girls, and later men or women.

Many parents, teachers, and youth-group leaders recognize the importance of preparing children for the physiological and emotional changes of adolescence; yet, they find it extremely difficult, if not impossible, to talk comfortably with youngsters about these things. In fact, many parents find the difficulty so great that they put off any discussion of these matters from year to year. Their children enter adolescence totally unprepared or with only the haphazard, and often erroneous, facts and attitudes picked up from peers, newspapers, movies, television, comics, or from adults' scattered remarks and innuendos.

Many teachers or group leaders are embarrassed or perplexed as to what they should say when boys and girls ask direct questions about sexual matters or when situations arise that involve problems of a sexual nature. Those adults who work with boys and girls may need to seek help in understanding their own feelings and attitudes before they can be sufficiently comfortable and clear in their own thinking and feelings to help a growing young person. Only those who are both comfortable and well informed in this area should have the responsibility for any planned course in the school curriculum or in the community.

Books can be a valuable aid in giving adults the correct information to pass along to children and the confidence to discuss sexual matters frankly. But they are only a supplement. They cannot take the place of the

day-to-day development of attitudes, the informal discussions, and the answering of questions as they arise in everyday life. If parents are too tense or embarrassed to talk informally with their child, then they probably will be wiser to read a well-written book with a young child or to provide an older child with a book to read for themselves. Even if the parents give their child a book to read, they should realize that they must still try to answer the questions that the reading may stimulate. Parents must always remember, too, that detailed factual information is not enough, that the child is learning attitudes as well as facts.

Whether the school should provide sex education or the broader course in family living through a formal plan of study is a question which cannot be answered categorically. It depends in great measure on the attitude and readiness of the community, on the teachers available, and on the religious background of the school. There is no question that the need for such education must be met in some adequate manner, because the ability of our children to understand their own sexual drives, and later to establish satisfactory marriage and family relationships is of vast significance. It would be desirable for parents to educate their children in this field, but some parents cannot or will not do so. Thus teachers often find

213

themselves having to guide or counsel not only the child but in many cases the parents as well. Such guidance must be given wisely and with understanding of the feelings and inhibitions of those involved.

Rushing into sex education with an enthusiasm which roughly pushes aside long-standing taboos or the sincere beliefs of the parents in the community is certainly unwise. If the school considers a formal course the most effective answer to the real needs of the children in the school or the community, it is best, first of all, to meet with parents, respecting their prior interest in this area and talk over the needs of the youngsters, the school's plan for meeting these needs, the factual material that will be covered, and the way it will be presented. Once parents' cooperation and support have been obtained, the school can proceed with parents and teachers working together for the benefit of the children. Such a preliminary procedure enriches the ensuing course of study for the students, whether it is given during one year or becomes a part of the total curriculum, because the parents often are able to add much by the type of support and approval given in the home. In addition, the materials presented in group meetings frequently give added insight to many parents, lessen their anxieties, clarify their attitudes, and even give them needed factual information.

SOCIAL INTERACTIONS  The gang or group is important to children of this age, whether they are nearing puberty or not. As part of a group they have the feeling they need of belonging and being like the others. But for youngsters who are nearing puberty, the character of the group is changing and will change even more. Such children lose much of their earlier interest in the secret code, the secret word, and all the mystery they used to enjoy. They become more interested in sports and in things the gang or the group can do together.

Friendships are important to the preadolescent. The more boys like one another, the more frequently they seem to get into fights. But they are

214

developing loyalty and the capacity to stand up for each other. Girls tend to have on-again-off-again relationships. They get angry at each other over little things and then make up again. They have long talks on the telephone, calling one another incessantly. Trouble and misunderstanding are likely to develop among youngsters of differing maturity levels. The more mature children tend to group together with interests of their own. Friendships, even of many years, may break up because of the difference in interests due to differing levels of both physical and social maturity.

Preadolescence may be a trying time for both parents and teachers, because the opinions of the peer group are becoming increasingly important. Acceptance by the peer group often means more to children of this age than their relationships with adults. "But all the other kids do it," is a recurring phrase. In the classroom, group contagion spreads quickly, and teachers may find a whole class up in arms against them. Parents, too, have a difficult time if their standards for their own child's behavior are different from the standards imposed by other parents. Youngsters are often quite unreasonable if they feel they are being asked to do something that will make them seem in any way different from their friends.

In our culture, early boy-girl social affairs sometimes begin before children really want them or are ready for them. Formerly, it was believed that boys' and girls' interests in each other began as a result of emotional feelings paralleling puberty and that this interest grew in intensity during the adolescent years. But today, fifth- and sixth-graders have been exposed to a cultural pattern through television, movies, books, and comics that emphasize boy-girl stories. Many adults also have accepted this pattern and push their youngsters into early social activities.

This premature social growing up usually is undesirable. If it is encouraged during preadolescence, youngsters may desire a faster pace of social life as they go through junior high. It also creates uneasiness among youngsters who are growing up at a slower pace, causing them to feel inadequate when, in fact, their interests and activities are the ones which are appropriate for most of this age group. The majority of fifth- and sixth-graders, especially boys, are not ready for such activities or really interested in them. But they often are made to feel that this is expected. Most children, if left to their own interests, would prefer to enter boy-girl relationships more slowly. A precocious social life, if permitted to flourish in the fifth and sixth grades, results in a vanishing childhood, depriving children of time in which to prepare themselves for their adolescent years.

This is the time for parents and teachers to meet together and set up standards for the children's social life. They should emphasize group activities. Preadolescents do enjoy informal activities—swimming, hiking, roller- or ice-skating, games, picnics, and hobby groups—in which both boys and girls can take part. Membership in organized groups such as Boy Scouts, Girl Scouts, Camp Fire Girls, and 4-H also should be encouraged.

Fifth- and sixth-graders are active, growing children who need many wholesome outlets for their energy and their expanding interests. They should not, however, be overloaded with after-school activities of adult choosing. Too many lessons after school, no matter how worthwhile, can

215

overburden children and leave them little time for free choice in developing their own interests.

Preadolescents are sometimes more difficult to live with than other children of the same age who are not so near puberty. Their moods change quickly. They may be eager to start a project in the morning, but by afternoon be depressed and uninterested in it. Girls may cry frequently over seemingly insignificant events or remarks. Preadolescents may become overcritical of parents and teachers, although at the same time they also may develop a crush on an adult to whom they are particularly attracted. They want to grow up, but they seem afraid to leave the security of childhood behind them. They may seem responsible and capable today, exceedingly childish tomorrow. They often expect and want help from their teachers or parents—yet they resent being told what to do.

The preadolescent is constantly contradicting, arguing, and taking issue with anything mother, father, brothers, sisters, teachers, or even friends say. They especially attack their mothers and disagree with them frequently. A preadolescent may rebel at going to bed and at keeping clean. They often are untidy, uncooperative, and sometimes use language which distresses adults. They are not interested in household chores and may be uncooperative when asked to help, yet they are likely to be polite and helpful to people outside the family. They resent being teased, but they love jokes and often try them out on their friends or on grown-ups. They respond best to teachers or to parents who crack jokes with them and laugh at their humor.

PREVENTING DELINQUENT BEHAVIOR Preadolescents often are overanxious and competitive, both in their play and in their schoolwork. If they are under too much pressure to excel in grades, sports, or some other activity, they may resort to cheating. It becomes increasingly important for teachers to recognize individual differences in ability to master schoolwork, so that the demands of the curriculum can be suited to the capacity of each child. Children who fail or are made to feel inadequate because the work assigned is beyond their abilities may seek compensation in group activities that border on delinquency. Groups of boys, and sometimes girls, may steal from a store and accuse the child who does not go along of being chicken. They may issue dares to each other that can have serious consequences, or they may share in the excitement of vandalism.

Children who get involved in even minor delinquent behavior need guidance to understand the seriousness of what they have done. Parents or teachers should help them take responsibility for their actions and to make amends, when that is possible. It is a mistake to allow potentially dangerous or destructive activities to slide by as merely "mischievous" or a "passing phase." This is the age of the alibi. Consequently, it is important that parents and teachers, if they find undesirable activities, try to discover the reasons behind them. If necessary and possible, both parents and child should receive professional counsel to help prevent more serious behavior

216

in the future. Sometimes delinquent behavior develops because a gang of boys has outgrown childish games and, with no new activities to take their place, hasn't enough to do. In this case, a better recreation program should be planned to meet the normal restlessness of this age group. Or, if there is an adequate program, these children need to be drawn into it.

It is wise to allow preadolescents to let off steam, to express their thoughts and their feelings. A listening adult needs to be understanding and to have a sense of humor to meet the ups and downs of this period, since scolding, nagging, or taking offense at signs of disrespect will only make matters worse. Adults must still be ready to exercise their veto, however, if the preadolescent gets out of bounds. They need to know that adults are still in control and that they are expected to behave in a responsible way. But it is better for the adult to respect these children's developing maturity and to trust that they can and will make adequately sound decisions than to treat them as difficult children or to show lack of confidence in them. When correction is necessary, it should be given in a friendly, matter-of-fact way with a firmness that will make it stick.

Those things that have given stability to the younger child also will give stability to the preadolescent—warm affection from parents and teachers, an understanding of a particular pattern of growth, recognition of individual personality needs, a vital school program, encouragement of skills and hobbies, being given a sense of belonging and of being accepted, and an opportunity to be as independent as maturity will permit. Proper support and encouragement are essential to help a youngster pass through the years of preadolescence and to leave childhood behind with self-esteem and self-confidence intact.

## Study of a child

*THE MATURING OF LISA*
*Puberty Can Be Puzzling*

That children change as they grow is recognized by everyone. But sometimes changes in behavior are so marked that they become disturbing to adults charged with the care of children. This is particularly true when the adults do not recognize the underlying causes of undesirable changes. Once they become aware of the reasons behind reactions, they can plan to help reach more acceptable ways of behaving. Until these reasons are uncovered, there may be long periods of puzzled concern and uneasiness for all involved.

That was the case with Lisa, who, as a bright nine-year-old, had performed well in fourth grade. Lisa was tall and well-built, the picture of sturdy physical health. She always seemed to get along well with her classmates; her parents were interested in her progress and activities. In general life seemed to go along smoothly.

But Lisa in fifth grade presented a vastly different and very worrisome picture. She had celebrated her tenth birthday just as school closed. Following an active summer, she came back enthusiastic and ready for the opening of the new school term. In the ensuing weeks, however, few of the desirable attitudes and behavior patterns so apparent during the previous school year were evidenced.

Once casually self-assured in manner, Lisa now seemed painfully self-conscious. She kept a mirror in her desk and examined her face frequently during class periods, worrying about her many freckles and pimples. She no longer enjoyed playing with her classmates. Instead she turned to a little clique of girls from seventh and eighth grades and sought to establish herself as one of them. Since they were older than Lisa, their interests had changed from activities typical of fifth-graders. Some of them accepted Lisa as a sort of pet, and though they often laughed at her, the group did not discourage her "hanging around" with them.

During class one day Miss Lewis, the teacher, corrected Lisa's poor posture. The child burst into tears. Another time, when Lisa stumbled against a table and upset a science exhibit, Miss Lewis suggested that she might be more careful. Lisa blushed furiously. She was so disturbed by the reprimand that she floundered in class discussion the following period. Soon after this, the other girls in the class began to tease her because of her obvious infatuation with Miss Lewis. Lisa gazed soulfully at the teacher, kept offering to do errands for her, brought her one small gift after another, and seemed unable to keep from touching her whenever an opportunity presented itself. She became interested in romantic TV plays and was embarrassed when her classmates laughed and ridiculed her ecstatic comments.

Her mother observed changes at home, too, and was perplexed and often irritated. Lisa demanded clothes that were inappropriate for a ten-year-old, and privileges that were unsuitable. She developed ways of behaving that she had never shown before—evasions and even deceptions, a haughtiness that was sometimes ludicrous, and a sensitiveness that made every day difficult for the entire family. Her parents were bewildered—worried and yet annoyed, concerned and yet impatient, too.

"She's just a child," said her father. "What are these notions she's getting? Why is she so hard to live with all of a sudden?"

"Maybe it's the big girls at school she's been tagging after," ventured her mother. "They're a bad influence. I'll talk to her about it."

When Lisa was urged not to go around with the older girls so much, matters seemed to get even worse. She became increasingly rebellious, flew into a temper when she was crossed, and often neglected the chores she had always attended to before. She was restless and sullen, and her frequent mood changes were unpredictable and irritating.

Lisa alternately tried standing on her dignity with her parents and cajoling them into permitting her to go out in the evening to another girl's house. Once she urged them to agree to an evening movie with one of her new friends and two boys from school.

"*Please* let me go. It's all planned. I can't stand not going with them. They'll think I'm a baby. They'll just *laugh*."

When her parents were firm in their refusal, Lisa withdrew. "Very well. If you insist. But you just don't understand, Mother! Things have changed since you were my age." And Lisa angrily left the room.

"It was funny, in a way," her mother said later, discussing the incident with her husband. "She tries so hard to be grown up. Of course she's right that things have changed since I was her age. She really felt upset, though, and I was sorry for her."

Lisa's schoolwork began to reflect the entire disturbed situation. Instead of being well up in her classes, she left work unfinished, was inattentive in class, and seemed unable to concentrate on new material. When Miss Lewis spoke to her about her increasingly poor achievement, Lisa breathlessly implored, "I'll try, really I will, Miss Lewis. *Please* don't think I don't want to please you. I'll do better." And she cried almost hysterically.

Finally teacher and parent talked things over together. Why the different and undesirable reactions in school after so successful an experience throughout the earlier grades? Why the changed emotional responses at home, the demand for greater freedom and for social relationships which were so inappropriate for a child her age?

Often when parents or teachers see a child day after day, they give little attention to physical changes that are taking place. Then something happens to bring the changes into focus—clothes suddenly seem too small, food demands change radically, complaints of lassitude or undue restlessness are so obvious they cannot be ignored, or a clear complexion becomes rough and blemished.

These alterations had actually been true of Lisa, but because they emerged gradually, they had not been especially noticed. On the first cold day, Lisa put on her last winter's coat and found that it was tight across shoulders and chest. Once eager for active outdoor play, Lisa had rarely seemed to fatigue, but now she seemed to tire easily and was listless and slow as she attended to her few chores about the house. Her always healthy appetite increased so that she usually was unsatisfied at meal times. Candy or cookies became routine after school. Before bedtime Lisa was sure to be heard at the refrigerator or the cookie jar. In her room there often were wrappings from candy bars or half-empty bags of potato chips.

The school records showed that Lisa's weight had increased markedly. She had grown twice as fast as girls her age generally do, and had gained nearly twelve pounds during the past year. And during the first few months in fifth grade, she had grown still another two inches and gained four more pounds. No wonder last year's coat could not possibly be worn. No wonder her once smooth face was marred with rough patches and pimples.

The changes in height and weight were accompanied by still other bodily changes. Lisa's hips were widening and her breasts were developing. Together with these evidences of an early puberty, she showed the muscular incoordination and clumsiness which often trouble pre-adolescents before they learn to manage their rapidly developing skeletal and muscular growth.

The frequent moodiness, the occasional angry outbursts, the restlessness, and the sensitiveness which had become characteristic of Lisa were all part of her approaching puberty and her confused feelings about herself. She did not see why she should look so different from her classmates; it bothered her and made her feel self-conscious. If she stood half stooped over, she thought she wouldn't seem so much taller than the boys in her class at school, and perhaps those embarrassing breasts would be less conspicuous. If she used make-up, maybe she could conceal the facial blemishes. If she sought the companionship of older girls—well along in their pubertal development, and thus more like her in appearance—she need not feel so different, so out of sorts with herself and her world.

When the reasons behind all of Lisa's annoying reactions became clear, neither parents nor teacher felt so helpless. They recognized that she needed aid in understanding and accepting herself in a new role.

"How could I have been so blind!" lamented her mother. "But somehow I never thought a ten-year-old was about to menstruate. I've been so wrong. I should have realized, and talked to her long ago about all this. I could have saved her a lot of misery."

It was clearly desirable for Lisa to learn more about how girls grow and develop, and the reasons for the changes in their bodies. Her mother explained matter-of-factly what was occurring, and that she was no different from other girls growing normally.

"It's only that you are maturing a little earlier than most girls," she was told. "It's nothing to be concerned about. Your menstrual periods will probably start before long. Mostly it occurs nearer thirteen, and sometimes later. There's a wide range that's perfectly normal; from ten to fifteen isn't an unusual span of years for the first period to start. All kinds of explanations are recognized: the climate where a girl grows up, inherited tendencies, and of course a particular girl's own growth pattern and health condition."

As they talked, Lisa sensed her mother's desire for her to understand.

"I knew a little about it all," she admitted, "but somehow I didn't connect what I knew with *me*. In school there was a talk once, just for the girls. It was in gym and the school nurse came to talk to us. I didn't think it was very interesting, and I didn't understand it anyway. And you know, sometimes I never really understood what some of the big girls were talking about, either. But I didn't like to say so, I couldn't admit it to them. They'd have laughed, and maybe they wouldn't have let me go 'round with them if they thought I was so dumb."

Their talk seemed to ease much of the tension which the entire household had been under. Lisa's rebelliousness was gradually replaced by a greater acceptance of the reasons why her parents felt they had to refuse some of her desires. As she was helped to develop new interests, her preoccupation with her changing appearance and her seeking older friends was no longer so all-absorbing. She voluntarily stopped constantly indulging in sweets, determined to lose her excess weight. She was enrolled in a swim class, and was promised ski lessons when her coordination and general physical condition improved. The Junior Drama Club at school intrigued her and she decided to try out "when there's a part for a big girl," she told her parents. "I guess it's not so bad being big."

With Lisa's energies absorbed by new and appropriate activities, the adults' worries lessened, and Lisa lost the feeling of being confused. Her school work reflected her greater inner relaxation. She concentrated more successfully on her lessons and therefore was more successful in completing them. She was definitely growing in her ability to live with her new maturity. Because she now realized that her differences from her classmates were temporary, she acquired a new perspective concerning them and herself. She no longer felt it necessary to be always on the defensive. Instead, with the help of her parents and her teacher, Lisa now was enabled to substitute for her half-ashamed awareness of her early maturity a kind of pride: "I got ahead of the other girls." Maturity became more than a matter of physical growth and functioning. There was an increasing maturity in social relationships and in emotional stability. Before the year was ended and she was ready for sixth grade, Lisa was again functioning more evenly both at home and in school.

221

chapter 14

# Not Quite Grown Up

LEAVING CHILDHOOD BEHIND Between the years of twelve and sixteen significant developmental changes take place in the physical, emotional, and cognitive development of our boys and girls. These changes are more striking and involve greater adjustment both on the part of the youngsters and of the adults who are guiding them, than at any other developmental point of life. Between these years all boys and girls must leave childhood behind and move toward the end of those adolescent years when they will be almost adult. They look backward and forward at the same time. They are not children yet they are not grown up.

MARKED PHYSICAL CHANGES Most boys and girls enter adolescence during their junior-high years, although a few, particularly boys, will not do so until they are in high school. The special problem of the junior high school is that it includes students in such different stages of development. In no other growth period is this variation in physical development quite so marked. In a single classroom, we find some youngsters still in the spindle-legged stage of late childhood and others with the developing figures of young men and women. By the eighth grade, approximately two thirds of the girls have matured and may be called adolescents, whereas two thirds of the boys are still preadolescents. By the ninth grade, almost all of the girls and a majority of the boys will have matured physically.

During these years from twelve through fifteen, adolescents' appearances change from that of children into that of young men or women. Adolescent girls gradually lose their childish appearances as their hips grow wider and rounder, and their breasts become larger and better formed. Boys also change in appearance as their muscles develop and their shoulders and chests broaden. Their voices gradually begin to change and early maturing boys often are embarrassed as their voices fluctuate between a childhood soprano and a developing bass or baritone. Growth in general continues to be uneven through the early years of adolescence, and the teen-ager may feel awkward and embarrassed because of it.

223

EMPHASIS ON APPEARANCE Many young adolescents feel generally uneasy and dissatisfied with their bodies or their appearances. Some of them are still concerned as to whether they will mature normally. Differences in body size, proportion, height, or weight now worry the developing adolescent in a new way—once they have matured they fear that this is the way they may always be. "I don't want to be a big woman like my mother." "I don't want to be a short guy." "My mother is awfully fat, and I'm getting heavy, too. I'm afraid I'll be fat by the time I'm twenty." Now they become aware that their height, bone structure, and general proportions are the ones they will always have, although they can, of course, gain or lose weight. Sometimes adolescents are very unhappy about their appearances and need help in accepting them. Again the cultural pattern, with its emphasis on small, slender girls and tall, manly boys, is not helpful. Body build is an inherited trait and many young people fall far short of the unrealistic ideal that may be so persistently held before them.

Acne or other facial blemishes, scars, birthmarks, or even freckles can distress adolescents and render them painfully self-conscious. Body odors which may be accentuated at this growth period embarrass them. The need to wear glasses or even the kind of hair they have may disturb them, especially at the beginning of adolescence. These things may seem superficial, but they may be serious to the youngster. Because of the dramatic changes that have taken place in their bodies, their attention is naturally focused on them. Often they will need greater maturity before they can value themselves primarily for what they are and what they can do rather than for how they look. It requires considerable maturity to be able to think of one's self as separate from one's appearance. Adults should take these feelings seriously if they occur, not criticizing or laughing at the adolescent, but giving constructive help and friendly reassurance. Some adolescents need help in growing toward the realization that the kind of person they are is determined by much more than how they look.

ADOLESCENTS' QUESTIONS AND CONCERNS The physiological changes that herald puberty are those that change the child's body into one capable of reproduction. These are gradual changes which are built upon the physical and psychological development that has been proceeding since birth. Adolescents begin to experience an intensity of certain drives and emotions that they have not known as children, ones that they will experience as adults. But with new physical maturity, even with the best of knowledge and attitudes, they still may lack the judgment that should accompany the capacity of reproduction. Young adolescents must be helped to understand that maturity of judgment doesn't automatically accompany physical maturity. During the young adolescent years they should be guided toward developing sound judgment and a responsible attitude about sexuality.

By the time boys and girls are physically mature, most of them know something about the physical facts of reproduction. They need opportunities, however, to talk through the emotional and social relationships be-

224

tween the sexes, and the values and attitudes that are important if they are to use their sexual drives with pleasure, responsibility, and wisdom. It is still the task of adults to help young adolescents to think through the complex feelings, attitudes, and responsibilities that face them when they have reached physical maturity.

Young teen-agers often ask questions dealing with feelings and emotions and with ways to get along with the opposite sex. But there are other questions that they do not ask as readily. Questions about the physiological changes that are so obviously taking place seem to embarrass them. At first, physical changes may seem strange and even distressing, especially if the young person has not been prepared for them. Some adolescents are disturbed and even resentful of their physical development if they have not learned to accept maleness or femaleness. Such children may need special help.

The development of the breasts and hips and the beginning of the menstrual flow can be bewildering experiences to growing girls and need careful interpretation and anticipation. Boys often are concerned about their developing genitals or their nocturnal emissions. Adolescents need time to adjust to these changes. Even if the facts have been given to them previously, now it has become a personal matter.

In spite of the many changes in traditional cultural roles of men and women, biological identification still remains desirable at this age for normal, healthy development. It is important, however, that the acceptance of the biological sex role should not be confused with the cultural sex role, although they are closely interwoven. For both boys and girls this is a time when an emphasis upon traditional cultural expectations may result in stereotyped behavior that may serve to limit the activities and goals, which in a changing society may be open regardless of sex.

## HOME, SCHOOL, AND COMMUNITY WORKING TO-GETHER

In every junior high school there are girls who become pregnant and both boys and girls who contract venereal disease. There are many other boys and girls who are aware of conflicting values and standards concerning sexual behavior, and are, themselves, frequently confused and sometimes frightened by the new sexual feelings which they are experiencing. Because of the discrepancy in the sexual development of boys and girls of this age, some are more involved both in feelings and actions than others. This makes for some difficulty in developing adequate and helpful programs in our communities, but does not relieve us of the responsibility. Even if all of the children are not yet adolescent, most of them are well aware of the emphasis upon sexuality in our culture. Some parents can be sensitive to this development in their own children, but all children do not have such parental guidance and may remain confused and uninformed unless plans are made to reach all boys and girls during these years. Home, school, church, and community organizations can work together to help young adolescents develop a respect for the human body, an understanding of sexual feelings and the role they play in our lives, appreciation for the rights of others, and an understanding of their own emotions. Thus, it may be possible to lessen the tensions, strains, and confusions accompanying the new kinds of personal relationships young adolescents will be meeting in the years ahead.

If a girl has matured early, she may have some problems, particularly in the seventh and eighth grades. Not only may she feel far ahead of other girls her age, but she may find boys her age uninteresting and unresponsive. Sometimes such a girl will be drawn toward older and more experienced boys. She may begin to date them and become involved in situations which remove her even farther from those of her own age. This may result not only in loss of interest and contact with the activities of junior high, but also involve her with experiences which she is not yet emotionally able to handle.

Early-maturing boys, on the other hand, are frequently in a much more favorable position. They are ready to enjoy some social activities with the junior-high girls. Often they are able and ready to move successfully into athletics in which their size and physical development is an asset. They can become leaders in junior-high activities. Some early-maturing boys who are having difficulties with their schoolwork may become restless and truant and turn toward activities with older boys outside of school, a group with whom they feel more comfortable and more successful.

Slow-maturing boys may be handicapped during these years. By eighth and ninth grades, the majority of the girls and many of the boys are developing physically, so the slow-maturing boys do not fit into the social or athletic activities of the junior high. Frequently they are worried, in spite of reassurances, as to whether they will ever grow up and be like the other boys. By ninth grade their physical immaturity may be a source of embarrassment to them. Many of them become timid and feel inferior among their peers. Many of them will catch up in size and strength while they are in high school, but often it is difficult for them to overcome some of their feelings of inferiority in relation to their peers. Some may become excessively bossy, overdoing their masculinity in order to compensate for the years when they felt left out.

Except for exceptionally late-maturing girls, the girl who is a slow maturer seems to have fewer problems. During seventh and eighth grades, there still are a number of girls and many boys who are also childlike in their physiques and interests. By ninth grade, most of the slow-maturing girls have become adolescent and have caught up with the other girls.

Teachers and parents need to be aware of the problems that may arise because of the wide differences in the age of maturing which separate youngsters not only in appearance but in their abilities and interests in responding to activities in junior high. Many different kinds of social programs will be needed. It is important not to let the needs of the early maturer overshadow the needs of those who are maturing more slowly. By ninth grade, since most of the youngsters have become adolescents, some school systems are returning the ninth grade to the senior high school and are thinking of combining the sixth, seventh, and eighth grades. This

226

would seemingly provide a school population which would allow for the planning of a program more nearly appropriate for developing youngsters. Even though many of the girls would have physically matured, the majority is not ready for the social life of the adolescent years. In many ways it would be beneficial for most thirteen-year-olds to have a less fast-paced social life than sometimes occurs when they are grouped with ninth graders who in their interests are more closely allied to high-school boys and girls.

By the time boys and girls are in the ninth grade, they usually want opportunities to be with the opposite sex. They need places where they can gather and get to know each other in informal surroundings. This is a different and more valuable experience than pairing off or going steady—experiences that should belong to the older adolescent. Parents should open their homes so that their young adolescent sons and daughters feel free to bring friends there. School, churches, and community agencies can provide opportunities for young teen-agers to participate in hikes, swimming parties, picnics, dances, dramatics, folk dancing, and hobby groups. Young people who are actively doing things together can get to know one another during early adolescence. This is good preparation for the social life of the high-school years.

DIFFERENCES IN SOCIAL MATURITY Even though many boys catch up with the girls in social maturity by the end of junior high, some boys and girls continue to be ill at ease with each other. Boys may stay aloof for fear of being turned down, of being clumsy, or of somehow embarrassing themselves. Many boys will date only popular girls, feeling too insecure to date the girl on the fringe of the group, however attractive she may seem. In the same way, many girls turn down a date with the "wrong" boy. Consequently, popular boys or girls may have many opportunities to date, while others just as attractive have none. Often young adolescents want to go steady as social security, as insurance against being left out. They change partners frequently and seldom feel any deep attachment for their current special friend.

Parents must continue to take considerable responsibility for guiding the activities of the younger adolescent, who is not always ready to judge wisely or to make sound decisions. They must sometimes use their veto quite firmly even in spite of anguished protests. There are times, indeed, when young adolescents want and need to rely on their parents' or on other adults' judgment and decisions. Sometimes this makes them strike out, resenting their own immaturity at the same time that they are seeking and accepting the security offered. Adolescents do not like the idea of controls, yet at times they want and must have the security controls can provide. "My mother won't let me go there" or "My father makes me get home at midnight" is sometimes a convenient shelter for the adolescent, even though the same teen-ager may storm at mother and father for being old-fashioned and too strict when the restrictions aren't so convenient.

## SELF-CENTEREDNESS, BELONGING, AND CONFORMING

In the early years of adolescence, boys and girls usually are self-centered. They are so deeply concerned with answering the question "Who am I?" that their thoughts often are focused on themselves. They use their friends as a mirror for themselves. They constantly ask them questions about themselves: "How do I look?" "Do you think Jim likes me?" "Did I do all

right?" "Let's have a truth session." When their friends start talking about some other subject, they listen to them just so long; then they must bring the conversation around to themselves again. They are self-conscious as well as self-centered. They use their friends for support. As they grow more mature and more sure of themselves, they will become increasingly able to turn from this self-questioning and to develop a real interest in other human beings, going out to them in genuine love and affection.

Belonging to a group reassures young adolescents. They seem to crave its security and its power to bolster waivering self-confidence. Often they will try to submerge themselves further in their groups by conforming to the group pattern—appearing and behaving as the group dictates. Adult standards of behavior do not matter nearly as much as the standards of the group. Frequently, boys or girls who do not really want to do everything the group is doing do not dare to be themselves but try instead to be what the others think they should be. Some are drawn into experimenting with drugs or enter into games of stealing and bragging about their antisocial achievements. They may do unwise and silly things in their efforts to be popular or at least accepted by the others. Group contagion is strong. At junior-high parties many youngsters get so excited and wound up that they behave in ways they would never think of as individuals. At school, normally friendly girls or boys may be unfriendly to those outside their group if group pressure demands it. They may feel unhappy about this and a bit ashamed, but they go along. As one girl said, "I have to pretend to be that way or I won't have any friends." Many young adolescents are so concerned about what others think of them that they can pay little attention to anything else, with the result that their schoolwork and their own real interests may temporarily suffer. They face an arduous, complicated task in living up to the demands of the group. They are often strained, unhappy, and worried during these years for fear they will not be accepted by others.

Often in their desire to make the grade socially, young adolescents may pass up friendships or acceptance in groups which could give them real companionship but which seem to lack prestige. Instead, they may hang on at the fringe of a supposedly better group, feeling left out and unhappy. A great deal of early adolescent tension and irritability stems from the worry over belonging. This anxiety has been heightened by a cultural pattern that puts a high premium on belonging to the right group, an emphasis felt not only by adolescents but by adults, who often consider conformity a virtue and in some instances a necessity for holding a job or attaining a promotion. Conformity is probably not an innate adolescent need but one that has been fostered as a cultural pattern. As the need for individual ability is reemphasized, we can hope to see a lessening of the pressures on the adolescent to be so completely like the others.

TEEN-AGE STANDARDS AND BEHAVIOR  By and large, junior-high school students are drawn toward boys who are good in sports, adequately attractive, and popular. They admire girls who are attractive by the particular standard of the group, talk easily, and enter into all the chatter and plans of the group.

The great loyalty boys often develop for members of their group or their team is less frequent among girls. Girls are more concerned with cliques, and can be quite cruel in excluding others and letting them know they are excluded. Many girls seem less secure and less motivated toward purposeful activity than boys, perhaps due to the fact that more activities— particularly sports—are open to boys of this age. Frequently the activities for girls are fewer and less challenging.

The junior-high boy or girl does not understand persons who do not conform to their own, usually narrow, standards and are often openly intolerant of them. They either wholly accept or wholly reject classmates— there is very little middle ground. If not guided and helped to develop an understanding of other people, they can, in their insecurity, be quite unkind and thoughtless toward a person who does not fit in. They may reject a member of a minority group or of a different religious belief, a youngster whose appearance or clothes are different, one who is especially successful academically or one who is a slow learner, one who has special talent or strong interests, or one who refuses to go with the group, or even a student who is too popular. Adolescents who are attractive and eager to be friendly sometimes are rejected because, for one reason or another, they do not fit in with a particular group pattern. Adults need to be aware of the heartaches suffered by those who are not accepted by their peers, in order to give them the support and guidance they need.

## ACADEMIC PROBLEMS AND OPPORTUNITIES

Because of the many emotional demands on a youngster during his junior high school years, schoolwork sometimes takes second place. A boy or girl who has done well in elementary school may begin to grow careless about homework and about handing in assignments. Yet many boys and girls respond positively to the wider academic program of the junior high school. Enthusiasm may be high—but interest may suddenly drop—as a new enthusiasm develops. They may become genuinely interested in a subject and may even find a major interest leading toward an eventual career. Most of them enjoy changing teachers, working in the laboratory and shop, and being assigned challenging projects. They often become attached to a particular teacher, developing crushes which they discuss avidly. Teacher influence is at a high point and can be most valuable in guiding the student in developing values and interests at this crucial period in development. Antagonisms toward certain teachers also are high, and a teacher who is disliked may have a difficult time. Friendliness and fairness are criteria used by the adolescent.

In spite of the difficulties encountered in working with boys and girls during these years, they can be good years for stimulating many young adolescents to confront issues and begin to develop their own points of view and their own judgments about situations, ideas, and events which occur. Between twelve and fourteen there is growth in the cognitive development of most children. They are beginning to be able to look at reality, to do some logical thinking, to see inconsistencies they had previously accepted, to realize that there may be more than one dimension to a situation. They are becoming increasingly able to organize their thoughts, to draw upon some of their experiences and some of the knowledge which they have accumulated. They are becoming more interested in abstract concepts and increasingly able to deal with them. If they are stimulated and encouraged, these abilities will grow and develop in depth during their adolescent years. Sometimes this may be uncomfortable for parents and teachers, for many of these young adolescents may argue or challenge statements which grown-ups make, or which they have read in an assignment. This is healthy growth and should be encouraged, for the capacity to think for oneself permits the beginning of thinking through the standards and values which young people will make part of themselves as they move toward adulthood. However, as one teacher of an alert ninth-grader said, "I have spent this year trying to teach him to challenge me politely!"

Individual differences in ability to do schoolwork become increasingly apparent in junior high school. The child who still cannot read well finds himself in very real difficulties. Now, even more than in preceding years, different programs of study suited to children's differing abilities and goals are essential. Each program must be offered as one of value, so that youngsters do not feel that they have failed because they are following one channel of study rather than another. In schools in which the major emphasis is an academic, college-oriented curriculum, many youngsters fail. If they feel little sense of achievement and rejection or nonacceptance by teachers, and particularly by peers, they may drop out of school entirely and turn to others like themselves for acceptance and assurance that they are able to belong. Such children, usually boys, form our delinquent gangs or become drifters. Some boys and girls run away from school and from home; others withdraw and become shadows in the school, seat-sitters—perhaps we should call them drop-outs in school. We seriously fail many boys and girls at this critical period in their search for values and identity.

CHANGING MOODS   The changing moods of the preadolescent period generally continue through early adolescence, sometimes with increasing intensity. Young adolescents may be happy and self-confident one day, despondent and self-doubting the next. Likes and dislikes often are strong. They are rarely tolerant of other people. They may be generous at one time, but revert to childish selfishness within the same hour. They want to be with friends, but at home they may bury themselves in their rooms, demanding utmost privacy, or they may withdraw within themselves, barely responding to their families. Moods are influenced by the heightened physical changes, by self-consciousness that comes from increased awareness of self, and by cultural pressures which demand acceptance from peers, parents, and teachers. The struggle to belong, to be accepted, puts an added strain on young adolescents as they become physically mature.

231

Adolescents' changing moods are difficult for teachers and parents to accept, even though they may have some understanding of the cause. Often young adolescents are easier to guide and live with in school than within the family; they may respond better to the group situation and to the guidance of teachers because they feel their parents are too close to them and too identified with their childhood. They are the ones upon whom they must become less dependent if they are to become adults. Although they may love their parents, frequently enjoy being with them, and often turn to them for support, they also rebel against them and push aside their attempts to help them as they struggle to grow up. They want their parents' interest, yet they often reject both their affection and their help.

This seems to be particularly true at about the fifteenth year, which might be considered the point at which the younger adolescents begin to grow up and feel that they are really becoming young adults. Living day in and day out with young adolescents while they are trying to break some of their home ties and establish their independence is not easy. Parents need encouragement during this period, but too often they receive condemnation.

## Study of an adolescent

*MISUNDERSTOOD MOTIVES AND HURT FEELINGS . . .*
*Lack of Communication Can Lead to Misunderstanding*

The background of behavior is not always readily apparent. Sometimes members in a family seem to be at odds with each other, and though they are confused and troubled by this, parents nevertheless may continue to accept difficult situations created by their children. No one benefits from such circumstances, least of all the children, who are generally wholly unaware of the basis and meaning of their actions.

Actions vary widely. Probably the most familiar way of manipulating parents is through temper tantrums. Very small children frequently use this method to get their own way. In the first school years, stomach upsets may succeed in keeping a child home and so avoiding a school situation which is frightening or embarrassing or in some way threatening. Later a boy or girl may respond to parental restrictions or to excessive solicitude with sullen or defiant behavior, making the parents apprehensive of what may follow. Or the youngsters may neglect studies or misbehave at school, especially if the parents place great emphasis on high grades and participation in school activities.

On both sides, with grown-ups confused and concerned and their children also confused and withdrawn or defiant, there will be hurt feelings. For both sides, help is needed to resolve the turmoil and bring greater satisfaction in living with each other and with themselves.

The Fuller family was faced with a situation that bewildered and disturbed them all. The parents had been lenient and forbearing. They now were distressed that their teen-age daughter was difficult to please and seemingly impossible to control.

Fifteen-year-old Leslie was confused and unhappy. She baffled the adults who knew her, both at home and at school. Her schoolmates wondered about her and although they sometimes envied her doing as she pleased, they did not admire or like her. Healthy and mentally alert, Leslie could have been attractive and popular. Instead she drew attention chiefly because she was sullen, scoffing, and rude. She had failed to establish friendly or even agreeable relationships with either grown-ups or her schoolmates. She was insolent when corrected or reproved, and she flaunted her disregard of school regulations. Her school record was poor, and she showed little desire to do anything to improve it.

To a teacher who had once tried to reach a responsive chord, talking sympathetically and warmly in an effort to break through her aloof manner, Leslie had given the defiant rejoinder, "Why should you care? I can get along." But thinking about the incident at home that evening, she was sorry and uncomfortable about it. "I shouldn't have said that," she murmured to herself.

"I don't understand that girl," the teacher said later at a faculty conference. "She *can* be pleasant. Yesterday I saw her being very helpful to a vis-

233

itor who stopped her to ask for information. And not long ago she calmed a frightened youngster who came to meet his big brother and got lost in the halls. But she's never been very pleasant to me!"

"I think she's unhappy," said another teacher, "but I can't imagine why. Her parents certainly seem interested in her. Why don't they do something? She really needs help."

"Perhaps they don't know what to do," ventured another faculty member. "Perhaps *they* need help, too."

And they did. The Fullers were greatly concerned about Leslie's attitude and behavior. She ignored all responsibilities at home—never making her bed or helping with the dishes or being reasonably cooperative with any household task. Yet she was constantly critical of her mother's housekeeping. She expressed dissatisfaction with the way the family lived, the car they drove, the clothes they provided, the size of her allowance. She seemed unaware of anyone's comfort but her own, turning up the television when others preferred quiet, insisting on listening to a program that only she found interesting.

The Fullers were worried, too, about some of Leslie's habits which they felt threatened her health. She had long since indignantly rejected the idea of a regular bedtime, saying she would go to bed when she felt tired. Mornings she usually had to be called several times before finally getting up. Then she would either hurry off without breakfast or sit down for an unnecessarily prolonged meal. As it got later and later her mother would hover about, half pleased at her appetite, half irritated that she would again be late for school.

Increasingly she left the house after the evening meal, often with no word as to where she was going. To any question she responded bluntly, "Just out," and left. Sometimes she added, "To Betty's," a school friend. Since they did not feel that she returned unduly late, they would make no further comment.

Once her mother raised the question of friends, saying she should know she could invite any of her friends to come to her house, and why didn't she? Leslie's only response was to shrug and go up to her room. Once alone, tears filled her eyes. "Who'd come?" she muttered to herself, and turned up her stereo so that her mother would not come in to talk further.

Occasionally her parents suggested going to a movie or to visit a relative. Leslie generally would say the picture wasn't interesting, or that she'd be bored visiting the family. But she would object to being left home alone. When, on occasion, they said in exasperation, "Well, we're going. You don't have to come," Leslie would go to her room until it became evident that they would actually leave without her. Then she would emerge, holding her head or her side and bewailing a pain and parents without feeling. The first few times this occurred her parents gave up their plan, expressing great concern and suggesting making an appointment to see a doctor. In the morning Leslie generally claimed she felt all right, and told them not to make any appointment for her. When they insisted that a phy-

234

sician be consulted, no physical problem had been found. The only comment offered was, "This is probably an emotional problem." When Mrs. Fuller reported this to her husband, he brushed it aside. "What's she got to be emotional about?" he said. And nothing was done about the suggestion of seeking other help.

Finally, however, when both the physician and the school counselor seemed in agreement that the situation should not be ignored, the parents agreed that "something" should be done. Leslie's poor scholastic record as well as her poor social adjustment had been brought to their attention more than once by the school. And it was all too apparent that she was not happy at home and that communication between them was ineffective. The idea of consulting a psychologist was accepted, although the Fullers had no clear notion of what was involved in psychological help. They were advised to contact the local mental health society, which could give them names of professional individuals qualified to aid in the situation. An appointment was arranged and the parents went to Dr. Barton's office.

It was something of a relief to hear that their daughter was not behaving in a totally unheard of manner. "Sometimes young people find growing up disturbing," Dr. Barton said. "Some of them cannot face becoming self-reliant and independent. That may be part of the trouble. And often we find that the difficulties young people have began years back, in early childhood. Then we must search carefully for the basis of whatever is troubling them, in order to give them the help and understanding that they have been needing for a long time."

In answer to questions, the Fullers reviewed the early years of Leslie's life. They expressed their dismay that what they had always thought was wise care and management somehow had not resulted in a happy girl.

"What did we do wrong?" the mother wondered. "We've given her everything she wanted. We haven't interfered with whatever she wanted to do. I've been home so much, trying to get her to talk to me, trying to find out what she seemed angry about. Seems I might as well have stayed on at the office, for all it's meant to her to have me home."

This took explanation, and Dr. Barton heard that for the first few years of Leslie's life her mother had worked full time, then half days until Leslie was about ten years old. "I wanted her to have everything I missed when I was a girl—good times, pretty clothes, a lovely home. I wasn't happy without them, but she isn't happy with them. I just can't understand it."

"We'll try to understand it all," said Dr. Barton. "I'd like to meet Leslie and get an idea of what she thinks about the total situation, both home and school. Could you come with her next week, and after we've met, you leave. It's better for her to keep appointments alone. After a time, when it seems she's ready for it, I'd like all of us to meet together. But let her feel these are her appointments, and let her arrange the times we'll meet. She'll tell you. There is probably some day during the week when she is out of school earlier than other days, or could be with school permission.

"When she comes home from an appointment, don't pry, don't ask her what she said and what I said. Take time to listen whenever she tells you anything, of course, but let her talk spontaneously, not in answer to questions. Leave it up to her. Her visits here will be much more helpful that way.

"And one more thing. Whatever the difficulties are, they aren't new. They've been with her for a long, long time. We can't expect that they will be cleared up immediately. We'll make progress as rapidly as possible, but when problems have had a long time developing, they need time to be unraveled."

After their meeting with the psychologist, the Fullers felt relieved. They hadn't been told it was all their fault, whatever the problem turned out to be. Nothing unusual or incredible had been suggested. Growing up was difficult. That they grasped, and felt they could rely on this warm and pleasant doctor to make things easier for Leslie, and for them.

Although they were uncertain how Leslie would react to the plan of seeing Dr. Barton, somewhat to their surprise she raised no objection. Actually, she welcomed an opportunity to reach for a pleasanter way of managing her life. She said little at home at first, but then offered an occasional brief comment or two: "She's OK." "She knows what I'm talking about. She doesn't think I'm so queer." "I'll ask Dr. Barton about that." Clearly a good relationship existed between them.

It was only after several meetings that Leslie began to feel really accepted, to sense that Dr. Barton was indeed interested in her, and wanted to help her. And as she became increasingly able to express her feelings, she was helped to understand the influences of her developing years. At first she protested that "all that happened a long time ago; it can't be important now." But Dr. Barton showed her many instances of how her teenage behavior was tied to situations remembered from her early childhood. There were scattered memories brought into the talks in the office. Sometimes Leslie was surprised at the hurt feelings she still had as she spoke of long past incidents.

She had never felt truly loved and wanted at home. She did not remember the baby-sitter in whose charge she had been left when her mother went to work, except to recall her as "not unkind but not affectionate." She saw her mother mornings when Mrs. Fuller was about to leave for the business she and her husband had established. "Be a good girl," Mrs. Fuller would say, with a quick kiss. Or sometimes, "Be careful, you'll muss my hair," when the child put up her arms for a hug. And in the evenings, Leslie remembered, her mother usually was tired and often irritable. "Be quiet for a while," she would say wearily. "Let Mommy rest."

When Leslie was old enough to go to kindergarten, Mrs. Fuller went to the office only in the mornings. The childish interpretation of this change was that the baby-sitter had not liked her enough to stay. Leslie was not happy in kindergarten. She had had very few contacts with other children or indeed with other adults, and was ill at ease in the group. Nor was she happy at home, although she now had more time with her mother, and more supervision from her than ever before.

236

"I seem to remember feeling Mother didn't want to be bothered with me," she told Dr. Barton one day. "I guess I wasn't a very nice little girl, or my mother would have played with me more. Or maybe she just would rather have gone to her office. I think I thought that," she added, reflectively.

"Did you and your father play games or do anything together?" asked Dr. Barton.

"I don't think so." Leslie hesitated. "I don't remember doing anything with him. He was a very quiet person. He brought me presents sometimes, but he didn't say much. I always thought he was worrying about something."

"About you, perhaps?" questioned Dr. Barton.

Leslie looked surprised. "I don't think so. I don't think he even thought about me. I didn't matter much to him."

She had missed several weeks of school during the middle years of elementary school; she had been ill, and there was a lengthy period of convalescence. This brought another change at home; her mother gave up all active contact with the family business and was at home most of the time.

Dr. Barton wondered to herself if perhaps the mother had come to recognize that the extra income she brought home could not provide everything the child needed to be happy. Possibly the apparently indifferent attention given her little girl was beginning to trouble her.

Whatever the reason for a changed attitude, Leslie remembered that during and after the illness, her mother was unusually solicitous, gratifying every whim expressed by the child. Leslie's reaction was not unmixed. Pleased though she was with this unusual attention, she also was puzzled and a little uneasy about interfering with her mother's work. This always had been impressed upon her as very important. She wondered how long it would be before her mother returned to the office. Evidently anxious to make the most of this new state of affairs at home, she became very demanding. She seemed to feel it necessary to keep testing the love which she now heard proclaimed. Her demands became more and more unreasonable, but they were rarely refused. It became something of a game she played with herself, trying to reach toward the first refusal. But she found little pleasure in the whole situation. She came to think her parents just didn't care about her; they would do as she asked as the quickest way of keeping her quiet and out of the way. Her distortion of the whole parent-child relationship continued.

Finally her attitude toward her parents was projected on others. She became convinced that no one had much use for her. She was both angry and disconsolate at feeling unwanted, but tried not to show her feelings. Her manner grew increasingly distant and aloof.

Dr. Barton was finally able to help her understand that her problems lay largely within herself. In her misinterpretation of others' attitudes and behavior, she developed attitudes and ways of behaving which were defenses against showing how miserable she felt. Fearful that acquaintances would not be attracted to her, she did not dare to like them. Fearful that

237

any warmth on her part would not be met with equal warmth, she was distant and cool. Ill at ease and expecting to be rebuffed, she rebuffed others first, protecting herself in this way from the slights or criticisms she dreaded.

"Your way has been a sort of shield," said Dr. Barton gently. "I don't think you want to be unfriendly, but you're afraid to be anything else for fear someone might not be friendly to you.

"You used to think your mother was unfriendly when she went to her office. Then later you were upset when she ignored the office for you. Really, she went to work and left you to earn money to get you nice things. She thought she was being a good mother. But you were too little to understand that. And later she gave up working because she really did love you very much and realized you needed her at home. But you didn't understand that either. You couldn't, because you were so mixed up in your feelings about her. And she found it hard to understand you, and evidently was unable to explain things to you."

Leslie's difficulties had not grown solely by reason of her mother working outside the home. To feel a warm love and a close bond with a parent, a child does not need to be in constant contact. Indeed, outside interests often are beneficial to both parent and child. But during their time together, real interest and affection must be sensed by the child. It is not the number of hours spent together, but the feeling-tone of those hours which is significant.

A child needs to feel assured of acceptance and love. To feel wanted and to sense approval help children's later interpersonal relationships. Establishing good contacts outside the home and feeling reasonably sure of one's ability to gain acceptance and approval from others have their start in early parent-child relationships.

Leslie came to understand her feelings and to recognize what had grown between her and her parents. Slowly she came to the conclusion that her discontent and unhappiness were not based on real facts. People did not dislike her at once. She just expected them to. Seeing herself, her parents, her teachers, and her schoolmates in new perspective gave her a different understanding of how people feel toward each other, and especially what the real feelings of her parents always had been. Gradually she developed the ability to show more friendliness, more overt responsiveness. Slowly her defensiveness was replaced by a warmer, easier manner both at home and elsewhere.

And Mr. And Mrs. Fuller needed to understand Leslie's problems. While at first they had said uneasily to each other that Dr. Barton's interpretations were exaggerated, they could not deny the changes in Leslie as the weeks went by. Her complaints of aches and her sullen antagonism stopped. Her provocative disregard of other people's wishes lessened. Her responsiveness to others increased. Finally accepting Dr. Barton's explanation of causes and effects, they began to readjust their own ways of feeling and of behaving toward Leslie.

Several interviews with the family together in Dr. Barton's office were enlightening to all of them. Free expression of how each had felt toward the others eased their hurt feelings as greater understanding developed. Family tensions lessened. Leslie felt more relaxed at home and also at school. She was able to concentrate more successfully on her schoolwork. She found, almost to her surprise, that more efficient studying came with more peace of mind. And she found that the changes within herself started to result in changes in the attitudes of classmates at school. She found herself making friends.

Crisscrossed motives and frustrations, wishes and anxieties, often tangle the lives of parents and children. The threads can be unraveled if the family members all learn to understand where the difficulty started. First, of course, they must accept the fact that difficulties exist, and that help is desirable. They must recognize that their cooperation is necessary. The attitudes of all concerned generally need rechanneling before relationships move smoothly. But when attitudes change, inner relief and satisfaction can be expected to replace confusion and discontent. Then outer evidences of inner feelings will be increasingly apparent in improved relationships with others and in greater success in daily tasks.

Behavior of young people usually can be redirected, if, without too long a delay, their excessive willfulness, contrariness, and seeming unreasonableness are correctly interpreted. These reactions are likely to be evidence not of defiance or rejection of authority, but of a need for help.

# chapter 15

# Almost Adult

APPROACHING PHYSICAL MATURITY  The older adolescent of high-school age is moving toward the end of adolescence and closer to the adult world. Physical changes are almost complete. Most high-school students have the bodies of adults. Few girls increase in height after their sixteenth year, although some boys continue to grow until they are almost twenty. Their body proportions are stabilizing, and the extreme awkwardness of early adolescence is passing. They no longer have as many physical adjustments to make. Growth slows down, and the symmetry of the body develops. Adolescents' heights or weights or general appearances may continue to cause anxiety, but many are beginning to learn that personality can be more important than mere physical attractiveness.

Sometime during high school a boy begins to show the first sign of a beard. This is an important time for a boy. He is proud of his beard whether he lets it grow or shaves it off. Unfortunately, many adults don't realize the significance of the first signs of a beard and treat its appearance with amusement and often ridicule. A boy's voice also completes its changes about this time.

CONTINUING CONFLICT WITH PARENTS  Adolescence, like other periods of normal growth, involves progress as the needs, problems, and interests of adolescents grow and change. Those of sixteen-, seventeen-, eighteen-year-olds, are quite different from those of young adolescents. High-school students chafe much more than younger adolescents under adult pressures and restrictions that deny them the right to grow up. Older teen-agers feel grown-up, and in many ways are, but the culture still treats them as though they were children even though most of them will attain adult citizenship during their senior year of high school. This pressure results in much of the moodiness and continued rebelliousness of the later adolescent years.

In their attempts to achieve adult status, older adolescents sometimes express their criticism of their parents quite frankly and freely. This, like so many other aspects of adolescence, may be hard on mothers and fathers. Parents are no longer seen through the eyes of childhood but are now compared with other parents and adults. Just as parents often see only the

241

problem side of their adolescent son or daughter, so older adolescents may temporarily see only what they feel to be shortcomings of their parents or their homes. Perhaps the need to establish their own identities makes it necessary for them to find fault with their homes, so that they will feel less guilty about breaking away from their childhood dependence upon their parents. During the final years of high school, many boys and girls experience considerable conflict over their very real attachment to their parents and their equally great need to become emotionally independent from them. They may feel anxiety and tension as they rebel against their parents, criticize them, or develop differing ideas and attitudes.

Too often parents and their older adolescent children come into unnecessary conflict because they lack understanding of each other's points of view. Parents are not always fully aware of their sons' or daughters' needs to assert their growing sense of independence. If they can allow their sons or daughters to express their points of view and their criticisms, without being too upset by their outbursts or taking their comments too personally, both parents and adolescents usually will be able to work their way through to more adult relationships. But if parents cannot take some measure of adolescent rebellion without growing angry, punitive, or rejecting, the conflict may increase and lead to a decisive break between parents and child. Parents must guard against losing patience with their older adolescents. It is wiser to listen as they try to work through their confusions and to provide them support and guidance.

BELONGING AND BREAKING AWAY High-school boys and girls usually will turn to others of their own age for support in their attempts to understand themselves. In their uneasiness about breaking away from dependence on their parents and childhood patterns of behavior, they feel reassured if they are surrounded by others similar to themselves in competence and experience. Those of their own age do not threaten the ability to decide for themselves, as adults so frequently do.

Older adolescents show a developing maturity as they offer sympathy to one another and try to help their friends along. They give each other advice, often better accepted than any adult's. Either in pairs or in groups they talk long, earnestly, heatedly, and often intelligently about their ideas and interests. They are all absorbed in the same problems of growing up and struggling to be free of adult domination. They are concerned over the same social successes or failures. They can talk together about their futures, their worries.

During their high-school years many adolescents will have gained enough self-confidence to begin to shake off some of the group influence. They will then be able to risk being individuals, making judgments and holding opinions of their own. They will be able to begin following their own interests and choosing people whom they enjoy for friends, rather than being limited to members of their groups. The insecure adolescent who never takes this step toward greater independence from the group,

242

but continues to need its support, may remain permanently in the stage of early adolescence and never become fully capable of thinking or acting as an individual.

Some young people, in their efforts to belong, develop feelings of inferiority. Some develop a man-of-the-world or woman-of-the-world attitude with which they try to impress their friends. In a loud voice, they boast and boss and criticize others, especially the leader of the group. They are sure they could run things better themselves. Or they try to attract attention by being different, by doing or saying startling things, by clowning or laughing at their own jokes. Some high-school boys and girls are afraid to express their own opinions at all and generally just parrot someone they admire. Others don't seem to fit into the group pattern, or don't want to. They withdraw too deeply into their books or hobbies or lose themselves in daydreams.

SOCIAL DEVELOPMENT Two channels of social development are involved in the needs of most older adolescents to find themselves acceptable to their peers. One is their continuing relationships with those of their own sex, and the other is their developing relationships with those of the opposite sex. Although we usually think of adolescence as the years of developing relationships between the sexes, we must not overlook the fact that friends of the same sex still are important. Even toward the end of adolescence, boys in particular, continue to feel great loyalty to the group. Often a boy of this age transfers his allegiance from the gang to the bas-

243

ketball team, the football team, or the baseball team. But where teams or other organized groups do not exist, gangs often continue to fill a boy's need for close companionship with a group of his own sex. Without purposeful activity, these gangs may develop serious delinquent tendencies during the senior high school years.

A girl tends to choose a confidante and personal friend within her larger group of girl friends. Although she continues to be part of a group of girls throughout high school, she no longer finds the group all-absorbing. She will readily turn down an activity with the girls for a date, and the other girls will accept her action as a matter of course. For boys of this age, the group still frequently comes first. Boys may have close personal friends, but the gang or the team often remains more important to them. A group of boys, furthermore, will continue to consider a member disloyal if he misses a team activity to take his girl out. A boy may even stand his date up if some plan of his group demands it. Despite the great loyalty among friends, young people of this age may criticize each other a good deal and even have serious disagreements and quarrels.

The high-school student is concerned about going steady, which may now mean much more than "I have someone to go to the next party with," as it did to the younger adolescent. High-school students sometimes think seriously about marriage—and an increasing number of them do marry, if not during their last years of school, then just as soon as school is over.

Older adolescents have serious questions to face, many of which they do not easily express. Should I go steady seriously? Shall I marry now or when I leave school? What about heavy petting? What about intercourse before marriage? What about birth control? If I am pregnant, what shall I do? What about abortions? What about homosexuality? Why doesn't anyone date me—is something the matter with me? What about venereal disease? If I remain a virgin will boys want to date me? Such questions are perturbing both to adolescents and to adults who may have to guide them.

GUIDING ADOLESCENTS   If parents and teachers are to be truly helpful in guiding adolescents, they must be aware not only of the heightened sexual drive, particularly among boys, but of the change in the cultural pressures that are being put on older teen-agers. Heavy petting and intercourse are becoming accepted activities in many adolescent and adult circles today. In some adolescent groups, participation in such experiences is played up and made to seem a highly desirable part of growing up. Adolescents who do not want to become involved in this kind of activity often are made to feel that they are behind the times and frequently are left out of social groups that they consider clever and sophisticated and fun. These boys and girls must feel the steady support of parents and teachers and the approval of the larger community if they are to withstand the pressures of this growing pattern of sexual intimacies. Many adults and young people take the position that where there is a real emotional attachment, sexual intimacies are part of the deepening feeling for one another and should be permitted. They feel that such relationships satisfy the need to feel close to another person. This needs thought, as the transient nature of the feelings many adolescents have for one another frequently may result in one involvement leading to another. There is genuine cause for concern in the increasing number of high-school marriages, often resulting in the disruption of education; in the high rate of divorce among those who have married under twenty; in the increasing number of illegitimate births, with all the resulting heartache; and in the growing incidence of venereal disease among young people.

One cannot underestimate the power of the drug culture on many of our high-school boys and girls. Even if they are not seriously involved themselves they are confronted with the responsibility of making a decision which may be different from that of some of their friends. The questions—"Shall I experiment with drugs; Am I missing something; What are they like; Will they make me feel better about myself?"—have to be thought through by most of our young people. The majority do not take part in the drug culture, but many may experiment once or twice. There are too large a number of high-school boys and girls who are seriously involved and in need of help in order to break away from a habit which may have started out as excitement and is verging toward disaster. Some boys and girls turn to drugs because they are unhappy, depressed, and seek some form of comfort. Others try drugs out to be part of the group and to share in the experience. All of our boys and girls need to understand the

245

effects of drugs of many kinds, but intellectual understanding must be followed with help for those who are tempted or who are already involved. Parents and teachers need to be aware of the signs which indicate that an adolescent is on drugs and call it to the attention of those who can help in a nonpunitive way.

Although older adolescents often seem noisy, rude, inconsiderate, and difficult, they also have another side. Many are in earnest about developing their abilities. They are anxious about their futures, wondering, planning, and daydreaming about what they are going to do with their lives. Many are concerned—"Will jobs be available; Can I plan a future; Will there be war again; Will the work I want to do still be needed?" These are important questions. These boys and girls now have realistic choices and decisions to make between an immediate job or further training in a vocational school or college. They are faced with questions of earning money and becoming self-supporting. Even in high school, most boys are up against the problem of having enough money for dates or for running a car. In fact, this has become one of the major distractions that may keep a boy from concentrating on his academic work, or may even result in drop-

246

ping out of school if owning a car seems more important than staying in school. Others face the problem of continually falling behind or failing in their work. If they try to solve this problem by dropping out of school, they run into even more serious problems of trying to make their way in an adult world that has no place for them.

Often adolescents who seem to lose interest in their schoolwork and do poorly because it has no meaning for them show surprising alertness and ability when they take courses relating to their own interests. They often respond, for example, to vocational courses or courses in which they have an opportunity to talk about things that are happening among young people or about social or political problems. Even students so disinterested in school that they have been truant regularly may respond to a half-day-school and half-day-work project in which their studies are related to their job. They may come to accept responsibility as they have never done before.

Adolescents who seem disinterested in school usually respond, too, to opportunities for assuming responsibility that has meaning for them. Many will work hard if they are allowed to plan some of their own activities, help develop their own programs, and make their own decisions and carry them out. They can do a capable job in school councils and committees, in club activities, and even in community affairs if they are made to feel that they are needed and wanted. Adolescents need a motive and a purpose in their work. If these are present, they frequently do a better job than many adults would believe possible.

Adolescents sometimes get into trouble because adults have not met them halfway in giving them opportunities to be mature. Studies have shown that most adolescents would prefer a real job after school, on Saturdays, or during the summer instead of extracurricular activities. But though high-school students want to work, even summer jobs are not readily available to them. We must do what we can to encourage growing young persons at each point where they are willing and able to take responsibility. Adolescents, like little children, should not be pushed too rapidly, but if responsibility is not offered to them as they show readiness for it, they may remain immature and continue to play the part of children, irresponsible and self-centered.

EXPANDING INTERESTS AND CONCERNS Many high-school boys and girls have a growing and intelligent interest in politics and in community, national, and world affairs. They are observant about what goes on. They form and discuss opinions often with a good deal of clarity of thought and judgment. Many of them will take a stand and speak out or demonstrate in support of a cause in which they believe. This interest should be encouraged by stimulating courses on current affairs and social problems, and in the home by thoughtful discussions of TV programs, news events, and current issues. Many of these discussions may become heated, for many older adolescents no longer agree with the points of view of their parents or other adults. Nevertheless the exchange of ideas is important as young people begin to clarify their own opinions and move toward their last year in high school when many of them will become adult citizens taking responsibility for the vote which they cast.

Some young people in high school are questioning the life-styles and goals of many of the people they see around them. They are beginning to question the materialistic emphasis of the goals which are presented to them as desirable. Some of them are seeking answers in experimenting with other approaches and different life-styles from the older members of their community. This is disturbing to many adults and has resulted in a lack of ability to communicate between such adults and youth. Yet many of these young people are sincere in trying to find a way of life which to them will be more satisfying than the life that they see being lived around them.

Other young people are ready and eager to move into the adult community and to fit into the established patterns with which they have grown up. These boys and girls also are thoughtfully and intelligently planning their own future way of life. Others will just settle in following whatever pattern of life is presented to them.

LEARNING RESPONSIBILITY  In learning to be responsible, adolescents will react better to guidance than to domination. Comments from members of their families, teachers, or activity leaders often help them to gain perspective and to sort out their thoughts as they become ready to make their own decisions. They need adults in the background to guide and encourage them without condemning, to give them the feeling that they are trusted to act on their own but are still ready to give help when they need it. They like to discuss ideas with older people who will listen to what they are trying to say and help them think things through. They will seek out those adults who take them seriously.

Many parents worry about their adolescent son or daughter and tend to become overrestrictive, thus making it more difficult for the young person to become responsible and independent. One reason for their fears is the realization that the mistakes of adolescence, unlike most mistakes of childhood, may affect their child's entire adult life. The couple who marries before they have finished high school, the boy or girl who fritters away time in high school and is then unable to enter college or get the job he or she wants, the girl who bears an illegitimate child, the youngster who chooses the wrong group of friends and gets drawn into activities that border on delinquency, and the boys and girls who get caught up in the drug culture—all of these naturally cause parents grave concern.

The parental role with sixteen-, seventeen-, and eighteen-year-olds will become one of counselor. It is usually too late for control. These teenagers look, act, and feel grown up, yet their judgment is not always so mature as their appearance would suggest, or as they think it is. They are seldom easy to guide, and they may make serious mistakes, despite the best efforts of parents, teachers, or counselors. If mistakes are made, the role of the adult is to help the young person face the reality of the situation and work it through toward greater emotional maturity. As one seventeen-year-old said, "It's not the trouble you get into, but the way you're helped to come through it that's so important."

What many adults do not see is that underneath manifestations of adolescent rebellion is the teen-agers' need to make decisions and to take more responsibility for themselves. This should be permitted and encouraged whenever the possible consequences of mistakes in judgment are not too serious. But with the greater freedom accorded, the older teen-agers must also be expected to shoulder more personal responsibility for decisions and actions. It is important that they become fully aware of this change in status, and that they fully realize that they will be held responsible in their own homes as well as in the adult world. But because the

249

older adolescent looks so mature, adults frequently find it hard to remain patient and to accept their mistakes. They forget that these young people are not yet adults. Their sprawling awkwardness, their morose and defiant moods, and their daydreaming often leave parents and teachers bewildered and baffled.

The adolescent's desire to be treated as an adult may serve as a cue for wise parents and teachers—although it is a cue that is frequently hard for them to follow, for today the high-school boy or girl may act like an adult and tomorrow return to childish, irresponsible behavior. Growth in the adolescent, as in the child, does not proceed equally at all times and in all areas. Even the older adolescent is often emotionally immature—"a full-grown body entrusted to an inexperienced mind." All this helps make adolescence a difficult period for both young people and adults. It is a challenge to adults not only to help adolescents but to *permit* them to achieve maturity and become part of an adult world which hopefully is ready to receive them.

## Study of an adolescent

### THE BACKGROUND OF FANTASY IS REVEALING
*A Parent's Own Relationship May Be Involved*

When it is possible to obtain a detailed picture of how a boy or girl has grown and developed and lived, clues are generally uncovered that help in understanding disturbing behavior. But sometimes even after a thorough study of the background, the behavior remains puzzling. The clues to its origin are not always in the son or daughter, but may be instead in parents' unconscious expression of their own problems and resultant tensions in the relationships within the home.

Such a concept may not be easy to understand, and such a situation is certainly not easy to resolve. If teachers sense problems which may not be within their experiences and skills to handle, they are wise to seek other professional help. Sometimes the involvement requires out-of-school professional consultation. In some instances, the school staff may include a psychologist whose training and clinical insight and experience are such that delicate situations can be skillfully eased.

Karl was sixteen when he entered high school. He had not been an apt pupil and had spent a great deal of time daydreaming when he should have been listening or studying. More than once he had been retained a second term in the same grade because he had not acquired the necessary facts and skills. He had seemed immature in many ways, including his physical size. Prominent also in the picture of his total development was his seeming inability to establish social relationships with his classmates. His teachers always hoped that the following year might find him more responsive and better able to cope both academically and socially.

250

In high school, his homeroom teacher, Mr. Spahn, found him a quiet boy whose vaguely acquiescent manner could have meant understanding of explanations and class discussions, but instead suggested a lack of understanding. Or was it a lack of interest? Karl disturbed his teacher, not as a disciplinary problem but because he did not feel he was reaching the boy. Checking with some of his teachers, Mr. Spahn found that Karl was making only fair progress, and sometimes his work was just on the borderline of failure. The math class was really a review of fundamentals. Karl was slow but careful, and although he often needed an explanation repeated, once he understood the method to be followed he usually managed to arrive at correct answers. In social studies he was hampered by slow reading, and the material did not always seem meaningful to him. The shop teacher was the only one who reported that Karl showed real interest in class procedures; he was careful and skillful in his work and unusually capable, as his completed projects showed. And that was the only teacher who did not comment on constant daydreaming.

Mr. Spahn was bothered by Karl's seeming to accept hopelessly his lack of success, whether in the classroom or on the athletic field. He felt that somehow Karl had to be helped to reach the satisfaction of real experiences and successful achievement in place of the vicarious contentment he evidently was finding in fantasy. The teacher did not think much progress would be made otherwise. Karl was not among the top students, but test results suggested that actually he did have the ability to do much better than he had thus far demonstrated.

One afternoon after school, Mr. Spahn made an opportunity to talk with the boy. Not very talkative at first, Karl became more responsive as obvious interest in him made itself felt. While he made no complaints, his teacher judged from one or two comments that his father was rather strict and demanding. An older brother, a day student at a local college, was not close to Karl, and there seemed some intimation that he was the favorite of their father. Karl spoke somewhat haltingly, but seemed to enjoy having a sympathetic listener.

"He seems so unsure of himself," thought the teacher. "He's so apologetic for everything." He sensed anxiety in the boy, and there was also a hint of hidden hostility. Karl's comments and his manner in speaking of family incidents gave his teacher the definite impression that further investigation would be helpful. Mr. Spahn spoke to the psychologist on the school staff, and although information was actually scanty, he aroused interested concern. The school psychologist readily agreed to talk with Karl, and an appointment was scheduled.

After a few preliminaries, Dr. Morton asked the boy how he enjoyed school subjects and activities, and inquired how he spent his time after school and during weekends. A series of facts emerged, with Karl increasingly offering spontaneous comments.

Finally the psychologist said, "Suppose we make another appointment. I think I can help with some ideas about your schoolwork."

The boy was pleased at the suggestion, and said, "My father would

251

like that, I think. He wants me to do better in school. He says he has plans for me." With a shy smile he left the office.

It was clear to Dr. Morton that while help for Karl in school was desirable, help at home might also be desirable. Talking things over with the family definitely seemed indicated. He recognized he had only the boy's impressions of the home situation.

The family lived on the outskirts of town in an area of small homes and truck farms. They were close enough so that the father, a widower, worked in town and the older brother attended the local college. The house had a wide lawn surrounded by a hedge. There was a vegetable garden, some chickens, and a few fruit trees. Karl thought his father was very proud of the house. He insisted on everything always being carefully tended. And it was Karl who was responsible for it all. He worked in the garden so that it always looked freshly weeded whenever his father inspected it. He fed the chickens and kept their quarters clean. He swept the porch or hosed it down daily. He also cut the grass in the summer, raked the leaves in the fall, and cleared the snow from the walk in the winter.

Sometimes he counted the number of chores he did and compared his jobs with those of his brother John. John trimmed the hedge occasionally, and painted the porch and steps each spring. But nothing else was expected of him.

When Karl pointed out that he was doing most of the work, his father rebuked him, reminding him that his brother had more important things to do. He was the one who would some day make them all proud; he was the student. Some day he would be a minister with his own church, and be recognized as a learned and important man. Now he needed all the time he could get to study.

"And you, Karl, you should study more. How did you do in school today? Bring your books and let me see," was the inevitable end of a conversation with his father.

That was why Karl had stopped protesting about the work he did. His father was never pleased with his grades and looked at every paper critically, asking why didn't he work for the same record John had when he was in high school. Karl, inwardly despairing and rebellious, would promise to try harder. The sessions usually ended with his father angry and Karl almost in tears. He became convinced that he was slow and stupid—he heard it so frequently. He wondered why he should even bother to try since his father was never pleased anyway.

"What can I do with you!" his father often exclaimed. "I told you, to use only your hands is not enough. You must study or you'll never amount to anything. What do you want to do, work with your hands all your life?"

Once Karl had ventured, "Dad, you work with your hands, don't you?" He quickly found it would be better not to mention that again; his father's temper seemed worse than usual. Karl gathered something about being respected in the community, being one's own boss, not depending on the whims of employers, and earning enough money to buy shoes for boys who always wore them out too fast. Part of the outburst was in Ger-

252

man, his native language, which his father often used when his temper was aroused. Karl understood only part of what he said, but the implication was clear enough. The boy was upset and decided it was easier to do just as his father demanded, than to raise any question about doing more than his share of the work. It was better just to listen quietly when his father was angry, than to try to say anything in his own defense.

He soon developed a way of letting his thoughts wander away from the tempest. He took *himself* away, even though physically he stood dejectedly before his father. He would let his imagination run. He would think of himself as being so strong that he could whip anybody, strike out at anyone who failed to follow his orders exactly. Or he would fantasy a world in which there were only cheery, pleasant people; among them there were never any older men. Everyone in his dream world was casual and easygoing, and no one cared about every weed being picked, every porch corner being free of dust. Everyone just kept busy at whatever he liked to do. His dream world was pleasant and comforting.

When daydreaming, fantasying, is indulged in often enough, it can become an habitual pattern of response. It can be a way of avoiding—at least in thought—something difficult or discomforting. Thus as Karl became more and more accustomed to using the defense of figuratively removing himself from his father's criticism and scolding, he soon found that he could evade just as easily teasing by the boys at school, or being reprimanded by his teachers. And, of course, the same escape was used when there were class recitations or explanations which he did not understand readily and which he felt were beyond him. A teacher might say, "Karl, you're not listening!" and he would obediently turn toward her. But he would not be listening even when he seemed to be. He would still be in his dream world, so satisfying and consoling.

The school psychologist wanted to meet Karl's father, and he was invited to come to the school. At the appointed time, Mr. Brandt came promptly. He asked bluntly, "What is it you want to talk about? That Karl is not doing good schoolwork? Is he in trouble?" He was plainly relieved to be assured there was no "trouble," but that Karl was capable of doing better schoolwork than his record showed, and the school was interested in helping him. Did the father know of anything that bothered the boy? Was he worrying about anything?

The father became greatly excited. "He must be punished!" he said firmly. "What has he to worry about?" With rising anger, he said that not a week went by that he did not talk with Karl about his studies, and tell him he must do better.

"I send him to his room to study, and when I go in later he is not studying. He is at his desk, making things with wood, with plastic—always working with his hands instead of with his brains. I have two boys. I always treat them just alike. But John listens to me. He studied when he was in high school, and now he goes to college. He will be a minister. Why Karl doesn't study I don't know. I want him to be an architect, but how can he go to college if he does poor work now? That my son should be like this!" His voice trembled in his agitation, but he went on. "He will be pun-

253

ished! He will not be allowed to make things." Half grudgingly he added, "His things are good—a bookshelf, a birdhouse, whatever—but he must study. What more can I do!" He shook his head helplessly.

He was assured that what he must *not* do was punish the boy. Dr. Morton continued, "Karl tells me he helps a great deal around the house. That's fine, but perhaps you expect too much of him? He didn't complain," he added quickly, "but he feels you are dissatisfied with him, and that troubles him. He wants to please you but feels he can't."

They talked then about the disappointment of parents when a child does not live up to expectations. "But," it was suggested, "sometimes when aims and goals have taken no account of individual abilities and interests, they need rethinking." Mr. Brandt nodded thoughtfully, but said nothing.

It is not an easy thing to convince a parent that his tactics are not helping but actually may be hindering a child from making progress. It is not easy for parents to relinquish plans which they have cherished with the best of intentions. As they talked, however, Karl's father did not deny that his two boys differed in interests and in aptitudes. He agreed it was not reasonable to hold one boy to the habits and achievement of the other. And he recognized that Karl was not mature enough to have any definite idea of what he would like to do when he finished school.

"Karl realizes that you are displeased with him. That makes him feel unhappy. It disturbs him, so that it isn't surprising that he finds it hard to concentrate on his studies. And he isn't finding his schoolwork easy, even without worrying," added Dr. Morton.

There was a long pause while the father was thinking over what had been discussed. His anger had passed. He said softly, "I will tell you something I am remembering."

His own father had been a professional man and was eager for him to follow the same career. But he had not been sufficiently interested in academic studies and had decided not to finish college. His father had never been reconciled to this decision, and often the son had regretted it in later years. He had long since felt remorse for having disappointed his father, and had felt he had never been forgiven.

"I think," he went on after another pause, "that all this time I have felt guilty for having disappointed my father. But I never told him so. Maybe I thought if my sons did not study, they would be as sorry as I have been. I did not think my father was right in what he wanted me to do, but maybe I was not right—I don't know."

"Not everyone finds satisfaction in the same kind of work," noted Dr. Morton. "And you say you have liked your work, enjoyed working out the problems you've met in it. It is your feeling about your father's reaction that has disturbed you and been so distressing. If you can help Karl begin to accept that you understand his interests, that you are not displeased with him, that you just want him to do his best in whatever he attempts, it will make a great difference in the way he feels. And feelings are important. They affect whatever we do, sometimes helpfully, but sometimes they get in the way and results are not good. Help Karl to feel better, and

254

you will find his performance in school will be better, I'm sure.

"And keep in mind, too, that Karl can have as satisfying a life *for him,* with his particular abilities and talents, as your older boy in his chosen work. Relax about Karl's future—see how he develops in the next couple of years—give him a chance to mature, and to try to find his own way. Parents should advise, but not always decide, I feel." Mr. Brandt nodded his agreement.

Changes in individuals do not come overnight. But by the end of that school year Karl was a much more relaxed and a much more contented adolescent. He was doing a more creditable job at school, he was finding greater acceptance and enjoyment with his classmates, and the dreaming-in-class habit was definitely lessened. And he had changed within himself. No one likes to feel unsuccessful, no one enjoys criticism and scolding, no one can accept easily the feeling of rejection. It was not strange that he sought to escape these discomforts—which, long continued, can be very traumatic—by building up soothing fantasies wherein he was capable and accepted and secure. He had felt inept and stupid; he had been discouraged and disheartened. Now he was able to sense his father's changed attitude and was encouraged by it to really make a greater effort, rather than continue the easier way of fantasying.

The search for reasons to explain Karl's daydreaming and difficult school adjustment led away from the boy himself. Without his teacher's recognition of an existing need, Karl might not have changed. Without his father's changed attitude and more affectionate relationship, Karl very likely would have continued uncertain and ill at ease, lacking in self-assurance.

part 5

# HOME, SCHOOL, COMMUNITY WORK TOGETHER

Although parents have the first responsibility for providing an environment suitable for the healthy development of their children, we cannot leave this to the parents alone. Many fathers and mothers carry their responsibility well. Others, however, are inadequate, and their children must not be deprived of their right to grow and develop as fully as possible. It is the responsibility of the community to see that no child shall be denied an opportunity for healthy growth.

Children are a part of their community. They cannot be isolated from the life around them. It is all the adults of the community, not only individual parents, who set the standards that influence children's developing concepts concerning education, religion, ethical values, and citizenship. Children will learn the prejudices of the adults in their communities, will copy the example that is generally set before them—even when parents would wish it otherwise. If there are slums, inadequate schools, low salaries for teachers, lack of support for law enforcement, or indifference to religion and moral order—it is *all* the children who suffer, not just those whose lives are intimately touched by the specific problems.

Therefore it is the task of the citizens in a community to see that no child goes hungry or lacks adequate shelter or clothing; that areas are set aside for wholesome, health-producing play activities; 257

that there is a seat for every child in a school where attention will be given to individual capacities; and that treatment centers are available not only for those who are physically ill or handicapped but also for those who have emotional problems that are too big to be solved by the family group. It is also the responsibility of the citizens in a community to see that no children are discriminated against because they are different from some of the other children—that the atmosphere in the community is such that there is compassion and concern for all children.

# chapter 16

# When Things Go Wrong

THE PROBLEMS OF GROWING UP  Growing up is especially difficult for some children. There are troubled youngsters in many homes and in all of our schools. Sometimes this is because of failure in the home, the school, or the community to provide adequately for the needs of these children. Many children face neglect or rejection by parents who are uninterested in them or too busy to give them adequate attention. Others experience the insecurity of a home broken by desertion or divorce. Still others feel pressured and discouraged because of the unrealistic demands imposed on them by their parents or their school. In some cases, factors beyond parents' control touch the lives of children, producing anxiety or problems that are difficult for the children to meet—the tensions of today's world; racial or religious prejudice; poverty. Some children, too, have physical or mental handicaps which make it necessary for them to have special understanding and help if they are to meet life successfully, making the most of whatever capabilities they may have.

Children have few inner resources and little practical experience to call on in meeting situations that are too difficult or pressures that are too great. Often they are not even conscious of the reasons for their hurt or distress. When children find themselves frustrated by a situation they cannot meet, they can move in either of two directions: They can pull back and withdraw into their own personal world, or they can hit back. In the latter case the child's aggressive behavior often is met with punishment or counteraggression on the part of adults. This, of course, tends to complicate the problem further.

There are many manifestations of these two basic ways of meeting problems that seem too difficult for solution, and children do not consciously choose one type of behavior over another. Various factors within themselves and their environment determine which pattern of response they will follow. For example, Mark's insecurity drove him into meeting his problem by running away. Johnny, whose parents demanded a standard of perfection he could not meet, protected himself by being obedient and never asserting himself. Leslie, who never felt really loved, rebuffed others because she expected that they would rebuff her; wanting friendship, she nevertheless pushed it aside when it was offered for fear that she would be hurt again. Karl, with his feelings of never being able to match his brother's achievements, withdrew into daydreams.

At some point in their lives, all children find growing up difficult, even if they come from homes in which they find loving support. But if the satisfactions of growing up outweigh the problems it entails, most children are able to cope with their disturbed feelings and to meet most situations adequately—though not always without a struggle within themselves. Children who have the support of their parents and other adults—who are encouraged and guided as they grow up—usually show the greatest resilience. When problems temporarily become too great for these children, they often can be helped to meet difficulties in a realistic and practical way by perceptive parents or teachers and sometimes even by other children.

THE EMOTIONALLY DISTURBED CHILD  Some children's defeats have so outbalanced their successes that they will need professional help in order to work through the conflicts between their own deep needs and the demands of situations they have been unable to meet. Russell and Mark were two such boys, both of whom might have become seriously delinquent if they had not received professional help in time.

In many communities such help can be obtained through mental health or child guidance clinics, through a physician specializing in psychiatry, or through a practicing clinical psychologist. School systems that have a psychologist or counselor should be able to guide parents to appropriate sources of help. Parents also can write to their state's Department of Mental Health for information about the resources available in or near their communities. Usually it is necessary to wait for an appointment, although many clinics have provisions for meeting real emergencies.

Emotionally troubled children can be found in all our schools—children whose problems, though deep, do not require hospitalization or placement in an institution. In some schools, special classes have been planned in which children with severe emotional disturbances, who are too disruptive to a normal classroom, can be taught in a smaller group with a specially trained teacher. When this is possible, their personal needs can be met more fully. But most emotionally disturbed children, even if they are under treatment, will attend regular classes. Many will remain the problem of the classroom teacher.

Providing an atmosphere of emotional stability within the classroom is important. Steadiness in classroom direction helps the withdrawing child to know what can be expected, and it shows the rebellious youngster that the teacher is in control and that certain standards of behavior are expected in the classroom. The disorganized teacher cannot successfully teach the confused child.

Every child's problem is individual. To give effective help, even the expert needs to know a great deal about the particular child: the background, the parents, the past experiences, the temperament, the needs and wishes, and the inner resources for dealing with pressure and strain. It is possible, nevertheless, to group some of the problems together and to find

260

common factors among them that are helpful as a guide in developing a program for the individual child.

## THE POORLY SOCIALIZED CHILD

One type of emotional problem is typified by rebellious children who dislike everybody, usually because they feel that people dislike them and are mean to them. They are poorly socialized children. Their way of trying to meet their needs is the clumsy, inadequate one of fighting the world indiscriminately. They are hostile and defiant. They have no sense of fair play. When they dare to, they attack or bully other children. Yet they feel they are being picked on, and indeed they are not well accepted by other children or by any gang. Usually they are loners. They are so difficult to manage and cause so much disturbance that they are sometimes called *undomesticated children.* They achieve little at home or school and, as a result, develop a discouraging self-image. They think they are no good and may say so.

Typically, such children lack sufficient mothering in their early years. Often they have had an immature or inadequate mother who considered her own needs and feelings rather than the developmental needs of her child. Typically, the child is unwanted at birth. The trouble is intensified when the child's activity becomes annoying to the mother, and over a period of time continual conflict develops as the pattern between the two. Sometimes the father becomes involved in the battle of wills, but often he is a rather inadequate parent who fails to back the mother in her attempts to control the child and thus gives the child tacit permission to continue his rebellion.

We also find rebellious, poorly socialized children among youngsters who have been raised in institutions that provide no stable child-parent relationships and among youngsters who have had frequent foster-care placements. Children with such backgrounds have lacked sufficient roots in any home. Adults have never seemed dependable to them, and they often give little return for kindness.

Rebellious, antisocial children may be helped to some degree by their classroom teacher or by someone else in the school system or community who can win their confidence. Great patience is needed, however, for the adult must not only try to win the child's trust but stand ready at the same time to disapprove behavior when it becomes objectionable. The prognosis for such a child will improve if the parents can be helped to gain understanding before the antagonism between them and the child becomes irreversible. Sometimes, however, it is necessary to remove the child from home before treatment can be successful.

In dealing with the rebellious child, kindness and understanding must be backed by firm control. Sometimes a female teacher will need the help of a male principal or some male teacher in critical situations, as when a physically strong troublesome boy becomes so difficult that he has to be removed from the classroom. When an unsocialized child has been in serious trouble with the juvenile court, the school should be informed, and the principal and the teachers should be aware of what kind of difficulty might be expected and how they should handle it if it does arise.

261

CHILDREN WHO DISLIKE OR MISTRUST ADULTS Children who dislike or mistrust adults may be well socialized as far as other children are concerned. As they get older they may become a member of a semidelinquent or delinquent gang. The youngsters who fall into this behavior pattern are almost always boys, rarely girls except when a girl is a hanger-on to a boys' gang. Where separate girl gangs do exist, they usually are more transient, more personal, and less likely to draw attention than are boy gangs.

The boy who dislikes or mistrusts adults is part of a rebellious group and he is loyal to his group, following the pattern that the gang builds up in defiance of the adult world. He will steal rather than chance disapproval from the gang. With his gang, he will participate in acts of vandalism, refuse to cooperate in the classroom, and generally tend to disturb and disrupt any situation he encounters. Emotional dissatisfactions contribute to a boy's desire for membership in such a gang. He is seeking the satisfactions that life has otherwise denied him by ganging up with other boys against adults.

In the classroom the influence of these boys may be a problem. Many of them are muscular, active, vigorous, and adventurous youngsters who, disliking school, find an outlet for their energy by disrupting their classes or playing truant. Frequently they fail to develop adequate reading skills, and this in turn contributes to school maladjustment. Sometimes the school itself is at fault in neglecting to provide a program geared to the interests, needs, and capabilities of this group. Few schools, for example, capitalize sufficiently on the interest that these youngsters may show in manual skills and shopwork. More can be done, too, by physical education departments in developing special programs for these boys. Obviously the school must set limits on the behavior of rebellious and trouble-prone youngsters, but it also has a responsibility to provide activities that will give them the experience of success and enable them to work off their energy.

Whatever teachers do in trying to meet the situation, they will have little chance of success unless they can reach the individual child through his group or separate him from it completely. The latter course usually is difficult to accomplish. A teacher or community leader who can capture the interest of the *group,* particularly that of the boys' leader, is often able to help redirect their energy and need for activity into more desirable channels.

Children who are hostile to adults but have close friends among other children are rarely as emotionally disturbed as the child who has been unable to establish any relationship with anyone. But although they are more normal in personality, they can get into serious difficulties and cause serious disturbances not only in the classroom but also in the community. It is from this group of boys who grow up with an increasing lack of interest in school that many of our dropouts come.

The child who dislikes adult authority often has a father who lacks any real interest in him and has therefore neglected him. Often he has experienced inconsistent discipline, failure of direction, and insufficient

262

warmth and affection from his father. An alcoholic father is not uncommon. Typically the mother has been adequately accepting of the youngster, at least in his early years, so that he has developed a capacity to like some people, but he directs this capacity toward other children rather than toward adults.

These children come most frequently from underprivileged areas, but they may be found in any neighborhood. Sometimes the parents of this kind of youngster can be awakened to see what is happening to their child. If they become aware that their child's activities with his group are bad for him and indicate a public failure on their part, they sometimes can be led to assume more responsibility for their child.

THE OVERANXIOUS CHILD  The overanxious children who suffer from severe inner conflict are the youngsters whom we often overlook in the classroom. Such children are insecure, too inhibited, too dutiful, and too sensitive to criticism and failure. They are apprehensive and unsure of themselves. As a rule they are overly concerned about examinations and grades. Such children maintain contact with reality and try to function effectively, but they are frightened, worried, and under strain. They are inclined to be timid, often more so with adults than with children. They sometimes literally worry themselves sick, undergoing spells of vomiting, stomachaches, and headaches. The child's deep concerns, if not recognized, may lead to neurotic illness such as incapacitating anxiety attacks.

Overanxious children create no problem of classroom control. They usually work hard in school and live up to their intellectual ability, sometimes even achieving beyond the level that might be expected. They often need help, however, in finding their places in the classroom group. It is unwise to force overanxious children into classroom situations that appear to distress them. Speed tests and competitive situations are undesirable. The teacher should make an effort to encourage them and help them relax. Because these children will need a great deal of help in learning that they are liked for themselves, the choice of a teacher for them is especially important. A warm, supporting teacher can help, but a rigid, scolding, or perfectionistic teacher can harm them and cause them to withdraw more deeply into themselves.

Overanxious children usually have parents who do not give much warmth and approval but hold very high standards for performance. These parents put so much value on achievement and grades that the children come to feel that they won't be accepted unless they are able to live up to their expectations. Such parents often are restrictive in what they permit the child to do, so that their child becomes dependent rather than self-reliant.

Many of these parents are interested in their child but fail to understand the level of anxiety. Sometimes it is possible to help them see that their child is too worried and anxious about schoolwork, that they must give more encouragement and praise. How much the child can be helped will depend largely on how the parents respond to their new insights.

263

Sometimes both the child and the parents will need professional help.

Overanxious children, particularly girls, may develop anxiety about attending school, although these children are willing and able to leave home in order to play with friends or go to other places. This is known as a *school phobia*. It usually begins with repetitive complaints of illness on the part of the child when it is time to go to school, or the child may panic when it is time to leave the house. If the child is persuaded to go to school, vomiting, stomachaches, or headaches may occur during the school day. The child may become so upset that remaining in the classroom is not possible. Frequently the mother of such a child is overprotective and fears that the school will not be sufficiently protective of the child, or she may have a deep inner need to keep the child dependent upon her. In her own anxiety she may convey these feelings to the child.

Some children develop a school phobia based on some very real school experience, or on their anxiety or fear they will not perform as well as they think they are expected to do. Whatever the cause, the phobia should be taken seriously, but the child should be returned to school as quickly as possible. In order to make this possible the child may need a refuge in school—a place to go and permission to go there—if the anxiety becomes too great. This should be with some adult in whom the child has confidence such as the office of the school nurse, a counselor, or the principal. Support for the child's anxiety will need to be given by teachers, counselor, principal, and other school personnel, so that if panic occurs the child always has someone to turn to for support. Both mother and child may need help in order that the child may overcome this crippling fear of going to school.

THE WITHDRAWN CHILD  Withdrawn children who pull away from reality into a world of daydreams are much more serious problems than the overanxious children. They cannot be reached easily by their teachers or by anyone else. But even though it is difficult to establish personal contact with such a child, the teacher must make a special effort to do so, showing warmth and friendliness even if the child does not respond. Sometimes a teacher takes this lack of response to mean a rebuff of kindness, but often the child is actually unable to respond. The problem is sometimes complicated because these youngsters do not relate well to the activities of the classroom. They may not keep their places in books. They may, like Karl, go on daydreaming when directions are given. Their schoolwork is rarely up to the level of their intelligence.

A friendly classroom atmosphere is likely to benefit withdrawn children if they are not lost in the shuffle. Even with great effort on their teachers' part, however, they seldom relate easily to others. They may attract the disapproval of other children because they do not fit into the classroom program. They are often considered odd. They do not rebel or refuse to take part. Rather, they just are not there.

Constant encouragement will be necessary in trying to hold the attention of such youngsters in the classroom, to bring them closer to reality,

and to help them find satisfaction outside their daydreams. Harshness and scolding will only work further harm. A teacher is usually able to help a little, but she must be prepared for the fact that she will have to make a large effort for a limited return.

A great deal still needs to be known about the withdrawn child. They are so hard to reach that it is difficult to understand the underlying causes of their problems. There are indications, however, that withdrawal from reality is more frequent with children of parents who have exerted strict control over their children without accepting them as persons in their own right. Usually the parents have not rejected them but rather have been unwilling or perhaps unable to let them develop individual personalities. Frequently they have made all the plans, laid down all the rules, directed every movement. They may regard their child as a possession or extension of themselves, thus making it difficult for the child to develop his or her own individuality. If professional counsel is sought, parents may be helped to modify their behavior toward the child. Both parents and such children may need long-term professional help.

THE APATHETIC CHILD  Some children do poorly in school because they are discouraged with themselves and refuse to try. Rather than withdrawing into daydreams, they tend to be apathetic. These children are found most frequently in deprived areas, in city slums and poverty-stricken rural communities—wherever the blight of extreme poverty and neglect is found. They come from homes where there is little money, poor clothing, inadequate food. Many are in poor physical condition, lacking muscular tone, and often are fatigued. Frequently their parents, too, are ill and, because of illness or general inadequacy, unable to give the encouragement and emotional support which children need. The children seem to have such a poor self-image that they no longer try—they just give up.

Such children are a responsibility of the community that has permitted neglected areas to continue to exist. Before these children can become alert and motivated to do schoolwork, they need attention to their physical needs, correction of their physical defects, clothing to encourage greater self-respect, and then, gradually, experiences in identifying themselves as individuals. Their apathy toward school can only be changed as we help them develop self-respect and a self-image which enables them to believe that the effort of learning is worthwhile—because they *can* learn.

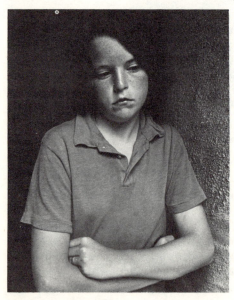

THE OVERACTIVE CHILD  Overactive children constitute a difficult problem in many of our classrooms. They disturb the rest of the class and often are difficult to manage. They have difficulty in conforming to classroom routine, in paying attention, and in sitting still. The majority of overactive children are boys.

266

Among these overactive children are those who have been called *unorganized children* because they have never developed an organized pattern of behavior. Such children usually have grown up in a haphazard fashion without adequate parental guidance. The expectation that they should conform to an acceptable pattern of behavior has not been made clear or has not been enforced. These children will need patient but firm direction as they are helped gradually to observe the behavioral limits that are essential in living and working with others.

With some other children overactivity has an organic basis. These children have suffered some damage to the brain. They have a quality of behavior which has appropriately been called *organic* "drivenness." Such children are constantly active, very distractible and impulsive. Their overactivity reaches such a high level that it has a different quality from the level of activity of a child without some brain damage.

There are other and even more numerous cases in which symptoms occur, but organic damage to the brain cannot be proven. This is called the *hyperkinetic reaction.* In many of these cases the child behaves as if there were some brain damage. In such cases the term *brain dysfunction* is used to suggest that the brain is not working quite as it normally would.

Obviously the diagnosis of brain damage or brain dysfunction is a medical one and cannot be made by observing behavior in the classroom. The classroom teacher *can,* however, recognize overactivity, distractibility, and a short attention span as possible signs of an organic problem. Indeed, a teacher may be the first person to realize the seriousness of the problem. In a classroom, the child's behavior can be seen in relation to that of other children. If this behavior presents a serious management problem and the child seems unable to respond to attempts to help control the overactivity, the teacher should discuss the situation with the principal and with the school psychologist, if one is on the staff. After further study it may be decided to contact the parents and suggest that the child be referred to a physician or a child-guidance clinic. Teachers are not qualified to suggest what the medical diagnosis might be, and it is advisable for them to stay out of this area. However, it is appropriate for them to ask for further medical or psychological study of a child when there is an unexplained problem in behavior.

At present, the child with minimal brain damage or brain dysfunction will often be taught in the regular classroom. Only in severe cases will a special class for severely handicapped children be indicated. Such a child does not belong in a class for the mentally retarded, for mental ability is usually normal and may even be superior. Sometimes, however, a special class is the only compromise available, because the child may have too much trouble in keeping up with normal children in school or is too disturbing in the classroom.

Scolding hyperkinetic children, telling them to pay attention and keep still, will not be effective. Their hyperactivity will crop out in one way or another. These children need a great deal of patience, tolerance, and steadiness, with as few distractions as possible. They should never be

267

placed in the room of a tense, nervous, or insecure teacher, for this will generate too much friction.

THE TEACHER'S ROLE   With both hyperkinetic children and with those children who are overactive because they have not developed a structured pattern of behavior, the teacher should carefully watch for signs of restlessness building up. The youngster may then be sent on an errand or given some other active job before the growing tension spills over into uncontrollable behavior. Perhaps such a child can be asked to put books away on the library shelves, clean out the fish bowl, take care of the plants, or help the custodian rake the leaves or wash the chalkboards. A wise teacher who sees tension mounting sometimes may even interrupt the class and have all the children do some exercises, or the classroom schedule may be arranged to provide more frequent breaks for physical activity and a change of pace, in order to keep one child's restlessness from being too upsetting to the entire group.

Having an overactive child in the classroom makes a difficult situation. The other children cannot understand the reason for the restlessness of the unorganized child, nor can they "see" the physical handicap of the organically damaged youngster. They are not likely to feel the same protective sympathy, therefore, that they do for an outwardly handicapped child, such as a youngster with a brace or one who is blind or deaf. A first step is for the teacher to understand the problem and the limits of what can be done for the child in the classroom. This means that the teacher should have continuing access either to the school psychologist or to some other professional person who understands the child's condition and acts as a guide as the youngster is worked with in the classroom. Teamwork involving the family, their physician, a psychologist, and the teacher is essential if the child is to be helped.

Teachers will find it easier to tolerate the problems that these children bring into the classroom if they can accept the youngsters without feeling personally threatened by their behavior. These are children in trouble, and their behavior is not always under their conscious control. Teachers should do what they can for these children, but remember that failure to help is not necessarily a personal failure.

CHILDREN WITH LEARNING DISABILITIES   In addition to their overactivity, many children with minimal brain damage or brain dysfunction must be considered, for teaching purposes, to have specific learning disabilities. Such children frequently have great difficulty in copying or even matching simple geometric forms, in spite of the fact that they usually have normal intelligence. This presents special difficulties in helping these children learn to read and write. If such a child is to function adequately in the regular classroom, the help of a special teacher trained in understanding learning disabilities will be needed. For such a child, like Ronnie, will not be able to master the basic skills of reading, writing, and often arithmetic by the teaching methods used with other children.

There also is another group of children, again mostly boys, who must have special help and understanding if they are to be able to learn to read adequately enough to keep up with their schoolwork. These are normal children in all respects other than that they have a specific disability in learning to recognize the symbols of reading. The cause of this difficulty is not agreed upon and is still being explored. In some cases, it may be inherited. It may be due to brain dysfunction, perhaps to some type of developmental lag. The answers are not yet in.

Some school-age children have mild or severe problems in this area. The problems involve such difficulties as confusing "b" and "d" beyond the age at which such letters are normally confused; the reversal of words such as "saw" and "was" or "no" and "on"; the skipping of words, or whole lines, or the adding of a letter to the beginning of a word. Some of these children may have difficulty in pronouncing words correctly. Spelling is very difficult for such children, and putting thoughts down on paper becomes a problem. Arithmetic also may be involved as some children have difficulty in recognizing the symbols used or in reversing them. Such problems are a genuine handicap in a culture in which so much learning depends upon the ability to read well and recognize symbols accurately. These children also will need special methods which combine visual, auditory, and kinesthetic experiences if they are to be able to gradually master their basic skills, particularly in reading. They must usually be taught individually or in small groups.

Many of these children naturally become discouraged when they see other children learning to read at a much faster pace and with greater ease. It is important to keep up motivation by using interesting materials and by offering encouragement and reward for success and even small signs of progress. It also is important to find other areas in which these very normal children can keep up with their peers, and to encourage any special strengths which they may have in other areas such as art, music, or athletics. Such children need to know that their inability to learn to read is not of their own making, that they are as intelligent as the other children, but that they have a problem with which they will need help. Methods of covering subject matter other than reading should be available for these children such as visual aids and tape recordings of chapters to be assigned. They can work successfully on projects which do not require reading, and should be given many opportunities to work with the other children in the classroom. Their parents should be helped to understand the problem so that they will not pressure their children to do better in reading or blame them for falling behind the other children. Such pressure can create great anxiety in youngsters with this handicap.

THE PHYSICALLY HANDICAPPED CHILD Many children are handicapped physically rather than emotionally, although emotional disturbance may become part of the picture if the physically handicapped child does not have adequate support and guidance. The epileptic child, the child with cerebral palsy, the child who has been crippled, the child

Growing up is especially difficult for some children. Perceptive parents and teachers and even other children can often help these children meet life successfully. Many mentally handicapped children (top left, bottom left) can benefit from an educational program planned to meet their particular capabilities. A rather different approach is necessary when emotional difficulties are of key concern as with the withdrawn child (top middle) or the autistic child (bottom middle). Physically handicapped children (bottom right) also need specific help to meet the problems of their handicaps. The family must initially respond to the individual demands related to each of these problems, but both school and community must join with the family in answering the special needs of these children.

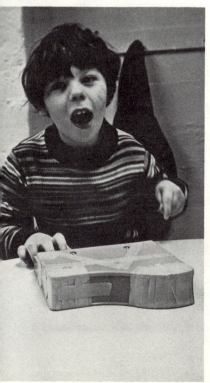

who is blind or deaf, the child who has diabetes or a heart condition—these are children who need special plans to help them meet the problems of their handicaps. Although most of these children are able to use their minds as competently as boys and girls without physical handicaps, there will be situations that they cannot meet unless special provisions are made. Parents and teachers must help physically handicapped children to accept their particular disabilities realistically and to meet the frustrations that they inevitably will face because of them.

We can help children with physical handicaps develop healthy personalities by accepting them as normal in other respects and by encouraging them to participate as much as possible in the activities of normal children. Encouraging them to be as independent as possible and to cultivate their own special interests and abilities helps them to develop a positive self-image and, as they grow up, to acquire an increasing degree of self-reliance.

THE MENTALLY HANDICAPPED CHILD   Another large group of children who will need special help are the mentally retarded. Three percent of our schoolchildren will test as mentally retarded, as approximately 120,000 mentally retarded children are born each year. Retarded children may be found in families of every level of intelligence. Fortunately, an increasing number of people no longer consider a retarded child a family disgrace. As scientific knowledge replaces superstition concerning the causes of mental deficiency, the stigma of mental retardation is diminishing.

Reseach has already uncovered many causes for this conditon. Heredity is now recognized as less important than was formerly assumed, while disease and injury of the brain are seen as more important. Even when heredity is definitely established as its cause, the mental defect is sometimes preventable with proper medical care. This is true, for example, in cases of phenylketonuria, or PKU—a metabolic disorder due to a hereditary enzyme deficiency which causes progressive mental retardation. When this defect is recognized in infancy by a chemical test of blood or urine, mental deficiency can be prevented by feeding the child a special diet during the first years of life while the brain is developing. This is only one of several hopeful breakthroughs in preventing mental retardation. The future is bright with hope for continuing progress in this field.

There are many degrees of mental retardation, and retarded children cannot be grouped together as if all their problems were similar. There are individual differences and needs among these boys and girls just as there are among children who do not have this handicap.

The *profoundly retarded* are so severely handicapped that they must have constant, kindly, nursing care throughout their lives. Only one of every thirty retarded children is in this group. Many of them will, of necessity, be cared for in institutions or special foster homes.

The *severely retarded* children, with I.Q.'s approximately between 25 and 39 also will need permanent care either in their own homes or in fos-

272

ter homes or foster group homes. They can never become capable of caring for themselves in an independent fashion. However, many of these severely retarded children can be helped to develop beyond previous expectations, if preschool and day-care experiences are available to them, with trained personnel who know how to encourage their development. Many of them can learn simple bodily care. Some, if a sheltered workshop is available when they become adults, may be able to do simple work in a protected situation. Although none of these children will be able to attend school in the usual sense, they do respond to a group situation and enjoy being with other children. These are children with the needs of children. These needs should be met through the public school system—so that education at their level can be provided for all of these children.

The *moderately retarded* or *trainable* children, as we call them when we think in terms of their educational needs, represent about four out of every thirty retarded boys and girls. These children will need constant supervision and care, but they are able to attend school in a special class, usually called a "trainable class." Presently, many of these classes are organized and supported by parents, but there is an increasing tendency for public schools to assume responsibility for such classes.

Trainable children can learn acceptable social behavior, useful work habits, and care of their personal needs. Most of them will not be able to learn to read and write, although some can learn to read simple signs, write their names, or master simple counting. They enjoy uncomplicated games and rhythms, finger painting, clay modeling, and many preschool and kindergarten activities. A few are able to go somewhat beyond this level. If a sheltered workshop is available to trainable children when they become youths and adults, many can become contributing members of society in a limited way. But they will always need someone who is responsible for their well-being, guidance, and protection.

The *mildly retarded* and many of the *borderline* children are the largest group of retarded youngsters. They are sometimes called the *educable* children. These are the boys and girls we find in the usual special-education classes in our schools. Some of the borderline children can manage in the regular classroom if they are provided with special help in the skill subjects. They can learn enough reading and arithmetic so that they can meet simple daily needs. Many of them will be able to function quite adequately in areas other than academic work, and some may show talent in special areas such as art or singing or athletics. There are many things that most mildly retarded children can do with other boys and girls. It is important that they should not be completely isolated from the other children. With an educational program planned to meet their special needs, most of them will be able to become self-supporting and to manage their own affairs quite adequately under circumstances that are not too complex. But they will continue to need help and guidance in their vocational adjustment and in situations that require judgment.

We are becoming increasingly aware that among children who test within the retarded range are many who have normal potentialities but are *culturally retarded.* They have grown up in disadvantaged areas in which

273

they have missed the opportunities most children have to build the concepts necessary to prepare them for success in schoolwork. Often their parents have been so culturally deprived themselves that they cannot provide for even the basic physical needs of their children. Some of these boys and girls have never seen themselves in a mirror or have never even realized that they have a name of their own or a personal identity. Some have had little opportunity to learn language, because in the crowded quarters where they have grown up parents seldom talk to their children and never read to them. Many of these culturally deprived youngsters can be helped to leave the group of the retarded if they are reached during their early years, if their physical needs are taken care of, and if they are provided with experiences that will help them develop their potential abilities. Programs like Head Start and special day-care centers are providing the experiences for some of these children.

MORE ALIKE THAN DIFFERENT Parents and teachers who are helping retarded boys and girls need to remember above all that these children are more *like* other children than *different* from them. They have the same needs for affection, achievement, and a feeling of personal worth. They need friends to play with, interests to follow, trips and experiences to open up the world to them. They need fun and laughter just as other children do. Retarded youngsters also will need special educational plans fitted to their mental abilities rather than to their chronological ages. They can never be expected to carry on the academic work that children their age experience in the regular classroom, to proceed at the same pace as more normal boys and girls, or to catch up with them unless they have been culturally retarded. When mentally retarded children are accepted at their own levels of performance, many of them can learn enough to become happy and productive citizens. They all have their own individuality and personality and their own needs. They will progress and develop at their own rate. They need to be known and appreciated as individuals rather than pigeonholed as "retarded children."

PARENTS NEED HELP Parents naturally feel deep grief over a handicapped child, whether the handicap is physical or mental, but by their own realistic acceptance of the handicap they can help their child to accept it, too. The earlier they recognize the problem, the earlier they can begin appropriate treatment, guidance, and education, and the better the prognosis will be for the child's learning how to accept and live with the handicap. It is unfortunate if parents, in their grief, are unable or unwilling to recognize the problem for what it is or if they put off facing the child's handicap, hoping that it will be outgrown.

Parents will not be able to meet all the needs of either a physically or mentally handicapped child by themselves. The community must help by providing both treatment and educational facilities that will make the care of these children possible. Small communities are not always able to afford all the necessary facilities, but these facilities usually can be supported by the larger units of county or state. The availability of such services should be called to the attention of all parents of handicapped children. If parents have not received such information and do not know how to secure it, they can write to their state's Department of Health and their state's Department of Education. These two departments will have information concerning all the possible help that handicapped children can receive within their state. There also are many national organizations to help the handicapped.

Parents of handicapped children also need opportunities to meet and talk with parents of other children who have similar problems. Through such contacts, parents are often able to support one another and share their solutions to some of the practical difficulties they must face in learning to live with their child's problem and the problems it makes for the whole family. The parents of retarded children, for instance, have helped one another immeasurably as they have come together across the country. They often have sponsored research on the causes and treatment of mental retardation. They have worked for the organization of schools for trainable children, special classes in the public schools, recreational and religious activities suited to the needs of their children, and sheltered workshops and vocational opportunities for their grown sons and daughters. Parents of children with other handicaps such as cerebral palsy or learning difficulties also are forming associations or local groups in which they can come together to share their concerns and plan for the needs of their children.

Now that families are becoming better able to accept their handicapped children without shame, many more parents are answering the special need of these children for love, affection, and a place in the family. This is the first and most important step in the emotional development of these children, as it is with all children. But there is still much to be done to obtain acceptance for the handicapped in the community, first as children and later as workers. This task begins in the schoolroom and in the neighborhood. Adults, through their own attitude toward the handicapped, set an example for children. Sometimes normal children need direct teaching in the schoolroom, in youth groups, in the church school, and in recreational activities if, because of their difficulty in accepting differences, they taunt or turn away from those who are handicapped. Discovering that many handicapped people have something of value to contribute provides an added dimension in a child's development.

THE BATTERED CHILD  Perhaps the saddest of all children are those who are victims of child abuse—those children whose parents have inflicted physical injury upon them as a result of abuse or physical neglect. Although 80 percent of these children are under three years of age, such abuse is found among elementary-school children and even adolescents. Little children cannot protect themselves from such abuse. Elementary-school children are sometimes afraid to tell; older boys and girls may run away from home or seek help in leaving such family situations.

Ten percent of all children taken to emergency rooms for treatment are there because their parents have hurt them and have then panicked and rushed the child to the hospital. This is a low figure for there are parents who take their child to the family doctor who may not report the case. Four percent of all abuse cases result in the death of the children, particularly of the little ones. Child abuse may be found in families of all income levels, although those that are reported usually are from low-income families.

Teachers, neighbors, and all who are interested in the welfare of children have an obligation to report evidences of child abuse such as bruises, welts on the body, or unusual evidences of neglect. Most states now have laws which protect those who do report such cases, and doctors are required to report them. In most communities the report should be made to the social-welfare agency which will have the authority to follow up and investigate what is happening to the child.

Many parents who abuse their children were themselves abused. They rarely mean to injure their child but are impulsive, easily angered, and usually lacking in self-control. Help is needed for such parents as well as their children. Sometimes it is necessary to place the child in a foster home, unless the parents are able to change and modify their actions. This is a serious problem for far too many children and one for which all members of the community must carry responsibility—a child cannot carry it alone.

chapter 17

# Living with Children at Home

THE IMPORTANCE OF THE FAMILY   Even in the rapidly changing world of today, the family is still the primary unit in our society. The outward forms of family life have changed and may change even more, but children still start life as members of a family group, and all boys and girls reflect the influence of their families on their lives. Their mothers and fathers, their grandparents, and even their great-grandparents leave their mark, not only through genetic influence on physique, basic temperament, capacities, and limitations but also through some of the attitudes, customs, and child-rearing practices that have been passed down from one generation to another. This family "lore" accumulates and is rarely discarded entirely, even though new cultural patterns may be added to it.

Those who work with problems of adjustment place a major emphasis on the effect of early emotional experiences in the home in determining how children will feel toward other people and in determining their capacities to withstand the strains and frustrations they necessarily will meet as they grow up. Research and clinical studies have been accumulating evidence that every child needs the security of belonging, of being accepted, and of being loved. These studies also have shown that juvenile delinquents and seriously disturbed children come less frequently from homes that provide a warm, affectionate, accepting atmosphere. Many of them come, rather, from unstable homes in which they have been unwanted or neglected. It also has been found that in many cases children who have grown up in institutions where they had no personal relationship with an adult have been retarded both in their mental growth and in their ability to relate warmly to other people. Research studies also have documented many cases of babies and young children who have suffered severe physical retardation when they have been deprived of sufficient mothering.

In our culture, no satisfactory substitute for a home has yet been found for supplying the kind of care that children need. A family still remains the first group in which children can feel that they belong and have the experience of being cared for in a warm and personal way. Children whose families fail them experience the deep void of being unwanted, a void which they may seek to fill all of their lives as they turn from one group or person to another in trying to satisfy their needs to belong.

Child-placement agencies are recognizing this need of children for a personal home and a personal parent-child relationship by trying to find foster homes for children whose homes have somehow failed them. When institutional placement seems the only available possibility, the placement-agency personnel look for institutions that try to give familylike experiences to the children in their care. Such institutions try to divide the children into small groups with a mother-substitute and, when possible, a father-substitute for each group. Some social agencies are trying in still another way to meet children's needs for a family by keeping impoverished families together, giving financial aid when necessary instead of taking children away from parents who cannot support them. It is now recognized that a home inadequate by many material standards may still be the best home for children if the parents are able to supply warmth and affection and interest in their children.

Children need parenting. They cannot thrive without it. But when we think of the family experience as important in the healthy growth of children, the emphasis upon a family structure of mother, father, and children as the only acceptable family group is unrealistic and hurts many boys and girls who are experiencing family life in diverse kinds of family groups. To recognize that there is change in the structure of many families does not necessarily mean that all provide the most desirable family setting for children. But it would seem to mean, that where there is genuine responsibility for the welfare of the children, other forms of the family may need to be accepted as capable of providing the parenting children need. There are successful one-parent families, foster-parent families, and commune families when the emphasis is upon responsible nurturing care of the children. There can be healthy experiences for a growing child in many different family situations, and there can be unhealthy experiences in the usual family group. Whatever changes occur in the structure of the family, the test of the continuing existence of the family will be found in the strength of the emotional bond which develops between nurturing parenting people and their children.

## PROVIDING AND DEMONSTRATING AFFECTION

A great deal of misunderstanding has arisen over the stress placed on the parent-child relationship. Some parents take this to mean that they must lavish physical and verbal expressions of love on their children. Other parents think that they must give children complete freedom to develop in their own ways, never expressing parental points of view and needs, or frustrating the children for fear their development will be blocked. Still others place great importance on the providing of material things for their children. Some parents make their children the center of the family's life to such an extent that the children never learn that belonging is only real when one shares in meeting the needs of the entire group.

Children need parents who are warm, mature adults. Such parents welcome a baby at birth; accept the heredity and build on it; try to provide the best conditions for physical growth; and try to understand the particular pattern of growth. Through affection, encouragement, and consistent guidance and example, they provide the child with the personal security that leads to self-confidence and mental health. Such parents may be found in almost every kind of home. Many children have grown to happy, competent maturity despite shortcomings in their physical surroundings, and many have grown into warped personalities in homes that supplied their physical needs in abundance. There are good homes and inadequate homes in every kind of community. Pleasant physical surroundings make growth easier, but it is the emotional relationships within the home that make the essential difference between a home in which growth proceeds freely and one in which it is hampered.

In a home good for children, parents want their children. They enjoy them. Even though family life engenders problems and worries and responsibilities, the parents feel that the rewards of having a family far outweigh the problems involved. In such a family, children receive affection, love, and the warmth of belonging. Affection is shown not only in the care given to the children but in the tone of voice, the arm around the shoulder, the fun together, the spontaneous laughter, the games, the stories at bedtime, and the willingness to listen and enter into each child's interests. Children are literal and so need the tangible proof of being loved that parents who enjoy their children can give.

As children grow up, the ways in which their parents show their affection and interest will naturally change. For example, small children love to roughhouse with their parents or to be taken for a piggyback ride, while elementary-school children are more likely to prefer their parents' help in making things. Teen-agers, while not always willing to confide in their parents, sometimes are anxious to have them listen and help with their prob-

279

lems. But sometimes parents unwittingly lose the opportunity to express their affection for their children by establishing an unbreakable pattern of "doing things together" instead of allowing for spontaneous opportunities and impulses. Plans should be flexible enough to be adapted to the family's growth and changing interests. Preschool children need and want the routine of always doing things in the same way, and even school-age children tend to cling to certain routines; but as children grow older it is the enjoyment of doing things together and being a part of the family group that is important, not the set time or plan. In fact, too rigid planning of family activities can even interfere with the enjoyment of them.

It is through the warm relationships established with their parents that children learn how to love and get along with other people, including their own brothers and sisters. In every family with more than one child, there will be some tensions among the children—quarrels, disagreements, and jealousy—as they seek to be first in the eyes of their parents. But parents can ease these tensions by gradually showing their children that they love and accept each one and that they will try to be fair with everybody. In such a family the underlying feeling of belonging to each other usually will be strong enough to balance the normal stresses of living and growing up together. When this feeling of belonging exists, the problems that do arise can be seen in perspective. Negative emotions, such as hostility and jealousy, may arise, but these will not constitute the family's basic emotional pattern.

Children need to feel that they are completely accepted by their mothers and fathers and that their love is not contingent on a particular

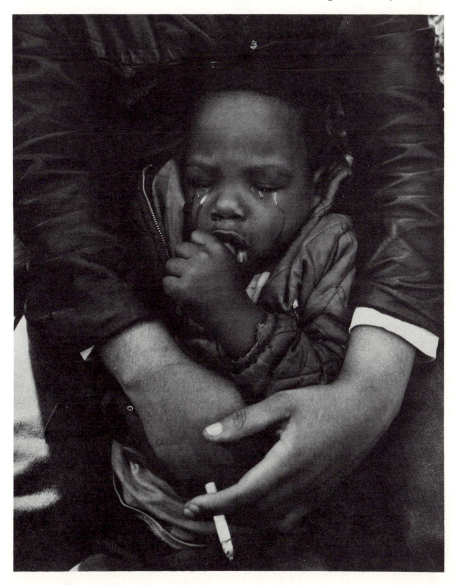

kind of behavior. They need to feel that they are loved not for looks or schoolwork or good behavior but because they are themselves. In a good home parents recognize each child's individuality and love their children as they are. They accept each child—the poorly coordinated child, the agile child, the child who learns easily in school, the child who has learning difficulties, the handsome child, the plain child, the handicapped or delicate child. If parents can accept their children as they are, they will then be able to help them grow within their own patterns. They will not try to turn them into the kind of children that they may have pictured before they were born, nor will they try to make a child like a brother or sister or the neighbors' child. They will help their children develop at their own speeds and in their own ways.

CONSISTENT ATTITUDES AND EXPECTATIONS Children should be able to count on the way their parents usually will react. Wise parents will not let moods interfere with basic feelings for their children or with the pattern of behavior they will expect their children to follow. They will realize that a child has many things to learn. Children are not born knowing what is right and wrong or what kind of behavior is considered acceptable in the part of the world where they live. These are things that they will learn gradually as they grow up. The first pattern of behavior that they learn is the one that parents teach them during early years. What parents say is right, children accept as right; what they are told is wrong, they believe is wrong. As they grow older, they will encounter other standards of behavior and will learn to make their own decisions about right and wrong. But if their parents' standards were inadequate or confused or inconsistent, they will have more trouble in knowing what they are expected to do and in learning to exercise sound judgment.

Whether youngsters will accept and follow the standards of their homes as children and later as adolescents will depend largely on the relationships that are built between them and their parents. If children feel that they are loved and accepted and if they respect their parents' standards, they are likely to accept their guidance and learn the behavior they are trying to teach. But if the children are unhappy in their relationship with one or both of their parents, they may seem to accept the pattern through fear but not make it really part of themselves, or they may rebel against their parents and refuse to do what they ask—whether it concerns toilet training or eating or coming home at a reasonable hour. Children who have warm feelings toward their parents are better able to resist being influenced by undesirable behavior which they may meet in their neighborhoods, through their gangs, or through questionable friends than are children whose need for affection has not been met at home. Youngsters who lack affection usually will turn to anyone who will offer them the satisfaction and security of belonging, and will be inclined to accept unquestioningly the standards and behavior of friends, even if the standards are ones they have been taught to consider unacceptable.

As parents teach their children desirable patterns of behavior, they will find it necessary to make rules and set limits. These will vary with the age of the children and with the particular family situation. Happy children are found both in families where parents are strict and in families where parents are lenient. Whether the home is strict or relaxed, the essential again is *consistency,* plus a warm, understanding relationship. Wise parents will not make a rule today that may be broken tomorrow because mother has a headache or father is busy and cannot bother to enforce it. If a small boy is forbidden to play in the street today, he should not be allowed to get away with it tomorrow. Inconsistency in rules is unfair to youngsters. It confuses them.

If children are old enough, they should be allowed to help make the rules, because then they will better understand the reasons for them. Rules should be well considered and should be kept at a minimum, involving only the essentials of safety and consideration for other people. There need to be rules, for example, about crossing streets and about letting parents know where you are going; such rules are reasonable and children usually will conform to them. But rules should not be made for situations that may change so frequently that the rule cannot be enforced.

As children grow rules have to be changed to meet new needs and situations. The yard may be a reasonable limit for two-year-olds, but four-year-olds will become restless and rebellious if confined to the yard. They will want to ride tricycles up and down the block and to play with other children a few houses away. School-age children will find the limits of the block too small and will want to go to the playground or to visit a nearby friend, while the adolescent will need the wider limits of the entire community and in some cases opportunities to go even farther away from home. Rules and limits should be made to fit the maturity of the child—the child should not be squeezed into the rules. Intelligent consistency and flexibility in setting limits give boys and girls a feeling of security. Children need to know what they may do and what is expected, and parents must expect of children only that which they are mature enough to give. Children respond better when a reason is given for the required behavior or for the veto which must sometimes follow a request.

MEANINGFUL PUNISHMENT  In all homes there will be times when a more forceful reminder, or punishment, is needed. Such a method of teaching should be reserved for times when youngsters have deliberately done what they know they should not have done. In considering punishment, parents should understand both the situation and what can fairly be expected at a particular stage of growing up. For example, parents should not scold toddlers for breaking a pretty object, even though they have been told not to touch; they should not always expect the four-year-old to tell the truth or the school-age child to remember consistently without a reminder; and they should not become too upset with the adolescent who sometimes seems irresponsible. Punishment should never be used to try to curb actions that indicate children may be under tension. Thumb-sucking, masturbating, nail-biting, stuttering, and failing in school are examples of behavior that cannot be helped by any form of punishment.

If punishment is to be at all useful, it must vary with the age of the children, with the thing they have done, and with the kind of children they are. One child can accept and understand the reasonableness of a punishment, but another who is more timid or sensitive may crumple under even a mild punishment. Punishment should be meaningful to children so that it really involves them in a learning situation and helps them remember the next time. The four-year-old who plays in the street might be restricted to the house or yard for a short time, and the nine-year-old who breaks a window because he played ball where he wasn't supposed to might make amends by mowing the neighbors' lawn or performing some other service to help pay for the damage he has done.

Parents must decide for themselves the kind of punishment that they feel comfortable in administering and that seems effective with their children. Physical punishment is rarely of value and may result in increasingly aggressive behavior. Some parents try to teach a child not to hit others by hitting the child. In every case the important thing is for children to feel that, despite being punished, they still have their parents' love and affection. If they detect hostility or indifference in their parents' behavior toward them, even the mildest punishment may be too hard for them to take. In such a case, punishment may increase the child's timidity or feed rebellion. Punishment which is too severe creates fear and anxiety. Rather than teaching children, it creates tensions that make teaching more difficult. To be of any value, punishment must be reasonable. It should never deprive children of their self-respect or make them feel that they, as people, are "bad." Punishment used too frequently often indicates that tensions are building between the parents and the child and that these tensions need thoughtful consideration.

Although punishment occasionally may be necessary as a reminder, children learn best by encouragement and approval. If parents notice when their children have been helpful, when they have shown good judgment, when they have tried to do a difficult task, or have done something especially kind, a word of approval encourages youngsters to act in the same way another time. Too often parents criticize behavior which they do not like rather than showing approval for that which they want to encourage.

PARTICIPATING IN FAMILY LIFE  Children grow best in a home in which they participate. Taking part increases their feelings of belonging, of being valued, of being wanted and accepted. From the time they are little, children need to feel that they are part of the family—sharing in work, in play, in family celebrations, and, later, even in problems. Instead of parents making all the rules, plans, and decisions, the children should be drawn into planning a picnic or a vacation, discussing the purchase of a new car or a new dog, or talking over the question of allowances or how to stretch the budget.

Each family has its own way of doing things, but in the homes in which children are the happiest and have the strongest family feeling the children usually take an active part in the work of the household. Parents can teach or fail to teach invaluable habits and attitudes toward work by their own feelings about it. Children easily come to feel that they don't like to work if their parents complain about doing the dishes or taking the garbage out or if they are always assigned the disagreeable jobs. Whenever possible, parents and children should work together as a cooperative unit. Work in the home rarely goes smoothly when children are *told* to do jobs. It is better to talk over the work to be done and let the family decide together how it will be distributed. An opportunity for children to change jobs as interest lags will help to keep up cooperation. It is not the specific job that is important but the fact that children have a valued contribution to make.

Competition within the family is lessened when members of the family have an opportunity to help with the planning and use their skills for the benefit of the family group. If one child likes to cook and does it well, the family may elect the youngster to help make the desserts. Another who is learning about electricity in school and is clever at electrical repair work may get the job of seeing that the electrical appliances are in order. Some families hold a regular family council in which everyone, even the littlest

285

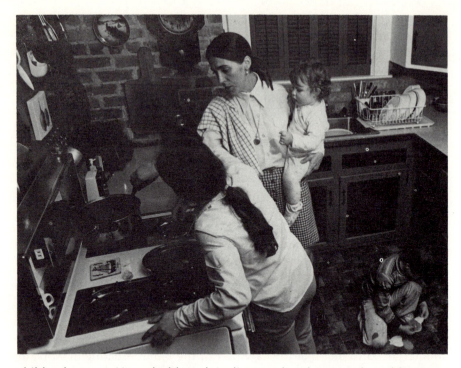

child, takes part. Household work is discussed and assigned, problems are talked over, complaints are aired, and plans are made. Other families have less formal discussions—perhaps around the dinner table when everyone is present and some special point has come up. But whatever method is used, children grow best when they are real participants. In all families there will be decisions that ultimately must be made by the parents, but the children's ideas can be welcomed, considered, and talked over before a decision is reached. Children follow decisions more readily and with greater understanding when they have had a part in making them, or talking them over.

Many compromises have to be made and accepted in every family, but in a family in which everyone takes part in making decisions, the compromises usually are better understood and more fully accepted. Both parents and children have to compromise for the benefit of the family group. For example, parents may have to be willing to put up with more mess and noise than they like, whereas children have to accept the fact that there are limits to the mess and noise which adults can tolerate.

As children grow old enough to understand, they are able to share in some of the serious family decisions, worries, and problems. Permitting children to know about family crises and to share in meeting them enables the children to come through the crises with the least possible strain. A conference behind closed doors or an anxious, abstracted look on a parent's face can worry and frighten a child more than a knowledge of the facts. "Daddy is having trouble with his job," or, "Mother is very sick with pneumonia; she may need to go to the hospital. Will you help by giving Timmie his supper?"—such straightforward explanations give a child a sense of worth, of responsibility in the family, that makes it possible to meet problems and troubles. Children who really share in the life of their family develop a family loyalty and a "we-feeling" which usually last throughout their lives and add to their emotional security. In addition, they receive invaluable practice in making decisions and in carrying responsiblity. Sharing the fun, the responsibilities, and the problems of the family is essential if growth is to be at its best.

HELPING CHILDREN MEET THEIR PROBLEMS   The wise parent remembers that growth does not always proceed smoothly. Even with the best of daily guidance, boys and girls will have problems and will sometimes get into trouble. Children need to feel that they can safely let their parents know what they feel and think and what they have done. If their real feelings and hurts must go unexpressed, the repressed emotions may fester and come out in undesirable forms of behavior. Withdrawal, bullying, quarrelsomeness, headaches, and stomachaches are some of the many channels through which hurt or anger may find their way to the surface. Children need the release that comes from being able to say how they really feel and the security of being allowed to explode when they are under too much pressure. But parents cannot always accept the form of release that their youngster uses. They may often have to let the child know that they understand the feelings but cannot allow the way of expressing them because, in the process, someone else is being hurt or someone else's property is being damaged.

Sometimes a youngster becomes so disturbed that parents are no longer able to give the help which is needed. It is not always easy for parents to realize that their child has reached this point and that they should seek the help of a guidance specialist. When children fail to learn from their own experiences or mistakes, or when they are unable to make adjustments, they need professional guidance. This also is true when their mistakes become too serious, when they pull away from life because of the pain their experiences give them, or when their relationships with their parents have become so tense that they don't respond to parents' efforts to help them. A child's problem is of a serious nature when any of the following behavior patterns become characteristic: withdrawal from others; preoccupation with health or with symptoms of illness; any other anxious preoccupation which interferes with schoolwork or effective living; delinquency; inability to accept his own sex or to be normally interested for his age in the other sex; chronic unhappiness or anxiety; troubled and obsessive thoughts; compulsive actions; irrational fears; or suspiciousness. Sometimes recognition of these symptoms may be gradual. At other times parents suddenly realize that a child's difficult behavior is becoming more frequent and marked—a customary pattern of behavior instead of an occasional one. It is important for parents to seek help for the child who shows any of these forms of behavior, for these are symptoms that indicate emotional tensions, tensions that cannot be relieved until they are fully understood.

287

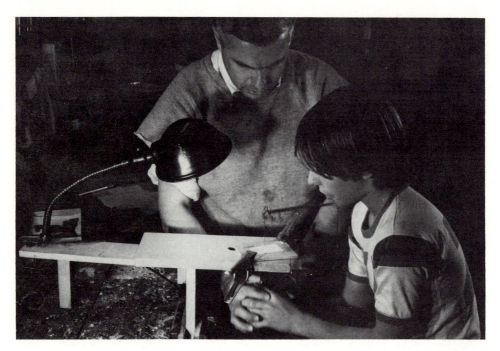

Being able to talk together, whether it is about feelings, interests, desires, or problems strengthens the parents' relationships with their children. The late Dr. Wendell Johnson wrote:

*What has impressed me most about people as I have been privileged to know them is their longing to be understood and to be understanding.**

This is what children want as they try to reach out to their parents who are the most significant adults in their lives. They try to communicate both through words and through their behavior. This is what most parents want as they try to communicate with their children. But barriers often come between parents and their children. Too often parents talk at children rather than with them. Children often say they feel that their parents do not listen. As a result they may grow up feeling that there is something wrong about asking questions. Adolescents may be rebuffed when they try to use their parents as a sounding board when they are sorting out their ideas about morality, religion, or politics. Yet open communication between parent and child which is based on mutual respect for the thoughts and feelings of the other person is an essential if parents are to be able to understand and guide their children as they are growing up.

To again quote Dr. Wendell Johnson:

*When you listen to understand you listen without preoccupation. You listen without irritation or anger. You listen without strong prejudice. You keep your own need to be understood from coming between you and the other person you are trying to understand. You listen not to*

288

*Johnson, Wendell and Moeller, Dorothy. *Living With Change: The Semantics of Coping.* New York: Harper & Row, 1972, p. 189.

*refute and not to persuade, but only to hear the speaker out, to understand just as well as you possibly can what he is trying to say. . . . Listen to the child well, to what he is saying, and not saying at all. He has something he wants to tell you, something that has meaning for him, that is important to him. . . . Respect him as a speaker. Listen to him enough to hear him out. It is wonderful for him as a growing person to feel that he is being heard, that others care about what he is saying.* **

The role of parents is constantly changing. Parents must move from full responsibility for their little children to counselor and guide, but not controller, as the child becomes a young adult. Parents have to learn to continue to love but to let go gradually as their children are able to assume more responsibility for their own behavior and decisions. Children must be given the opportunity to learn to become independent in both thought and actions, otherwise they cannot function effectively as adults.

Children need parents who are people with their own interests, who develop themselves as persons. As they get older they do not need twenty-four-hour parenting. They do need parents who love them and care about what happens to them. Being an effective parent does not mean that parents must give up everything they want to do and feel a need to do in order to meet the wishes and wants of their children. It does mean that the children must be aware that there is room for them in their parents' lives. Children need to know, in ways that children can understand, that their parents care for them deeply and will be supporting and responsible guides as they are growing up. Children must know that they can count on their parents.

**Johnson, Wendell and Moeller, Dorothy. *Living With Change: The Semantics of Coping.* New York: Harper & Row, 1972, p. 193.

chapter 18

# Teachers and Parents Work Together

UNDERSTANDING THE WHOLE CHILD   In understanding individual children, their needs and their problems, teachers and parents should meet and share their knowledge of the children whenever possible. Parents must help teachers see youngsters as they are in their families and neighborhood groups; teachers must bring to the parents their insights into the children's capacities to learn in the classroom and to live and work with others in the school environment. Teachers and parents must work in harmony—each has the welfare of the children in mind, and each has a special contribution to make to the children's growth and development.

Parents are responsible for providing the emotional support and individual guidance their children will need as they are growing up. Their concern for their children should be deep and personal. The bonds of affection must be strong if children are to feel the security of belonging to their family groups. This is essential if they are to become emotionally healthy adults.

Teachers, too, feel deep concern for the individual child, but their responsibilities are in two directions. Their primary responsibility is to teach. They must see that all children are equipped, insofar as possible, with the skills and knowledge that will enable them to meet their responsibilities as adults in a complex world. In working toward this end, they must pay attention not only to *what* is to be learned but also to the individual boys and girls who are the learners. Only as they understand and recognize that children's emotional needs must be met if they are to learn effectively will they be able to fulfill their roles as teachers.

When parents and teachers feel able to communicate with one another, realizing that each has the welfare of the child in mind, the child can be seen as a whole person, not segmented between school and home. Experiences can be brought together and seen in perspective so that parents and teacher, planning together, can help develop capacities as fully as possible. Many potential problems never develop if, through the years, parents meet with teachers to discuss the needs and characteristics of their children. Through such meetings parents can learn about the classroom program which has been planned or is being developed, and the teacher

291

can gain valuable insights into the child's relationships with parents and into home conditions.

PARENT-TEACHER CONFERENCES The keynote of cooperative relationships with parents is not teachers' professional training nor their understanding of learning processes or even of child psychology. Rather, it is their willingness to talk with the parents and to listen to them, in order to seek and understand more fully the reasons behind a child's behavior. If the child is having trouble at school, what do the parents think the problem is? Have they any idea how the problem arose? What action have the parents taken and what do they think the school should do? What can school and home do together? Thoughtful discussion between teacher and parents may seem to make little headway at times, but the conclusions they reach together are much more likely to lead to a successful plan for attacking the problem than are conclusions reached by the teacher alone.

The importance and benefit of teachers giving parents a complete and detailed progress report on their children can hardly be overemphasized. A report, whether it is written or given at a parent-teacher conference, can give perspective both on the child's progress and on problem areas—perspective from which parents and teachers can then plan intelligently for the child. Such a report should be based, of course, on a child's own record rather than on comparisons with other children. (See "Guide for Parent-Teacher Conferences," page 313.)

Unfortunately, teachers can seldom get to know the parents of all the children in their classes. Often the parents whom they would most like to know will not come to school. Some are afraid of the teacher—a carryover, perhaps, from their own school days. Others are too busy or not sufficiently interested. Some are embarrassed to come to school because of inadequate clothing, work-roughened hands, or inarticulate language. Still others might like to come to school but do not realize that they would be welcomed by the teacher.

It should be made easy for parents to come to school—the door of the school should always be open. Parents should be informed, however, about when they can most conveniently confer with a teacher or principal. In some schools a parent may drop in at any time, but in others the teachers set aside special hours to see parents or to talk on the phone. Whatever the arrangements are, they should be clearly stated at the beginning of the year so that no parents need suffer embarrassment or be put off because they happen to come to school at an inconvenient time. Special arrangements should be provided if both parents work and neither can get to school at the times regularly scheduled for conferences.

THE SCHOOL IN THE COMMUNITY It is easy to blame parents who never come to school for lack of interest in their children, but before doing so the school personnel should study their own policies. Has the school become part of the community? Parents in middle- and upper-class neighborhoods usually take it for granted that they may go to school. But in impoverished neighborhoods and in some neighborhoods with large numbers of minority parents, the school must reach out toward the parents and encourage them to feel that this is *their* school.

Teachers need to become familiar with the disciplines, traditions, customs, taboos, and attitudes of the communities in which they teach, especially those of the homes of children in their classes. Children who are well accepted in their own homes or neighborhoods may face a problem when confronted with a school situation where they meet for the first time a completely new set of social and ethical standards. Most teachers come from the middle socioeconomic level and are accustomed to middle-class standards of language, behavior, and values. But many children come to school from homes in which these standards do not exist. Children from lower socioeconomic level homes may use words that seem offensive to their teachers. Yet these may be the only words they have learned, words that are commonly used within their families and their neighborhoods. If teachers take these children's efforts to express themselves in their own language as deliberate disrespect, communication between children and teacher inevitably will suffer.

Many communities also include national and racial groups that have customs different from those of the community as a whole. If these customs—many of which have a traditional value—are ignored or undermined at school, children may lose their moorings to their families and even come to look down on their own parents. All parents are quick to sense whether their child's teachers respect their traditional ways or reject them as being different from their own.

Although teachers may want to help all children achieve the values and patterns of behavior they consider desirable and appropriate, they will be making a mistake if they fail to recognize the cultural pattern of the community—the reason and often the necessity for behavior considerably different from their own. They must choose carefully the behavior and attitudes that they will try to change and learn to recognize those that are better left undisturbed.


UNDERSTANDING PROBLEMS AT HOME  Parents sometimes hesitate to talk with their child's teacher for fear that the teacher will be critical of them because their child has failed in some respect. Often teachers do blame parents when things go wrong with children they are teaching. This is easy to do and at times is justified. But as professionals, teachers should have some understanding of the causes behind parental behavior and should be able to accept parents of all kinds with patience and insight. By openly showing their disapproval of parents, they may lose the opportunity to gain an understanding of the home problem and may completely destroy any possibility of effective communication concerning the child's problem.

Many parents are on the defensive. Most of them want to love and understand their children; they would like to give their children the essen-

293

tials for healthy emotional growth, but they may be unable to do so because of conflicts, problems, or lack of emotional, intellectual, or financial resources. Even some parents who can accept their children's needs intellectually are unable to show the warmth and affection they feel. Perhaps they themselves as children were never really helped to learn how to show affection. Others have unresolved conflicts of their own which make them resent the burdens of parenthood and interfere with their enjoyment or understanding of their children. Some children receive the brunt of their parents' tensions resulting from their own marital problems or from negative feelings that they still harbor toward their own parents and their own childhood. Sometimes parents cannot seem to love a child or give adequate care because they are reminded of undesirable or disappointing qualities in themselves or in a husband or wife or parent. There are parents, too, who need to exert authority over a child to make up for their own feelings of inadequacy and insecurity. Such parents may be unnecessarily harsh. Others would like to be kind to their children and to guide them well but fail because they interpret behavior exclusively in terms of "good" and "bad" or in relation to themselves—"Does it annoy me?" Such parents usually are unaware of their failure to interpret their child's behavior in relation to developmental needs.

Unfortunately parents sometimes are so hampered by their own problems or inadequacies that they are unable to do what is best for their children. But as professional people, teachers should take an understanding attitude toward the parents' failures as well as the children's failures. In condemning a parent the teacher only widens the gap between home and school and makes fruitful cooperation virtually impossible. Teachers must be able to recognize the point at which they cannot reach a parent or hope to obtain the parental help that they feel a child needs. If teachers anticipate that their inability to communicate with the parents is likely to have serious consequences for the child, they will want to talk with the principal, the school psychologist, or the counselor to see what plans can be made for the child. Sometimes, too, these individuals can suggest ways to steer parents toward the help that they need in working through their own problems.

Teachers cannot change an undesirable home environment. Yet by knowledge of students' home conditions, they can do much to give them the help and the support they need. Russell, Johnny, and Mark suffered from emotional insecurity as a result of their parents' difficulties. In each case their feelings affected their schoolwork. A fairly stable home basis was eventually established for Mark and Johnny, but Russell's original insecurity was aggravated by his abnormal family situation. The harsh and eccentric grandmother, the aloof aunt, the rejecting father made a happy adjustment impossible for the boy. A number of children, like Russell, are subjected to the influence of many relatives in the home and to all the conflicts of in-laws who disagree with one another. Perhaps the household is divided by friction or divorce has created a problem, as it did for Russell. Special problems are created, too, if one of the parents is physically handicapped—deaf, blind, or trying to direct the household from a wheelchair or

294

invalid's bed. A father or mother may be bringing up the family alone. A mother may be working and thus have to be away from her children immediately before and after school. Sometimes an older child, particularly a girl, may be doing most of the housework and taking care of the younger children, or a boy may be holding down an after-school job to help the family finances. Such heavy responsibilities are likely to affect the preparation of schoolwork. Knowledge of a child's home life cannot help but make a difference in teachers' attitudes, patience, and the techniques they will find useful when problems arise.

Home visits are not always possible, and in some school systems they are not considered advisable. In some schools, a social worker or a visiting teacher is assigned to gather information about the backgrounds of the children, particularly those who have problems and need help. A cumulative record of home visits, if it is properly kept, can be a useful source of information. Any information included in the cumulative record must be treated professionally, of course, and should never become a subject of discussion in the teachers' room, or placed in files available to others than professional school personnel.

Because children from the same family attend the same neighborhood school, a great deal of information can be compiled from their various records. Teachers who have known other children from the same families, and teachers who have taught a child in previous years can be valuable sources of information, as can the principal. The knowledge gained from these sources can then be added to the teacher's own assessment of the family situation. Care must be taken that the material included is factual rather than based on personal bias or judgmental statements.

## UNDERSTANDING PROBLEMS AT SCHOOL
At times parents come to a conference at school feeling that the school rather than their child is at fault. When this happens, many teachers react indignantly. Although some parents blame teachers unreasonably for a child's failure, there are times when the teacher or the methods or policies of the school may indeed be at fault.

Although children's growth is influenced first and most strongly by their homes, even adequately adjusted children may develop personality difficulties or fail in schoolwork if the school environment is unsuitable. Children who have always done well in school may become anxious and discouraged if they have a harsh, uncompromising teacher or one who is inadequate and ill-prepared. Children who are constantly expected to accomplish work that is beyond them by teachers who set a single standard for all the children in their classes may become unhappy, withdrawn, or disturbed. A parent is justified in questioning whether the class atmosphere or a relationship with a particular teacher is the cause of a child's problem, if the child has shown a marked difference in behavior and attitude toward school when moved into a new class. Such changed behavior may serve as a cue for thoughtful teachers to question themselves, to reexamine their classroom methods and, perhaps, their feelings for particular children.

295

Communication between parents and teachers helps both home and school to view the child as a whole person. Through conferences, parents can learn about classroom programs, and the teacher can gain valuable insights into home conditions and the child's relationship with parents. Teachers can also gain insight into their own teaching by taking an objective look at taped classroom activities (bottom right). But only as parents and teachers understand one another can each child's best educational growth be attained.

Teachers are people, too. They bring to the classroom not only their knowledge and training but their personalities as well. Just as the parents' personalities help to create a child's home environment, so teachers' personalities determine in great part the climate of the schoolroom. Sometimes teachers find themselves unable to be patient and warm with their students, even though they desire to do so. They may be under strain and tension themselves. They may have home problems and worries which crowd into their minds during the school day in spite of their attempts to forget them and to think only of their classes. Or they may feel insecure because they lack experience or adequate training. They may be afraid that their classes will get out of hand, that they will not maintain proper discipline, or that a supervisor or principal will walk in at a critical moment. This may make them brusque and irritable, to the detriment of all students and especially of those who are particularly sensitive or insecure.

Some teachers will be worried, strained, or anxious as a result of past experiences or present difficulties. Nevertheless, teachers must be aware of how deeply their personalities and anxieties can affect the children in their classes. If problems or anxieties are not a passing thing but result in a pattern of behavior that prevents achievement of a pleasant, calm atmosphere in the classroom; and, if irritabilities affect teaching, they should seek help and try to reach an adjustment that will make life more comfortable both for themselves and for the youngsters in their classes. Teachers' own mental health must be good if they are to teach children effectively.

HOMEWORK AND EXTRACURRICULAR ACTIVITIES The everyday practices of school life can result in friction between home and school if parents and teachers do not discuss them and agree on them. The assignment of homework, for example, frequently becomes a cause of tension and misunderstanding. Teachers often feel themselves caught in the middle between parents who want their children to have a lot of homework—who gauge progress by the amount of work brought home—and other parents who are concerned because their children have to work too late in the evening. Parents have a right to be concerned if homework interferes with needed outdoor recreation or sleep. Every child needs time to participate in the family group as well as in the school group, to do a share of work in the home, and to enjoy a hobby, music, books, and even some television.

Teachers must think through the relationship of homework to the total life of the child. Where a departmental system is used, teachers in the different departments need to check with one another to see whether the overall amount of homework required is realistic or whether each is making an assignment without regard to what the others are requiring. It also is important to differentiate assignments for children of different abilities. A fast learner may cover a long reading assignment in less time than it takes a slow child to read even a few pages.

Sometimes parents are justifiably irritated by assignments requiring the use of reference material that all homes do not have, especially if a library is not readily available. They also are likely to resent having their child encouraged to undertake a project involving expenses they cannot meet without financial strain, such as an elaborate project for a science fair.

If homework is to be assigned, particularly in the elementary grades, the school should help the parents understand their expected roles. Many teachers would be surprised if they could look into the homes of their students and watch the tension that frequently develops over getting homework done. Many parents dread the evening hours—which should be a pleasant family time—because of the nagging and pressures they feel obliged to use to make their children get their homework done. Many parents, too, try to help with homework but only succeed in confusing their children by using methods different from those that the school is using. Other tensions crop up in homes so crowded that boys and girls, particularly of high-school age, have trouble finding a quiet spot in which to work.

Homework that has a real purpose may have a place in the school program, but homework that is just busy work is unjustified. Both parents and children resent assignments that are given to be done at home but are never looked at, corrected, or returned by the teacher.

Extracurricular activities also may cause tensions between school and home. A play rehearsal scheduled too near suppertime, costumes that take money and time to buy or make, committee work, band practice, or even punishment scheduled for after school with no thought of how the children will be able to get home—these may all prove potential points of irritation if parental cooperation has not been sought beforehand.

Parents also have a right to expect that school activities will be open to all boys and girls. Lack of money or suitable clothing should not form a barrier between students within the school. Activity fees, expensive uniforms, trips, or parties that are too expensive for some of the children in the school can upset and embarrass these children and their parents, especially if the children are forced to miss the event.


EXPLAINING THE SCHOOL PROGRAM TO PARENTS   Much of the misunderstanding that arises between parents and teachers revolves around the parents' feeling that their children are not learning enough. Parents are proverbially fearful that their children will not learn to read and do arithmetic. They need reassurance based on facts. Methods change, and parents need answers to their questions about why certain subjects are taught in certain grades and why others are held until later. They need to understand the reasons behind new methods of teaching, new organization of classrooms, and building plans. Many parents would appreciate more interpretation by the school of the aims and goals of the whole school program and, in particular, of their child's class. They want to know the policies of their school system. Parents can be informed in PTA meetings and, even more effectively, in small classroom meetings, or in specially planned discussion groups. Written presentations sent out to each parent also may help, but they are not as effective as meetings in which parents and teachers talk over together the school's aims and methods.

Thoughtful parents are genuinely concerned about school policies and their effect on the education of their children. Teachers should not be afraid of parents' honest questions or their honest criticisms. If school personnel show a willingness to talk over controversial matters and back their policies with factual statements, they usually will find that the questioning parent and the school can come to a better understanding of one another. This does not mean that groups of parents should be encouraged to run the schools—the actual educational direction must remain in the hands of the superintendent and the staff who have been professionally trained for this task, and teachers must be free to teach according to the methods that have been found to work best. But only as parents and teachers understand one another can each child's best educational growth be attained.

## BUILDING COOPERATION BETWEEN SCHOOL, HOME, AND COMMUNITY

Parents can be drawn into the life of the school in many ways. In some schools parents are employed as aides or as helpers in the cafeteria. In some they may be volunteer helpers in the library or classroom, or be invited into the classroom to share a hobby, a skill, or some experience they have had—such as personal knowledge of a country the children may be studying. Some schools make the school a community center to which parents and children can come separately or together for many activities. A school building should be in constant use, symbolizing the place of learning in the community. Parents, children, and adults without children need to feel welcome, not only for classes but for other community experiences. Some schools have hobby nights when whole families work together in the shops and the art room. Many schools are open in the evenings for adult-education classes, thus drawing the parents into the building for educational interests of their own. Other schools open their doors for all kinds of meetings, for forums and community groups, for classes in citizenship. Some schools share their facilities with the recreation department for summer or after-school play. One city has opened a new school building which houses a county health clinic and a branch of the library. Parents who come to the school for many purposes usually have a much closer feeling for the teachers and the work of the school.

The relationship between the school and the parents may affect the work of the school as a whole as well as the way in which an individual child is helped to learn. When the school and the parents are not in sympathy and are not working together, the program of the school may be seriously damaged. Working for cooperation between school and home takes time, especially when classes are crowded and teachers are overburdened, but the effort can result in mutual respect and support.

reference manual

# STUDYING CHILDREN

This section presents additional material to be used in studying children. This material will highlight and reinforce important points already presented in *These Are Your Children* and will foster insights and skills not obtainable from reading alone. It will also provide a means of evaluating and checking statements given in the text.

# Individual Study Guide

UNDERSTANDING CHILDREN As the emphasis in today's schools turns more and more toward helping individual children achieve wholesome adjustment, it becomes increasingly important that teachers have a thorough understanding of the children in their charge. In order that each child be given counsel and guidance according to particular, specific needs, each must be understood as *an individual reacting in a social environment.* To be so understood, the complexity of factors inherent in each child and present in each background of situations, experiences, and people must be discerned. These are the influences through which each child has become an individual personality.

Every child differs from all other children. Genetic factors, environmental factors, or the impact of either on the other, may be involved in such differences. Thus physical development, mental ability, emotional maturity, and social adjustment are unique for every child. So, too, are interpersonal relationships. In the interaction of abilities and limitations, situations experienced and people known, lies the explanation of behavior characteristics of the child. This may be desirable or undesirable behavior.

*Behavior problems may occur in all children.* Such problems are easily detected when the overt behavior is unacceptable; for example, when a child has temper tantrums, steals, or is truant. But they may not be so readily noted when other people are not disturbed or affected, as when, for instance, a child is excessively timid or shy or fearful. In both kinds of responses—one shown primarily in overt behavior, the other more in inner personality trends—the child's conduct is problem conduct.

When a problem exists, when the behavior is considered maladjusted, effort should be directed toward making it more acceptable. It must be recognized that the *overt behavior is only a symptom* of underlying maladjustment. It is a manifestation that something is in need of change, that the child is less than happy and at peace in the world. To treat a symptom without understanding its cause—or, more correctly stated, its causes—is futile. Probably no more common error is made in dealing with problems of both children and adolescents than to stress the symptom and ignore its underlying basis.

The causal elements of problem behavior are not always readily identified. Frequently they are so intricately concealed that only the trained and experienced clinician is successful in bringing them to light. But before they become so complicated they usually exist in less potent form, and are discernible to one alert to their significance. It is at this time that an observant teacher armed with understanding can often forestall the development of more serious maladjustment.

If there are classroom or playground circumstances which might be contributing to a child's difficulties, the teacher generally is in a position to alter the circumstances. For instance, a child may be so self-conscious and unsure, that reciting before the class is almost a traumatic experience. Or there may be a child who is the clown of the room, looking for admiring attention from classmates. On the playground there is often seen a girl or boy who stands alone; watching a group activity but rarely participating. The explanation may be that the child feels inept, awkward; or disliked by the other children; or afraid of being hurt in rough and tumble play.

If a family situation seems to be involved, a meeting with one or both parents is often desirable. A chance remark of the child may alert the teacher to such a situation. It may be that an older sibling in the same school is scholastically superior. When two children in a family show widely different achievement in school, some parents become greatly concerned. They may urge the slower one to give more time and attention to schoolwork. They may deprive the slower one of some privilege until marks "as good as your sister's" are brought home. Loss of parental approval often means to a child loss of parental love, and is extremely threatening. Sometimes a very capable child has several additional activities urged by parents—music or art lessons, skating or tennis lessons—making for stress and tension as well as physical fatigue. Whatever home circumstances exist, the youngster's reactions at school may be affected in either social relationships or academic achievement or both.

Clearly it is important to recognize that *behavior disturbing to the progress of the class is not the only behavior which should alert a teacher.* Early recognition that understanding help is needed by a child is part of a teacher's responsibility. Should teachers feel that their skills or opportunities are not sufficient to manage a situation, they will be wise to consult with guidance counselor, adjustment teacher, or principal, depending on the school's organization. Cooperative consideration of the circumstances can then suggest steps which seem desirable, involving both school and home, and, in some instances, a specialist or a mental-health clinic whose aid is to be sought by the child's parents. The teacher should be familiar with some of the steps taken by the specialist, and provide whatever pertinent information is available.

There are many possible elements which need investigation before complete understanding of a problem can be reached. These should be in every teacher's awareness, even though it is not the teacher's role to investigate the total picture of involvement. Specialized training is a necessary prerequisite in seeking to aid the more troublesome and more serious situations which threaten a child's present and future well-being.

PURPOSE OF THE INDIVIDUAL STUDY GUIDE  The Individual Study Guide reproduced on pages 307–12 is designed to gain a clearer understanding of actual and potential adjustment of children. The Guide comprises what may be termed the *minimum essentials* of understanding behavior maladjustment. By no means does it indicate a restriction of investigation to the items it includes, for there will often be cases where even more detailed knowledge will be needed; but it does indicate the areas that should not be neglected in studying any child showing evidence of emotional and/or social maladjustment. These areas—the minimum essentials of understanding—are: (1) a clear formulation of the problem; (2) a survey of the child's physical development, including the present condition of health; (3) the home environment—parents and brothers and sisters, the attitudes and interrelationships of the entire family, and the physical elements that make up the home and the neighborhood; (4) the child's social and emotional characteristics and reactions; (5) interests, experiences, and hobbies; (6) a record of progress and adjustment in school; and (7) the results of whatever standardized tests of intelligence, achievement, and personality may have been given. The compilation of this information may then be viewed as an overall picture of the child as a total individual.

The interaction and interdependence of the many items of inquiry covered by the Guide need to be comprehended before correct interpretation can be evolved. The inexperienced investigator of human behavior frequently grasps at the first apparent cause of maladjustment and initiates a plan of management prematurely, only to discover later that the apparent cause had little significance for the real problem. More often the actual causes are bound up in a complexity of details, no one of which seems, at first, particularly vital in itself, but many of which assume real importance when considered in their effects on one another.

OBTAINING ESSENTIAL INFORMATION  Information is ordinarily obtained from the individual child, from parents, and from teachers; sometimes additional knowledge may be obtained from other members of the household, from a club leader, or from a playground supervisor.

It is desirable that, whenever possible, all angles of investigation suggested in the Guide be covered as far as possible. Generally, the free conversational comments of the person interviewed will provide information to be inserted in the various sections. The classroom teacher is not the one to seek all of this information; the student is never qualified to undertake such an investigation. The school psychologist or counselor is better equipped to proceed with any extensive inquiry into a child's problem after referral by the teacher. Such special help is not always available in the school, hence many times it may be desirable to recommend to the parents that the aid of a mental-health clinic or a specialist in private practice be sought, even though all the information desirable for such a recommendation cannot be obtained by school personnel. However, it is usually the principal rather than the classroom teacher who will make the recommendation.

# INDIVIDUAL STUDY GUIDE

Date _____

Name _____ Age _____

Address _____

Birthdate _____

Phone _____

Father's name _____

Occupation _____ Phone _____

Mother's name _____

Occupation _____ Phone _____

School _____ Grade _____

Study requested by _____ Reason for study _____

Resumé of problem: _____

_____

_____

_____

_____

Resumé of recommendations: _____

_____

_____

_____

_____

Signed _____

Date _____

# PHYSICAL DEVELOPMENT

Early Years

Birth normal _____

    instrumental _____

    premature _____

Walked at _____ months

Talked: single words at _____ sentences at _____

    baby talk _____ any defect _____

Bladder control: days _____ nights _____

Defects of development _____

Injuries _____

Operations _____

Diseases _____

Allergies _____

Present Health

Height _____ Weight _____

Underweight for body build _____ Overweight _____

Vision _____ Hearing _____

Speech _____ Fatigues easily _____

Muscular coordination _____

Characteristic physical reactions:

    energetic _____

    slow-moving _____

    lethargic _____

General appearance _____

Vaccination and Inoculation _____

Anecdotal comment: _____

# HOME BACKGROUND

|  | Age | Educational Background | Health | Relationship with child |
|---|---|---|---|---|
| Mother | _____ | _____ | _____ | _____ |
| Father | _____ | _____ | _____ | _____ |
| Siblings | _____ | _____ | _____ | _____ |
|  | _____ | _____ | _____ | _____ |
|  | _____ | _____ | _____ | _____ |
|  | _____ | _____ | _____ | _____ |

Lives in house _____ Apartment _____ Others in home _____

Own room _____ Shares with _____ Place to play _____

Language spoken at home _____

Mother at home _____ Employed _____

Neighborhood _____

_____

Supervision when mother at work _____

_____

Anecdotal comment: _____

_____

_____

_____

# INTERESTS, EXPERIENCES, HOBBIES

Likes to read _____

Prefers being read to _____

Reading materials at home _____

Reading skill _____

Kinds of stories preferred _____

Records: _____ hours per day

favorites _____

_____

TV: _____ hours per day.

favorite programs _____

_____

Has some familiarity with:

farm _____ concerts _____

city _____ zoo _____

museums _____ circus _____

travel _____

Has lessons in music _____ art _____ dancing _____

other _____

Regular allowance _____

Job experience _____

_____

Ambition for future _____

Parents' ambition _____

_____

Anecdotal comment: _____

_____

_____

## EMOTIONAL AND SOCIAL REACTIONS

Friendly _____   Shy _____

Cooperative _____   Negativistic _____

Self-assured _____   Dependent _____

Reliable _____   Careless _____

Cheerful _____   Sullen _____

Anxious _____   Rebellious _____

Excitable _____   Placid _____

Temper _____   Fearful _____

Daydreams _____   Nightmares _____

Other _____

Enough time for play _____

Parents join in play _____   Plays with siblings _____

Good athlete _____

Place to play _____   Play equipment _____

Prefers solitary play _____

     group play _____

     active games _____

     solitary games _____

Resourceful in play _____

Imaginative in play _____

Favorite pastime _____

Prefers older playmates _____

     younger playmates _____

     playmates same age _____

Accepted by peers _____

Popular _____

Anecdotal comment: _____

_____

_____

_____

# RECORD OF SCHOOL PROGRESS

Nursery school _____ At age _____

Kindergarten _____ At age _____

Schools attended _____

Grades repeated _____

Reasons for retardation _____

Grades skipped _____

Reasons for acceleration _____

Early adjustment _____

Reasons for transfer _____

Best work in _____

Difficulty with _____

Preferred subject(s) _____

Disliked subject(s) _____

Adjustment in general _____

Anecdotal comment: _____

_____

_____

# STANDARD TEST RESULTS

| Intelligence tests | C A | M A | I Q | Examiner |
|---|---|---|---|---|
| Binet Rev. _____ | ___ | ___ | ___ | _____ |
| WISC _____ | ___ | ___ | ___ | _____ |
| Group _____ | ___ | ___ | ___ | _____ |
| Achievement tests | C A | E A | GR. Equivalent | Examiner |
| | ___ | ___ | _____ | _____ |
| | ___ | ___ | _____ | _____ |
| Other tests: | ___ | ___ | _____ | _____ |
| Anecdotal comment: | | _____ | | |

312

# Guide for Parent-Teacher Conferences

Most schools today use the parent-teacher conference as a means of reporting to parents on the progress of their children. These conferences are usually scheduled twice or sometimes three times a year. The time for each conference is limited; therefore, it is important that the teacher should plan for each conference if the time is to be well spent.

## GUIDEPOSTS TO A SUCCESSFUL CONFERENCE

1. *The note home, inviting the parents to come to school, should be very friendly and informal. It should make clear to the parents that the teacher is interested in their child and that the conference is for the purpose of making things better for him. A note should never contain anything which could conceivably put the parents on the defensive or bring them to the conference in a hostile mood.*

2. *When the parents arrive, the teacher should greet them in a friendly way, putting them at ease as quickly as possible. An expression of appreciation for their coming and other cordial remarks are quite in order. It is essential that a good feeling be established before the interview really gets under way.*

3. *In getting into the conference, the teacher should make some very positive remarks about the child of these parents, relating some specific incident as an illustration. A humorous anecdote often gets things off to a good start. Most certainly an expression, on the part of the teacher, of her interest in the child helps considerably to establish a good rapport.*

4. *In getting into the conference, the teacher should make some positive remarks about the child, as a person; it is important for the teacher to begin her remarks about his work from a positive angle, pointing up his strengths before indicating where he needs to most improve. In this way she keeps the parents with her and can move into the more doubtful areas with a little more assurance of their cooperation and good feeling. Naturally, some discussions will be about children at the bottom of the class who are seemingly achieving nothing. To talk with their parents is a difficult thing for the teachers, but, even so, surely these children have done something of merit, whether in subject matter or human relationships. The teacher must have something good to say about them, with specific examples to back it up.*

5. *As the teacher talks of the academic achievements of the child, she should show the parents some of his paperwork and then indicate how she arrived at*

313

*his rating on the report card. As she shows the written work, she has an excellent opportunity to indicate the methods used in teaching the particular subjects and of interpreting the program. Many parents are skeptical of the modern methods of teaching. . . .*

6. *The teacher must not be afraid to indicate the areas in which the child needs to improve. If it is a subject-matter area in which he is weak, she should show how she is attempting to help him to improve and what the parents might do to help him at home. If it is a behavior problem, she must explain this in a kindly, positive way, being very careful not to put blame of any kind on the parents. She should let the parents know that she is seeking their help and enlightenment on the matter and should help them to feel that this problem should be a shared part of responsibility in which she is most happy to do her part. . . . The child should be presented as an immature person who needs additional guidance and help to work out the specific problem he presents.*

7. *The teacher must make a conscious effort through the interview to listen. Parents often have good ideas and are much more likely to be willing to carry them out than those a teacher might impose on them. . . . The teacher should be willing to listen, too, if the parents wish to voice their criticism. Some parents will be highly critical, but if the teacher is able to accept their feelings without becoming defensive or argumentative, she will be able to make more progress in the long run. . . . It is better to accept the criticism, letting the parents get things off their chests and then gradually and quietly getting around to interpreting the kind of thing which will help them to understand the "why" of the program and the "why" of the methods used.*

8. *In concluding the interview, the teacher should summarize the conference rather briefly, again indicating the child's strengths, where he needs to improve, and what she and the parents can do to help him to improve in all phases of his growth.*

9. *The teacher should again indicate her appreciation of the parents' visit and invite them to drop in whenever they can find a convenient time. She should also let them know that she is willing to send home a note from time to time if necessary to indicate lack of progress or outstanding progress.*

314    Adapted from PARENT-TEACHER CONFERENCES by Bailard and Strang. Copyright © 1964 by McGraw-Hill Book Company. Used with permission of McGraw-Hill Book Company.

# PARENT CONFERENCE AGENDA

Name _____ Age _____

Date _____ Grade _____

Who was present? _____

Areas to be discussed during the conference:

1. _____    6. _____

2. _____    7. _____

3. _____    8. _____

4. _____    9. _____

5. _____    10. _____

Parent Comments: _____

_____

_____

Specific Agreements or Recommendations:

1. _____

2. _____

3. _____

4. _____

5. _____

Conclusion and Miscellaneous Information:

Follow up:

# Theories of Development

ERIK ERIKSON: The Eight Stages in the Life Cycle

"Personality," Erikson has written, "can be said to develop according to steps predetermined in the human organism's readiness to be driven toward, to be aware of, and to interact with a widening social radius, beginning with a dim image of a mother and ending with an image of mankind. . . ." Following are the steps he has identified in man's psychosocial development, and the special crises they bring. In presenting them, he has emphasized that while the struggle between the negatives and positives in each crisis must be fought through successfully if the next developmental stage is to be reached, no victory is completely or forever won. . . . In each crisis, under favorable conditions, the positive is likely to outbalance the negative, and each reintegration builds strength for the next crisis. But the negative is always with us to some degree in the form of a measure of infantile anxiety, fear of abandonment—a residue of immaturity carried throughout life, which is perhaps the price man has to pay for a childhood long enough to permit him to be the learning and teaching animal, and thus to achieve his particular mastery of reality.

I. INFANCY: Trust Vs. Mistrust. *The first "task" of the infant is to develop "the cornerstone of a healthy personality," a basic sense of trust—in himself and in his environment. This comes from a feeling of inner goodness derived from "the mutual regulation of his receptive capacities with the maternal techniques of provision"—a quality of care that transmits a sense of trustworthiness and meaning. The danger, most acute in the second half of the first year, is that discontinuities in care may increase a natural sense of loss, as the child gradually recognizes his separateness from his mother, to a basic sense of mistrust that may last through life.*

II. EARLY CHILDHOOD: Autonomy Vs. Shame and Doubt. *With muscular maturation the child experiments with holding on and letting go and begins to attach enormous value to his autonomous will. The danger here is the development of a deep sense of shame and doubt if he is deprived of the opportunity to learn to develop his will as he learns his "duty," and therefore learns to expect defeat in any battle of wills with those who are bigger and stronger.*

III. PLAY AGE: Initiative Vs. Guilt. *In this stage the child's imagination is greatly expanded because of his increased ability to move around freely and to*

From Erikson. Erik, in interview with Kathryn Close. Youth and the life cycle. *Children*, March-April 1960, p. 45.

communicate. It is an age of intrusive activity, avid curiosity, and consuming fantasies which lead to feelings of guilt and anxiety. It is also the stage of the establishment of conscience. If this tendency to feel guilty is "overburdened by all-too-eager adults" the child may develop a deep-seated conviction that he is essentially bad, with a resultant stifling of initiative or a conversion of his moralism to vindictiveness.

IV.   SCHOOL AGE: Industry Vs. Inferiority. The long period of sexual latency before puberty is the age when the child wants to learn how to do and make things with others. In learning to accept instruction and to win recognition by producing "things" he opens the way for the capacity of work enjoyment. The danger in this period is the development of a sense of inadequacy and inferiority in a child who does not receive recognition for his efforts.

V.   ADOLESCENCE: Identity Vs. Identify Diffusion. The physiological revolution that comes with puberty—rapid body growth and sexual maturity—forces the young person to question "all sameness and continuities relied on earlier" and to "refight many of the earlier battles." The developmental task is to integrate childhood identifications "with the basic biological drives, native endowment, and the opportunities offered in social roles." The danger is that identity diffusion, temporarily unavoidable in this period of physical and psychological upheaval, may result in a permanent inability to "take hold" or, because of youth's tendency to total commitment, in the fixation in the young person of a negative identity, a devoted attempt to become what parents, class, or community do not want him to be.

VI.   YOUNG ADULTHOOD: Intimacy Vs. Isolation. Only as a young person begins to feel more secure in his identity is he able to establish intimacy with himself (with his inner life) and with others, both in friendships and eventually in a love-based mutually satisfying sexual relationship with a member of the opposite sex. A person who cannot enter wholly into an intimate relationship because of the fear of losing his identity may develop a deep sense of isolation.

VII.   ADULTHOOD: Generativity Vs. Self-Absorption. Out of the intimacies of adulthood grows generativity—the mature person's interest in establishing and guiding the next generation. The lack of this results in self-absorption and frequently in a "pervading sense of stagnation and interpersonal impoverishment."

VIII.   SENESCENCE: Integrity Vs. Disgust. The person who has achieved a satisfying intimacy with other human beings and who has adapted to the triumphs and disappointments of his generative activities as parent and co-worker reaches the end of life with a certain ego integrity—an acceptance of his own responsibility for what his life is and was and of its place in the flow of history. Without this "accrued ego integration" there is despair, usually marked by a display of displeasure and disgust.

## ROBERT HAVIGHURST: Developmental Tasks

Origin of Developmental Tasks "As the individual grows, he finds himself possessed of new physical and psychological resources. . . . The individual also finds himself facing new demands and expectations from the society around him. The infant is expected to learn to talk, the child to learn to subtract and divide.

"These inner and outer forces contrive to set for the individual a series of developmental tasks which must be mastered if he is to be a successful human being. . . . Some tasks arise mainly from physical maturation. . . . Other tasks arise primarily from the cultural pressure of society."

## DEVELOPMENTAL TASKS OF INFANCY AND EARLY CHILDHOOD
*Learning to walk*
*Learning to take solid foods*
*Learning to talk*
*Learning to control the elimination of body wastes*
*Learning sex differences and sexual modesty*
*Forming concepts and learning language to describe social and physical reality*
*Getting ready to read*
*Learning to distinguish right and wrong, and beginning to develop a conscience*

## DEVELOPMENTAL TASKS OF MIDDLE CHILDHOOD
*Learning physical skills necessary for ordinary games*
*Building wholesome attitudes toward oneself as a growing organism*
*Learning to get along with age-mates*
*Learning an appropriate masculine or feminine social role*
*Developing fundamental skills in reading, writing and calculating*
*Developing concepts necessary for everyday living*
*Developing conscience, morality and a scale of values*
*Achieving personal independence*
*Developing attitudes toward social groups and institutions*

## DEVELOPMENTAL TASKS OF ADOLESCENCE
*Achieving new and more mature relations with age-mates of both sexes*
*Achieving a masculine or feminine social role*
*Accepting one's physique, and using the body effectively*
*Achieving emotional independence of parents and other adults*
*Preparing for marriage and family life*
*Preparing for an economic career*
*Acquiring a set of values and an ethical system as a guide to behavior, and developing an ideology*
*Desiring and achieving socially responsible behavior*

Copyright 1952 by Longmans Green and Co. Inc. From the book *Developmental Tasks and Education* by R. J. Havighurst, 3rd edition. Published by David McKay Co. Inc. Reprinted with permission of the publishers.

## AGENTS PRINCIPALLY INVOLVED IN TASKS OF MIDDLE CHILDHOOD AND ADOLESCENCE

| Task | Self | Family | Peer Group | Television and Other Media | School | Religious Group | Economy |
|---|---|---|---|---|---|---|---|
| 1. To get along with age-mates | | | x | | x | ? | |
| 2. Learning an appropriate masculine or feminine role | x | x | x | x | x | | |
| 3. Developing basic intellectual skills | | | | ? | x | | |
| 4. Choosing and preparing for an occupation | x | x | | | x | | x |
| 5. Developing attitudes toward social groups and social institutions | | x | x | x | x | x | |
| 6. Becoming independent of parents and other adults | x | | x | | x | | |
| 7. Developing conscience and moral judgment | x | x | x | | x | x | |
| 8. Forming a system of ethics and a scale of values | x | x | x | x | x | x | |

## JEAN PIAGET: Stages of Intellectual Development

Paralleling growing interest in cognitive processes, Piaget's theory has been very influential. Piaget's main concern has been to study how children understand nature and the world about them. He has characterized intellectual development in terms of the four stages presented here.

| Stage | Approximate Ages | Characterization |
|---|---|---|
| I. Sensorimotor period | Birth to 2 years | Infant differentiates himself from objects; seeks stimulation, and makes interesting spectacles last; prior to language, meanings defined by manipulations, so that object remains "the same object" with changes in location and point of view. |
| II. Preoperational thought period | | |
| Preoperational phase | 2-4 | Child egocentric, unable to take viewpoint of other people; classifies by single salient features: if A is like B in one respect, must be like B in other respects. |
| Intuitive phase | 4-7 | Is now able to think in terms of classes, to see relationships, to handle number concepts, but is "intuitive" because he may be unaware of his classification. Gradual development of conservation in this order: mass (age 5), weight (age 6), and volume (age 7).* |
| III. Period of concrete operations | 7-11 | Able now to use logical operations such as reversibility (in arithmetic), classification (organizing objects into hierarchies of classes), and seriation (organizing objects into ordered series, such as increasing size). |
| IV. Period of formal operations | 11-15 | Final steps toward abstract thinking and conceptualization; capable of hypothesis-testing. |

*Ages for 50 percent passing, according to Kooistra (1963). The ages given by Piaget and Inhelder (1941) are generally higher.

Condensed from Piaget's *Stages of Intellectual Development* in Irving E. Siegel, "The Attainment of Concepts," Review of Child Development Research, Vol. I, edited by Martin L. Hoffman and Lois Wladis Hoffman, © 1964 by Russell Sage Foundation, New York. This condensation first appeared in *Children and Youth: Psychosocial Development*, by Boyd R. McCandless and Ellis D. Evans, © 1973 by the Dryden Press.

320

# LAWRENCE KOHLBERG: Stages of Moral Development

On the basis of theoretical and philosophical considerations and from *listening* to children of all ages and backgrounds explain their judgments about hypothetical moral dilemmas, Kohlberg constructed the six stages of moral development defined below. The six stages fall into the three levels shown: the premoral, conventional, and principled.

I.  PRECONVENTIONAL LEVEL  *At this level the child is responsive to cultural rules and labels of good and bad, right or wrong, but interprets these labels in terms of either the physical or the hedonistic consequences of action (punishment, reward, exchange of favors) or in terms of the physical power of those who enunciate the rules and labels. The level is divided into the following two stages:*

STAGE 1:  The punishment and obedience orientation. *The physical consequences of action determine its goodness or badness regardless of the human meaning or value of these consequences. Avoidance of punishment and unquestioning deference to power are valued in their own right, not in terms of respect for an underlying moral order supported by punishment and authority (the latter being Stage 4.)*

STAGE 2:  The instrumental relativist orientation. *Right action consists of that which instrumentally satisfies one's own needs and occasionally the needs of others. Human relations are viewed in terms like those of the marketplace. Elements of fairness, of reciprocity, and of equal sharing are present, but they are always interpreted in a physical, pragmatic way. Reciprocity is a matter of "you scratch my back and I'll scratch yours," not of loyalty, gratitude, or justice.*

II.  CONVENTIONAL LEVEL  *At this level, maintaining the expectations of the individual's family, group, or nation is perceived as valuable in its own right, regardless of immediate and obvious consequences. The attitude is one not only of conformity to personal expectation and social order but of loyalty to it, of actively maintaining, supporting, and justifying the order and of identifying with the persons or groups involved in it. At this level, there are the following two stages:*

STAGE 3:  The interpersonal concordance or "good boy–nice girl" orientation. *Good behavior is that which pleases or helps others and is approved by them. There is much conformity to stereotypical images of what is majority or "natural" behavior. Behavior is frequently judged by intention—"he means well" becomes important for the first time. One earns approval by being "nice."*

STAGE 4:  The "law and order" orientation. *There is orientation toward authority, fixed rules, and the maintenance of the social order. Right behavior consists of doing one's duty, showing respect for authority, and maintaining the given social order for its own sake.*

III.  POSTCONVENTIONAL, AUTONOMOUS, OR PRINCIPLED LEVEL  *At this level, there is a clear effort to define moral values and principles that have validity and application apart from the authority of the groups or persons holding these principles and apart from the individual's own identification with these groups. This level again has two stages:*

STAGE 5:  The social contract, legalistic orientation. *This stage generally has utilitarian overtones. Right action tends to be defined in terms of general individual rights and in terms of standards that have been critically examined and agreed upon by the whole society. There is a clear awareness of the relativism of personal values and opinions and a corresponding emphasis upon procedural rules for reaching consensus. Aside from what is constitutionally and democratically agreed upon, the right is a matter of personal "values" and "opinion." The result is an emphasis upon the "legal point of view," but with an emphasis upon the possibility of changing law in terms of rational considerations of social utility (rather than freezing it in terms of Stage 4 "law and order"). Outside the legal realm, free agreement and contract are the binding elements of obligation. This is the "official" morality of the American government and Constitution.*

*STAGE 6:  The universal ethical-principle orientation. Right is defined by the decision of conscience in accord with self-chosen ethical principles appealing to logical comprehensiveness, universality, and consistency. These principles are abstract and ethical (the Golden Rule, the categorical imperative); they are not concrete moral rules like the Ten Commandments. At heart, these are universal principles of justice, of the reciprocity and equality of the human rights, and of respect for the dignity of human beings as individual persons.*

The full definition of stages is more detailed than is shown here and is based on separate treatments of thirty basic moral concepts that can be found in any culture.

From Lawrence Kohlberg in CRM Books, *Developmental Psychology Today,* © 1971 by Ziff-Davis Publishing Co.

# Charting Development

Together with the Summary of Normal Development (pages 349–53), the graphic materials in this section provide a rapid overview of the various areas and stages of growth. In referring to these summaries, the reader should bear in mind several concepts that are basic to any discussion of "normal" development. First, even though all children progress through the same sequence of growth, each individual child grows at a unique rate. Second, there are no clear boundaries between the so-called *stages* of development or between the various *areas* of development. Successive periods of growth merge gradually and almost imperceptibly one into another, and at each stage there is a complex intertwining of physical, mental, emotional, and social development.

The graph at the right of the page illustrates yet another concept underlying any generalization about "normal" development. Whatever characteristic we consider—whether height, weight, intelligence, self-reliance, or any other—we find in a large group selected at random that most people possess the trait in an average amount, with about 68 percent falling within a normal range in the middle of the distribution. Similarly, the development norms established for any age level are those which a *majority* of children—but not all of them—display at that age. Many children will reach this developmental level much earlier than the average, and many will reach it much later.

In short, the following summaries of normal development are dependable and meaningful only if correctly interpreted with the understanding that (1) individual children vary; each being like no one else; (2) "development" refers not to any single area of growth, such as physical growth, but to the overall pattern of growth; and (3) "normal" means not a point on a scale but a *range*, extending over a relatively wide portion of a measure. When interpreted in the light of these qualifications, the charts, graphs, diagrams, and word pictures on the following pages should extend the reader's understanding not only of "normal" development but of the developmental patterns of particular children.

THE "NORMAL" DISTRIBUTION OF SCORES  This is the distribution of scores that would be expected if 1000 randomly selected persons were measured on any biological or psychological trait. Each dot represents one individual's score. Curves actually obtained only approximate this curve, of course, but they come remarkably close to it.

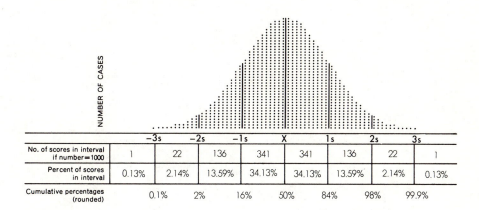

| | | | | | | | | |
|---|---|---|---|---|---|---|---|---|
| No. of scores in interval if number=1000 | 1 | 22 | 136 | 341 | 341 | 136 | 22 | 1 |
| Percent of scores in interval | 0.13% | 2.14% | 13.59% | 34.13% | 34.13% | 13.59% | 2.14% | 0.13% |
| Cumulative percentages (rounded) | 0.1% | 2% | 16% | 50% | 84% | 98% | 99.9% | |

325

# PHYSICAL DEVELOPMENT

## DEVELOPMENT OF MOTOR ABILITIES

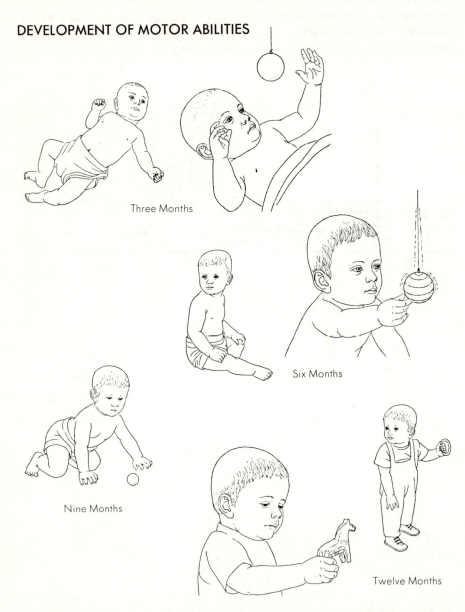

Three Months

Six Months

Nine Months

Twelve Months

FIGURE 1. Development of motor abilities in growing infants is controlled by maturation of the nervous, muscular, and other body systems. Most infants can roll over at about three months of age, sit erect between six and eight months, crawl by ten months and stand by twelve months. The order of motor development is rarely altered. Certain cognitive developments (bottom row) appear to be linked to maturation of the central nervous system. As early as the second month infants begin forming "schemata," or mental representations, of events and objects. For the next six months they pay attention to events and objects that differ moderately from these schemata. They pay less attention to familiar or totally novel events. At about eight or nine months appear the first signs of active mental work, in which the infant tries to generate hypotheses to explain novel events.

326

# SKELETAL MATURATION

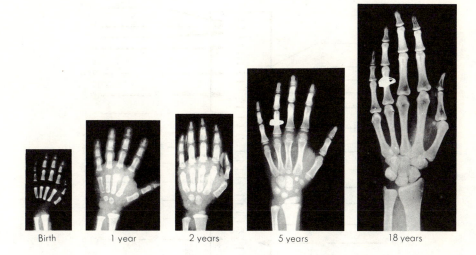

Birth 1 year 2 years 5 years 18 years

FIGURE 2. Bone development begins during the sixth week after conception and is not generally completed until the individual is around twenty. These X rays of hand and wrist show skeletal maturation of girls at various stages of development between birth and early adulthood. The development of the wrist (carpal development) is one commonly used measure of skeletal maturation.

Figure 2:   Reproduced from Radiographic Atlas of Skeletal Development of the Hand and Wrist, 2nd edition, by William Walter Greulich and S. Idell Pyle. With the permission of the publishers, Stanford University Press, © 1950 and 1959 by the Board of Trustees of the Leland Stanford Junior University.

327

# GROWTH CHART

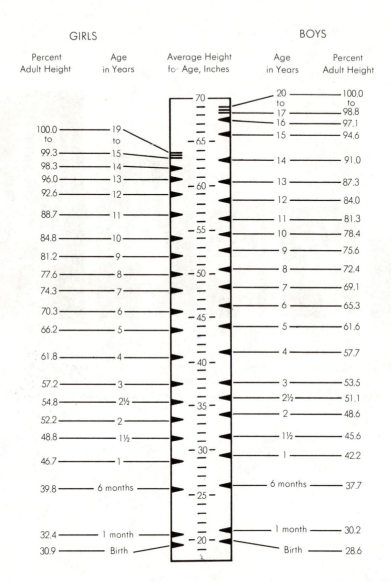

FIGURE 3. This Growth Chart shows (in the middle column) the average height, at different ages, of girls from birth to nineteen years as shown on the left, and of boys from birth to twenty years as shown on the right. This chart can be used for predicting probable adult stature by taking the height of a child at a given age and figuring from the percentage indicated. A seven-year-old girl, for example, has already attained about 74.3 percent of her growth in height. If she is an inch taller than average (49 instead of 48), she may grow to be almost 66 inches tall. An eight-year-old boy has attained about 72.4 percent of his adult height. If he is an inch shorter than the average for his age (50 inches instead of 51), he may grow to be 68 inches tall.

*Figure 3: From "How Children Grow" by Nancy Bayley, from the book,* The Encyclopedia of Child Care and Guidance *edited by Sidonie Matsner Gruenberg; © 1954, 1956, 1959, 1963 by Doubleday and Company, Inc. Reprinted by permission of the publisher.*

# PHYSICAL GROWTH RECORDS

PHYSICAL GROWTH RECORD FOR GIRLS

PHYSICAL GROWTH RECORD FOR BOYS

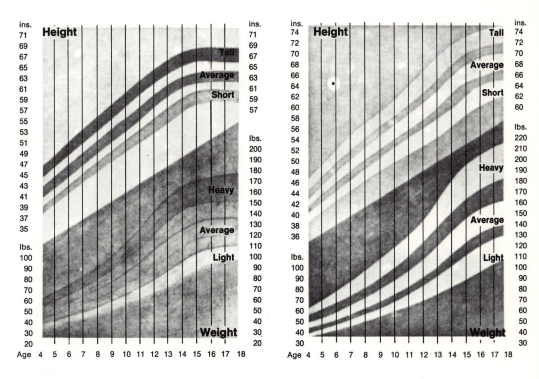

FIGURES 4 and 5.   These physical growth records indicate normal height and weight ranges for ages six through eighteen. Weight ranges are given for different body builds, while height ranges characterize a child in short, average, and tall categories.

Figures 4 and 5:   (left) Adapted from "Physical Growth Record for Girls" from Physical Growth Record for Girls by the Joint Committee on Health Problems in Education of the NEA and AMA. Reprinted by permission of the American Association for Health, Physical Education, and Recreation.
(right) Adapted from "Physical Growth Record for Boys" from Physical Growth Record for Boys by the Joint Committee on Health Problems in Education of the NEA and AMA. Reprinted by permission of the American Association for Health, Physical Education, and Recreation.

# A GIRL'S GROWTH

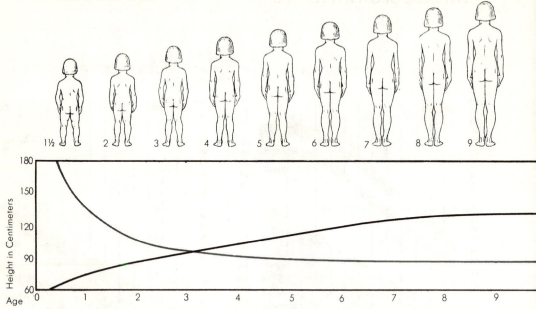

FIGURE 6. A girl growing up is shown at regular intervals from infancy to maturity. The figures show the change in the form of her body as well as her increase in height. The height curve (gray) is an average for girls in North America and western Europe. Superposed on it is

# A BOY'S GROWTH

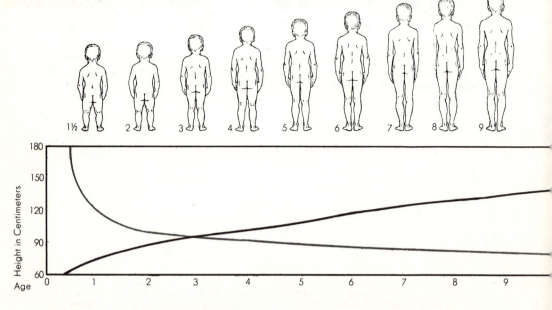

FIGURE 7. A boy growing up is shown at the same age intervals as the girl. Again the height curve and velocity curve of his growth are below the figures that show the development of his body. His adolescent growth spurt comes some two years later than the girl's.

330

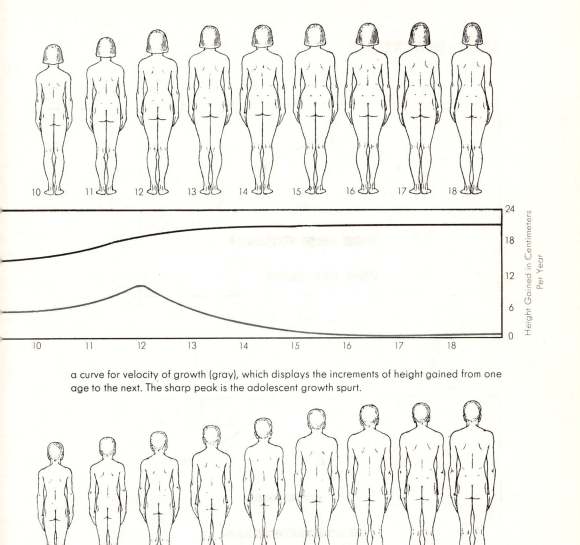

a curve for velocity of growth (gray), which displays the increments of height gained from one age to the next. The sharp peak is the adolescent growth spurt.

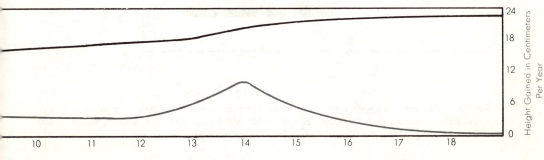

The human figures in both of these illustrations (Figures 6 and 7) are based on photographs in the longitudinal-growth studies of Nancy Bayley and Leona Bayer of the University of California at Berkeley.

331

# ADOLESCENT GROWTH

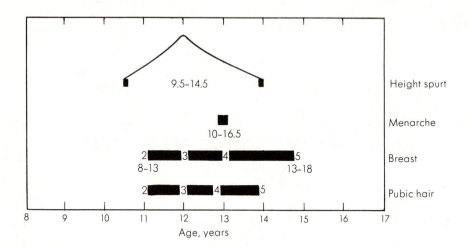

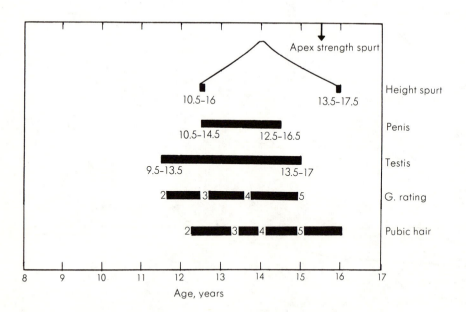

FIGURE 8. Diagram of sequence of events at adolescence in boys and girls. The average boy and girl are represented. The range of ages within which each event charted may begin and end is given by the figures placed directly below its start and finish.

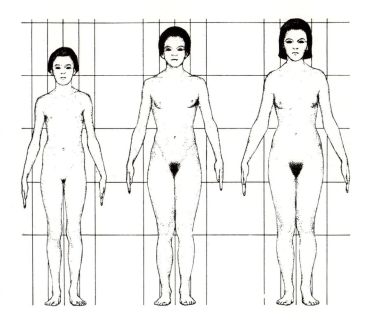

FIGURE 9.  Three girls, all with the chronological age of 12.75 years, differed dramatically in development according to whether the particular girl had not yet reached puberty (left), was part of the way through it (middle), or had finished her development (right). This range of variation is completely normal. This drawing and the one in Figure 10 are based on photographs made by J. M. Tanner and his colleagues at Institute of Child Health of University of London.

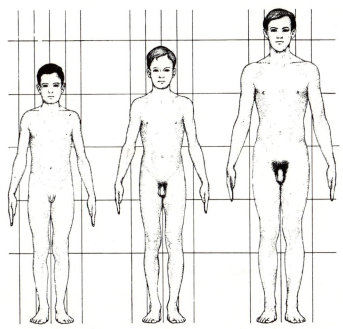

FIGURE 10.  Three boys, all of the chronological age of 14.75 years, showed a similar variation in the range of their development. Evidently some boys have entirely finished their growth and sexual maturation before others even begin theirs.

# LANDMARKS OF NORMAL BEHAVIOR DEVELOPMENT

| Age | Motor Behavior | Adaptive Behavior | Language | Personal and Social Behavior |
|---|---|---|---|---|
| Under 4 weeks | Makes alternating crawling movements<br>Moves head laterally when placed in prone position | Responds to sound of rattle and bell<br>Regards moving objects momentarily | Small, throaty, undifferentiated noises | Quiets when picked up<br>Impassive face |
| 4 weeks | Tonic neck reflex positions predominate<br>Hands fisted<br>Head sags but can hold head erect for a few seconds | Follows moving objects to the midline<br>Shows no interest and drops objects immediately | Beginning vocalization, such as cooing, gurgling, and grunting | Regards face and diminishes activity<br>Responds to speech |
| 16 weeks | Symmetrical postures predominate<br>Holds head balanced<br>Head lifted 90 degrees when prone on forearm | Follows a slowly moving object well<br>Arms activate on sight of dangling object | Laughs aloud<br>Sustained cooing and gurgling | Spontaneous social smile<br>Aware of strange situations |
| 28 weeks | Sits steadily, leaning forward on hands<br>Bounces actively when placed in standing position | One-hand approach and grasp of toy<br>Bangs and shakes rattle<br>Transfers toys | Vocalizes "m-m-m" when crying<br>Makes vowel sounds, such as "ah, ah" | Takes feet to mouth<br>Pats mirror image |
| 40 weeks | Sits alone with good coordination<br>Creeps<br>Pulls self to standing position | Matches two objects at midline<br>Attempts to imitate scribble | Says "da-da" or equivalent<br>Responds to name or nickname | Responds to social play, such as "pat-a-cake" and "peek-a-boo"<br>Feeds self cracker and holds own bottle |
| 52 weeks | Walks with one hand held<br>Stands alone briefly | | Uses expressive jargon<br>Gives a toy on request | Cooperates in dressing |
| 15 months | Toddles<br>Creeps upstairs | | Says 3 to 5 words meaningfully<br>Pats pictures in book<br>Shows shoes on request | Points or vocalizes wants<br>Throws objects in play or refusal |
| 18 months | Walks, seldom falls<br>Hurls ball<br>Walks upstairs with one hand held | Builds a tower of 3 or 4 cubes<br>Scribbles spontaneously and imitates a writing stroke | Says 10 words, including name<br>Identifies one common object on picture card<br>Names ball and carries out two directions, for example "put on table" and "give to mother" | Feeds self in part, spills<br>Pulls toy on string<br>Carries or hugs a special toy, such as a doll |
| 2 years | Runs well, no falling<br>Kicks large ball<br>Goes upstairs and downstairs alone | Builds a tower of 6 or 7 cubes<br>Aligns cubes, imitating train<br>Imitates vertical and circular strokes | Uses 3-word sentences<br>Carries out four simple directions | Pulls on simple garment<br>Domestic mimicry<br>Refers to self by name |
| 3 years | Rides tricycle<br>Jumps from bottom steps<br>Alternates feet going upstairs | Builds tower of 9 or 10 cubes<br>Imitates a 3-cube bridge<br>Copies a circle and a cross | Gives sex and full name<br>Uses plurals<br>Describes what is happening in a picture book | Puts on shoes<br>Unbuttons buttons<br>Feeds self well<br>Understands taking turns |
| 4 years | Walks downstairs one step per tread<br>Stands on one foot for 4 to 8 seconds | Copies a cross<br>Repeats 4 digits<br>Counts 3 objects with correct pointing | Names colors, at least one correctly<br>Understands five prepositional directives—"on," "under," "in," "in back of" or "in front of," and "beside" | Washes and dries own face<br>Brushes teeth<br>Plays cooperatively with other children |
| 5 years | Skips, using feet alternately<br>Usually has complete sphincter control | Copies a square<br>Draws a recognizable man with a head, body, limbs<br>Counts 10 objects accurately | Names the primary colors<br>Names coins: pennies, nickels, dimes<br>Asks meanings of words | Dresses and undresses self<br>Prints a few letters<br>Plays competitive exercise games |

FIGURE 11.  Normal behavior development must be considered in terms of the individual as a functioning whole. The indicators presented here for motor development, adaptive behavior, language, and personal and social behavior can serve as general guidelines of a normal developmental pattern from infancy through five years.

334

# EMOTIONAL AND SOCIAL DEVELOPMENT

## DEVELOPMENTAL TASKS

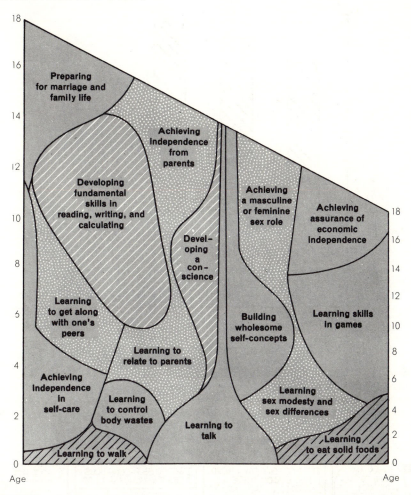

FIGURE 12. At each period of growth, the individual is confronted with certain developmental tasks—skills, attitudes, and understandings which must be acquired to meet society's expectations and to satisfy a person's own needs for growth and accomplishment. The characteristics and continuity of these developmental tasks are represented schematically in the diagram above. Some tasks are compressed into a short period of time (areas striped in black); others persist for many years and span several phases of development (areas striped in white); and some alter and merge into predominant tasks of a given phase of development (adolescence, for example), as can be seen by reading across the age scales. The relative importance of a task at any particular age is indicated by its width. The diagram does not represent all of the developmental tasks for any given age.

# AGGRESSION

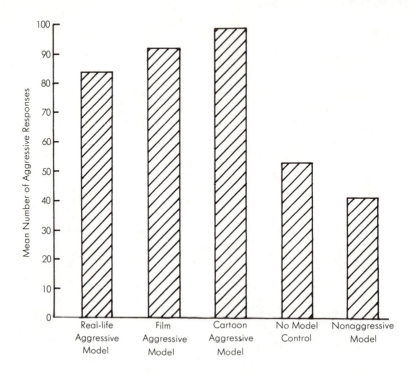

FIGURE 13. Mean number of aggressive responses performed by children in each of five groups. Experiments by Bandura, Ross, and Ross (1961, 1963) show that young children who have been exposed to real-life film or cartoon models of aggressive behavior show more aggressive responses in a frustrating situation following the exposure than do children who had no model or a nonaggressive model to follow.

FIGURE 14. Overt aggression, though a very natural response, is almost never a satisfactory way of dealing with frustration. The mature individual is more likely to seek ways of overcoming the obstacles in his or her path or to find other compensating sources of satisfaction.

| Study* | Age | Differences | Comments |
|---|---|---|---|
| OBSERVATIONAL STUDIES | | | |
| Dawe 1934 | Nursery school | Boys | Boys participated in more quarrels. |
| Green 1933 | Nursery school | Boys | Boys had more quarrels. |
| Sears et al. 1953 | Nursery school | No diff. | Total aggressive responses—boys slightly higher, but not significantly so. |
| Sears et al. 1965 | Nursery school | Boys No diff. | In 7 out of 10 types of aggression. Verbal disapproval, tattling, and prosocial aggression. |
| Jersild and Markey 1935 | 2-5 | Boys No diff. | More physical quarrels. Verbal quarreling. |
| Muste and Sharpe 1947 | 2-5 | No diff. | Boys slightly more physical and girls slightly more verbal aggression. |
| McKee and Leader 1955 | 3-4 | No diff. | Pairs of children playing. |
| Siegel 1956 | 3-5 | Boys | Like-sex pairs playing. |
| McCandless et al. 1961 | 3½-5 | Boys | Initiated more conflicts and resisted attack more frequently. |
| Seigel et al. 1959 | 5 | Boys | In type of interaction, aggression was rank order 3 for boys, and 7 for girls, out of 9 possible categories. |
| Walters et al. 1957 | 2-5 | Boys | Aggressive contacts with peers. |
| Whiting and Whiting 1962 | 3-6 | Boys | Physical aggression in six cultures. |
| RATING STUDIES | | | |
| Hattwick 1937 | 2-4½ | Boys | Negativistic behavior. |
| Beller and Neubauer 1963 | 2-5 | Boys | Mothers' reports of hyperaggression and hyperactivities in clinic children. |
| Beller and Turner 1962 | Preschool | Boys | Several subscales of aggression. |
| Sears et al. 1957 | 5 | No diff. | Mothers' reports. |
| Beller 1962 | 5½-6 | Boys | General aggression. |
| Digman 1963 | 6-7 | Boys | Teachers' ratings—more negativistic, aggressive, noisy. |
| Feshbach 1956 | 5-8 | Boys | Teachers' ratings. |
| Toigo et al. 1962 | 8 | Boys | Nominated by peers as more aggressive. |
| Tuddenham 1952 | 8 and 10 | Boys | Considered more quarrelsome by peers. |
| Sanford et al. 1943 | 5-14 | Boys | Teachers attributed aggression more to boys. |
| EXPERIMENTAL STUDIES | | | |
| Bandura et al. 1961 | Nursery school | Boys No diff. | Imitative physical aggression. Imitative verbal aggression. |
| Bandura et al. 1963 | Nursery school | Boys | Total aggression and nonimitative aggression. |
| Bandura et al. 1963 | Nursery school | Boys | Imitative and nonimitative aggression. |
| Bandura 1965 | Nursery school | Boys | Aggressive acts. |
| Hartup and Himino 1959 | Nursery school | Boys | More doll-play aggression with isolation as a precondition. |

*See source of chart for complete references to studies.
Source: E. E. Maccoby (Ed.), *The development of sex differences*, Stanford, Calif.: Stanford University Press, 1966. Pp. 323-24.

FIGURE 15. Summary of research findings on sex differences in aggression.

*Figure 15: Excerpted with permission of the publisher from "Classified Summary of Research in Sex Differences," in* The Development of Sex Differences, *edited by Eleanor E. Maccoby (Stanford: Stanford University Press, 1966), pp. 323-324.*

# CHILDREN'S FEARS

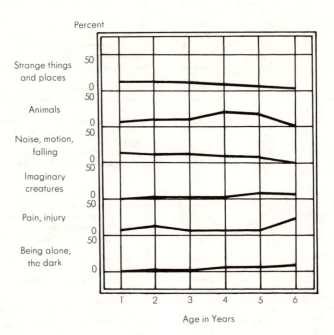

Age in Years

FIGURE 16. Situations in which children show fear change with age. As the child's imaginative abilities increase in addition to the understanding of potential danger, the range of situations found frightening will widen.

# SOCIALIZATION ACROSS THE LIFE CYCLE

| Life cycle stage | Approximate ages | Most significant others | Major dilemma of value-theme differentiation and integration security/challenge |
|---|---|---|---|
| I. Infancy | 0–12 months | mother | AFFECTIVE GRATIFICATION/ SENSORIMOTOR EXPERIENCING |
| II. Early childhood | 1–2 years | mother, father | COMPLIANCE/SELF-CONTROL |
| III. Oedipal period | 3–5 years | father, mother, siblings, play-mates | EXPRESSIVITY/INSTRUMENTALITY |
| IV. Later childhood | 6–11 years | parents, same sex peers, teachers | PEER RELATIONSHIPS/ EVALUATED ABILITIES |
| V. Early adolescence | 12–15 years | parents, same sex peers, opposite sex peers, teachers | ACCEPTANCE/ACHIEVEMENT |
| VI. Later adolescence | 16–20 years | same sex peers, opposite sex peers, parents, teachers, loved one, wife or husband | INTIMACY/AUTONOMY |
| VII. Young adulthood | 21–29 years | loved one, husband or wife, children, employers, friends | CONNECTION/SELF-DETERMINATION |
| VIII. Early maturity | 30–44 years | wife or husband, children, superiors, colleagues, friends, parents | STABILITY/ ACCOMPLISHMENT |
| IX. Full maturity | 45 to retirement age | wife or husband, children, col-leagues, friends, younger associates | DIGNITY/CONTROL |
| X. Old age | Retirement age to death | remaining family, long-term friends, neighbors | MEANINGFUL INTEGRATION/ AUTONOMY |

FIGURE 17. A stage developmental model of the ideal-typical life cycle in contemporary urban, middle-class America.

Figure 17: Chad Gordon, "Socialization Across the Life-Cycle: A Stage Developmental Model," Department of Social Relations, Harvard University, 1969, and "Role and Value Development Across the Life-Cycle," in "A Symposium on Role Theory" edited by John Jackson, Sociological Studies IV: Role (London: Cambridge University Press, © 1971.) Reprinted by permission of W. W. Norton and Company, Inc.

# PARENT-CHILD INTERACTIONS

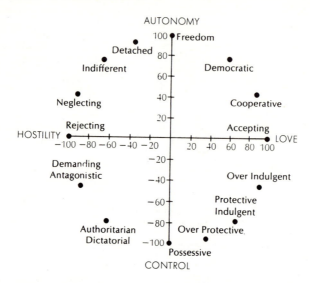

FIGURE 18. A two-dimensional model of parent-child interactions as proposed by Schaefer. The four combinations of love-hostility and autonomy-control produce very different children. The types of parental attitudes characteristic of the various combinations are outlined along the perimeter of the figure.

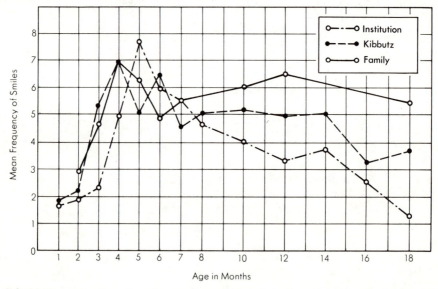

FIGURE 19. As family patterns become more diverse, behaviors of developing children will no doubt show greater variation. In as early a response as a smile, frequency of smiling varied among infants raised in three different environments—institution, kibbutz, and family.

Figure 18: From Schaefer, E. S., "Parental Attitudes and Child Behavior," 1961, J. C. Glidewell (ed.). Courtesy of Charles C Thomas, Publisher, Springfield, Illinois.
Figure 19: From J. L. Gewirtz, "The Cause of Infant Smiling in Four Child-Rearing Environments in Israel." In B. M. Foss (ed.), Determinants of Infant Behavior, Vol. III. London: Methuen, 1965. By permission of the publishers and the Tavistock Institute of Human Relations.

# A CHILD'S NEED FOR PROTECTION

## THE CHILD'S BEHAVIOR
Is the child aggressive, disruptive, destructive? Such a child may be acting out of need to secure attention. He may be shouting for help. His behavior may reflect a hostile or emotionally destructive climate at home, or he may be imitating destructive parental behavior.

Is the child shy, withdrawn, passive, or overly compliant? This child may be as emotionally damaged as the aggressive child. He has internalized his problem; his cry for help is a whisper instead of a shout. He may be inattentive; he may daydream; he may be out of touch with reality.

Is the child a habitual truant—chronically late or tardy? Is he frequently absent for flimsy reasons and lame excuses? This behavior points to problems of adjustment—problems at home, in school, within the child, or in combination.

Does the child come to school much too early? Does he loiter and hang around after school is dismissed? This child may be seeking to escape from home—he may lack normal satisfactions at home. On the other hand, he may be "pushed out" in the morning and has no place to go after school because there is no one to supervise or care for him.

## THE CHILD'S APPEARANCE
Is the child inadequately dressed for the weather? Is his clothing torn, tattered, or unwashed? Is the child not clean; is he unbathed? Do other children refuse to sit next to him because he smells? These are all signs of physical neglect, a condition not related to poverty. It reflects a breakdown in household management and in concern for the child.

Is the child undernourished? Is he coming to school without breakfast; does he go without lunch? Again, this is often a problem unrelated to poverty.

Is the child always tired? Does he sleep in class? Is he lethargic or listless? Such conditions are symptomatic of parental failure to regulate the child's routines, or of family problems which disrupt family routines.

Is the child in need of medical attention? Does he need glasses or dental work?

Does the child bear bruises, welts, and contusions? Is he injured frequently? Does he complain of beatings or other maltreatment? Is there reason to suspect physical or sexual abuse?

## PARENTAL ATTITUDES
Are the parents aggressive or abusive when approached about problems concerning their child?

Are they apathetic or unresponsive?

Is parental behavior, as observed by school personnel, or as related by the child, bizarre and strange?

Do the parents show little concern about the child? Do they fail to show interest in what he is doing? Do they fail to participate in school activities or to permit the child to participate?

FIGURE 20.   With a growing recognition of children's rights each person should be aware of indications that a child might need protection. A child's own behavior and appearance as well as parental attitudes can help reveal a child's need for help.

---

Figure 20:   By courtesy of The American Humane Association—Children's Division.

# INTELLECTUAL AND COGNITIVE DEVELOPMENT

## DEVELOPMENT OF LANGUAGE BEHAVIOR

| Indicators | Age expected (months) |
|---|---|
| I. PRESPEECH VOCALIZATIONS | |
| Crying—explosive sounds, grunts, sneezes, sighs, coughs, guttural sounds | 0–2 |
| Vowel sounds—"a" as in "fat," "i" as in "fit," "e" as in "set," "u" as in "up," and "u" as in "food" | 4 |
| All speech sounds, random vocalization | |
| Babbling stage—sounds "uttered for the mere delight of uttering them" | 8 |
| Lalling period—phoneme practice, imitation of heard sounds, "ma ma," "da da," "ba ba" | 11 |
| | |
| II. SPEECH | |
| Understands assortment of action words—"drink," "go," "come," "give," "bye bye" | 12 |
| Generalized meaning of nouns—"da da" may refer to any man | 12 |
| Single-word sentences—"give," "ball," "dog" | 12 |
| Early sentence stage—nouns, verbs, and some adverbs and adjectives, "good," "nice," "hot." No prepositions or pronouns | 17 |
| Understands simple sentences—"Where is the ball?" "Give mother the spoon." "Want to go bye bye?" Active vocabulary about twenty words | 18 |
| Short sentence stage—two-word sentences, excess of nouns, lack of articles, prepositions | 24 |
| Comprehends simple requests and is able to carry them out—"Give me the kitty." "Put the spoon in the cup." Stanford-Binet Test | 24 |
| Identifies objects by use | 30 |
| Question-asking stage—questions asked mainly for pleasure of asking | 36 |
| Complete sentence stage—five-word sentences, virtually all parts of speech present | 48 |
| Counts three objects (Stanford-Binet) | 60 |
| Knows meaning of numbers | 72 |
| Knows meaning of "morning," "afternoon," "night," "summer," "winter" (Stanford-Binet) | 78 |

FIGURE 21. Indicators of progress in speech development start with such prespeech vocalizations as crying and babbling and develop to more and more complex vocalizations. Language maturity is estimated in terms of articulation, vocabulary, adaptive use, and comprehension.

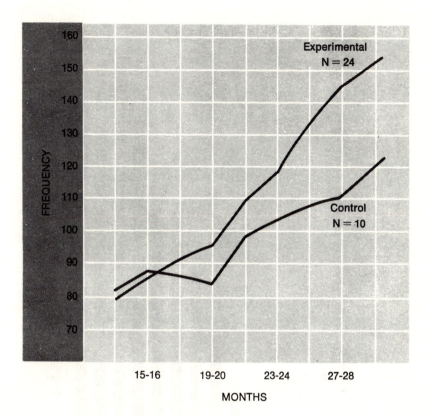

FIGURE 22. A child's experience of being read to can enhance language development. The mean phoneme frequency scores of read-to and non-read-to children indicate the growing advantage of the read-to child.

Figure 22: Reproduced from Orvis C. Irwin, "Infant Speech: Effect of Systematic Reading of Stories," Journal of Speech and Hearing Research, 1960, 3, Figure 1, p. 189. With the permission of the author and the American Speech and Hearing Association.

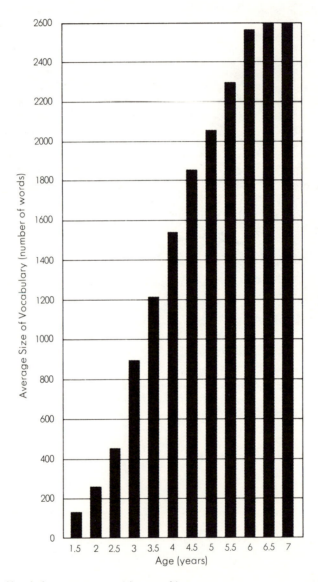

FIGURE 23. Vocabulary size is one indicator of language maturity. Here average vocabulary sizes at various ages are shown from ten sample groups of children used in the study.

Figure 23: From Biological Foundations of Language, Figure 4.1, page 133. Graph showing "Emergence of Various Developmental Milestones in the Acquisition of Language" by E. H. Lenneberg. From John Wiley & Sons, 1967.

# CHILDREN'S USE OF THE MASS MEDIA

FIGURE 24.  AVERAGE NUMBER OF HOURS PER WEEK VIEWED BY CHILDREN, FEBRUARY 1970 (IN QUINTILES)

| Quintile | Ages 2-5 | Ages 6-11 |
|---|---|---|
| 1 (heaviest) | 56 | 46 |
| 2 | 36 | 30 |
| 3 | 26 | 23 |
| 4 | 17 | 15 |
| 5 (lightest) | 4 | 5 |
| | | |
| Composite Feb 1970 | 28 | 24 |
| Composite Nov–Dec 1969 | 28.4 | 23.6 |
| Composite Jan–Feb 1970 | 30.41 | 25.49 |
| Composite Jan–Feb 1974 | 30.16 | 26.92 |

FIGURE 25.  TELEVISION VIEWING EACH WEEK IN THE FOUR WEEKS' PERIOD ENDING FEBRUARY 24, 1974*

A.  Average number of hours viewed by children

| Period of Usage | Ages 2-5 | Ages 6-11 |
|---|---|---|
| Monday–Friday 4:30 to 7:30 PM | 5.76 | 5.19 |
| Saturday 7:00 AM to 1:00 PM | 2.45 | 2.18 |
| Monday–Sunday 7:30 to 8:00 PM | 1.56 | 1.71 |
| Monday–Sunday 8:00 to 11:00 PM | 6.24 | 8.65 |

B.  Percentages of television usage

| Period of Usage | Households | Ages 2-5 | Ages 6-11 |
|---|---|---|---|
| Monday–Friday 7:30 to 8:00 PM | 60.4 | 43.2 | 47.3 |
| Saturday 8:00 AM to 1:00 PM | 22.9 | 42.6 | 42.1 |
| Monday–Sunday 8:00 to 11:00 PM | 64.2 | 29.7 | 41.2 |
| *Program Type:* | | | |
| General Drama | 19.9 | 10.9 | 13.4 |
| Suspense and Mystery Drama | 20.4 | 8.1 | 11.5 |
| Situation Comedy | 21.2 | 11.0 | 16.2 |
| Western | 20.2 | 12.1 | 15.5 |
| Variety | 21.1 | 11.7 | 15.0 |
| Feature Films | 19.9 | 6.9 | 12.1 |
| Children's Weekend Daytime | 6.0 | 13.1 | 12.0 |

*The Nielsen data cited are derived from Nielsen television audience measurements,and like the data in reports of these measurements,are estimates of the size and makeup of TV audiences and other characteristics of television usage. The amounts and percentages as used here should not be regarded as a representation by Nielsen that the measurements are exact mathematical values.

FIGURES 24 and 25.  The information and ideas to which children are exposed by the mass media comprise an important part of their learning environment. Of special concern to parents and teachers is the impact of television, the one medium that children use almost universally. In January–February 1974, children two to five years old averaged 30.16 hours every week before the TV; children six to eleven averaged 26.92 hours (see Figure 24). This chart (Figure 24) divides the children into two age groups (ages 2-5 and ages 6-11) and each of these groups into fifths, or quintiles, by the degree of their television viewing. One prime factor accounting for differences reported in Figure 24 appears to be parental supervision or lack of it. Figure 25 indicates the heaviest watching periods for young people and types of programs viewed.

# INTELLIGENCE AND CREATIVITY

HIGH I.Q

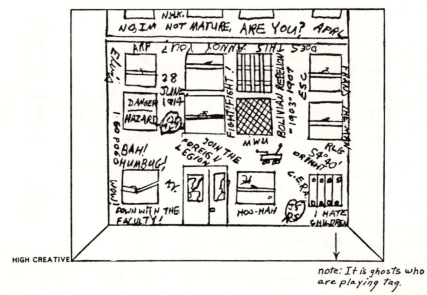

HIGH CREATIVE

note: It is ghosts who are playing tag.

FIGURE 26.   Although a high IQ is necessary to creativity in fields such as science and mathematics, creativity is not simply a matter of intelligence. People who are highly intelligent may rank very low in creativity, and, conversely, people who are highly creative do not always have exceptionally high IQ's. What distinguishes the creative individual more than intelligence level is originality and independence of thought. Some of the differences between intelligence and creativity are suggested by the drawings on this page. The first was made by an adolescent who was highly intelligent but not highly creative; the second, by one who was highly creative but not highly intelligent. The directions to both youngsters were identical: "Draw a picture appropriate to the title, 'Playing Tag in the School Yard.' You may draw any picture you like—whatever you may imagine for the theme." The highly creative adolescent has used these instructions merely as a point of departure for self-expression. This drawing is not only freer than that of the highly intelligent youngster, but also more playful and humorous.

Figure 26:   From Creativity and Intelligence: Explorations with Gifted Students by Jacob W. Getsels and Phillip W. Jackson, John Wiley & Sons, Inc., 1962.

# RETARDATION IN INFANCY

## MOTOR BEHAVIOR

| *Showing No Retardation* | *Showing Retardation* | *Showing Unusual or Deviant Behavior* |
|---|---|---|
| 0 mo. Reflex responses | Kicking activity | Failure to adapt to holding |
| Arm activation | Support of weight on lower extremities | |
| Hand engagement<br>Rolling: prone to supine | Head control: pull to sit | Rocking (excessive) |
| Emergence of hand-to-mouth maneuver | Rolling: supine to prone | Disappearance of thumb-sucking |
| Maturation of grasping patterns | Foot play (hand-foot; foot-mouth) | Absence of self-touching |
| Lifting legs high in extension (supine) | Sitting erect | Decreasing skill in coordination of movements |
| Head control in prone | Changing position: sitting to prone and back; pivoting | Unusual motility patterns: hand waving, hand posturing, "athetoid" movements |
| | Reaching out to people, toys | Inhibition of movement |
| | Creeping (mild retardation) | Poor modulation of movement (poor modulation of motor impulse |
| | Pulling to stand | discharge) |
| 12 mo. | Walking | |

## LANGUAGE BEHAVIOR

| | | |
|---|---|---|
| 0 mo. Early *ah, eh, uh* sounds | Cooing | |
| Emergence of vowel sounds | Vocal social responses—chuckling and laughing | Quietness |
| Emergence of consonants | Spontaneous vocalization to toys, to self, to adult | |
| Changes in tonal range of voice (high pitch, low pitch, etc.) | Use of voice to initiate social contact | |
| | Differentiation of vocal signs (pleasure, eagerness, recognition, displeasure, anxiety, etc.) | |
| | Use of language for communication | |
| | Specificity of mama, dada words | Discrepancy between maturation and |
| 12 mo. | Understanding verbalizations of others | function |

## RESPONSES TO PEOPLE

| | | |
|---|---|---|
| 0 mo. Visual attentiveness | See also Motor Behavior and Language Behavior | Intensity of visual regard of adult |
| Responsive smile | Recognition of nurse | |
| Spontaneous smile | Discrimination of face versus mask | Failure to establish a personal attachment: tenuousness of emotional ties |
| | Reflection of facial mimic | |
| | Anxiety to the stranger | |
| | Participation in social games (peekaboo, pat-a-cake, etc.) | Failure to seek out the adult either for pleasure or when in distress |
| | Initiation of social games | |
| 12 mo. | Reaching out to adult to touch, caress, explore, or act aggressively | |

## RESPONSES TO TOYS (Inanimate Objects)

| | | |
|---|---|---|
| 0 mo. Visual and acoustic attention | | |
| Early grasping efforts | | |
| | Memory for hidden toy | Decreasing interest in toys |
| | | Rarity of spontaneous play with toys |
| | Investigatory behavior | Rarity of mouthing of toys and other objects |
| | Combining of toys | |
| | Simultaneous attention to two or more toys | |
| | Preference for one toy over another | |
| | Recovering toy when obstacle is introduced | |
| 12 mo. | | Absence of transitional object. |

Source: S. Provence and R. Lipton. *Infants in institutions.* New York: International Universities Press, 1962. Pp. 173-176.

FIGURE 27. Institutionalization in infancy affects the total developmental pattern of the growing child. As seen in this chart, intellectual as well as motor and social skills show retardation.

*Figure 27:* *From Infants in Institutions by S. Provence and R. Lipton, p. 173-176. © 1962 by International Universities Press.*

## PERCEPTION OF A BRAIN-INJURED CHILD

What does this drawing represent? Two rectangles. It seems to.

And here we have a V.

And here, a trough, or an exaggerated letter M.

And here, two signal flags.

Ah, but here is an envelope.

Back where we started—the two rectangles become an envelope with a stamp on it.

The normal person sees the progression:

The brain-injured may see this:

Would brain-injured children be led to perceive the rectangles as an envelope? Perhaps not. Does this mean they are less intelligent? No, it indicates they are not perceiving what normal persons perceive.

FIGURE 28. How the brain-injured child's perceptual handicap alters his or her view of the world can be determined to some extent by psychological tests. It may be illustrated, for example, by the response of a brain-injured child to the above sequence.

348

Figure 28: From The Other Child—The Brain Injured Child by Richard S. Lewis with Laura E. Lehtinen and Alfred A. Strauss. Grune and Stratton, Inc., 1960. Reprinted by permission of the publisher and author.

# A Summary of Normal Development

But allowance must always be made for individual differences

## THE INFANT

*Physical Development*
Continued neuromuscular development. Progression from head downward—gains control of eye movements, swallowing, smiling, and using hands before he gains control of leg movements.
Most rapid growth rate of any period—often triples birth weight by age one.
Develops from crying as only form of language expression to smiling, cooing, laughing, babbling, using one or two words.
Gradually develops some motor control—from random movements to ability to pick up small objects with fingers.
Begins to cut teeth by six or seven months.
Sleep pattern changes from almost constant sleep to twelve hours a night and one or two naps.
Learns to eat solid food, drink from a cup.

*Characteristic Behavior*
Develops from no social perception to recognizing parents, brothers, sisters, environment, and routine.
Responds to people he knows. Usually withdraws from strangers.
Gradually becomes social—likes watching people and being played with, talked to, or held.
May be startled or cry at sudden, loud sounds or voices. May pull back or cry at strange objects. Disturbed by sudden movements.

*Special Needs*
Physical care—is dependent on adults for satisfaction of all physical needs. Should have prompt response to his needs.
Certainty of parents' love. Consistency and patience in handling. Cuddling, holding, rocking.
Consistent care by one or two people.
Verbal response to his babbling to help his language development.
Activity, opportunity to move about and to develop the large muscles.

## THE TODDLER

*Physical Development*
Growth rate slower than during infancy.
Decrease in appetite from infancy.
Walks between twelve and eighteen months. Runs awkwardly and may fall.
Tries to feed himself, but manipulating spoon and cup still difficult. Finger feeds. Will be messy.
Constantly in motion. Into everything. Explores his environment—pushing, pulling, climbing, dragging, lifting everything within reach.
Learns by touching, feeling, and putting in mouth.
Short attention span.
Vocabulary increase in second half of year. May use words, but can't always express his wants.

*Characteristic Behavior*
Responds to his mother and likes to be near her. Enjoys his father and siblings, but usually wants his mother to do things for him.
Unable to play cooperatively with others.
Likes simple stories about himself, jingles, rhymes, and picture books.
Beginning to be negativistic and may develop some fears. Developing likes and dislikes.
Becomes angry when frustrated.

*Special Needs*
Love, affection, and a secure, happy relationship with parents.
Acceptance of his constant activity. Patience and encouragement as he tries to learn to do things for himself.
Training with a light touch rather than by commanding and scolding.
A safe environment in which to explore, with dangerous objects put out of reach. Also a fenced-in, outdoor play area. Playpen outgrown near beginning of period.
Recognition that the toddler is not old enough to be responsible for himself, even though he may seem to understand directions.

349

# THE RUNABOUT

*Physical Development*
Motor skills unevenly developed—marked development in large muscle coordination, but small muscles and eye-hand coordination still not well developed.
Full set of temporary teeth by three years.
Gradually acquires ability to feed and dress himself with greater skill.
Rapid language development—from a few words to an average of 2000.
Change in sleep pattern—twelve hours needed at night with daytime naps gradually given up. But still needs rest period because children of this age fatigue easily.
Toilet habits established. Child usually takes care of his own needs by end of period.

*Characteristic Behavior*
Learning to understand his environment and comply with many of its demands.
Often negativistic at beginning of period, but gradually becomes able to accept necessary limits and restraints. Wants adult approval.
Likes to be close to his mother, but his father is becoming increasingly important to him.
Likes to help around the house.
Imitative in language, manners, and habits.
Constantly active, but capable of longer stretches of quiet activity toward end of period.
Shows fatigue by being irritable or restless.
Gradually learning what is acceptable behavior and what is not.
Great curiosity. Asks countless questions.

*Special Needs*
Security of love and affection from parents.
Guidance and a pattern of behavior to follow.
Time, patience, understanding, and genuine interest from adults.
Simple, clear routines. Limited choices.
Opportunity to learn to give and take, to play cooperatively with other children.
Wider scope of activity. Limited freedom to move about and to move away from immediate home environment by end of period.

# ABOUT FIVE

*Physical Development*
Period of slow growth. Body lengthens out and hands and feet grow larger. Girls usually about a year ahead of boys in physical development.
Good general motor control, though small muscles not so fully developed as large ones.
Sensory-motor equipment usually not ready for reading. Eye-hand coordination improving, but still poor. Apt to be farsighted.
Activity level high.
Attention span still short, but increasing.
Little infantile articulation in speech.
Handedness established.

*Characteristic Behavior*
Stable—good balance between self-sufficiency and sociability.
Home-centered.
Beginning to be capable of self-criticism. Eager and able to carry some responsibility.
Noisy and vigorous, but activity has definite direction.
Purposeful and constructive—knows what he's going to draw before he draws it.
Uses language well, enjoys dramatic play.
Can wash, dress, eat, and go to the toilet by himself, but may need occasional help.
Individuality and lasting traits beginning to be apparent.
Interested in group activity.

*Special Needs*
Assurance that he is loved and valued.
Wise guidance.
Opportunity for plenty of activity, equipment for exercising large muscles.
Opportunity to do things for himself, freedom to use and develop his own powers.
Background training in group effort, in sharing, and in good work habits that he will need next year in first grade.
Opportunity to learn about his world by seeing and doing things.
Kindergarten experience if possible.

# ABOUT SIX

*Physical Development*
Growth proceeding more slowly, a lengthening out.
Large muscles better developed than small ones.
Eleven to twelve hours of sleep needed.
Eyes not yet mature, tendency toward farsightedness.
Permanent teeth beginning to appear.
Heart in period of rapid growth.
High activity level—can stay still only for short periods.

*Characteristic Behavior*
Eager to learn, exuberant, restless, overactive, easily fatigued.
Self-assertive, aggressive, wants to be first, less cooperative than at five, keenly competitive, boastful.
Whole body involved in whatever he does.
Learns best through active participation.
Inconsistent in level of maturity evidenced—regresses when tired, often less mature at home than with outsiders.
Inept at activities using small muscles.
Relatively short periods of interest.
Has difficulty making decisions.
Group activities popular, boys' and girls' interests beginning to differ.
Much spontaneous dramatization.

*Special Needs*
Encouragement, ample praise, warmth, and great patience from adults.
Ample opportunity for activity of many kinds, especially for use of large muscles.
Wise supervision with minimum interference.
Friends—by end of period, a best friend.
Concrete learning situations and active, direct participation.
Some responsibilities, but without pressure and without being required to make complicated decisions or achieve rigidly set standards.
Help in developing acceptable manners and habits.

# ABOUT SEVEN

*Physical Development*
Growth slow and steady.
Annual expected growth in height—two or three inches. In weight—three to six pounds.
Losing teeth. Most seven-year-olds have their six-year molars.
Better eye-hand coordination.
Better use of small muscles.
Eyes not yet ready for much close work.

*Characteristic Behavior*
Sensitive to feelings and attitudes of both other children and adults. Especially dependent on approval of adults.
Interests of boys and girls diverging. Less play together.
Full of energy but easily tired, restless and fidgety, often dreamy and absorbed.
Little abstract thinking. Learns best in concrete terms and when he can be active while learning.
Cautious and self-critical, anxious to do things well, likes to use hands.
Talkative, prone to exaggerate, may fight verbally instead of physically, competitive.
Enjoys songs, rhythms, fairy tales, myths, nature stories, comics, television, movies.
Able to assume some responsibility.
Concerned about right and wrong, but often prone to take small things.
Rudimentary understanding of time and monetary values.

*Special Needs*
The right combination of independence and encouraging support.
Chances for active participation in learning situations with concrete objects.
Adult help in adjusting to the rougher ways of the playground without becoming too crude or rough.
Warm, encouraging, friendly relationships with adults.
Acceptance at own level of development.

## ABOUT EIGHT

*Physical Development*
Growth still slow and steady—arms length-ening, hands growing.
Eyes ready for both near and far vision. Near-sightedness may develop this year.
Permanent teeth continuing to appear.
Large muscles still developing. Small muscles better developed, too. Manipulative skills are increasing.
Attention span getting longer.
Poor posture may develop.

*Characteristic Behavior*
Often careless, noisy, argumentative, but also alert, friendly, interested in people.
More dependent on his mother again, less so on his teacher. Sensitive to criticism.
New awareness of individual differences.
Eager, more enthusiastic than cautious. Higher accident rate.
Gangs beginning. Best friends of same sex.
Allegiance to other children instead of to an adult in case of conflict.
Greater capacity for self-evaluation.
Much spontaneous dramatization, ready for simple classroom dramatics.
Understanding of time and of use of money.
Responsive to group activities, both spon-taneous and adult-supervised.
Fond of team games, comics, television, mov-ies, adventure stories, collections.

*Special Needs*
Praise and encouragement from adults.
Reminders of his responsibilities.
Wise guidance and channeling of his interests and enthusiasms, rather than domination or unreasonable standards.
A best friend.
Experience of belonging to peer group—oppor-tunity to identify with others of same age and sex.
Adult-supervised groups and planned after-school activities.
Exercise of both large and small muscles.

## ABOUT NINE OR TEN

*Physical Development*
Slow, steady growth continues—girls forge fur-ther ahead. Some children reach the plateau preceding the preadolescent growth spurt.
Lungs as well as digestive and circulatory sys-tems almost mature. Heart especially subject to strain.
Teeth may need straightening. First and sec-ond bicuspids appearing.
Eye-hand coordination good. Ready for crafts and shop work.
Eyes almost adult size. Ready for close work with less strain.

*Characteristic Behavior*
Decisive, responsible, dependable, reasonable, strong sense of right and wrong.
Individual differences distinct, abilities now apparent.
Capable of prolonged interest. Often makes plans and goes ahead on his own.
Gangs strong and of one sex only, of short du-ration and changing membership.
Perfectionistic—wants to do well, but loses in-terest if discouraged or pressured.
Interested less in fairy tales and fantasy, more in his community and country and in other countries and peoples.
Loyal to his country and proud of it.
Spends a great deal of time in talk and dis-cussion. Often outspoken and critical of adults, although still dependent on adult ap-proval.
Frequently argues over fairness in games.
Wide discrepancies in reading ability.

*Special Needs*
Active rough and tumble play.
Friends and membership in a group.
Training in skills, but without pressure.
Books of many kinds, depending on individual reading level and interest.
Reasonable explanations without talking down.
Definite responsibility.
Frank answers to questions about coming physiological changes.

# THE PREADOLESCENT

*Physical Development*
A "resting period," followed by a period of rapid growth in height and then growth in weight. This usually starts sometime between 9 and 13. Boys may mature as much as two years later than girls.
Girls usually taller and heavier than boys.
Reproductive organs maturing. Secondary sex characteristics developing.
Rapid muscular growth.
Uneven growth of different parts of the body.
Enormous but often capricious appetite.

*Characteristic Behavior*
Wide range of individual differences in maturity level.
Gangs continue, though loyalty to the gang stronger in boys than in girls.
Interest in team games, pets, television, radio, movies, comics. Marked interest differences between boys and girls.
Teasing and seeming antagonism between boys' and girls' groups.
Awkwardness, restlessness, and laziness common as result of rapid and uneven growth.
Opinion of own group beginning to be valued more highly than that of adults.
Often becomes overcritical, changeable, rebellious, uncooperative.
Self-conscious about physical changes.
Interested in earning money.

*Special Needs*
Understanding of the physical and emotional changes about to come.
Skillfully planned school and recreation programs to meet needs of those who are approaching puberty as well as those who are not.
Opportunities for greater independence and for carrying more responsibility without pressure.
Warm affection and sense of humor in adults.
No nagging, condemnation, or talking down.
Sense of belonging, acceptance by peer group.

# THE ADOLESCENT

*Physical Development*
Rapid weight gain at beginning of adolescence. Enormous appetite.
Sexual maturity, with accompanying physical and emotional changes. Girls are usually about two years ahead of boys.
Sometimes a period of glandular imbalance.
Skeletal growth completed, adult height reached, muscular coordination improved.
Heart growing rapidly at beginning of period.

*Characteristic Behavior*
Going to extremes, emotional instability with "know-it-all" attitude.
Return of habits of younger child—nail biting, tricks, impudence, day-dreaming.
High interest in philosophical, ethical, and religious problems. Search for ideals.
Preoccupation with acceptance by the social group. Fear of ridicule and of being unpopular. Oversensitiveness and self-pity.
Strong identification with an admired adult.
Assertion of independence from family as a step toward adulthood.
Responds well to group responsibility and group participation. Groups may form cliques.
High interest in physical attractiveness.
Girls usually more interested in boys than boys in girls, resulting from earlier maturing of the girls.

*Special Needs*
Acceptance by and conformity with others of own age.
Adequate understanding of sexual relationships and attitudes.
Kind, unobtrusive, adult guidance which does not threaten the adolescent's feeling of freedom.
Assurance of security. Adolescents seek both dependence and independence.
Opportunities to make decisions and to earn and save money.
Provision for constructive recreation. Some cause, idea, or issue to work for.

# SUGGESTED READINGS

ALMY, MILLIE (Ed.) *Early Childhood Play: Selected Readings Related to Cognition and Motivation.* New York: Associated Educational Services, 1968.

ALMY, MILLIE, CHITTENDEN, EDWARD A., and MILLER, PAULA. *Young Children's Thinking: Studies of Some Aspects of Piaget's Theory.* New York: Teachers' College Press, 1966.

ANTHONY, ELWYN JAMES, and BENEDEK, THERESA (Eds.) *Parenthood: Its Psychology and Pathology.* Boston: Little, Brown and Company, 1970.

ANTHONY, ELWYN JAMES, and KOUPERNIK, CYRILLE (Eds.) *The Child in His Family.* Vol. 2. *The Impact of Disease and Death.* New York: John Wiley & Sons, 1973.

ARIES, PHILLIPE. *Centuries of Childhood, a Social History of Family Life.* (Trans. by Robert Baldick) New York: Alfred A. Knopf, 1962.

ARNSTEIN, HELENE S. *What to Tell Your Child About Birth, Death, Illness, Divorce, and Other Family Crises,* Indianapolis: Bobbs-Merrill, 1962.

AUERBACH, ARLINE B., and ROCHE, SANDRA *Creating a Preschool Center: Parent Development in an Integrated Neighborhood Project.* New York: John Wiley & Sons, 1971.

BAKER, KATHERINE READ, and FANE, XENIA F. *Understanding and Guiding Young Children.* New York: Prentice-Hall, 1967.

BANDURA, ALBERT, and WALTERS, RICHARD A. *Social Learning and Personality Development.* New York: Holt, Rinehart and Winston, 1963.

BARROW, HAROLD M. *Man and His Movement: Principles of His Physical Education.* Philadelphia: Lea & Febiger, 1971.

BEARD, RUTH *An Outline of Piaget's Developmental Psychology for Students and Teachers.* New York: Basic Books, 1969.

BERNARD, HAROLD W. *Mental Health in the Classroom.* New York: McGraw-Hill, 1970.

BERNHARDT, KARL SCHOFIELD *Being a Parent: Unchanging Values in a Changing World.* Toronto: University of Toronto Press, 1970.

BERNHARDT, KARL SCHOFIELD *Discipline and Child Guidance.* New York: McGraw-Hill, 1964.

BILLER, HENRY B. *Father, Child and Sex Role: Paternal Determinants of Personality Development.* Lexington, Mass.: D. C. Heath, 1971.

BLODGETT, HARRIET E. *Mentally Retarded Children: What Parents and Others Should Know.* Minneapolis: University of Minnesota Press, 1971.

BLOOM, BENJAMIN *Stability and Change in Human Characteristics.* New York: John C. Wiley & Sons, 1964.

BOWER, ELI M. (Ed.) *Orthopsychiatry and Education.* Detroit: Wayne University Press, 1971.

BOWLBY, JOHN *Attachment and Loss.* New York: Basic Books, 1969.

BOWLBY, JOHN *Separation, Anxiety, and Anger.* New York: Basic Books, 1973.

BRAZELTON, T. BERRY. *Infants and Mothers: Differences in Development.* New York: Delacorte Press, 1969.

BRIGGS, DOROTHY. *Your Child's Self-Esteem: The Key to His Life.* New York: Doubleday, 1970.

BRODY, EUGENE B. *Minority Group Adolescents in the United States.* Baltimore: Williams and Wilkins, 1968.

BRONFENBRENNER, URIE *Two Worlds of Childhood: U.S. and U.S.S.R.* New York: Russell Sage Foundation, 1970.

BRUNER, JEROME S. *Processes of Cognitive Growth: Infancy.* Heinz Werner Lecture Series, Vol. 3. Barre, Mass.: Barre Publishers, 1968.

BUTTON, ALAN DeWITT *The Authentic Child.* New York: Random House, 1969.

CALDWELL, BETTYE M., and RICCIUTI, H. (Eds.) *Review of Child Development Research.* Vol. 3. Chicago: University of Chicago Press, 1973.

CAPLAN, FRANK, and CAPLAN, THERESA *The Power of Play.* Garden City, New York: Doubleday, 1973.

CASAVIS, JAMES V. *Principal's Guidelines for Action in Parent Conferences.* West Nyack, N.Y. Parker, 1970.

CASS, JOAN E. *Helping Children Grow Through Play.* New York: Schocken Books, 1973.

CASSE, ROBERT M., Jr., SCAFF, MARILEE K., and PACKWOOD, WILLIAM T. *Drugs and the School Counselor.* Washington, D.C.: American Personnel and Guidance Association, 1972.

CERVANTES, L. *The Drop-Out: Causes and Cures.* Ann Arbor, Mich.: University of Michigan Press, 1965.

CHANDLER, CAROLINE A., and DITTMANN, LAURA (Eds.) *Early Child Care: The New Perspectives.* Chicago: Aldine, 1968.

CHURCH, JOSEPH (Ed.) *Three Babies: Biographies of Cognitive Development.* New York: Random House, 1966.

CLARK, KENNETH BANCROFT *Prejudice and Your Child.* (2nd ed.) Boston: Beacon Press, 1963.

COHEN, DOROTHY H. *The Learning Child.* New York: Pantheon Books, 1972.

COLES, ROBERT M.D. *Children of Crisis: A Study of Courage and Fear.* Boston: Little, Brown and Company, 1967.

COLES, ROBERT M.D. *Children of Crisis: Migrants, Mountaineers and Sharecroppers.* Boston: Little, Brown and Company, 1970.

COLES, ROBERT M.D. *Children of Crisis: The South Goes North.* Boston: Little, Brown and Company, 1971.

COLES, ROBERT M.D. *Teachers and the Children of Poverty.* Washington, D.C.: Potomac Institute, 1970.

COOPERSMITH, STANLEY *The Antecedents of Self-Esteem.* San Francisco: W. H. Freeman, 1967.

CRAIG, ELEANOR. *P.S. You're Not Listening.* New York: Richard W. Baron, 1972.

CURTIS, JEAN *A Parent's Guide to Nursery Schools.* New York: Random House, 1971.

DOUVAN, E., and ADELSON, J. *The Adolescent Experience.* New York: John Wiley & Sons, 1966.

DUNN, LLOYD M. (Ed.) *Exceptional Children in the Schools: Special Education in Transition.* New York: Holt, Rinehart and Winston, 1973.

ELKIND, DAVID *A Sympathetic Understanding of the Child: Six to Sixteen.* Boston: Allyn & Bacon, 1971.

ERIKSON, ERIK H. *Childhood and Society.* New York: W. W. Norton, 1963.

ERIKSON, ERIK H. *Identity, Youth and Crisis.* New York: W. W. Norton, 1968.

ERON, LEONARD D., WALDEN, LEOPOLD O., and LEFKOWITZ, MONROE N. *Aggression in Children.* Boston: Little, Brown and Company, 1971.

EVANS, E. D. (Ed.) *Adolescents: Readings in Behavior and Development.* Hinsdale, Ill.: Dryden, 1970.

EVANS, E. D. *Contemporary Influences in Early Childhood Education.* New York: Holt, Rinehart and Winston, 1971.

FONTANA, VINCENT M.D. *Somewhere a Child Is Crying.* New York: Macmillan, 1973.

FREEDMAN, ALFRED M. M.D., and KAPLAN, HAROLD I. M.D. (Eds.) *The Child: His Psychological and Cultural Development.* Vol. 1. *Normal Development and Cultural Development.* New York: Atheneum, 1972.

FROST, JOE L., and HAWKES, GLENN R. *The Disadvantaged Child: Issues and Innovations: A Book of Readings.* Boston: Houghton Mifflin, 1966.

GESELL, ARNOLD, and ILG, FRANCES *The Child from Five to Ten.* New York: Harper & Row, 1946.

GIL, DAVID *Violence Against Children: Physical Child Abuse in the U.S.* Cambridge, Mass.: Harvard University Press, 1970.

GLASSER, WILLIAM *Schools Without Failure.* New York: Harper & Row, 1969.

GORDON, IRA J. *Readings in Research in Developmental Psychology.* Glenview, Ill.: Scott, Foresman, 1971.

GOWAN, JOHN CURTIS, and TORRANCE, E. PAUL (Eds.) *Educating the Ablest: A Book of Readings on the Education of Gifted Children.* Itasca, Ill.: F. E. Peacock, 1971.

Group for the Advancement of Psychiatry. *Humane Reproduction.* New York: Publications Office, Group for the Advancement of Psychiatry, 1973.

Group for the Advancement of Psychiatry. *Joys and Sorrows of Parenthood.* New York: Publications Office, Group for the Advancement of Psychiatry, 1973.

Group for the Advancement of Psychiatry. *Normal Adolescence.* New York: Charles Scribner's Sons, 1968.

HAIMOWITZ, MORRIS L., and HAIMOWITZ, NATALIE R. *Human Development: Selected Readings.* (3rd ed.) New York: Thomas Y. Crowell, 1973.

HARTUP, WILLARD W. (Ed.) *The Young Child: Reviews of Research.* Washington, D.C.: National Association for the Education of Young Children, 1972.

HAVIGHURST, ROBERT J. *Developmental Tasks and Education.* (3rd ed.) New York: David McKay, 1972.

HEFFERNAN, HELEN, and TODD, VIVIAN EDMISTON *Elementary Teachers Guide to Working with Parents.* Englewood Cliffs, N.J.: Prentice-Hall, 1969.

HELFER, RAY E. M.D., and KEMPE, C. HENRY M.D. *The Battered Child.* Chicago: University of Chicago Press, 1968.

HERZOG, ELIZABETH, and SMITH, CECELIA E. *Boys in Fatherless Families.* (Department of Health, Education, and Welfare) Washington, D.C.: U.S. Government Printing Office, 1971.

HOLT, JOHN. *Freedom and Beyond.* New York: E. P. Dutton, 1972.

HOFFMAN, MARTIN L., and HOFFMAN, LOIS WLADIS (Eds.) *Review of Child Development Research.* Vols. 1 and 2. New York: Russell Sage Foundation, 1964, 1966.

JENKINS, GLADYS G. *Helping Children Reach Their Potential.* (2nd ed.) Glenview, Ill.: Scott, Foresman, 1971.

JENKINS, RICHARD L. M.D. *Behavior Disorders of Childhood and Adolescence.* Springfield, Ill.: Charles C Thomas, 1973.

JOHNSON, WENDELL, and MOELLER, DOROTHY *Living with Change: The Semantics of Coping.* New York: Harper & Row, 1972.

JOSSELYN, IRENE M.D. *Adolescence: A Report Published Under the Auspices of the Joint Committee on Mental Health of Children.* New York: Harper & Row, 1969.

KAGAN, JEROME *Personality Development.* New York: Harcourt Brace Jovanovich, 1971.

KAGAN, JEROME *Understanding Children's Behavior, Motives and Thoughts.* New York: Harcourt Brace Jovanovich, 1971.

KAGAN, JEROME, and COLES, ROBERT M.D. (Eds.) *Twelve to Sixteen: Early Adolescence.* New York: W. W. Norton, 1972.

KAGAN, JEROME, and MOSS, HOWARD A. *Birth to Maturity.* New York: John Wiley & Sons, 1962.

KAPLAN, LOUIS *Education and Mental Health.* New York: Harper & Row, 1971.

KEMPE, HENRY C., and HELFER, RAY E. *Helping the Battered Child and His Family.* Philadelphia: J. B. Lippincott, 1972.

KENNEDY, WALLACE A. *Child Psychology.* Englewood Cliffs, N.J.: Prentice-Hall, 1971.

KEYSERLING, MARY DUBLIN *Windows on Day Care: Report of a Survey.* New York: National Council of Jewish Women, 1972.

KILANDER, H. FREDERICK *Sex Education in the Schools.* New York: Macmillan, 1970.

KIRK, SAMUEL A. *Educating Exceptional Children.* (2nd ed.) Boston: Houghton Mifflin, 1972.

KOCH, HELEN L. *Twins and Twin Relations.* Chicago: University of Chicago Press, 1966.

KOCH, RICHARD, and DOBSON, JAMES C. (Eds.) *The Mentally Retarded Child and His Family: A Multidisciplinary Handbook.* New York: Brunner/Mazel, 1971.

KOHLBERG, L. *Stages in the Development of Moral Thought and Action.* New York: Holt, Rinehart and Winston, in press.

LANDRETH, CATHERINE *Early Childhood Behavior and Learning.* New York: Alfred A. Knopf, 1967.

LAVATELLI, CELIA STENDLER, and STENDLER, FAITH *Readings in Child Behavior and Development.* (3rd ed.) New York: Harcourt Brace Jovanovich, 1972.

LeMASTERS, E. E. *Parents in Modern America.* Homewood, Ill.: Dorsey Press, 1973.

LERNER, JANET W. *Children with Learning Disabilities: Theories, Diagnosis and Teaching Strategies.* Boston: Houghton Mifflin, 1971.

LEWIS, M. M. *Language, Thought and Personality in Infancy and Childhood.* New York: Basic Books, 1963.

LICHTENBERG, PHILIP, and NORTON, DOLORES G. *Cognitive and Mental Development in the First Five Years of Life, A Review of Research.* (National Institute of Mental Health) Washington, D.C.: U.S. Government Printing Office, 1970.

LIEBERT, ROBERT M., NEALE, JOHN M., and DAVIDSON, EMILY S. *Effects of Television on Children and Youth.* New York: Pergamon Press, 1973.

LOURIA, DONALD B. *Overcoming Drugs: A Program for Action.* New York: McGraw-Hill, 1971.

MACCOBY, ELEANOR E. (Ed.) *The Development of Sex Differences.* Stanford, Calif.: Stanford University Press, 1966.

MAIER, HENRY W. *Three Theories of Child Development.* New York: Harper & Row, 1969.

MARZOLLO, JEAN, and LLOYD, JANICE *Learning Through Play.* New York: Harper & Row, 1972.

McCANDLESS, BOYD R., and EVANS, ELLIS D. *Children and Youth: Psychosocial Development.* New York: Holt, Rinehart and Winston, 1973.

MELODY, WILLIAM H. *Children's Television: The Economics of Exploitation.* New Haven: Yale University Press, 1973.

MORRIS, NORMAN S. *Television's Child.* Boston: Little, Brown and Company, 1971.

MOUSTAKAS, CLARK *The Authentic Teacher: Sensitivity and Awareness in the Classroom.* Cambridge, Mass.: Howard A. Doyle, 1967.

MUSSEN, PAUL HENRY (Ed.) *Carmichael's Manual of Child Psychology.* (3rd ed.) New York: John Wiley & Sons, 1970.

MUSSEN, PAUL HENRY, CONGER, JOHN JANEWAY, and KAGAN, JEROME *Child Development and Personality.* (4th ed.) New York: Harper & Row, 1973.

OTTO, HERBERT A. *The Family in Search of a Future.* New York: Appleton-Century-Crofts, 1970.

PATTON, ROBERT GRAY M.D., GARDNER, LYTT I. M.D., and RICHMOND, JULIUS M.D. *Growth Failure in Maternal Deprivation.* Springfield, Ill.: Charles C Thomas, 1963.

PECK, R. F., and HAVIGHURST, R. J. *The Psychology of Character Development.* New York: John Wiley & Sons, 1960.

PIAGET, JEAN. ELKIND, DAVID (Ed.) *Six Psychological Studies.* New York: Random House, 1968.

POLLARD, MARIE B., and GEOGHEGAN, BARBARA. *The Growing Child in Contemporary Society.* Beverly Hills, Calif.: Bruce, 1969.

PROVENCE, SALLY M.D., and LIPTON, ROSE C. *Infants in Institutions: A Comparison of Their Development with Family Reared Infants During the First Year of Life.* New York: International Universities Press, 1962.

Public Health Service, Department of Health, Education, and Welfare. *Perspectives on Human Deprivation: Biological, Psychological, and Sociological.* Washington, D.C.: U.S. Government Printing Office, 1968.

Public Health Service, Department of Health, Education, and Welfare. *TV and Growing Up: Impact of Televised Violence.* (Report to the Surgeon General's Scientific and Advisory Committee on TV and Social Behavior) Washington, D.C.: U.S. Government Printing Office, 1972.

PULASKI, MARY SPENCER *Understanding Piaget: An Introduction to Children's Cognitive Development.* New York: Harper & Row, 1971.

PURKEY, WILLIAM W. *Self-Concept and School Achievement.* Englewood Cliffs, N.J.: Prentice-Hall, 1970.

RASMUSSEN, MARGARET (Ed.) *Feelings and Learning.* Washington, D.C.: Association for Childhood Education International, 1965.

RASMUSSEN, MARGARET (Ed.) *Readings from Childhood Education: Articles of Lasting Value.* Washington, D.C.: Association for Childhood Education International, 1966.

RATHS, LOUISE E. *Meeting the Needs of Children: Creating Trust and Security.* Columbus, Ohio: Charles E. Merrill, 1972.

RIESSMAN, FRANK *The Culturally Deprived Child.* New York: Harper & Row, 1962.

ROFF, MERRILL, SELLS, S. B., and GOLDEN, MARY M. *Social Adjustment and Personality Development.* Minneapolis: University of Minnesota Press, 1972.

ROGERS, DOROTHY *Adolescence: A Psychological Perspective.* Monterey, Calif.: Brooks/ Cole, 1972.

ROGERS, DOROTHY *Issues in Adolescent Psychology.* (2nd ed.) New York: Appleton-Century-Crofts, 1972.

SAPIR, SELMA G., and NITZBURG, ANN C. (Eds.) *Children with Learning Problems: Readings in a Developmental-Interaction Approach.* New York: Brunner/Mazel, 1973.

SARASON, SEYMOUR B., et al. *Anxiety in Elementary School Children.* New York: John Wiley & Sons, 1960.

SARASON, SEYMOUR B. *Culture of the School and the Problem of Change.* Boston: Allyn & Bacon, 1971.

SCHREIBER, D. (Ed.) *Profile of the School Drop-out.* New York: Random House, 1968.

SEARS, P., and SHERMAN, V. *In Pursuit of Self-Esteem: Case Studies of Eight Elementary School Children.* Belmont, Calif.: Wadsworth, 1964.

SEGAL, JULIUS (Ed.) *The Mental Health of the Child: Program Reports of the National Institute of Mental Health.* Washington, D.C.: U.S. Government Printing Office, 1971.

SENN, MILTON J., and SOLNIT, ALBERT J. *Problems in Child Behavior and Development.* Philadelphia: Lee & Febiger, 1968.

SILBERMAN, C. E. *Crisis in the Classroom: The Remaking of American Education.* New York: Random House, 1970.

STONE, L. JOSEPH, and CHURCH, JOSEPH *Childhood and Adolescence: A Psychology of the Growing Person.* (3rd ed.) New York: Random House, 1973.

STOTT, LELAND H. *Child Development: An Individual Longitudinal Approach.* New York: Holt, Rinehart and Winston, 1967.

STUART, IRVING, and ABT, LAWRENCE (Eds.) *Children of Separation and Divorce.* New York: Grossman, 1972.

THOMAS, ALEXANDER, CHESS, STELLA, and BIRCH, HERBERT G. *Behavioral Individuality in Early Childhood.* New York: New York University Press, 1963.

THOMAS, ALEXANDER, CHESS, STELLA, and BIRCH, HERBERT G. *Temperament and Behavior Disorders in Children.* New York: New York University Press, 1968.

VAZ, E. W. (Ed.) *Middle-class Juvenile Delinquency.* New York: Harper & Row, 1967.

WEINER, FLORENCE *Help for the Handicapped Child.* New York: McGraw-Hill, 1973.

WELLS, LEORA WOOD *The Acquisition and Development of Values: Perspectives on Research.* (National Institute of Mental Health) Washington, D.C.: U.S. Government Printing Office, 1968.

White House Conference on Children and Youth. *Profiles of Children.* Washington, D.C.: U.S. Government Printing Office, 1970.

WOLFF, SULA *Children Under Stress.* London: Allen Lane, 1969.

YAMAMOTO, KAORU (Ed.) *The Child and His Self Image: Self Concept in the Early Years.* Boston: Houghton Mifflin, 1972.

YARROW, MARIAN, CAMPBELL, JOHN, and BURTON, ROGER *Child-Rearing: An Inquiry into Research and Methods.* San Francisco: Jossey-Bass, 1968.

# index

## A

1 2 3 4 5 6 7 8 9 10-KP-80 79 78 77 76 75 74